Financial crises

Financial crises

Theory, history, and policy

Edited by
Charles P. Kindleberger
and
Jean-Pierre Laffargue

Cambridge University Press

Cambridge
London   New York   New Rochelle   Melbourne   Sydney

& Editions de la Maison des Sciences de l'Homme

Paris

CAMBRIDGE UNIVERSITY PRESS
Cambridge, New York, Melbourne, Madrid, Cape Town, Singapore, São Paulo, Delhi

Cambridge University Press
The Edinburgh Building, Cambridge CB2 8RU, UK

With Editions de la Maison des Sciences de l'Homme
54 Boulevard Raspail, 75270 Paris Cedex 06, France

Published in the United States of America by Cambridge University Press, New York

www.cambridge.org
Information on this title: www.cambridge.org/9780521243803

First published 1982

A catalogue record for this publication is available from the British Library

Library of Congress Cataloguing in Publication data
Main entry under title:
Financial crises:
Includes index.
1. Depressions – Congresses. 2. Business
cycles – Congresses. I. Kindleberger, Charles
Poor, 1910– . II. Laffargue, Jean-Pierre
HB3722.F55 332.4′1 81–17111

ISBN 978-0-521-24380-3 hardback
ISBN 978-0-521-06871-0 paperback

Transferred to digital printing 2009

Contents

Contributors

The following were the participants in the colloquium "Financial Crises and the Lender of Last Resort," on which this book is based, which was held at Bad Homburg, May 21-3, 1979.

Arthur I. Bloomfield *University of Pennsylvania*
Knut Borchardt *Universität München*
Paul Coulbois *Université de Paris I*
Jean-Claude Debeir *Université de Paris VII*
Rudiger Dornbusch *Massachusetts Institute of Technology*
J. S. Flemming *Nuffield College, Oxford*
Wolfram Fischer *Freie Universität, Berlin*
Jacob A. Frenkel *University of Chicago*
Raymond W. Goldsmith *Yale University*
Carl L. Holtfrerich *J. W. Goethe-Universität, Frankfurt/Main*
Charles P. Kindleberger *Massachusetts Institute of Technology*
Serge C. Kolm *Ecole des Hautes Etudes en Sciences Sociales, Paris*
Jean-Pierre Laffargue *CEPREMAP, Paris, and Université de Lille II*
Pierre-Marie Larnac *Université de Paris-Dauphine*
J. F. Lepetit *Banque de l'Indochine et de Suez, Paris*
Vivien Lévy-Garboua *Banque de France*
Maurice Lévy-Leboyer *Université de Paris X, Nanterre*
Eduard März *Johannes Kepler Universität, Linz*
R. C. O. Matthews *Clare College, Cambridge*
Warren D. McClam *Bank for International Settlements, Basel*
Jacques Melitz *I.N.S.E.E., Paris*
Joël Métais *Université de Paris-Dauphine*
Hyman P. Minsky *Washington University, St. Louis*
D. E. Moggridge *University of Toronto*
Robert E. Mundell *Columbia University*
Jurg Niehans *Universität Bern*

Peter Oppenheimer   *Christ Church, Oxford*
L. S. Pressnell   *University of Kent*
Robert M. Solow   *Massachusetts Institute of Technology*
Wolfgang Stützel   *Universität des Saarlandes*
Alexander K. Swoboda   *Institut des Hautes Etudes Internationales, Geneva*
Peter Temin   *Massachusetts Institute of Technology*

Professor Franco Bonelli of the Ente per gli studi monetari, bancari e finanziari "Luigi Einaudi," Roma, could not attend this meeting but wrote one of the chapters for this book.

Acknowledgments

The idea of publishing this book arose at the Maison des Sciences de l'Homme in the spring of 1978. The Maison des Sciences de l'Homme sponsored several seminars on the general subject, a three-day conference in Bad Homburg with an international group, and made possible the publication of this volume. The editors wish to express their gratitude especially to the Maison des Sciences de l'Homme and to its head, Professor Fernand Braudel, and also to Professor Clemens Heller for his help and encouragement.

A particular word of thanks is due to the Werner-Reimers-Stiftung, which made it possible to hold a conference, gathering more than 30 participants in the beautiful setting of its Bad Homburg building. The head of the Stiftung, the late Dr. Konrad Muller, and Mrs. Sönntgen did their utmost to make our stay pleasant and creative.

The linguistic assistance of Mrs. Christine Laffargue was helpful in the preparation of the conference and of this volume. A great deal of administrative work was done at CEPREMAP and some at the Centre d'Economie Quantitative et Comparative, both in Paris. The National Science Foundation in Washington financed the participation of the American participants to the conference. The editors are grateful to all of them.

1. Introduction

CHARLES P. KINDLEBERGER
AND JEAN-PIERRE LAFFARGUE

This book is based on the conference "Financial crises and the lender of last resort," held at Bad Homburg in the house of the Werner-Reimers-Stiftung (Foundation), May 21–23, 1979. The conference was sponsored by the Maison des Sciences de l'Homme in Paris, which expressed interest in a book by Charles P. Kindleberger, *Manias, Panics and Crashes, A History on Financial Crises*,[1] sponsored several seminars on the subject by Kindleberger, Carl Holtfrerich, and Hyman P. Minsky, and organized a committee to prepare a conference to go deeper into the subject.

The conference was originally intended to be divided into theory, history, and policy, with one day devoted to each. In the event, it was virtually impossible to separate these aspects, although perhaps history got more than its share of time and attention, and theory was somewhat underrepresented in the list of participants. Nor was policy separable from theory and history. However imprecise, a division among theory, history, and policy is convenient for the purposes of this introduction.

I. Theory

The major theoretical issues turn on whether the financial system (of a nation, or of the capitalistic world as a whole) is fragile or robust. According to one view, which assumes a supply of money set by rules, markets functioning efficiently with rational expectations that take account of all the information available to the system, stabilizing speculation, and foreign-exchange rates converging to purchasing-power parities determined by price levels in various countries, no crises are possible. Crises will then occur only when governments depart from sensible rules and fall into error. Dornbusch's comment following Chapter 8 presents a model of such a crisis on the exchange market: A successful speculative attack by rational speculators drives a country from a fixed to a flexible exchange rate, as a result of an excessively loose monetary policy. In the other view, the previous assumptions have heuristic value for the very long run. In the dynamic short run, however, departures may and occasionally will occur and lead to financial crises.

The conference participants occasionally worried how to define a financial crisis: as sharp changes in interest rates, asset prices, or bankruptcy rates (Goldsmith), a threat to the stability of the system (Swoboda), or a rush to test the convertibility of assets into money, or of one money into another (Mundell). No precise agreed definition was reached, but perhaps a financial crisis is like a pretty girl, difficult to define but recognizable when seen.[2] In any event, financial crises were distinguishable from crisis of unemployment or crises of wartime devastation and were associated with changed expectations that led owners of wealth to try to shift quickly out of one type of asset into another, with resulting falls in prices of the first type of asset, and frequently bankruptcy. The crisis is particularly acute if the asset newly sought is limited in quantity, so that one's chances of getting it are increased by being early. The lender-of-last-resort function usually consists of providing the sought-after liquid asset in abundant amount, and thus slowing down the stampede.

Why crises? Minsky, who insists on the fragility of the financial system, and elsewhere emphasized an exogenous shock leading to euphoric expectations, in Chapter 2 attributes the crisis to unstable debt structures built by years of tranquility that lull firms and households into speculative and Ponzi finance, the latter consisting of a situation such that current earnings do not meet payment commitments except for some distant future. In this case, solvency of the agent requires a not too large increase of the interest rate and a continuous increase of the debt to meet its current service. This view and the language met strong resistance from a number of participants and from the commentators, who conceded that such crises could occur, but did not necessarily occur. Minsky himself had to explain that the financial system, for all its fragility, had been sustained since 1960 by last-resort lending and by the government deficit in the United States. Flemming asked if, as Minsky believes, there exists a feedback from observed tranquility to more fragile financial structure, why has this policy not encouraged banks to take still higher risks? Would not Minsky be more consistent by suggesting that in order to enforce financial stability the authorities should intervene randomly in financial markets, that is, increase their uncertainty? A different criticism by Melitz concerned the independence of Minsky's argument from institutional arrangements. Would it be still valid in capitalist countries like Japan and France, where every financial intermediary automatically has heavy access to the lender of last resort?

Matthews, at one stage in the discussion, suggested that wars were a cause of instability in finance: 1974, he asserted, was linked to the finance of the war in Vietnam, 1929 and 1921 to World War I, 1873 to the Franco-Prussian War, and so on earlier in the nineteenth century. The period of limited crises from 1873 to 1907 was a period of few and limited wars. Without the financial strain of war, banking systems were stable.

A second theoretical question is how national crises spread between countries. This topic is considered in most historical papers, and although no specific report was written on it, it gave rise to much discussion at this conference. Mundell linked it to the world supply of international monies on the one hand and to their parities on the other hand. The scarcity of gold and silver in 1790, 1850, 1870, and 1890 produced the 40-year cycle of crises in 1811, 1851, 1891, 1931, and 1971. The scarcity of gold in 1950 produced the 1951 agreement between the Federal Reserve System and the United States Treasury. The crisis of 1974 was the result of the release of the "golden brake" in August 1971 and the ensuing Smithsonian agreement. The troubles of 1890, 1893, and 1907 were the consequence of the abandonment of bimetallism.

Oppenheimer's discussion of the propagation of crises ran, in less cosmic terms, to the spread of information and misinformation, with learning and knowledge not always cumulative, to foreign-trade multipliers and capital flows that built up and then were frequently interrupted, to sudden recourse to protection that interfered with debt service, and to pure coincidence. In the discussion of the 1830s, Matthews emphasized the unpredictable impact of bad harvests, which, like weather, spread beyond national boundaries.

An unresolved question was which was the more crisis-prone: fixed or floating exchanges? Ten years ago it was claimed by many economists that the adoption of floating exchange would minimize crises. The flexible exchange-rate system was acknowledged to have the advantage over the fixed system, that it did not provide speculators with a one-way option, large gains if they drove the exchange rate off par, but limited losses if they failed. Kolm defended the opposite thesis. What counts is the effect of the exchange-rate system on the degree of synchronization of business cycles in various countries. Such synchronization had been absent in the fifties and the beginning of the sixties, because under fixed rates, one country in deficit, engaged in restraint, was likely to be matched in its external effects by a surplus country in expansion. Under flexible exchange rates, this mechanism was missing, and business cycles moved into greater synchronization. In 1974, all countries tried to deflate together, which produced the largest crisis since the 1930s. Niehans added that under flexible rates, overshooting of exchange-rate fluctuations (e.g., destabilizing speculation) spread crises from a country with a weak currency to other countries with strong currencies.

II. History

The 1907 crisis in Italy, which is investigated by Bonelli in Chapter 3, had all the ingredients of the typical national financial crisis. Speculation took place in equities. First it fed on the industrialization of Italy, then on itself. The money supply increased steadily as a result of a favorable and stable balance of payments. Distress appeared in the fall of 1906, when interest rates increased on foreign money markets and when speculators met difficulties in financing their positions. When the Banca d'Italia increased its discount rate in order to protect its reserves, speculation became bearish. The Società Bancaria d'Italiana (SBI), deeply engaged in the financing of speculation, faced strong deposit withdrawals in September 1907. The other banks cut their credit, and the liquidity of the economy decreased sharply. The Banca d'Italia had neither the legal power nor the means to play the role of a lender of last resort alone. Its attempts to organize a bank consortium were not well received by the other banks at first. But when the panic threatened to spread to the whole financial community, an agreement was reached, with active participation of the Treasury. This strong and credible commitment of the banks and the government was enough to stop stock prices decreasing and save the SBI. One of the consequences of this crisis was a better under-standing by the financial community of the need for a strong central bank. Stringher, the director of the Banca d'Italia, and the most effective character in this story, was to succeed in using this mood to orient his bank better in this direction.

The 1830s, investigated by Lévy-Leboyer in Chapter 4, furnish a good case of the international transmission of financial crises. They also show the disappointment experienced by the Bank of England in its attempts to regulate the financial system, which was already an international one, by discretionary monetary policy. In 1832 Palmer devised what appeared as sound guidelines for the Bank's operations: widespread discounting in times of discredit, short of a threat to the convertibility of the pound. The difficulty was in the application of "Palmer's rule." The cotton boom of the early 1830s and the resulting increase in U.S. imports from the world as a whole were financed largely in England, and in particular by American banks in Liverpool (Wiggins's, Wilson's, and Wilde's, the three W's). The Bank of England discounted too freely in this speculative period, fueling the boom. A sharp decrease in cotton prices in 1837 put many banks in difficulty, and the three W's had to suspend payments. A drain on the Bank of England's reserves led it to raise discount rates and to limit credit to the market. This increased the troubles of the system, and the Bank soon had to make an about-face and buy a great deal of bank paper, much of which was never honored. In 1839 speculation in U.S. government bonds and private equities took place in London. Again the finance of speculation was assisted by a low discount rate. By the time the bank rate was raised to limit the drain of the Banks reserves, it was already too late. Once again the Bank of England had to act as a lender of last resort and refinance a lot of paper, although at a penalty rate.

Temin does not believe that the Bank of England lent to an exaggerated extent in the early 1830s. But he gives some responsibility in the crises of the late 1830s to the active interventionism of the Bank: Its tight monetary policy in 1836 precipitated the fall in the cotton price and the panic that followed.

Lévy-Leboyer believes that the Bank of England learned in the 1830s the danger of discretionary policies. This led to the more mechanical and rigorous policy enshrined in the Bank Charter Act of 1844 and the financial-stability period that followed 1866.

Now, did this stability result from the new monetary policy of the Bank of England? Matthews notices that other factors acted in a stabilizing way: repeal of the Corn Laws and the speeding-up of communications. But, more important, Matthews does not believe that the policy of the Bank became so rigorous and so new after 1844. No governor could leave a crisis to run its course without intervening, and the "chancellor's letters" gave him the right of intervening. But this new procedure may have created uncertainty regarding if, when, and how the Bank would act as a lender of last resort and may have discouraged speculative excesses – the "moral hazard" that Solow analyzes. On the other hand, at this conference Kindleberger was skeptical that the Bank had learned to handle its monetary machine efficiently. He quoted the Baring crisis of 1890, which had repercussions in Australia in 1893. He pointed out that the burst of foreign lending from 1910 to 1913 strongly resembled those of 1825, 1857, and 1887–90 that had led to crises, and it had all the earmarks of a major boom-and-bust in foreign lending when it was cut short by the outbreak of World War I and an entirely different kind of crisis in August 1914.[3]

Only the Holtfrerich–Frenkel colloquy (Chapter 5) involves a discussion of econometrics and theory. Holtfrerich believes that foreign holders of German marks in 1919–22 had an essentially speculative demand for this currency. The conviction by foreigners that the mark was undervalued was based on a quite unreasonable analysis (i.e., on irrational expectations). Some had faith in the return to the prewar gold parity; others noticed that exchange depreciation of the mark ran ahead of the rise of German internal prices, and they made a naive application of the purchasing-power-parity doctrine. The technical question is whether foreign and domestic holders of marks can be aggregated into a single demand function, as if they were motivated by the same information and purposes, or whether their demands had widely different characteristics. Debeir and Frenkel doubt that the great shift of expectations and the bearish speculation against the mark that followed June 1922 and drove the German economy into hyperinflation were due only to non-Germans. Debeir tries to show that part of the foreign-capital outflow from Germany resulted from the buoyant business situation in England.

A factual problem is to determine when the ordinary inflation became hyperinflation. Some participants thought the date of the change must reflect a sharp change in time-series data. Using somewhat different price series, both Cagan and Holtfrerich put the hyperinflation start in June 1922. Others participants believed it was better to choose the date of an occurrence of a crucial event that changed expectations and caused the hyperinflation. Goldsmith (the only participant in the conference who could claim to have experienced the hyperinflation, first as a student and toward the latter days as a bank clerk) believed it was the Ruhr occupation in January 1923 and the huge government deficit that followed. Borchardt considered it to be the London reparations agreement amounting to an ultimatum to Germany in May 1921. In his comment, Frenkel proposes the rise to power of Poincaré in France in January 1922, the Treaty of Versailles, and the sharp increase in the debt financing of war in Germany as early as 1916.

Pressnell (Chapter 6) presents the interesting cases of countries in the sterling area: Australia, Ceylon, Mauritius, and India, where crises were handled by borrowing on outside financial markets, in particular in London. These measures often were taken on the initiative of local British authorities. They also acted as central banks would have done (banks that did not exist or were limited to a currency board in these countries); suspension of convertibility, guarantee of notes issued by banks in difficulty, declaration of bank holidays. The parent houses in London of local banks also played an important role in this respect. The market of large financial centers appeared then as the lender of next-to-last resort that came to the rescue as part of its regular business. By the same token, Czarist borrowing of 1.5 billion francs in 1906 after the twin disasters of revolution and defeat saved a regime from bankruptcy, although a decade later the sovereign risk involved loomed more ominously. What was the extent of the role of the London center and of the Bank of England? Fischer's belief is that it was overestimated. Other financial centers and central banks played essential (even if more regional) roles, and the Bank of England would never have been strong enough to assume the role of the world lender of last resort alone.

III. Policy

Moggridge (Chapter 7) criticizes Kindleberger's view that the crises of 1921 and 1929 were so damaging because of the nonexistence of an international lender of last resort, a function that Britain could not and the United States would not assume. The 1921 crisis was not a financial one. What would have been needed was an international reconstruction program (like the Marshall plan), a choice of reasonable parities, a progressive return to convertibility and decontrol, a more balanced evolution of government budgets, and a more sensible U.S. monetary policy. During the crisis that started in 1929, many financial salvage operations were attempted, even though they often came too late and not in the best places. But if these mistakes had not been made, the deep causes of disequilibrium should have been dealt with, especially U.S. monetary policy, overvaluation of the French franc and gold accumulation by France, and weakness of the British balance of payments, which was suffering from a more and more overvalued pound in a world of depression in which many currencies were depreciating

One might further wonder whether or not an international lender of last resort in 1920 could have made return to normal conditions possible without having to pay the price of deflationary policies. Would not the 1929 crisis have been less deep if the Federal Reserve System had played its role of lender of last resort at home by preventing the Wall Street crash from spreading to the whole economy and by limiting credit cuts? Finally, the idea that the function of lender of last resort cannot be assumed by international cooperation, in a world in depression divided by international rivalries, is surely a lesson to be learned from the 1929 crisis.

On a more contemporaneous level, Métais (Chapter 9) notes the financial fragility of the less developed countries in the face of increasing short-run indebtedness, large fluctuations in interest rates and in the prices of raw materials, and the increase in the price of oil. Private banks try to limit their risk by countries. They spread it among them by bank consortia and by better sharing of risk among U.S., European, and Japanese banks. Most lending relates to a small number of rich or rapidly developing and diversified countries, such as Brazil and Korea. The banks use sophisticated methods of risk evaluation and credit rationing. Central banks act on their own. They try to gain better knowledge and control of the international operations of their banks. They agreed under the auspices of the Bank for International Settlements to play the role of lender of last resort for Euromarket operations of their banks. Finally, case-by-case salvage operations are organized under the Paris agreement in countries facing risk of bankruptcy. These consist of refinancing or rescheduling of the debt linked to an agreement between the country and the International Monetary Fund (IMF) on the basis of policies of adjustment worked out with the financial help of the IMF. Such operations are necessary to prevent a crisis on the Eurocurrency market and a sharp decrease in the exports of industrialized countries. But they require accommodating policies of central banks (first the Federal Reserve System), and they increase world liquidity and inflation.

These operations are of the same kind as the international stabilization scheme decided in Geneva under the auspices of the League of Nations in 1922, which is investigated by März. The largest countries supplied credit at a cheap rate to Austria to allow it to reestablish first its budget, then its balance of payments. This was at the price of international control on Austrian public finance. Other similarities with the interwar period are seen in the cases of France of 1924 and Britain in 1931.

Coulbois (Chapter 8) focuses on the issue whether the "cambist" approach or the "academic" approach to forward-exchange-rate determination was the more accurate and what this meant for the treatment of foreign-exchange crises by central banks' operations in forward exchange. To the academic, a central bank can drive the forward rate to a level different from interest parity and induce a flow of arbitrage capital in one direction or another. The cambists deny this, asserting that the forward rate is set directly by dealers from the interest differential and is therefore not subject to this manipulation. Commentators think that the distinction is perhaps overdrawn and is without much practical consequence for the management of exchange rates.

Forward operations in foreign exchange as a device for countering a crisis, however, lack an essential ingredient. A lender of last resort faces the need to reverse expectations. Forward operations are, on the whole, a quiet, even secret, means of intervention, designed to prevent a loss in reserves showing up. But what is needed, Dornbusch asserts, is a countercrisis, a squeeze of the speculators, a show of force that makes them head for cover. The $30 billion swap line used to protect the dollar on November 1, 1978, furnished an example of an appropriate response. Edward März, in commenting on the 1929 depression, notes that the Austrian banks had been weakened by their losses in speculation against the French franc in the squeeze undertaken by the Banque de France in March 1924 with the help of a Morgan $100 million loan.

Solow's discussion of the role of the lender of last resort (Chapter 10) focuses on two issues: the nature of the public good to be furnished, and the "moral hazard" that the knowledge that financial institutions in trouble will be saved in straits may make them more reckless. On the first score, the precise nature of the public good involves externalities. In the absence of a force to halt spreading deflation, external diseconomies are realized in bankruptcies that need not occur. Laffargue believes that one origin of these externalities is that the customers of a bank do not have precise information on the risk facing their bank. Rather, they have a general idea of the risks in the whole financial community. In order to discourage each bank from taking inordinate risk and so destroying the credibility of the whole system, regulation and bank inspection are necessary.

On the moral-hazard issue, Solow presents a model of partial indemnification related to what can be observed of the level of care taken by the insured, under various circumstances, emphasizing again the need for bank inspection and regulation as an aspect ensuring that banks exercise appropriate caution.

Of course, if these precautions are not taken or fail, the lender of last resort must assure a soft landing instead of a crash. Such soft landings have occurred in the United States since the 1960s, successively, one at a time, in the stock market, in the bond market, in real estate investment trusts (called REITs), and in banking lending on mothballed jumbo airplanes such as the Boeing 747s and unemployed tankers "on the mud" in Norwegian fjords or Greek bays, and they are prospectively faced in a few specialized credit markets such as those for house mortgages, consumer debt, and lending to less developed countries.

McClam (Chapter 11) notes that if lender-of-last-resort actions help to limit the spreading of panics and bankruptcies, they cannot prevent the decrease of the private demand for credit, and consequently the decrease of the demand for commodities and of the supply of money. What is required is the government's acceptance of a large money-financed deficit (i.e., to be the borrower of last resort). The fact that this double function has been assured efficiently since 1950 explains the present relative stability of the economy compared with the interwar period. But the fact that public-authority interventions have been made more on a continuous basis than on an exceptional basis helps to explain the current inflation. The moral-hazard issue is far from having found a solution.

The identity of the lender of last resort is fairly clear in a domestic setting, with which Solow is concerned, although McClam makes the suggestion that ultimately not the central bank but the government as a whole is the lender of last resort. In an international context, the position is not so clear, and the free rider that inhibits the production of public goods more generally may take over. McClam underlines that in the Herstatt episode, central banks under the leadership of the Bank for International Settlements asserted the doctrine of national or parental responsibility. Each central bank is responsible for the liabilities of its banks and their subsidiaries, wherever in the world such subsidiaries may be located. Parental responsibility was intended to stabilize the Eurocurrency market after Herstatt. There remains, first, a small ambiguity in the case of subsidiaries jointly owned by banks headquartered in several countries, and, second, the possibility that in a crunch, one or more authorities may decide that the contingent liabilities implied by parental responsibility are too large or are inappropriate to the domestic policy of punishing local malefactors. The private banker Lepetit notes that the German authorities wanted to teach the speculators a lesson at the time of Herstatt, and they created a dangerous situation in which one large international bank had to switch off its computer so as not to observe that its capital was impaired, whereas other banks created liquidity by exchanging checks. Lepetit adds that parental responsibility and the conviction that central banks would not allow large bankruptcies or the failure of large borrowers have progressively encouraged banks to bear excessive risks. This calls for more regulation and control of the banking industry.

Perhaps the most awkward issue in the lender-of-last-resort function is the choice of what banks and companies get rescued. The Bagehot rule calls for lending to all solvent borrowers, albeit at a penalty rate to discourage the less necessitous. But who is solvent is an acute question when prices are falling rapidly. In discussing Austrian financial history, März points out that the Austrian National Bank limited its lender-of-last-resort operations to members of the establishment, insiders, those with connections to the monarchy or the financial oligarchy. The public good in these cases become confused with the private.

The International Monetary Fund is the lender of last resort for developing countries, if not for financial centers for which its resources are too limited except as part of a larger package. The "penalty rate" in its operations, and the picking and choosing of whom to aid, are converted into the question of conditionality. "The Lord helps those that help themselves." Both conditionality and picking emphasize the political element in world central banks. Much as economists would wish to work out rules and deny that politics enters into what they regard as essentially technical issues of financial stability, there is no escape from the conclusion that the provision of stability to the world macroeconomy is an art, and a political work of art, at that.

Notes

1. New York, Basic Books, 1978.
2. The male social scientist may be troubled by this simile, however, if he recalls the story of the two anthropologists standing on a street corner when a pretty girl went by. The first anthropologist said to the second, "Wow, that's a pretty girl," but recovered himself in time to add, "in our culture."
3. He also told the story of the young diplomat who went to the old diplomat in 1939 and asked what he should tell tourists and others who kept asking if there was going to be a war. "Tell them no," said the veteran, "I have been telling them no for forty years, and I was only wrong once."

Part I. Theory

2. The financial-instability hypothesis: capitalist processes and the behavior of the economy

HYMAN P. MINSKY

I. Introduction

Financial instability and crises are facts of economic life. Precise definitions are not necessary, for the major episodes of instability, whether runaway inflation, a speculative bubble, an exchange crisis, or debt deflation, can be identified by pointing (Kindleberger, 1978). Analytically, financial instability can be defined as a process in which rapid and accelerating changes in the prices of assets (both financial and capital) take place relative to the prices of current output. Of particular importance for this chapter is the relationship between financial instability and the deep depressions of history. On the debt-deflation side of financial instability, which is a major focus of what follows (although the theory is symmetrical with respect to inflations and deflations), the critical element in explaining why financial instability occurs is the development over historical time of liability structures that cannot be validated by market-determined cash flows or asset values. Thus in a free market, wide and spreading bankruptcies can occur, but in an economy with big government and an alert lender of last resort, the thrust to debt deflation can be overridden. One of the implications of the theory that is labeled the financial-instability hypothesis is that there are "costs" to overriding the thrust to debt deflation in the form of an aggravated instability and a tendency toward stagflation.

Financial instability is a nonevent, something that just cannot happen, insofar as the standard body of today's economic theory is concerned. If economic theory were just an abstract game played by some who were moderately gifted in mathematics, such ignoring of observed reality would be only a minor nuisance. However, each era's standard theory is the guide to the era's economic policy. The floundering of the capitalist economies in the 1970s reflects the irrelevance of the theoretical framework that the economists of the policy establishments apply when they advise and instruct political leaders. In part, the malaise of capitalist countries is iatrogenic – the disease has been induced in the patient by physicians.

Standard theory will not do because it ignores essential facts and cannot explain important observations. Therefore there is a need to replace standard theory. Fortunately we do not have to start such a reconstruction of theory from square zero. Before theory became a victim of mathematics and observations were replaced by printouts, economists recognized that financial crises occurred and set their minds to explaining why they took place and their effects on system performance.[1]

There are interpretations of *The General Theory* (Keynes, 1936) that differ from the interpretation in the standard literature (Chick, 1973; Davidson, 1972; Keynes, 1937; Kregel, 1973; Minsky, 1975a; Robinson, 1971; Weintraub, 1966). One implication of these interpretations is that *The General Theory* points to, even if it does not fully realize, an economic theory that is relevant for a capitalist economy because it fully integrates the behavior of what standard literature labels the real economy with the financial system. One implication of these interpretations is that the processes of a capitalist economy that finance investment and asset holdings lead to the endogenous development of conditions conducive to a financial crisis. This means that Keynes provides us with the shoulders of a giant on which we can stand as we try to understand how capitalist economies behave.

II. The financial-instability hypothesis in relation to standard theory

During recent years there has been a discussion as to the "true meaning" of Keynes. My contribution is a little book in the Columbia essays on the great economists. In that book I hold "that *The General Theory* does embody a revolutionary change in economic theory, but that in the process of arriving at today's standard version of what Keynes was about the revolution was aborted" (Minsky, 1975a). I argued that "the missing step in the standard Keynesian theory was the explicit consideration of capitalist finance within a cyclical and speculative context. Once capitalist finance is introduced and the development of cash flows (as stated in the interrelated balance sheets) during the various states of the economy [is] explicitly examined, then the full power of the revolutionary insights and the alternative frame of analysis that Keynes developed becomes evident" (Minsky, 1975a:129). The events since the book was written bear out the virtue of looking at capitalist economies from the perspective of their financial relations.

Standard interpretations of Keynes virtually ignore his analysis of financial markets and interrelationships. They are strangely ahistorical. It is not necessary that one wholeheartedly embrace the view that anomalies are the driving force behind scientific revolutions (Kuhn, 1962) to recognize that the collapse of the American and world financial systems between 1929 and 1933 was a powerful factor tending to concentrate the mind of anyone who was trying during those years to explain the behavior of capitalist economies. The impact of the financial collapse on the formation of a new theory would be especially marked if the principal adventurer in the quest for new understanding was a political animal who was deeply involved both in the "city" and along corridors of power. In order to understand *The General Theory* we need to recognize that the financial collapse of 1929–33 was recent history when *The General Theory* was being formulated. It is necessary to believe that Keynes understood and appreciated the interactive process that Irving Fisher described so well (Fisher, 1933).

Those who describe Keynes as mainly concerned with labor-market disequilibria in which real wages are "too high" seem unaware that persistence of unemployment was not the critical problem when *The General Theory* was formulated. The critical problem was that unemployment kept increasing even though money wages and prices were falling rapidly. If unemployment equilibrium occurred, it was only after the downward plunge was halted in 1933; until then the critical labor-market development was the unprecedented increase in unemployment.

The disequilibrium interpretation of Keynes (Malinvaud, 1977) holds that unemployment results from a combination of market functions and constraints that lead to a rationing of jobs among workers. Fixed-price sellers, inflexible money wages, and a floor to interest rates are some of the forms disequilibrium-inducing constraints can take. This constrained-equilibrium approach to macroeconomics ignores the problem of the functioning of a system in which various facets of today's behavior are determined by variables that reflect quite different time horizons.

Keynes divided the economic problem of a capitalist economy into a primary problem, the determination of various budget constraints, and a secondary problem, the determination of individual outputs. Once the primary problem is solved, the secondary problem can be described as the determination of an equilibrium within constraints.

A proposition that emerges from a disequilibrium approach such as that of Malinvaud is that Keynesian unemployment exists because money wages and output supply prices are too high, and persists because money wages and prices do not tend to fall with the rationing of jobs and sales. A key proposition of Keynes's analysis is that when inadequate aggregate demand leads to unemployment, wage and price flexibility makes things worse. This is because price and wage declines make it an ever-increasing burden for debtors to acquire cash to fulfill payment commitments due to debts. Keynes's dynamics explicitly include the repercussions on demand of financial interrelationships; standard theory largely ignores them. Any theory of employment that does not integrate aggregate-demand formation with the financing of investment and positions in capital assets cannot be called

Keynesian. Furthermore, an analysis that ignores finance cannot catch the essential cyclical features of a capitalist economy in which Wall Street exists and is important.

Standard economic theory does not examine the possibility that there are endogenous disequilibrating forces within a capitalist economy because of the way prices of capital assets are determined or how positions in capital assets and investment activity are financed. The issue is whether or not propositions relevant to a capitalist economy's development can be derived by studying theoretical constructs that ignore essential features of a capitalist economy. If economic theory is to explain financial crises, the inter-relationships between financial crises and business cycles, and how finance affects system behavior, then economic theory must examine an economy that is explicitly capitalist.

To a standard economic theorist such as Edmond Malinvaud, the proto-typical economy consists of consumers, producers, and an autonomous sector called government. It deals with only three commodities, called goods, labor, and money. It concerns the operations during one given period, which is analyzed independently of past and future periods (Malinvaud, 1977:38). Each item in this specification does violence to Keynesian perceptions of what must be studied and what must be explained and understood. Theorems about the stability of capitalist processes valid for a capitalist economy with sophisticated financial institutions cannot be developed in the framework of Malinvaud's prototype model (Arrow and Hahn, 1971:Chapter 14). The existence of capital assets, financial instruments, financial institutions, and money means that economic theory must deal with intertemporal relations in which the time frames differ for various decisions that determine system behavior. For standard theorists to study the problems of a capitalist economy, they must abandon their normal operating procedure of modeling village-fair economies and turn to modeling economies with a Wall Street. In such economies, financial instability that has occurred in a variety of specific institutional frameworks becomes a key fact to be explained. No theory of the behavior of a capitalist economy has merit if it explains instability as the result either of exogenous policy mistakes or of institutional flaws that can be readily corrected. Instability existed long before there was anything now recognized as economic policy and under a wide variety of banking and financial institutions.

A theory that links investment to the prices of capital assets, the prices of capital assets and the pace of investment to the functioning of financial markets, and the functioning of financial markets to profit opportunities in financial businesses will readily explain financial instability. Persistent unemployment is explained as the result of financial crisis that is allowed to lead to debt deflation. Thus persistent unemployment is an unconstrained, though transitory, state of monetary economy with a history that includes recent financial crises and debt deflations.

The fundamental ingredients of a theory of the capitalist process are in *The General Theory*. The lesson from Keynes is that if the behavior of a capitalist economy is to be understood, money cannot be introduced into the argument as an afterthought. Nevertheless, this is what standard theory does. The first step in developing a theory of the behavior of a capitalist economy is to model money and financial relationships as integral parts of the determination of aggregate demand. One way is to model the money (or cash) flows that are set up by the financial structure and the way income is distributed.

Malinvaud introduced money as follows: "Let us consider an economy with r commodities ($n = 1, 2, \ldots r$), the last one being money" (Malinvaud, 1977:18). Arrow and Hahn wrote: "Let the subscript 'n' stand for money that we now regard as the non-interest-paying debt of some agency outside our formal system, say the government" (Arrow and Hahn, 1971:349). It is clear that the money of these theorists has no relevant resemblance to the money of capitalist economies. Arrow and Hahn recognized that they were violating reality in their definition and offered apologies for the primitive monetary ideas they explored; Malinvaud did not apologize, even as he offered his work as being relevant to the analysis of policy.

Wages and gross capital income are cash flows that result from the way income is determined. Gross capital income consists of rents, interest, taxes, conventionally labeled profits, and some, perhaps almost all, of the "executive and overhead" wages of business. Kalecki (1971:Chapter 7) showed how gross capital income is related to investment, government spending, the foreign balance, consumption financed by profits, and savings out of wage income. The Kalecki equations show the various conditions under which the profits of business can be large enough to enable business to fulfill its payment commitments on financial instruments. The linkages among business profits, fulfillment of commitments on financial instruments, investment, and financing enable us to understand why conditions conducive to financial crises emerge from the normal functioning of a capitalist economy.

The Kalecki equations also show why a full-blown interactive debt-deflation process has not occurred since World War II. An understanding of capitalist financial relations enables us to see the importance of lender-of-last-resort operations and why the postwar economy, which has been free of debt deflation, is now subject to chronic inflationary pressures. The financial-instability hypothesis is a variant of Keynesian theory closely linked to insights about profit formation most clearly stated by Kalecki.

III. Legacies from the past and endowments
for the future

In every economy, today's capital assets and labor force are inherited from the past, and tomorrow's capital assets and labor force are partially determined by today's activity. A financial structure, related to ownership of capital assets and production of investment, is also a legacy from the past and an endowment for the future. Such intertemporal financial links and the payment commitments they embody are special to capitalism. In standard economic analysis, capital assets collected into plants are worked by labor to yield outputs. For simplicity, money wages are assumed to be given so that marginal and average out-of-pocket cost curves can be derived for outputs This analysis ignores the conditions imposed on the functioning of a capitalist economy by the need to fulfill commitments on financial instruments and to use financial instruments to finance investment and the ownership of capital assets.

We start with a modern capitalist economy that has a complex and sophisticated financial structure. The decision units and financial relations of such economies take many different institutional forms. The theoretical result that inherited financial relations determine the relative stability or instability of an economy holds for a wide range of specific financial structures. In complex and sophisticated financial systems claims are layered and there is specialization in financing practices. In particular, financial systems allow for a range of techniques by which firms control capital assets. A capitalist economy has markets in which real and financial assets are sold; markets and prices exist for current output, labor services, capital assets, and financial instruments. We also deal with an economy in which innovation (Schumpeter, 1934) exists in financial as well as in production processes and products (Minsky, 1957a).

As Keynes noted, "when a man buys an investment or a capital-asset, he purchases the right to a series of prospective returns, which he expects to obtain from selling its output, after deducting the running expenses of obtaining this output, during the life of the asset. The series of annuities $Q_1, Q_2, \ldots, Q_n$ it is convenient to call the *prospective* yield of the investment" (Keynes, 1936:136). The Q values are a series of cash flows that, as defined by Keynes, are the total revenues minus out-of-pocket costs (the running expenses of production). The Q values are a gross profit or a gross capital income. They provide the cash that the owners of capital assets are free to dispose of as they will – after providing for debts and taxes.

Production is carried on by firms. Capital assets, however, are collected into plants. Wages of variable labor and costs of materials yield running costs for a plant. The liabilities that a firm uses to finance capital assets and materials that flow through the plant may be linked to specific capital assets or plants (i.e., by a mortgage) or to the general worth of the firm. In either case, the cash flow available to meet payment commitments on debts will arise from the total operations of the firm.

Debts commit a firm to money payments. These money payments are on both income account (interest, rent) and for the repayment of principal (because debts are due or are amortized). Modern accounting practice leads to a division of the gross income of capital net of taxes into income and capital-consumption portions. The capital-consumption portion can be likened to the repayment of principal of a debt. In essence, in a capitalist economy, capital assets (plant, equipment, and inventories) are like bonds; Keynes identified the quasi rents produced by such assets as a series of annuities.

In addition to producing firms that receive "annuities" from profits earned by capital assets, a capitalist economy includes a wide variety of firms that receive their annuities as cash flows generated by debts and other financial instruments they own. In a capitalist economy, two sets of profit-maximizing institutions exist: One owns capital assets and makes profits by producing and selling goods and services; the other owns financial assets and makes profits by producing and selling debts, both its own, which others hold, and others', which it holds.

As a result of their debt structure, firms operate today with cash-payment commitments inherited from the past. Furthermore, current investment and ownership of capital assets require financing, which sets up payment commitments for the future. Economics is a strange discipline in which present, past, and future coexist in time. A cash-flow approach to economic theory helps unravel some of the problems associated with time.

Profits are a central concern of the economic theory based on an integration of Kalecki and Keynes. This theory leads to the proposition that instability results from the normal functioning of a capitalist economy. Profits are determined by investment, enable business to honor payment commitments on financial instruments, and enter the determination of views as to future profits. Current views of future profits help determine current values of capital assets and decisions to invest. Inasmuch as future investment determines future profits, it is evident that business invests today because business is expected to invest in the future. But investment requires financing. Thus the terms on which financing is now available and is expected to be available determine investment. New financing is available only as past financing is validated by current profits. A key to understanding the behavior of a capitalist economy is the precise statement of the payments required by the liability structure and how cash to meet such commitments is generated.

IV. Cash flows, present values, and cash kickers

In standard economic theory, firms are characterized by the outputs they produce and perhaps by the technical, physical inputs they require for production; economic reality is analyzed by studying markets for commodities and services. The fundamental insight that guides standard theory is that an economy can be analyzed as if it were a village market.

For a study of the capitalist process, the structuring of economic reality into commodities and markets is of secondary importance. The analysis of cash flows (receipts and payments) has primary importance. Whereas standard theory views an economy as producing and consuming outputs, a Wall Street perspective views an economy as producing and allocating profits. The economy consists in a set of balance sheets in which assets generate cash receipts and liabilities state payment commitments. The problem that theory addresses is how assets generate cash and how relations among cash-payment commitments, anticipated cash flows, and realized cash flows affect system performance.

The gross flow of cash to a firm from its current participation in production is its sales revenues; these revenues, minus what Keynes called "running expenses," yield gross profits before taxes, which, following Keynes, we call Q. We ignore government spending and taxes for the moment. We therefore have a set of anticipated quasi rents or gross profits that we will label $AQ_1, \ldots, AQ_n$. Firms may also own financial assets that yield cash flows as contracts are fulfilled.[2]

Liabilities set up demand, dated, and contingent cash payments. With more or less precision the current day's (0's) liability structure leads to a time series of payment commitments, $PC_1, \ldots, PC_n$. We therefore have two time series: one of anticipated gross profits, AQ_i, the second of payment commitments due to the liability structure, PC_i. Before an investment is viable, it is necessary that

(1) $$\sum_{i=1}^{n} AQ_i > 0$$

(2) $$\sum_{i=1}^{n} AQ_i > \sum_{i=1}^{n} PC_i$$

Cash in must exceed payment commitments.

We can split both anticipated quasi rents and payment commitments into two parts: $AQ(a)$, $AQ(y)$, and $PC(a)$, $PC(y)$, where $AQ(a)$ is the amount of quasi rents that represent the wastage or consumption of capital, $PC(a)$ is the amount of the payments on debts that is a repayment of principal, and $AQ(y)$ and $PC(y)$ are the net income part of the cash flows.

(3) $AQ(y) = AQ - AQ(a)$
        $PC(y) = PC - PC(a)$

A *hedge-finance unit* is one for which

(4) $AQ_i > PC_i$

for all i, so that

(5) $AQ_i - PC_i > 0$

for all i. The value of the firm, E, is a capitalized value of the cash flows

(6) $E = \sum\limits_{i=1}^{n} k_i(AQ_i - PC_i)$

k_i takes into account the felt assuredness, which Keynes called uncertainty, of the cash flow to the firm and depends on the market interest rates on different risk or uncertainty classes of assets. This relation is a variable over business cycles (Temin, 1976). For a hedge unit, a present-value reversal cannot occur as a result of a change in interest rates.

Consider an ordinary business firm that has payment commitments due to contracts of PC_i ($i = 1, \ldots, n$). Ordinarily the cash to fulfill these payment commitments will accrue to the firm from current profits. However, a firm will find it advantageous to keep some cash or cash-equivalent assets on hand as insurance against interruptions in its cash receipts. These holdings will be related to sales revenues and payment commitments on debts. Thus a money position (which may consist largely of short-term financial assets) exists that is related to near-term running expenses X_i and payment commitments on contracts PC_i

(7) $M_D = \sum\limits_{i=1}^{m} (T_i(X_i) + L_i(PC_i))$ (m small)

For a hedge firm, anticipated total revenues exceed running expenses and cash payments in every period; the need for M, except to bridge time gaps, is small.

For a *speculative-finance* unit

(8) $AQ_i < PC_i$ ($i = 1, \ldots, m$, m small)
        $AQ_i > PC_i$ ($i = m + 1, \ldots, n$)

Furthermore, over the first m periods,

(9) $\sum\limits_{i=1}^{m} AQ_y(y) > \sum\limits_{i=1}^{m} PC_i(y)$

the income portion of quasi rents exceed the income (interest) portion of payment commitments. Such a unit has a portion of the principal on debt falling due in the near term, and this debt repayment exceeds the capital-consumption or debt-repayment funds that its assets generate. Such a firm can fulfill its payment commitments only as it runs down its money assets or succeeds in placing new debts.

Speculative finance characterizes banks, other financial institutions, treasuries with floating debts, and ordinary business firms that roll over bank debt and commercial paper. The continuing normal functioning of such units depends on their ability to place liabilities; they depend on the normal functioning of financial markets. Whereas the value of a hedge-finance unit is positive for all interest rates, the value of a unit that engages in speculative finance depends on interest rates. The value will be positive for low interest rates and negative for high interest rates: A rise in interest rates can lead to a present-value reversal.

For a speculative-finance unit the demand for money is still given by equation (7). However, for such a unit, $PC_i/X_i (i = 1, \ldots ,m)$ is greater than for a hedge unit. The demand for money and money-market assets is more a function of the payment commitments due to debts for units engaged in speculative finance than for units engaged in hedge finance. Speculative-finance units tend to hold money as insurance against refinancing failures. Because of this, we would expect L_i for speculative firms to be negatively related to interest rates.

There is a special kind of speculative-finance unit, a *Ponzi-finance unit*, for which the current income portion of payment commitments exceeds the current income portion of cash receipts, and such payment commitments exceed the anticipated cash receipts for all periods except some terminal periods. Symbolically, we have

$$(10) \quad AQ_i < PC_i \quad (i = 1, \ldots ,n-1)$$
$$AQ_i >> PC_i \quad (i = n)$$

Furthermore,

$$(11) \quad AQ_i(y) < PC_i(y) \quad (i = 1, \ldots ,n-1)$$
$$AQ_i(y) >> PC_i(y) \quad (i = n)$$

For all except some end points of the horizon, current earnings do not meet payment commitments. The outstanding face value of debt increases as time goes by.

I have labeled such financial arrangements "Ponzi finance," recalling a Boston "swindler." However, these financial relations are much more widespread than the label I give them, which relates to pyramiding schemes. Ponzi finance characterizes any investment program with a significant gestation period. Furthermore, deals that involve holding assets the carrying costs of which exceed the income earned, so that the "deal" is profitable only if the asset appreciates, are examples of Ponzi finance. The thin-margin stock market of the 1920s is an example of Ponzi finance.[3]

The present value of units engaged in Ponzi finance is sensitive to interest rates. Because $AQ_i(y) < PC_i(y)$ ($i = 1, \ldots, n-1$) and because $PC_i(y)$ increases when (short-term) interest rates rise, the outstanding debt of a unit engaged in Ponzi finance increases at a faster rate the higher the interest rates; furthermore, if AQ_n reflects the value of a capital asset, AQ_n will fall with rising interest rates. A unit engaged in Ponzi finance is especially vulnerable to present-value reversal.

Because Ponzi-finance schemes are always in the money market to finance positions, they might be expected to carry a significant amount of money and money-market assets. However, the pressure on such units to control financing costs by minimizing borrowing is great. Ponzi units often will be economizing on cash as well as dependent on refinancing conditions.

The formalization of cash-flow relations throws light on the emergence of financial instability. A hedge-finance unit, with its financial commitments in place, can fail to meet commitments only if the actual Q_i values fall short of anticipated Q_i values. However, in a simple capitalist economy, actual Q_i values depend on investment. Financial difficulties for a hedge-financing unit can thus occur only if a prior fall in income occurs. Inasmuch as financial crises do not depend on a prior fall in income, hedge-financing units cannot cause downward financial instability.

A speculative unit is constantly refinancing a portion of its liability structure. Its normal functioning depends on the normal functioning of financial markets. Its interest costs reflect changing conditions in financial markets. In particular, a rise in interest rates on debts will raise payment commitments even as there is no change in the quasi rents. A speculative unit can become a Ponzi unit, in the sense that for some periods $AQ_i(y) < PC_i(y)$ will be true when financial markets tighten.

Ponzi-finance units are especially vulnerable to changes in money-market conditions. Not only can their payment commitments increase beyond anticipated levels when interest rates rise, but a rise in interest rates may lead to a fall in the nth-period receipts that are expected to validate liabilities. This is so because the payoff receipts of a Ponzi scheme often reflect the value of a capital asset that will be delivered or sold, and this value is inversely related to interest rates.

Ponzi-equivalent finance characterizes the financing of much of investment in process. An investment project yields no revenues until the project is finished. The cost of production includes the interest costs on early expenses. The value of the project on completion is the present value of anticipated profits, which is inversely related to interest rates. When interest rates rise, the present value of Ponzi schemes can become negative; the value of the

AQ_n that makes the entire scheme viable decreases even as the accumulated debt, because of the excess of current costs (including interest charges) over early quasi rents, increases.

V. Robust and fragile financial systems

A financial system is robust when modest changes in cash flows, capitalization rates, and payment commitments do not appreciably affect the ability of private units to fulfill their financial commitments. Conversely, a financial system is fragile when modest changes in cash flows, capitalization rates, and payment commitments adversely affect the ability of private units to meet their financial commitments. However, a financial system does not exist in isolation. Its robustness or fragility does not depend solely on interactions within the financial system. Whether or not investment, employment, and profits are strongly affected by (1) small changes in financial variables and (2) the success or failure of debtors in fulfilling financial contracts is important in determining the robustness or fragility of the financial system. Neither finance nor income determination can be treated in isolation; the connections between them are strong.

The robustness or fragility of a financial system depends on two relations: the cash-flow characteristics of the financial system and the way financial-system behavior affects the cash flow that enable businesses, households, and financial institutions to fulfill their obligations. Furthermore, analyses of the stability of the financial system and the interactions between the financial structure and income determination need to examine whether the fragility (and thus the stability) of the system is an invariant characteristic of the economy or whether it evolves (and if it evolves, what determines its evolution).

The financial-instability hypothesis holds that changes in cash-flow relations occur over a run of good (or tranquil) years and transform an initially robust financial system into a fragile financial system. The debt-deflation process identified by Irving Fisher during the 1930s presumably transforms a fragile financial structure into something more robust, whereas the financial changes over a run of good times transform a robust financial structure into a fragile one. The fragility/robust status of the financial system comes down to two questions: What determines the quasi rents that enable units to fulfill financial commitments? Does the structure of financial relations set limits to system performance that enable units to satisfy financial commitments?

Hedge, speculative, and Ponzi firms are all affected by changes in quasi rents. A shortfall of quasi rents from anticipated levels can make a hedge unit a speculative unit and a speculative unit a Ponzi unit. Inasmuch as a Ponzi unit's validating quasi rents result from selling out a position, such a shortfall means that payment commitments on debts cannot be fulfilled. A decline in quasi rents can mean that the cash-receipt expectations of some debt owners will be disappointed.

A shortfall of quasi rents of a Ponzi unit from anticipated values can also mean that the cash receipts of a debt owner fall short of those anticipated. This refers to financial institutions that own such debts. The ability of these institutions to fulfill their stated commitments depends on a continuing flow of payments toward them on owned financial instruments. The degree of layering of financial institutions and the asset–liability mix of these institutions are parameters of the aggregate robustness or fragility of a financial system.

In the simplest Kalecki case, where aggregate gross profit (aggregate Q) equals aggregate investment, the shortfall of realized profits below anticipated profits requires a logically prior shortfall of investment. This leaves the generation of financial crises and deep depressions essentially unexplained, for it is the decline of investment that has to be explained. History records examples of triggering events in the form of collapse of some financial institution or business enterprise that led to financial crisis. There are also examples of financial institutions and business enterprises that collapsed, leaving masses of unpaid debts, that did not lead to a financial crisis. The failure of particular units to meet their payment commitments does not necessarily lead to generalized financial crisis. If a financial crisis is triggered by a particular event or failure of policy, the overall financial structure must be such that individual failure can trigger a chain reaction of failures.

A rise in interest rates lowers the capitalized value of a hedge unit but does not alter its payment commitments. A hedge unit's capitalized value (the E of equation 6) will decrease with a rise in interest rates. A rise in interest rates that lowers the market value of the firm also lowers the margin of safety that the excess of market value of shares over the nominal value of debt provides. Whereas this does not affect the ability of the firm to meet its payment commitment, it may well affect the terms on which additional debt can be issued. Inasmuch as the terms on which debt can be issued affect investment activity, investment will be reduced.

A rise in interest rates affects payment commitments and can thus transform a positive present value into a negative present value for speculative and Ponzi financial units. Speculative and Ponzi units must issue debt in order to meet payment and commitments. This means that they must always meet the market. Furthermore, they are vulnerable to any disruption, in the form of transitory unfavorable financing terms, that may occur in financial markets. A rise in interest rates that severely affects the value of a firm engaged in speculative or Ponzi finance will compromise its ability to issue debt and will move a speculative or Ponzi unit to a higher risk class.

The risk class of a firm reflects views as to the likelihood that it will not meet its payments. If a rise in interest rate compromises the value of a speculative or a Ponzi unit, refinancing of maturing debt and issuance of additional debt will occur at terms that reflect this compromised net worth. Such higher terms further compromise the net worth. The process may not converge; before terms high enough to compensate the lender for increased default possibilities are reached, the terms may be such that borrowers and lenders alike will believe that default is inescapable. The existence of risk-compensated financing terms for a particular class of units may well depend on the level of riskless or default-free interest rates.

The stability of a financial system depends on the weight of hedge finance in the total private financial structure. The smaller the weight of hedge finance (the greater the weight of speculative and Ponzi finance), the greater the possibility of a financial crisis, because the greater the likelihood that rising interest rates will lead to present-value reversals. Present-value reversals lead to the abandonment of investment projects that are under way and a decrease in new investment undertakings.

A financial structure that is dominated by hedge finance offers both inducements to invest and incentives to engage in speculative and Ponzi finance. Banks and other financial institutions are merchants of debt. They merchandise their debts to asset holders and finance various types of activities. Idle or excess cash balances in portfolios are potential raw materials for their lending. The substitution of short-term debt for long-term debt in financing asset holdings and investment in process provides a market for their loans. Banks and other financial institutions therefore have an incentive to induce speculative and Ponzi finance.

Stability is destabilizing, not initially to a recession but first to an expansion of investment. The determination of today's financing structure by the past behavior of the economy means that the financial structure becomes more susceptible to a financial crisis even as businessmen and bankers extrapolate success in fulfilling financial commitments into diminished protection against a financial crisis.

VI. The generation of profits

There is no need to repeat Kalecki's demonstration that gross profits = gross investment + capitalists' consumption (Kalecki, 1971:78–92). Furthermore, these relations can be generalized, so that the following equation will hold: gross profits net of taxes = gross investment + export surplus + budget deficit − workers' savings + capitalists' consumption. These latter relations, in which profits are generated by the way in which the system works in terms of investment, government size and scope, foreign balance, consumption habits of workers, and the distribution and use of profit incomes, link the income-generating process under capitalism to the cash flows needed to validate the financial structure. Kalecki's gross profits after taxes are the realized cash flows that enable firms that use debt to finance control over capital assets to satisfy their payment commitments. Whereas current profits determine whether or not units can fullfill their financial commitments, anticipated profits determine the willingness of bankers and businessmen to extend and to take on financial commitments.

In capitalist economies, prior to the 1930s, peacetime governments were small. There was no potential budget deficit that was large relative to gross investment. In such an economy variations in gross investment were well-nigh fully transformed into variations in gross profits. Thus a decline in investment led to an equal fall in gross profits, which could transform hedge units into speculative units, and speculative units into Ponzi units, even as net worths decreased. Such changes, along with an extrapolation of a decline in current profits into a decline in anticipated profits, lower investment. A recursive process in which a decline in investment yields a deterioration of cash-payment relations, which leads to a further decline in investment, will take place in a small-government capitalism.

If government is big, a fall in investment leads to falls in income, employment, and profits and to a substantial rise in the government's deficit. How big the deficit becomes and how rapidly it increases depends on the structure of the tax system and the nature of the government spending programs. In a modern welfare state, the income-maintenance schemes are such that expenditures rise rapidly with unemployment, and the tax system is such that a sharp decline in revenues takes place when income falls. Even without discretionary measures, the government deficit will increase rapidly when income turns down.

Big government acts as a breaker of the recursive process by which a decline in investment leads to a decline in profits. In the United States in 1974–5 the government deficit exploded to an annual rate of more than $100 billion in the second quarter of 1975. It is no accident that the second quarter of 1975 was the bottom of the recession and that an expansion that continued for at least 15 quarters (through Q1 1979, as this is written) started in 1975 III.

Big government is a powerful stabilizer of income and employment because of the direct impact of spending and taxes on demand and because a government deficit sustains business profits.

The other items in the extended Kalecki formula for profits are important determinants of system behavior and help explain business-cycle experience. Note that the export surplus shows up as positively related to profits. When a country expands its budget deficit and this leads to a rise in imports, both domestic profits and profits of its trading partners are increased. The United States' balance of trade deficits after 1975 sustained both income and profits in its trading partners.

If workers buy consumption goods on credit, declines in income, employment, and business profits will be amplified as employed workers cut down on debt-financed spending. On the other hand, the evidence indicates that once unemployment stops rising, workers who experienced little or no unemployment increase their purchases of debt-financed consumer goods; this diminishes worker savings and increases income, employment, and profits.

There is an ambiguity in Kalecki's formulation of the determination of profits. Whereas the level of profits in consumption-goods production is determined by the condition that profits in the production of consumer goods equal the wage bill in the production of investment goods ($\pi_c = W_I N_I$), no such straightforward relation rules for the determination of profits in the production of investment goods. Total profits equal profits in the production of consumption goods plus profits in the production of investment goods ($\pi = \pi_c + \pi_I$). The value of investment output is the wage bill in investment-goods production plus profits in investment-goods production ($I = W_I N_I + \pi_I$). It therefore follows that total profits equal investment output ($I = \pi_c + \pi_I$ for $\pi_c = W_I N_I$). However, to determine profits in the investment-goods industries it is necessary to refer to the supply conditions of investment output.

A large part of investment goods consists of unique items, tailor-made to the specification of the purchase. Furthermore, the production of investment goods often involves significant gestation periods. Thus investment ties up liquid financial resources in work in process. These liquid financial resources often are borrowed from banks. In any case, an explicit contractual or an implicit opportunity-cost interest charge on the labor and material costs of producing investment goods must be covered by the supply price.

Bankers lend on a margin of safety. The expected sales proceeds from the production of investment goods should exceed costs of production, including interest charges on funds tied up over the gestation period, by some amount. This bankers' margin leads to a markup on costs that exceeds the interest charges by a substantial ratio. If the project is successful, the markup leads to realized profits. Thus the need to protect bankers leads to a supply price of investment goods that exceeds by a substantial margin the running costs of production.

To complete the story of profit determination in investment-goods production, demand conditions are needed. Once again banking and finance enter into the process in an essential manner. Debts to banks, other financial institutions, and the open market are used by firms to finance positions in capital assets. Keynesian liquidity preference can be interpreted as a market view, depending on past experience and current expectations, of the appropriate liability structure for the financing of positions in debt.

The terms on which finance is available for the holding of capital assets determines the market price of capital assets. In Keynesian theory, asset and liability preferences yield, for a given structure of financial institutions, a financing structure for business. This financing structure of business is the proximate determinant of the prices (explicit or implicit) of the capital assets that yield quasi rents (Minsky, 1975a:Chapter 4). That is, Keynesian theory is a two-price-level theory: one for capital assets and the second for current output. A link between the two is the way the price of capital assets becomes the demand price for investment. Financial-market conditions enter into the determination of investment in two ways: They determine the supply price of investment output, because they are a cost that must be recovered, and they determine the demand price, because the price of capital assets depends on the way positions in capital assets can be financed.

In modern capitalist economies, firms with market power have offer prices that involve a predetermined markup on out-of-pocket costs, although, as the preceding argument indicates, markup pricing is a natural outcome of a banker's or finance officer's view of the economic process. Firms without market power earn a markup on out-of-pocket costs only if demand is "strong" (i.e., realized markups depend on aggregate investment). Such price-takers produce an unchanging output as long as demand price equals or exceeds out-of-pocket costs.[4]

In the simple Kalecki case, output is determined by the condition that the sum of all profits equals financed investment. Financed investment yields the wage bill in investment output, which in turn must be reflected in the realized markups over wage costs in the prices of consumer goods. How realized profits are distributed among the various fixed and flexible markup outputs depends on the preferences of wage earners and other purchasers of consumer goods.

In a capitalist economy, prices, outputs, and employment are determined by the condition that profit equals investment (allowing for the modifications specified in the generalized profit equation). Investment depends on what is financed, which in turn depends on an excess of the demand price for investment over the supply price of investment output. The demand price of investment is derived from the market price of capital assets. The market price of capital assets depends on relations that Keynes identified under the rubric of liquidity preference, one of which is the liability structure that is "acceptable" for the financing of positions in capital assets. All other things being the same, the easier the cash-flow constraints embodied in balance sheets, the higher the price of capital assets. The supply price of investment output includes financing costs during gestation periods and the bankers' margin of safety in financing such outputs.

In a capitalist system the terms on which bankers (broadly defined to include commercial, investment, and merchant bankers) finance positions in capital assets and the production of investment output are critical determinants of system behavior. Such financing directly affects profits and thus whether or not current income validates the inherited liability structure.

VII. The turning points: upper and lower

In business-cycle analysis it was usual to consider two cumulative processes (expansion and contraction) and two turning points (upper and lower) (Haberler, 1937). In the study of financial crises, the upper turning point is of special interest, for a financial crisis often occurs in the neighborhood of the upper turning points of deep-depression cycles. It is convenient to distinguish between the evolutionary process that leads to the emergence of balance-sheet relations that are conducive to financial crises and the events that trigger it.

The profit equation of banks and the profit opportunities from holding leveraged capital assets for income or appreciation together show that even an initial condition dominated by hedge financing is unstable.[5] In an economy dominated by hedge finance, there are profit opportunities in shifting toward a larger mix of speculative arrangements. This is so because the supply conditions for short-term finance lead to lower financing costs for those who can qualify. A rise in the mix of speculative finance in the total increases demand for and thus the price of capital assets. This leads to increases in investment demand, in investment that is financed, and in profits. During a shift to speculative finance, profits increase in the aggregate. This validates the decisions of those who lent and those who borrowed to engage in speculative finance (Minsky, 1975a:Chapter 4 and 5).

Banks and other financial intermediaries are both lenders and borrowers. As lenders on short term, they induce speculative finance in others. As borrowers, idle hoards of cash are the raw materials for expanding loans. They have an incentive to develop liabilities that enable those who would otherwise hold cash to dispense with cash. As a result, banks stand ready to furnish cash to two sets of clients: their borrowers and their depositors. Banks need to have secure means for acquiring cash at their own initiative. In the theory of banking, assets that enable banks to acquire cash are often called secondary reserves. In a world where banks are active profit-making institutions that manage their liabilities, the instruments used to acquire cash when needed are the position-making instruments. The cash manager of a modern corporation or bank has a variety of position-making instruments and actively juggles short-term debts and assets among a range of them.

For an instrument to qualify as effective in position making, sizable transactions in it must be executed without generating large changes in its price. The market for the instrument must be broad, with many buyers and sellers, and, in many cases, a residual market maker. The residual market maker is usually (but not necessarily) the central bank.

Some assets and liabilities are not good generators of cash at the initiative of the money-position manager. If financial positions develop in which managers of the cash of corporations or banks are forced to try to raise cash by selling out such assets or issuing such liabilities, the cash realized by such sales or by such liabilities can fall short of anticipated levels. In particular, a wide attempt to make position by selling an asset that is not usually used for the purpose can lead to a large fall in the market price of such assets. This happened in 1966 when banks tried to make position by selling municipal bonds. Such an attempt to make position by selling out positions characterized the rapid stock-market decline in 1929, the sales of foreclosed real estate in the years of the Great Depression, and much of the difficulties of real estate investment trusts in 1974–5.

The shift of a financial system from a structure that is inhospitable to financial crises to one that is hospitable has two characteristics; one is an increasing weight of speculative finance; the second is greater dependence of banks, financial institutions, and ordinary businesses on their ability to make position by the sale of liabilities rather than by the use of money or liquid and guaranteed assets.

The flow-of-funds data prepared by the Federal Reserve yield ample evidence that the weight of short-term and therefore presumptively speculative finance in the total financial structure of nonfinancial corporations in the United States has increased over the years since 1946. The same body of data shows that the money (demand deposits and currency) holdings of nonfinancial businesses have decreased relative to sales, profits, and financial obligations. Any chronicle of developments in banking and finance shows that position-making techniques have become more complex; in particular, bank position making has shifted from operations on an asset traded in a highly protected market (Treasury bills) to operations in a variety of liabilities. Furthermore, active liability juggling has spread from commercial banks to finance companies, other financial institutions, and nonfinancial businesses. The greater the need of units to manage their liabilities, the greater the susceptibility of the system to financial failures. That the shift to a financial structure conducive to financial crises is consistent with the profit opportunities that exist from managing liabilty structures in a regime of robust, predominantly hedge finance is borne out both by the numbers and by chronicles (Minsky, 1966, 1973, 1975a, 1975d, 1977).

An investment project is like a contract to make payments along a more or less precisely defined timetable. Although not all investment is as large scale and complex as a nuclear power plant, construction of a nuclear power plant can serve as a model. A large or even an ordinary human-scale investment project involves the "on-the-site" construction and assemblage of components in a relatively well defined sequence. This requires coordinated production of components that go into the plant. Thus a payment schedule by contractors and manufacturers to workers and suppliers is an integral part of the investment process. Ongoing investment involves a maze of financing relations. An investment boom is accompanied by increases in the volume and complexity of financial relations.

The financial arrangements of an investment project conform quite closely to the characteristics we have identified with Ponzi finance. Over the construction period, committed payments exceed revenues from the project. Furthermore, at the end of a period, lump sums are paid by the purchaser that presumably cover payments made by the builder during construction. The financing arrangements in the American construction industry, where there is a clear distinction between construction and take-out financing, conform to the relations that have been characterized as Ponzi finance.

The cash-flow relations in investment in progress make Ponzi finance an essential and not a peripheral characteristic of the financial structure of capitalism. The cost of the investment output that is produced and must be recovered by the sales price of the investment good as a capital asset is positively related to the short-term rate of interest, even as the market price of the capital asset is negatively related to the long-term rate of interest. If investment-goods financing conforms to our model of Ponzi finance, if an investment boom leads to an increase in both short-term and long-term interest rates, and if such investment boom takes place in a financial structure heavily weighted by speculative and Ponzi finance, the upper turning point is completely endogenous. Under these circumstances a rise in interest rates will cause present-value reversals; the present value of some Ponzi-financed investment in process will change from positive to negative. Similar reversals will happen for some units that are speculatively financed but are not financing investment. Furthermore, the rise in interest rates will lead to declines in the values of firms that are hedge financed; this decreases margins of safety and lowers credit standing. Increases in specific financing terms relative to the rates typically chronicled by the time series will take place.

The rise in the cost of investment projects above the expected value of the completed capital asset leads both to a decrease in new investment undertakings and to failure of ongoing investment projects to obtain the cash needed for completion. Inability of units engaged in speculative and Ponzi finance to refinance their positions means that cash receipts of banks and other financial institutions fall short of contract net amounts. Such units now have to acquire cash by issuing new liabilities or selling assets. Meanwhile, units with refinancing problems try to stay afloat by selling assets. Under these circumstances the prices of assets used in attempts to make position fall, and the terms on liabilities that are offered in the market increase.

The drying up of finance and cash shortages decrease investment, which cuts profits. Realized quasi rents fall below anticipated quasi rents. The fall in profits leads to a further decline in the present values of firms.Conservative hedge units become embarrassed speculative units.

The upper turning point is completely endogenous once it is accepted that interest rates rise in an investment boom and that the successful functioning of the economy induces profit-seeking bankers and their customers to engage in speculative financial arrangements and to economize on holdings of money and protected financial assets. For interest rates not to rise during an investment boom, the supply of finance must be infinitely elastic, which implies either that a flood of financial innovation is taking place (Minsky, 1957a) or that the central bank is supplying reserves in unlimited amounts. But this, in turn, implies that investment is an ever-increasing proportion of output and that accelerating inflation is tolerable (Minsky, 1957b).

Although endogenous market processes lead to incipient financial crisis and an upper turning point, the extent of the financial crisis and whether or not a debt-deflation process takes place depend on how quickly and aptly the central bank intervenes as a lender of last resort and whether or not government deficits stabilize profits. In 1974–5 the Federal Reserve and the giant banks promptly intervened as lenders of last resort and so allowed the profit-generating effects of the massive 1975 government deficit to take hold. This led to an early and high lower turning point. In 1929–33 the Federal Reserve dithered, and government tried to balance its budget. This led to a delayed and deep lower turning point. The 1975 lower turning point was followed by a quick, although perhaps incomplete, recovery, with continuing inflation. The 1933 lower turning point was followed by a long and deep trough.

VIII. The lender of last resort

In a capitalist economy with a complex, sophisticated, and responsive financial system, the dynamics introduced by profit seeking into the balance-sheet structures of banks, financial institutions, business organizations, and households assure that a run of good times will be accompanied by an increase in the importance of position-making activity as well as by changes in the instruments and markets used. The passive management of liability structures that characterizes a highly liquid financial structure dominated by hedge finance is a transitory state that follows either a deep and prolonged depression after a debt deflation or a large increase in government debt due to a great war. Active liability management means that a modest shortfall of cash from operations or a rise in other claims on quasi rents will lead to a need to raise cash by operations in position-making instruments.

In the first decade after World War II, position-making activity was carried out mainly by operations using Treasury bills. Any rise in the need by banks or others to raise cash by selling Treasury bills led to an infusion of Federal Reserve credit, either directly through an open-market operation or indirectly through the support of bond dealers at the discount window. The Federal Reserve prized orderly conditions in Treasury debt markets and remained in close and continuous contact with the money market. Position making took place by means of operations in a market protected by the Federal Reserve. Because the Federal Reserve was operating in the Treasury security market, both as fiscal agent for the government and in its effort to control the economy, the Federal Reserve was a constant participant in the position-making market.

As position making became more a matter of liability management, the Federal Reserve lost its day-to-day contact with the markets in which positions were made, and position-making instruments were no longer protected by the Federal Reserve. As a result, rapid swings in the price, terms, and even the availability of cash through markets that were being used for position making became possible. Furthermore, any rise in interest rates or restrictions on availability of reserves led to an active exploration by units needing cash for new or exotic sources of cash. Complex convoluted procedures were adopted. Markets for new instruments grew rapidly. Inasmuch as these markets were exposed to rapid fluctuations and lacked central-bank protection, "local failure" could lead to sharp rises in financing terms and restrictions on the availability of bankers' cash.

. With the development of closely articulated cash management, the need for central-bank constraints to control and restrict speculative finance increased. However, the Federal Reserve was not in touch with the emerging financial markets, and its seems to have missed the significance of the evolutionary changes that were taking place. In the closely articulated cash-management system that developed, not unusual events triggered serious financial market disruptions in 1966, 1969–70, and 1974–5. In each episode episode the Federal Reserve was forced to intervene to protect the viability of the financial system by acting as a lender of last resort that made cash available or promised to supply cash.

Three distinct aspects of the lender-of-last-resort function can be identified. One is the provision of funds to the money market when position-making activity leads to a sharp fall in the price (or a sharp rise in the interest rate) of position-making instruments. The second is the restructuring of the finances of various organizations in the aftermath of a crisis, so that the weight of Ponzi and speculative finance is decreased. The third is to guide the evolution of the financial system so that the central bank remains in touch with the position-making markets and so that the weight of speculative and Ponzi finance is constrained. The first or emergency intervention is the traditional lender-of-last-resort intervention (Kindleberger, 1978:Chapter 9).

When the price of the asset normally used in making position falls so that the required cash cannot be raised by dealing in that asset, the cash-short organization will turn to the sale or hypothecation of other assets. Asset prices can fall rapidly and across a wide spectrum of assets as organizations try to make position by selling out position. Once this spreads, the ability to borrow, and even the solvency, of many institutions is impaired. The central bank has a responsibility to prevent a generalized fall in asset values by providing funds for position making through conventional assets or by extending credit to organizations with refinancing problems. The central banks' primary responsibility is to assure that asset values are sufficiently high so that insolvency is always a local condition, not a general condition; in particular, the lender-of-last-resort function aims to assure that a generalized fall in capital-asset values will not occur when such assets are offered for sale by units that need cash to make position.

A central bank's lender-of-last-resort function is of greater importance the greater the proportion of speculative and Ponzi finance in the structure of financial relations. Once an investment boom that is associated with a sharp increase in speculative and Ponzi finance breaks, business organizations with profit expectations that can support a long-term debt structure at normal interest rates may be unable, through cash flows and refinancing at boom or crisis financing terms, to validate a debt structure heavily weighted by short-term finance. It is the responsibility of the central bank as the lender of last resort to facilitate the restructuring of debts so that in the aftermath of a crisis the weight of hedge financing increases in the total financial structure.

In short, the internal dynamics of a capitalist economy lead to financial structures that are conducive to financial crisis and income instability. It is the lender of last resort's responsibility to prevent the position-making difficulties of some institutions to lead to a generalized fall in asset values and to facilitate a recovery from a recession by aiding and abetting the restructuring of debts so that the weight of speculative and Ponzi finance in the system is decreased.

It is also a responsibility of the central bank to guide the evolution of the financial system, either by legislation or by its operations, so that the actual and potential weights of speculative and Ponzi finance are constrained. The Roosevelt-era reforms that changed the nature of the standard American mortgage and cut down on the ability of investors to finance positions in common stocks with thin margins were financial reforms that diminished the potential for instability by erecting barriers to speculative and Ponzi finance.

Over the past decade, the Federal Reserve has been remiss in its responsibilities to guide the evolution of American finance so that the development of conditions conducive to financial crisis would be slowed, if not reversed. In particular, the Franklin National crisis of 1974–5 indicated that positive steps to control and constrain the offshore banking community were necessary. In the years since 1975 the Federal Reserve and other central banks have been remiss in doing little or nothing to constrain the further expansion of offshore speculative financial relations.

IX. Conclusion

The financial-instability hypothesis is an economic theory that emphasizes the financial relations that are special to capitalism. As such, it is an alternative to today's standard theory, which attempts to derive truths about capitalist economies from theories that ignore the capitalist aspects of the economy.

The financial-instability hypothesis leads to important propositions about system behavior beyond those emphasized here: that the internal workings of a capitalist economy generate financial relations that are conducive to instability and that the price and asset-value relations that will trigger a financial crisis in a fragile financial structure are normal functioning events. One further proposition that follows from the financial-instability hypothesis is that if the debt-deflation interactive process that leads to deep depression is quickly aborted by the deficits of big government and by lender-of-last-resort intervention, then an inflationary recession will take place. The financial-instability hypothesis leads to the view that money prices reflect the basic operating characteristics of the economy; they are not something that is tacked on to a prior-determined set of relative prices.

A major implication of the financial-instability hypothesis is that policy for a capitalist economy must recognize the limitations and flaws of capitalism if it is to be successful. In particular, as long as an economy is capitalist, it will be financially unstable; however, as a comparison of the unstable mid-1920s and the unstable mid-1960s to date shows, the overall behavior of the economy can be quite different. That is, all capitalisms are unstable, but some capitalisms are more unstable than others. Furthermore, the system characteristics that result from the underlying instability can be quite different.

Notes

1 As Professor Kindleberger notes, the financial-instability hypothesis, which, flattering me, he calls the Minsky model, has a distinguished ancestry, for "it is a lineal descendant of a model, set out with personal variations by a host of classical economists including John Stuart Mill, Alfred Marshall, Knut Wicksell and Irving Fisher" (Kindleberger 1978:15). Karl Marx and John Maynard Keynes belong on the list of great economists who held that the capitalist process is endogenously unstable.

2 The most detailed analysis of cash-flow relations that I have set out is for financial institutions (Minsky, 1975a).

3 At the Bad Homburg conference Raymond Goldsmith and Robert Solow took exception to my label "Ponzi Financing" for financial relations that can be validated only if at some later date a sufficiently large payment is received. Raymond Goldsmith went so far as to use the term "demagogue." In the initial formulation of these ideas I emphasized the "fraudulent" and "bubble" aspects of this type of finance, but the experience of the real estate investment trusts and an appreciation of the sequential relations in the financing of investment led me to recognize that the type of financial relations that I label Ponzi finance is a quite general and not necessarily fraudulent characteristic of a capitalist financial structure. Financial relations the validation of which depends on the selling out of positions are a normal functioning part of the capitalist process. Furthermore, every "bubble" or stock-market speculation in which profitability depends on the timing of entry and exit is of the nature of a "Ponzi scheme."

However, the label attached to the financing relations I identify as Ponzi is not important. What is important is whether or not such structures exist and what effect such financing has on system behavior. In particular, if Ponzi financing exists, if the extent of Ponzi financing determines the domain of instability of the economy, and if Ponzi financing is a normal adjunct of investment production, then there are normally functioning endogenous factors that make for significant instabilities.

Incidentally, what in retrospect appears to be a fraudulent operation often has its roots in a "speculative" or "honest Ponzi" financial arrangement where the "payoff" is not forthcoming as anticipated. "Fraud" often is an ex-post result and is not always ex-ante in conception.

4 The chronic problems of agricultural credit under free-market conditions may reflect the banker's abhorrence of price structures in which price is not built up by suppliers out of costs. Agricultural producers cannot offer bankers the protection that a firm offer price provides. Hence the reform of agriculture in a market economy involves some combination of two "forces" – the promotion of a cartel by government or the provision of finance outside of normal banking channels.

5 A bank's profit identity can be written as

$$\frac{earnings}{assets} \times \frac{assets}{equity} = \frac{earnings}{equity}$$

Earnings = revenues − cost of money − operating costs. Bankers operate on their assets/equity ratio and their earnings ratio; bankers and those who oversee banks are often in conflict as bankers operate to increase their assets/equity ratio.

References

Arrow, K., and Hahn, F. 1971. *General Competitive Analysis.* San Francico: Holden-Day.

Chick, V. 1973. *The Theory of Monetary Policy.* London: Gray-Mills.

Davidson, P. 1972. *Money and the Real World.* New York: John Wiley & Sons.

Fisher, I. 1933. "The Debt-Deflation Theory of Great Depressions." *Econometrica* 1:337–57.

Haberler, G. 1937. *Prosperity and Depressions.* Geneva: League of Nations.

Kalecki, M. 1971. *Selected Essays on the Dynamics of the Capitalist Economy.* Cambridge University Press.

Keynes, J. M. 1936. *The General Theory of Employment, Interest and Money.* London: Macmillan.

　　1937. "The General Theory of Employment." *Quarterly Journal of Economics* 51: 209–23.

Kindleberger, C. P. 1978. *Manias, Panics, and Crashes: A History of Financial Crisis.* New York: Basic Books.

Kregel, J. A. 1973. *The Reconstruction of Political Economy.* London: Macmillan.

Kuhn, T. 1962. *The Structure of Scientific Revolutions.* Chicago: University of Chicago Press.

Malinvaud, E. 1977. *The Theory of Unemployment Reconsidered.* Oxford: Basil Blackwood.

Minsky, H. P. 1957a. "Central Banking and Money Market Changes." *Quarterly Journal of Economics* 71: 171–87.

　　1957b. "Monetary Systems and Accelerator Models." *American Economic Review* 57: 859–85.

　　1966. "The Evolution of American Banking: The Longer View." *The Bankers' Magazine* 202: 325–30, 397–400.

　　1973. "Problems of U.S. Monetary Policy." *The Bankers' Magazine* 216: 63–8.

　　1975a. *John Maynard Keynes.* New York: Columbia University Press.

　　1975b. "Financial Instability, the Current Dilemma and the Structure of Banking Finance." In *Compendium on Major Issues in Bank Regulation,* pp. 310–53. United States Senate, Committee on Banking, Housing, and Urban Affairs, 94th Congress, 1st session. Washington, D.C.: U.S. Government Printing Office.

　　1975c. "Financial Resources in a Fragile Financial Environment." *Challenge* 18: 6–13.

　　1975d. "Suggestions for a Cash Flow Oriented Bank Examination." In: *Conference on Bank Structure and Competition,* pp. 150–84. Federal Reserve Bank of Chicago.

　　1977. "Banking in a Fragile Financial Environment." *Journal of Portfolio Management* 3: 11–22.

Robinson, J. 1971. *Economic Heresies.* London: Macmillan.

Schumpeter, J. 1934. *The Theory of Economic Development.* Cambridge: Harvard University Press.

Temin, P. 1976. *Did Monetary Forces Cause the Great Depression?* New York: W. W. Norton.
Weintraub, S. 1966. *A Keynesian Theory of Employment, Growth and Income Distribution.* Philadelphia: Chilton.

Comment

J. S. FLEMMING

Minsky's chapter presents two arguments relating to economic stability, but although both have a financial dimension, neither is a distinctively financial (as opposed to monetary) mechanism. Clearly, in making this statement, I am rejecting claims implicit in Minsky's exposition. Unfortunately, that exposition is so deficient in clarity and precision as to obscure the constructive content. Malinvaud (1977), on whom Minsky is quite unnecessarily harsh, is a model of the explicit theorizing that is missing in this essay – an omission not made good in the author's other works to which we are referred.

To mention but two such problems, Minsky consistently identifies income concepts (usually defined on an accruals basis) with cash flows. If financial instability is associated with price-level instability, this identification is particularly unfortunate: a sources-and-uses-of-funds statement contains a lot more information on cash flows than does a balance sheet. Minsky also persists in giving a causal significance to Kalecki's famous arrangement of the national-income identities.

Perhaps more important than these problems is Minsky's failure to do justice to those mainstream macroeconomists who have emphasized both finance and stability. Tobin's approach (1969) to investment through the financial-valuation ratio q is entirely in the spirit of Minsky's remarks and has been implemented empirically by Ciccolo (1975) and von Furstenberg (1977). Minsky's explanation of investment relies, I believe appropriately, on a two-sector model. This is not novel; Sir John Hicks's famous 1935 interpretation of *The General Theory* was explicit on the point, as was Witte's account (1963). Moreover, contrary to what is said in Section II, mainstream economists have examined the possibility of instability when there are many assets (Hahn, 1966), some of which may be financial.

Minsky misrepresents the new "disequilibrium" approach of Barro and Grossman (1976) and Malinvaud (1977) when he says that it suggests that Keynesian unemployment exists because money wages and prices are both too high and too inflexible. Their analyses equally support the view that it is due to too small a supply of money. Minsky nowhere substantiates his implicit claim that unemployment can be explained in terms of financial disequilibrium without reference to wage stickiness or other reasons for nonclearance of the labor market.

I share Minsky's view that Keynes rightly asserted that wage and price flexibility may make things worse. However, it is not true that this mechanism depends on the existence of a sophisticated financial structure – money is enough. Keynes's own argument (1936:265) appears to rely on extrapolative expectations of deflation raising the ex-ante real interest rate depressing investment even if the nominal interest rate falls to zero (see also Tobin, 1969). It can be shown (Flemming, 1979) that increased wage flexibility may destabilize employment even if expectations are rational. Such destabilization is particularly likely if wage flexibility is low and monetary policy is aimed at stabilizing nominal interest rates. Although, as mentioned, these arguments do not require a complex debt structure, deflation-induced bankruptcies would presumably aggravate the instability.

Similarly with Minsky's argument for the endogeneity of crises. He refers several times to the following mechanism: Suppose an economy is, in fact, subject to random shock generated in a stationary way. A chance period of stability will be misinterpreted as implying that fewer precautions need be taken, thus increasing the economy's vulnerability to the next "normal" shock. As applied to financial structures, enterprises adopt excessively exposed geared, levered positions in a period of stability that does not, in fact, reflect a favorable shift in the economy's stochastic environment.

This mechanism is, of course, extremely general; it may account for wars and certainly plays a role in epidemiology. A period of random quiescence by the influenza virus may reduce participation in immunization programs and increase the severity of the next outbreak. Both of these examples have implications for economic stability – as, more directly, does the case of farmers who respond to a temporarily stable weather pattern by planting less robust or less diversified varieties. Whether the financial version of this story is economically more significant than the real version, with which it is compatible, is not clear, but the economic relevance of the mechanism is by no means restricted to capitalism.

In either case, the argument depends on agents failing to distinguish a run of good luck from a favorable structural shift in their environment. Such errors are not only identifiable but also optimal if agents attach the correct nonzero probability to structural changes. If Minsky believes that people are too willing to believe that such changes have occurred, he should consider suggesting to the authorities that they intervene randomly in financial markets – by increasing their variance, such intervention would hinder the recognition of genuine shifts and should also inhibit false inferences.

This suggestion depends on agents not being able to observe the authorities' interventions. More generally, interventions of the kind Minsky advocates for the lender of last resort encounter the objections of the rational-expectations school that the stabilization policy will be offset by individuals adopting a more risky position. Minsky does not address this position explicitly, and his own remarks are inconsistent. As we have just seen, he does stress an argument relying on a feedback from observed tranquility to more fragile financial structures. Presumably, this would apply to policy-induced tranquility, rendering the latter unfeasible. Yet Minsky attributes postwar stability to the enlarged role of government. Clearly, a more explicit and quantitative development of the presently ambiguous theory of financial instability is called for.

References

Barro, R. J., and Grossman, H. I. 1976. *Money, Employment and Inflation.* Cambridge University Press.
Ciccolo, J. H. 1975. "Four Essays on Monetary Policy." Ph.D. dissertation, Yale University.
Flemming, J. S. 1979. "Wage Flexibility and Employment Stability." Unpublished Manuscript, Oxford University.
Hahn, F. H. 1966. "Equilibrium Dynamics with Heterogeneous Capital Goods." *The Quarterly Journal of Economics* 80: 633–46.
Hicks, J. R. 1937. "Mr. Keynes and the Classics." *Econometrica* 5: 147–59.
Keynes, J. M. 1936. *The General Theory of Employment, Interest and Money.* London: Macmillan.
Malinvaud, E. 1977. *The Theory of Unemployment Reconsidered.* Oxford: Blackwell.
Tobin, J. 1969. "A General Equilibrium Approach to Monetary Theory." *Journal of Money, Credit and Banking* 1: 15–29.
von Furstenberg, G. M. 1977. "Corporate Investment: Does Market Valuation Matter in the Aggregate?" *Brookings Papers on Economic Activity* 2: 347–408.
Witte, J. G. 1963. "The Micro-foundations of the Social Investment Function." *Journal of Political Economy* 71: 441–56.

Comment

RAYMOND W. GOLDSMITH

I entirely agree with Professor Minsky's opening plea for an integration of theory of the financial system with that of the real economy, and for the need to understand financial development in any analysis of the modern economic process. That, however, unfortunately, is almost where our agreement ends. I do not believe that his hypothesis of endogenous financial instability, notwithstanding some interesting observations and suggestions, provides an explanation of the financial development of a modern economy.

For brevity's sake I shall mention only three of the many doubts I have about Professor Minsky's theories, facts, and interpretations that I regard as important: the lack of a definition of financial crisis, the conflict of the implications of his hypothesis with economic history, and his choice of terminology. I shall thus pass by several other important criticisms (e.g., his failure to distinguish adequately between financial crises and business-cycle upper turning points and his undue reliance on oversimplified, aggregative Kaleckian identities).

Failing to find a definition of financial crisis in Professor Minsky's chapter (or, for that matter, in Professor Kindleberger's book), I shall offer one of my own for discussion: a sharp, brief, ultracyclical deterioration of all or most of a group of financial indicators – short-term interest rates, asset (stock, real estate, land) prices, commercial insolvencies, and failures of financial institutions. This definition would exclude several of Professor Minsky's so-called financial crises, particularly the minor financial difficulties experienced in the United States in the 1960s and 1970s, on which he puts so much emphasis, erroneously I feel, as they were at most potential or near-crises. Note that I do not regard foreign-exhange difficulties as a necessary concomitant of a financial crisis.

My main empirical argument against Professor Minsky's hypothesis is that its implications run counter to the evidence of economic history. It is implied in the hypothesis, more clearly in his recent evidence before the Joint Economic Committee (*Special Study of Economic Change*, 1978: 847 ff.) than in the chapter before us, that the larger a financial system grows in relation to the economy and the more complex and layered it becomes, the greater its fragility and its proneness to financial crisis, and the more serious its effects on economic development. Now it is a fact that over the past century and a half the financial systems in practically every country, developed or less developed, have become relatively larger and more complex by any measure we may want to apply, such as the relation of all financial instruments or of the assets of financial institutions to national product or wealth or to the size of the financial superstructure. It is also a fact that financial crises have become rarer and less acute and indeed have almost disappeared since the early 1930s, a period of nearly half a century, in sharp contrast to the decennial recurrence in the preceding century. Financial crises are a childhood disease of capitalism, not an affliction of old age. This contradiction alone is sufficient, it seems to me, to invalidate the financial-instability hypothesis.

Finally, the question of terminology. It may be argued that an author is free to paste any name he wants on the phenomenon he describes. I do not think so. We must, I believe, remain as close as possible to the common and common-sense usage of the terms we employ, and shun terms that are definitely misleading. From this point of view, the use of the term *speculative finance* for activities that are as widespread and basically sound (because based on the law of large numbers) as the business of a savings bank or any other financial institution whose assets have legally a longer maturity than its liabilities is unfortunate. To apply the term *Ponzi finance,* derived from a fraudulent and basically unsound (because inherently defective) scheme, to as commonplace an operation as construction loans, for example, which work out perfectly well year-in-year-out in more than 99 out of 100 cases, is irresponsible. It is, I am sorry to have to use a harsh word as the author seems unwilling to abandon his terminology, demagoguery. *Amicus Hyman, magis amica veritas.*

Comment

JACQUES MELITZ

In arguing from a non-Marxist standpoint that capitalism is increasingly prone to financial crises, Minsky undertakes a courageous and thankless task. Fellow non-Marxists will only take offense, and the encouragement of Marxists will bring him few new friends. Minsky maintains that individual balance sheets under capitalism tend to evolve in such a way as to make random economic shocks likely to generate a cumulative percentage fall in aggregate financial wealth. In other words, the elasticity of influence of plausible negative shocks on aggregate financial wealth is sizably greater than one. His hypothesis is one of "financial fragility" rather than "financial instability," though he uses the terms interchangeably. That is, according to him, crises are not inevitable; they merely become more likely. Metaphorically, it is not that the patient will predictably become ill; he just gets more and more susceptible to illness. Even this susceptibility is perfectly clear only if we abstract from certain kinds of antibodies (essentially remedial actions by a "lender of last resort") or if we consider them as events from outside the system.

Some parts of Minsky's argument, I confess, evade me completely. This encompasses most everything he has to say about the real sector of the economy, and in particular his references to Kalecki's equations, which strike me as accounting relationships that are compatible with all possible states of events. Accordingly, I shall confine my remarks to the financial side, where his meaning comes across more clearly to me. My comments will bear on three aspects: (1) Minsky's emphasis on "speculative" units, (2) the supposed tendency of expansionary phases of business cycles to heighten the financial fragility of capitalism, and (3) the generality of the fragility thesis, or, more exactly, its supposed application to capitalist economies generally.

1. Minsky's starting point is a distinction between "hedging" and "speculative" units, the "Ponzi finance" units being an extreme example of the speculative ones. Specifically, the distinction revolves around the time profile of the individual's anticipated income receipts in relation to the time profile of his contractual debt payments over a near-term horizon. The speculator is someone who does not foresee enough income to cover his contractual debt obligations in the short run. Therefore he necessarily plans to sell assets or to borrow in order to meet his obligations. That makes him vulnerable to current conditions in asset markets, which is the basic source of danger to him. Minsky agrees also that "speculators" do not borrow with the intention of running down their capital *permanently*. Hence for any given flow of expected income receipts, the extent of speculative finance, in his conception, depends entirely on the term structure of the debt. The shorter the term structure, the larger the aggregate of current debt payment obligations that run ahead of the aggregate of current income receipts.

As a starting point, we may note that this view has some paradoxical implications. For example, we know that the term structure of the debt is, at least partly, a creature of the time profile of interest rates. When long-term rates are below short-term rates, the market tends to manufacture debt of a higher average term to maturity. It then follows, in the terms of Minsky, that a falling term structure of interest rates means a more robust financial structure. Accordingly, conditions of anticipated price deflation, such as ruled in the late nineteenth century, are then healthy ones for the financial system. These are not particularly convincing results. But over and above this, Minsky's concept of speculative finance (his index of the fragility of the financial system) depends entirely on the time unit in which income is measured (or the duration of the "short run" of the preceding paragraph). If we take a long enough income period, all debtors are "hedgers." Similarly, if contractual debt payments are lumpy and income receipts continuous, then for short enough income periods, all debtors are "speculators." For any given length of income period, an individual is likely to change status automatically from a hedger to a speculator as his maturity date approaches. Can any measure of speculative activity of this sort really provide a useful index of the robustness or fragility of the financial system?

What Minsky is essentially trying to get at is the extent to which capital losses resulting from rises in interest rates will trigger a cumulative, cascading effect on wealth stemming from efforts to meet outstanding debt commitments. From a general economic standpoint, this will depend mainly on two factors that Minsky's classification between hedgers and speculators fails to consider: first, how much people *choose* to sell assets of *variable nominal price* in order to meet debt commitments; second, what are the wealth and price elasticities of the net stock demand (the stock demand minus the stock supply) for these assets. One fact that Minsky tends to disregard, in this connection, is that people dispose of money or debt assets of fixed nominal price. Those who decide to meet debts out of capital over any time interval may decide to do so by decumulating money. If they have stored enough money for this purpose, they may then not envisage ever selling even a penny's worth of variable-price assets in order to meet their obligations, and thus may not pose any threat at all from Minsky's point of view. On the other hand, those who need not pay out of capital (or, more precisely, those who anticipate income receipts in excess of contractual payments at all future intervals) nonetheless may plan to sell bonds and equities at some points in the future in order to meet their payments, preferring to allocate their contemporaneous future income receipts to some other ends.

It is highly noteworthy also that a shorter average term of the debt lowers the fall in capital values that can be generated by a rise in interest rates. Thus, although, as Minsky says, a lower average term to maturity implies more debt to be financed during any given time interval (more speculative finance, in his sense), it also means a smaller fall in capital values for any given rise in interest rates. This is further reason to think that a shorter average term need not spell a higher risk of financial catastrophe.

The usual balance-sheet index of the soundness of a financial position has nothing to do with the term structure of the debt; it concerns the total debt relative to total assets, or the debt–equity ratio. Perhaps this is sensible.

2. What about Minsky's argument that capitalist economies become financially more vulnerable during expansions? Even if we reject his notion of speculative finance, this argument deserves careful attention, because there is clearly good sense in his assertion that a succession of good years will increase optimism and therefore readiness to assume risk. In fact, even without supposing that people become more sanguine toward risk-bearing during good times, it follows from standard assumptions that the rise in expected returns over the short run during those times will induce the ordinary risk averter to hold a riskier position. What implication does this have for the harm that a negative shock will perpetrate on the economy? Obviously a negative shock will have a negative effect, and if the elasticity of influence is greater than 1, this negative effect will be more than proportional. But what Minsky must mean is that the elasticity of influence will be higher near the peak than near the trough (or otherwise there would be no reason why the economy would be more vulnerable to negative shocks during good times than bad times). Yet I do not think that he offers adequate support for

this view. The higher riskiness of individual portfolios during good times simply means a higher variance of expected returns on the portfolios. By no stretch of the imagination does this imply a higher proportional loss if interest rates rise (or any other negative shock takes place). From a strict empirical standpoint, it has never been shown that the sensitivity of aggregate equity and bond values to interest rates grows systematically in the expansionary phase of the cycle. Thus, even if we grant Minsky that individuals take more risks during expansions, he still lacks a clear argument for higher *collective* risk during these periods.

3. Finally, what about Minsky's claims to discuss capitalism as a whole? This assertion is puzzling in a work in which the basic examples derive solely from the U.S. experience. In fact, I find Kindleberger's book (the other primary text for this conference) to be largely a foil for Minsky's chapter, because it calls to our attention the wide range of historical and international experience of crises that Minsky pretends to encompass.

One limiting factor in Minsky's reasoning is his unqualified view of the essential contribution of financial intermediaries to financial crises. Commodity-market speculation is a fact of life, and Kindleberger reminds us of many commodity bubbles in the past. Does a financial crisis then necessarily require the help of financial intermediaries? Why may such intermediaries not be a stabilizing element in a commodity-market crash? Of course, there are historical examples of financial systems that were notoriously unstable. However, this may be the result of the specific institutional arrangements at the time. Is this a Panglossian view, and, if so, where is the evidence? The only general reply by Minsky seems to be that banks are intrinsically speculators. But this can be challenged on his own grounds, because most deposits have no maturity date and, more generally, because banks are a type of firm that rests on the insurance principle of a pooling of risks. It might be argued then that banks lead to greater safety than would be present without them. Doesn't this view at least deserve an answer?

Further doubts about the independence of Minsky's arguments from the precise institutional arrangements arise for several reasons. Assume, for example, circumstances where every financial intermediary automatically has heavy access to the lender of last resort, much like the situation in certain capitalist countries such as Japan, France, and some of the Scandinavian ones. To what extent would Minsky's reasoning still apply? Imagine, also, a capitalist environment where bank deposits constitute the bulk of financial assets held outside the banking system (where the banks, in turn, possibly hold a large proportion of quoted securities). Once again, to what extent would Minsky's reasoning apply?

In sum, a financial-fragility argument is one thing; the application of the argument to all capitalist countries is another. Minsky skips over this distinction with his appeal to formal classifications, test examples, and his general pronouncements about capitalism, including an occasional reference to "the Federal Reserve" as a generic term. If he, or anyone else, would only fully specify any one financial-fragility model with plausible application somewhere, perhaps we could think more clearly about the potential scope of the argument. As things now stand, we are in the dark about such elementary questions as whether or not destabilizing expectations are necessary in his argument, to what extent differences in relative speeds of adjustment in different markets are essential for him, and whether or not he requires asymmetric behavior by lenders and borrowers. Are we then in a position even to discuss the general application of his thesis to all capitalist economies?

Part II. History

3. The 1907 financial crisis in Italy: a peculiar case of the lender of last resort in action

FRANCO BONELLI

Contrary to what happened in other countries, the 1907 crisis in Italy remained essentially a financial fact as regards both its origins and its consequences. It had the character of a long-lasting depression of the share market that plunged into difficulties even the largest of the banks that granted both commercial and industrial credits (the so-called mixed blanks), to the point that one of them came close to suspending its business with the public. The incipient bank crisis was faced up to by a series of measures taken at various moments that permitted its consequences to be circumscribed before it became uncontrollable and burst into a full-blown industrial crisis. The Banca d'Italia, the principal of the three issuing banks operating in Italy at that time, played an outstanding part not only as lender of last resort but also as coordination center for agreeing and concerting the anticrisis measures, and the events of that year represent a very significant step forward as regards the maturing of the Italian central bank. The topic with which we are here concerned has already been subjected to detailed study[1] and lends itself to examination from various points of view. In this chapter we shall limit ourselves to aspects that highlight the propagation mechanism of the crisis, as well as the policy that was adopted at the time in order to safeguard the stability of the Italian banking system and to ensure that it would continue to discharge the particular and original function it had up to then performed in the capital-accumulation process.

The scenario that we have to imagine is the one that sees a sector of the Italian banking system engaged in financing industrial investments in a phase that is generally considered as one of the crucial moments of an industrialization process. The protagonists on which we have to concentrate our attention are mixed banks and the Banca d'Italia.[2]

Ever since the beginning of the ascending phase of the cycle, that is, from about 1897 onward, these mixed banks had been engaged in a vast action of channeling capital for the creation of the productive base, especially (but not exclusively) in some new capital-intensive sectors. The accumulation process was based on a containment of aggregate domestic consumption, including wages, and also on the balance of foreign payments ensured by unilateral transfers of resources from abroad on current account (remittances from Italian emigrants and payments for tourist services in Italy). The inflow of resources from abroad was integrated with the resources formed within the country, which by themselves would have been insufficient to finance the formation of industrial capital, and was the true linchpin of the mechanism. Moreover, the very manner in which this inflow took place ensured that Italy was no longer exposed to the destabilizing effects of sudden capital withdrawals, as had happened on other occasions. Having eliminated her position as a debtor in the international monetary market, Italy was in a very solid position as far as her currency was concerned. Taken on the whole, undoubtedly, the country was only barely involved in international financial circuits and occupied a marginal (and almost residual position) in the capital market, this in the sense that foreign capital spilled over into Italy only at moments of exceptional liquidity in European markets, whereas an outflow of Italian savings toward foreign parts constituted a rather unlikely contingency that could take place only in the event of exceptionally high differentials in discount rates. The unilateral transfers of resources from abroad, on the other hand, performed an important monetary function, because in the absence of policies capable of sterilizing the liquidity of foreign origin, this liquidity became transformed into increments of the monetary base through the mediation of a "neutral" and therefore substantially permissive policy of the issuing banks and the far more aggressive lending policy of the mixed banks. These liquidity inflows from abroad therefore sustained the domestic business cycle and propelled it forward. The state, for its part, refrained from fund-raising activities during these years and permitted domestic savings to remain available for private loans.

The mixed banks, not least thanks to these particularly favorable circumstances, performed a strategic role in the allocation of resources and were fundamental instruments for mobilizing and transferring resources among various sectors of the economy, among various geographic areas of the country, and from abroad toward the domestic market. It was the mixed banks, above all, during the course of these years that enlarged the geographic and social basis of fund raising through financial saving. They financed a limited number of large enterprises by means of bill discounting and especially by granting overdrafts on current account and the continual renewal of contango (carry forward) operations; what is more, they financed speculation based on the expectation of a bullish trend in the stock market, this to the point where they could be defined as manipulators of the market valuation of equities. But this market also had some special characteristics. Thanks to the support given by banks, an experiment was going on (and there were many people who believed in it), aimed at developing a financial market on the model of those in other capitalist countries, with direct channels for financing industrial investments. But this experiment was taking place in conditions that were not exactly ideal; by about 1906 it had to all intents and purposes failed, even though a long time passsed before the fact was realized. The continuous issues of new shares made from 1898 onward could not be placed in a stable manner because the Italian bourgeoisie (for reasons interesting to analyze, although space prevents this being done here) still preferred to immobilize its funds in government bonds. More than 70% of the share capital of joint-stock companies was quoted on the stock exchange, but the "floating volume" was enormous and continued to go forward and backward between financial operators with the help of systematically renewed contango operations. Consequently, a growing proportion of the loan funds of the mixed banks became concentrated and immobilized not only in financing industrial investments but also in speculative operations that caused the volume of stock-exchange business to increase of its own accord. The demand for means of payment originating on the stock-exchange front conditioned the pattern of monetary movements, conferring a decidedly convulsive appearance on it, and every ripple that occurred in the stock market, given the concentration of risks and the oligopolistic structure of the supply, ran the risk of involving large areas of the credit market and requiring the banks of issue (in actual practice only the Banca d'Italia) to offset the monetary tensions that derived from it.

On account of its size and operating capacities, and also by virtue of its relations with the Treasury, the Banca d'Italia was the only one among the three issuing banks that had the task and, indeed, was in a position to perform any kind of incisive action on the money market. The instruments that it could use to this end were rather limited by the institutional constraints imposed by banking law and by its own statutes, but even more so by the structural characteristics of the Italian bank market. This latter was extensively segmented, and there was but little communication between its various sections; the two principal mixed banks (Banca Commerciale Italiana and Credito Italiano, which we shall henceforth refer to as COMIT and CREDIT) were not in the habit of rediscounting. The Banca d'Italia therefore entered into a relationship with the money market almost exclusively through rediscounts granted to minor institutes, banking firms, individual bankers, and the smallest of the three mixed banks, the Società Bancaria Italiana (henceforth to be referred to as SBI), which was about to become the protagonist of the crisis. In addition, of course, the Banca d'Italia was in touch with the market through advances to the clearing houses of the stock exchanges and open-market operations (sale and purchase of government bonds). It was in competition with the mixed banks and other institutes for obtaining its share of the small amount of really liquid paper generated by the Italian market. Rediscount was not a normal feature of the Italian market, but rather was considered as the instrument to which the weaker operators had recourse, and other banks only in moments of acute monetary tension. It was an operation that the Banca d'Italia was called on to perform under difficult conditions (i.e., on the riskiest, poor-quality securities in Italian portfolios). Changing the discount rate, moreover, meant in the first place changing not the general rate but the special "accommodation rates" for different types of securities. Above all, discount policy served ex post to penalize various sections of the money market, and particularly to enforce liquidation of the highest-risk operations, rather than to guide the market in advance by smoothing out the peaks and troughs of movements in monetary indicators.

Even though its action was limited by these constraints, essentially due to the structure of the Italian credit market and the fact that it was not sufficiently involved in the market, the Banca d'Italia nevertheless had in its favor a number of by no means negligible strong points; some were of a legal and monetary nature, whereas others were of a political order, and one might even say moral order. Owing to a wise and prudent administration of its business and to the external processes mentioned at the beginning of this chapter, the Banca d'Italia had become the depository of the growing mass of reserves that the country had been accumulating and therefore had a greater freedom of movement in the creation of money than it had enjoyed at any time in the past. This was true in the sense that it could cope with substantial peaks in the demand for money while maintaining a high degree of gold coverage and substantially ensuring the "de facto" convertibility of its circulation. Moreover, Bonaldo Stringher, its director general (the office of governor had not yet been created), had earned for himself unquestioned prestige among the country's banking and industrial circles and, above all, enjoyed this prestige with the most powerful and expert of the heads of the mixed banks (Otto Joel of COMIT). He also worked in harmony with the government and enjoyed the confidence of the prime minister, Giovanni Giolitti. Stringher expressly asserted that his institute and its money-issuing policy should play a more incisive part in regulating the money market and promoting the industrial development of the country. Quite independently of his aspirations, however, the Banca d'Italia at that time was being pushed in this direction, or rather "dragged by its hair," by the mechanisms working in the context just described. On the external front it was being pushed along by continuous inflows of liquidity that it could not and, indeed, did not want to sterilize and that translated themselves into increments of the monetary base with all the inevitable multiplier effects as far as bank management was concerned; on the internal front, too, it had for some years past been induced to intervene with injections of liquidity every time the monetary market had become involved in the incidents of the onward march of stock-exchange speculation and, more generally, in the race of the large mixed banks to lend money for industrial and financial investments. The Banca d'Italia was a private joint-stock company, and it was therefore natural that its managers should endeavor to reconcile the need for making a profit typical of private enterprise with the "public" functions of guiding the market. However, the public function, on occasion, required the bank to forego profit opportunities in the form of increases in outstanding loans. In 1907 the Banca d'Italia's experience led to a sharp increase in its role as a responsible public institution, at the expense of its profit-making purpose.

We thus begin to have at our disposal the several elements that help us to understand the various factors in the Italian situation that could have had a destabilizing effect under certain conditions. The chronicles of Italian financial life of those years are highly instructive and provide us with punctual confirmation of certain expectations that we shall here endeavor to outline in an abstract manner.

The neuralgic area of the market was that of the large mixed banks financing stock-exchange business. It is quite true that the Italian monetary market cannot be said to have been vulnerable to the external factors that generally derive from dependence and/or integration based on capital movements and position of indebtedness; and yet it suffered such vulnerability on account of the fact that increases in the cost of money abroad provoked a rapid falling in line of the leading Italian operators and therefore penalized the more risky speculative positions. Monetary tensions in world markets, no matter how temporary, had the effect (even in the presence of a continuous surplus in the balance of payments) of triggering off a process of liquidation of marginal operations and therefore always gave rise to complications in Italian stock exchanges as a result of the fall of those operators whom their financiers had abandoned to their fate, preferring to bear the cost of the liquidation rather than to accept even greater risks. Whenever these incidents ran the risk of spreading, the banks were ready to collaborate with the Banca d'Italia, which was called on to intervene with injections of liquidity in order to smooth out the position of operators who would otherwise have had to be declared insolvent at the end-of-the-month settlement. In the aftermath of such incidents the banks themselves got business moving again by financing further bullish speculation. The persisting possibility of transforming foreign assets into means of payment for granting of loans and the increasing funds raised by the banks were further factors that permitted the stage managers of the market not to worry unduly about the increasing volume of loans, the ever lengthening period of repayments of these credits, and the growing concentration of risks.

The chronicles of Italian financial life permit us to verify that this "script" was punctually followed on various occasions, and they enable anyone who observes these events today to imagine the conditions that would cause the entire process to be repeated. In fact, for the banks to be induced to change their attitude it was by no means necessary to arrive at a negative balance of payments, an industrial crisis, or some other event capable of suddenly and unexpectedly depriving the banks of further possibilities of increasing their fund raising; far less proved to be quite enough.[3]

Contrary to what could easily have happened, a reversal of trend in the movement of business did not come about suddenly but rather matured over several months as 1906 turned into 1907.

In the autumn of 1906 an increase in the cost of money in the international markets once again had the effect of forcing speculation to liquidate some of its outposts, and, consequently, the Banca d'Italia (on the occasion of a stock-exchange collapse at Genoa) intervened once more to circumscribe and limit the conflagration by means of massive injections of liquidity, enjoying the collaboration of the banks as on previous occasions. But the sequel of this episode did not follow the script as it had many times before. A number of new and by no means negligible facts had to be recorded even before the year came to an end. The rising cost of money had caused speculative deposits to take to their heels, and the minor ordinary credit institutes had begun to fall back. Even the large mixed banks closed the year with a volume of carryovers that remained at the level of 12 months earlier, and this while the Banca d'Italia, for the third year running, continued to supply means of payment at an increasing rate. And yet there were many people who expected the triumphal march of stock-exchange speculation to resume. What actually happened in the next few months, however, was a kind of deadlock among the principal forces engaged in the fray. The idea that a liquidation of the recent speculative past was needed gained ground even among those who had reason to fear its consequences. It was difficult indeed to imagine how some form of withdrawal could be avoided. The two largest mixed banks were standing by the window, as it were, to observe the cost of money in world markets as if this could suggest a line of action. At the beginning of the year Stringher had publicized the fact that the Banca d'Italia was limiting its loans in view of the rate-of-exchange tensions that occurred each spring to damage the lira, and he multiplied his sermons to the effect that banks should not resume their financing of bullish speculation.

The situation became clear toward March and April 1907. Information arriving from abroad indicated that the monetary tensions of the previous year had been the forerunners of a trend that was not merely momentary. The policy of foreign central banks, which increased their discount rates, was promptly imitated by the Banca d'Italia; the mixed banks began to limit their lending, indicating a desire to withdraw from stock markets. It was then said that tens of millions of liras would be pulled out of the stock exchanges, and, consequently, the stock-exchange list began to record appreciable price declines. In May, Stringher proposed that the banks should agree to and jointly administer a kind of withdrawal designed to limit the cost of liquidating the past and to contain the damage. The instrument he suggested was a consortium financed by the Banca d'Italia and capable (by virtue of its composition and the means at its disposal) of propping up the quotations of the more important shares. This proposal was not accepted, and when a new stock-exchange crash occurred at Genoa at the end of June, the Banca d'Italia found itself practically alone in facing up to the situation. Following a new and massive emission of liquidity, the Banca d'Italia raised its discount rate (on 8 July) and, in answer to the protests against the measure, made it known that it had adopted the measure to defend its reserves, that it "would not fail to provide the means necessary to satisfy the needs of industry and commerce," but that it would not intervene to "rescue" speculation.

Because the attempt to organize an agreed liquidation of the past had failed as soon as it was made, it became clear in July that all parties had chosen their own paths. The two strongest banks (COMIT and CREDIT) indicated that they were sure of themselves and did not fear events. The third mixed bank (SBI) was the subject of rumors, in view of the involvement of some of its administrators in the Genoa stock-exchange complications, and it seemed to have the most to lose from a drop in price of the shares held by the speculators it had financed. It was the only one not to spare means in defense of its position. With the help of some minor operators styled as its "friends," the Banca d'Italia organized two consortia as best as it could at Milan and Genoa to counteract the continuous decline in the market that had by then been abandoned to itself. During the summer a further drop of share quotations occurred as a result of bearish speculation. The continuous decrease of stock prices began to push increasing numbers of operators out of the game and continued to erode the assets of the banks, especially the one (SBI) that had persisted in its attempted defensive action. Almost as if some disaster was being expected, the specialized press began to talk about "salvage operations" after 15 years of silence on this matter. There were also frequent requests for changes in the banking law that would permit the Banca d'Italia to increase the amount of money in circulation. Whereas the action of the two consortia had lost all effectiveness, the SBI experienced an attack on its own shares in the stock exchanges (not least, it would seem on the initiative of the rival banks), and its credibility was called into doubt, at first in the eyes of the more experienced observers and depositors and later also as regards the general public not accustomed to reading stock-exchange news.

Deposit withdrawals became insistent during September. As the depositors of the SBI appeared on the scene, events assumed an ever more pressing rhythm. Those interested in arresting the chain reactions triggered by the drop of share prices were forced to exert their efforts along a wider front.

Fear was the true protagonist of this new phase, and this fear was far more generalized than that of a restricted number of stock-exchange operators on the verge of insolvency or of bank executives conscious of the latent losses stemming from their past operations. Whereas several months had been needed before the continuous drop of share prices had sapped the resistance of the weakest of the three banks, two weeks were now sufficient to bring it into real peril, and just a few more days would have sufficed to create the conditions for a bank disaster of vast proportions.

In September, therefore, the SBI found itself in difficulty. It had not attempted to reduce the volume of its lending or obtain repayment on past loans in order not to have to reveal its losses; its shares had been the subject of bearish speculation, and it had lost credibility and was suffering a hemorrhage of deposits, with a consequent grave unbalance between receipts and payments. In short, it was suffering a liquidity crisis and was running the risk of having to go out of business. It was leaning heavily on the Banca d'Italia, but the day on which it would no longer have at its disposal eligible paper to discount was approaching fast and inexorably.[4] At this point the other two large mixed banks became worried, fearing that the collapse of their rival might spread lack of confidence among their own depositors. After having cut off finance to stock-exchange speculation, they also began to ration disbursements to commercial and industrial customers as a means of widening the margin between receipts and payments. Their conduct was immediately imitated, to the point of exasperation indeed, by the minor institutes, the banking firms, and individual bankers. A sharp credit squeeze thus took hold, and the last 10 days of the month saw the Banca d'Italia flooded with credit requests from all sides. The first moment at which the policy of the central bank could decide the course of events had thus arrived. At this point, in fact, some incisive and perhaps altogether decisive decisions were taken by the Banca d'Italia. It began to provide liquidity in all directions by means of discounts and advances, to all intents and purposes taking the place of the ordinary credit banks, at the same time foregoing an increase in the cost of money that everybody was expecting in imitation of what was happening abroad; it also announced that its reserves were increasing, that it could issue money without any difficulty, and that it could even count on the government's readiness to take any extraordinary measures that might become necessary (to wit, removal of the ceiling established by law as regards the volume of circulation not enjoying full metallic coverage). Stringher dwelt insistently on the fact that his institute would never allow commerce and industry to become deprived of the necessary means, but that it was not willing to come to the help of speculation. In fact, the directors of the local offices of the Banca d'Italia did everything possible to select the portfolios submitted to them with a view to preventing the disbursed funds from ending up on the stock exchange rather than being used to finance productive activities.

At the end of the month the heads of the COMIT and the CREDIT began to show signs of fear, and through an intermediary they let Stringher know that they were ready to collaborate to avoid a bank disaster. This move also had the purpose of warning the Banca d'Italia that they themselves might yet stand in need of help. At this point, in any case, Stringher no longer found himself in an isolated position, but rather disposed of interlocutors who were bound to inform him about what was happening in Milan and Genoa, interlocutors whom he could commit vis-à-vis the government in the search for ways and means of intervening in aid of the bank in peril and to stem the stock-exchange landslide. A consortium to help the SBI (in effect, a salvage consortium) was set up on 12 October with the participation of the two mixed banks, some minor banking houses, and the two other institutes of issue, although this latter was little more than a symbolic presence. Naturally, this consortium was financed by the Banca d'Italia and began to function right away. But in this phase Stringher did not succeed in counteracting the bear speculation and thus arresting the "free fall" of stock-exchange quotations.

What happened during the next two weeks made it clear to the protagonists that the danger had not yet been averted and that both the instruments and the means employed were insufficient. Within the space of 10 days or little more the SBI used up the funds from the consortium and practically confessed that it had not completely revealed the gravity of its situation. The supply of liquidity was therefore insufficient, the intervention did not have the desired effect, and matters remained exactly as before. The Banca d'Italia remained alone once more to plug the gap, so much so that its shares began to suffer. At this point the heads of the two banks found it easy to ask that the SBI should be liquidated, but Stringher succeeded in convincing them to enter into new agreements (7 November).

Further assistance was to be provided, but this time on the explicit condition that the bank's management was subject to a kind of guardianship entrusted to the Banca d'Italia.

On other fronts the situation became further aggravated. With the SBI now completely hors de combat, the managements of the two mixed banks, like the minor bankers, were paralyzed by fear of a coming run of depositors to their counters, and they kept in their coffers millions in ready cash that had been subtracted from the monetary circuits and that the Banca d'Italia had been obliged to reinject, Moreover, having stopped lending for some weeks past, they even found themselves without a discountable portfolio. On the other hand, business enterprises were also beginning to feel the pinch, there was open talk about an industrial crisis, and pressure groups and politicians were entering the field. Both the Banca d'Italia and the government gave further assurances that financial means would be provided, and there were further generalized injections of liquidity. Without anybody knowing about it, the Treasury transferred to the Banca d'Italia about 40 million lire in gold (the equivalent of the finance granted to the SBI). The Banca d'Italia thus increased the note issue enjoying full metallic cover, and the ratio between its reserves and circulation remained unaltered. The only effective help that Stringher received from the public and the banking system during this phase was represented by the inflow of current-account deposits, which served to provide a far from negligible flywheel effect in the service of the monetary maneuver.

For the rest, the money-market front was now characterized by a veritable rush for liquidity, although this race was being run not by savers but by those (businessmen and enterprises) who had become "orphans" of their banks and who, after being penalized by the high cost of money and finding themselves deprived of credit, were having recourse to their deposits (mostly in current accounts) and selling their governement bonds to obtain the required liquidity. Furthermore, even though the fear of losing their savings remained confined to the depositors of the SBI, the fear of finding themselves without means of payment for current operations induced a far larger number of people to engage in hoarding. Among the public there were people who sold bonds, the quotations of which suffered therefrom, and complications were feared as regards the rate of exchange. Even during these weeks, however, the monetary market continued to receive its liquidity injections without the Banca d'Italia running the risk of losing credibility. This happened because, as we have already pointed out, the issues were fully covered thanks to the Treasury's transfer of reserves and the continuing inflow of remittances from abroad.[5]

The latest episodes in the war that foreign central banks were carrying on by successive blows of raised discount rates, the 5.5% that had to be paid in London even on first-class bills, the historical fact that even Paris had increased the discount rate to 4%, the 7.5% payable in Berlin, the news (7 November) that the Banque de France had lent a helping hand to the Bank of England, the blockage of operations by the mixed banks (which were then thinking of nothing but accumulating liquidity), the news that these banks were asking enterprises to issue bills in respect of credits in current account, the pressures of a group of large enterprises that the banks invited to approach the prime minister with a view to obtaining finance from the Banca d'Italia, the general outlook that Stringher might see his institute transformed into an ordinary credit bank (because it had been conceding loans for a good month by then) – all these things made people think that the Banca d'Italia was exhausting, if not its means of intervention, at least its possibilities of intervening without its own prestige suffering as a consequence.

But the share market by then represented the front that had been left without defenses and therefore gave rise to destabilizing blows for the banks. New insolvencies had occurred on the occasion of the settlement at the end of October.

It began to seem intolerable that in a situation that promised to become even more dramatic the protagonists proved incapable of arriving at some agreement to oppose the ever faster downward trend of the entire stock-exchange list. This complex situation gave rise to a series of initiatives of a new type, initiatives in which there appeared factors of a political nature and also administrative instruments. On 29 October Stringher had given extensive assurances that he was in a position to help the market, and he let it be understood that he would not raise the discount rate. Evidently impressed by what was happening, irritated by the obstructionism that delayed effective intervention in the share market, and possibly suspecting (not without reason) that a part of the means he was disbursing ended up financing further bear-market speculation, he eventually announced that the official rate for all discount and advance operations would be increased from 5% to 5.5%.[6]

During the next few days the prime minister himself began to play a direct part. On 11 November he clearly told COMIT's top executive, Otto Joel, how irritated he was by the fact that nothing had been done to commence market interventions (obtaining an immediate and effective commitment by COMIT). Two days later, on 13 November, a decree (judged to be at the very limit of constitutionality) introduced the *diritto allo sconto*[7] in an effort to put an end to bearish speculation. On 19 November the Treasury entered the battle and announced advance payment of its interest coupons from 25 November onward. Another 100 million lire and more were thus put at the disposal of capitalist savers in the expectation that a part of this sum would find its way into the banking system.

The monetary tension came to an end during the second half of November. In a certain sense this fact provided an a posteriori confirmation of the destabilizing function that the continuous fall of share prices had exerted during the preceding weeks, and it also confirmed that, just as the non-collaboration of the "stage managers" of the market was by itself sufficient to leave the field wide open for the speculators, the mere announcement of their firm intention to oppose further speculation was quite enough to bring about a change of trend. Probably the *diritto allo sconto* also produced its effects. But it was the news that the COMIT was intervening to sustain the market (as part of the consortium at last set up with the full support of the Banca d'Italia) that brought to an end the chapter that had begun during the spring. On the other hand, this rather rapid slackening of the monetary tension can also be taken as evidence of two equally significant facts: first of all, that the monetary tension had essentially affected only a very restricted area of the Italian economy, namely the area in which the big ordinary credit banks come into contact with industrial enterprises and the share market. To all intents and purposes the rush for liquidity had infected only particular groups of savers and businessmen, that is to say, depositors of the SBI and businessmen who had fallen victims to the credit squeeze of their banks. Those who had deposited their savings with savings banks, with cooperative banks, and in postal accounts, as well as the migrants, had not become gripped by fear.[8] But undoubtedly this happened because the SBI did not close its doors and because at the right moment there was money for all. The conflagration had been substantially circumscribed, and the decisive battle was fought within the area occupied by the mixed banks. This meant that the Banca d'Italia had not vainly run the risks it shouldered when it decided to take their place.[9]

This gives some idea of the quality of the events. As regards their dimension, an attempt to measure it is difficult and perhaps even useless, because the events were not disastrous, although they could have become so. An immediate idea can perhaps be had by bearing in mind that the increase in circulation that occurred in Italy during 1907, and in particular between September and November of that year, was of such an exceptional nature that no increase of similar magnitude was ever recorded before or after that time, this being true at least until the increase of the summer and autumn of 1914 that coincided with the end of the gold standard.

There are various reasons why the events of 1907 are important in Italian banking history. Among others, they represent a testing ground for the banking structures that had come into being about the middle of the 1890s on the basis of nineteenth-century experiences. The events of 1907 put to the test not only the functionality of the mixed bank of the German type (in the form in which it had been adapted to the Italian environment) but also that of the Banca d'Italia, which had desired to shape itself in the image and likeness of the banks of issue of France and England. Here we shall therefore limit ourselves to some reflections about the reasons that make 1907 a decisive moment along the difficult and original road that was to lead Italy to the creation of a modern central bank.

On the eve of the crisis, notwithstanding the successes it could boast in connection with the administration of its assets and in spite of the "services" it had rendered to the market and the Treasury, the Banca d'Italia still occupied a noncentral position within the general framework of the financial system. In the aftermath of the crisis, albeit exploiting the emotion of the moment, Stringher easily obtained from the government and from the Parliament a number of important modifications of the rules that regulate the activities of the Bank and thus came to enjoy greater freedom of movement in connection with the control of the monetary market.[10] But quite apart from these institutional facts, the Banca d'Italia emerged from the crisis a little more a "central bank" than it had been on its eve, for very different and weightier reasons. It strengthened its hierarchical position at the summit of the Italian financial system because the crisis had enabled the banking system and the country's industrial and political forces to discover its strategic function in avoiding a blockage of the credit mechanism. As time has shown, this strategic function is represented by its capacity of intervening in the guise, as we would say today, of lender of last resort. At this point we have to ask ourselves what it meant in concrete terms to act as lender of last resort in Italy at the beginning of the century. What mainly strikes one from this point of view is that, in the case here considered, the Banca d'Italia took the place of the banks granting ordinary credit and thereby shouldered risks that would have been quite inconceivable, say, for the Banque de France or the Bank of England. The fact that these risks did not lead it into real danger does not mean that they were of little account or that suitable instruments for controlling them were available (as the vicissitudes of the next 30 years were to show).

It is precisely this circumstance that leads one to reflect on the importance of a whole series of conditions that do not depend on the behavior of the lender of last resort but that constitute essential "permissive" conditions for the purposes of action in opposing a given trend. Among these conditions, the one that seems to us to have the most significant and direct impact is represented by the manner in which the inflow of foreign resources into Italy took place (and we have already had occasion to dwell on this aspect), but many others could and perhaps should be taken into consideration. For example, we could ask how the oligopolistic market structure functioned in triggering and propagating the crisis and whether it facilitated or hindered its eventual solution. Let us not forget that the two leading mixed banks each agreed to collaborate with Stringher only after its fear for its own fate had got the upper hand of its desire to see its competitor go to ruin. In fact, as many as six months (from June to December) went by before the head of the COMIT decided to collaborate effectively in sustaining the share market. What is more, this happened only after the introduction of an administrative measure (the *diritto allo sconto*) and after the government had exerted pressure. Certainly it would be highly instructive to "simulate" situations that could have been created if Stringher had succeeded right away, at the end of May, that is, in obtaining an agreement for a planned and concerted management of the "liquidation" of the speculative positions. In particular, one may imagine what might have happened if an immediate start had been made with the great consortium visualized by Stringher, which was to bring peace back to the stock exchange and share the risks, the damage, and the cost of the withdrawal, as well as make possible the "survival" of the most valid shares, and which was thereby to become an instrument for the direct finance of the investments of the enterprise. Undoubtedly, such an instrument would immediately have become a great factor in the stabilization of the market. But probably it would not only have meant that the mixed banks would quickly have renounced behaving like "finance companies with the right to conduct over-the-counter business," as P. Saraceno has put it, but also would have led to the Banca d'Italia becoming involved in the management of share portfolios, and that might also have meant the state becoming an "entrepreneur state" about 30 years earlier than in actual practice.

As can be seen, these are problematics that are very familiar even to those who have little knowledge of the economic history of a latecomer country like Italy and that by themselves are sufficient to indicate the extent to which a theory of the behavioral models of financial operators has to take account of the context in which the various institutional types (which comprise, of course, also the lender of last resort) have to operate.

Notes

1   Bonelli, F. 1971. *La crisi del 1907. Una tappa dello sviluppo industriale in Italia.* Turin: Fondazione Luigi Einaudi.
2   Anyone who requires information more detailed than the necessarily summary remarks included in this chapter may consult the basic and well-documented work by A. Confalonieri, *Banca e Industria in Italia. 1894–1906,* 3 vols. (Milan: Banca Commerciale Italiana, 1974, 1975, and 1976), and the references quoted therein. As regards my own sources, I avail myself (in addition to Confalonieri's results) also of indications given in the study cited in Note 1 and of elements acquired in the course of my research for a biography of Bonaldo Stringher, director general of the Banca d'Italia from 1900 to 1930, shortly to be published by the UTET publishing house of Turin.
3   For a more detailed account of the facts related in the following pages the reader is referred to pages 39 to 148 of the work cited in Note 1.
4   The imbalance between receipts and payments came about because the bank executives "could not ask the re-entry of the disbursed funds or did not do so because they thought it harmful" (Bonelli, Note 1, p. 95). But the psychological effect of the loss of credibility proved to be fundamental on account of the suspicions that were making the rounds as regards the latent losses in the speculative operations in which the bank had been involved.
5   Owing to the economic crisis in the United States and the lack of confidence in the banks there, the remittances coming from that country included also transfers of savings made with a view to an early homecoming.
6   This measure was probably also affected by the preoccupation that the

differential between the Italian discount rate and those practiced elsewhere (especially in Berlin) might cause some of the funds disbursed by the Banca d'Italia to emigrate abroad.

7   The *diritto allo sconto* ("immediate settlement rights") gave the purchaser of equity the right to have them consigned to him at no more than two days' notice.

8   The following data should be borne in mind:

Percentage share of the national total

	Fund raising	Lending[a]
COMIT, CREDIT, SBI	13.9	24.3
SBI only	1.9	3.9

[a]Almost exclusively in credit to enterprises.

9   Percentage variations between 30 June and 30 November 1907 in the amount of:

	Fund raising	Lending[a]
COMIT	−10.1	− 5.9
CREDIT	− 9.8	−10.0
SBI	−64.7	−22.0

Percentage variations between 30 June and 30 November 1907 in the amount of:

"Circulation and debts on sight" of the Banca d'Italia	Credits to the domestic private sector
+11.2	+23.1

[a]Almost exclusively in credit to enterprises.

10   Bonelli, Note 1, pp. 106–7.

4. Central banking and foreign trade: the Anglo-American cycle in the 1830s

MAURICE LÉVY-LEBOYER

It would be unrealistic to question the role that the Bank of England (the Bank) played in the early part of the nineteenth century as a lender of last resort. From the end of the Napoleonic wars, with capital and deposits equal to about one-third of those of all the other banks in London[1], besides the exclusive right to issue notes within a 65-mile radius around the city, the Bank was in a position to exert a decisive influence on credit in the various stages of the business cycle. More specifically, it could step up rates in the money market so as to restrict speculative excesses when overtrading was becoming general, but also give extra facilities in order to limit the pressure for liquidity that used to develop in times of acute crisis, as inventories were run down and debts were cashed in by merchants. Actually, on the assumption that in the late 1830s bills under discount in the London market were about £75 million to £80 million (out of some £100 million for the country as a whole), the Bank could easily have doubled or trebled its share, from £2 to £4 million up to £11 or £12 million, to prevent a panic or reduce its amplitude.[2] Moreover, the directors were well aware of the necessity for the Bank "to uphold the credit of the country."[3] It was with this aim in view that its management had been reorganized shortly after the return to gold. During the suspension period, when the pound was inconvertible and at a discount, the Bank had been somewhat too liberal in its credit operations. However, with the crisis of the mid-1820s it had been realized that the same policy (coupled with a lowering of Bank rate) might endanger the convertibility of the currency and cause an internal drain on the reserve. New guidelines were therefore devised to give a rational framework to the Bank's discounts. The new rule that was presented in 1832 by J. Horsley Palmer, the governor of the Bank, while fully acknowledging the responsibility of the institution to the public, limited lending in two ways. It required, first, that "as an exclusive bank of issue in the capital, the Bank should not discount to any great extent, except in times of discredit, since competition with private bankers might lead to excess." And, second, if called on to assist the market, it should do so, but only up to the period of "full currency," that is, when the reserve was about to fall in consequence of an unfavorable state of the

66

foreign exchanges. The principle, thereafter, was to keep the amount of the securities constant and to let notes in circulation be contracted passively with the export of gold. In short, although its action had been restricted, there developed in the 1830s, to use the words of one of the directors, "a general expectation that the Bank of England was to be looked to as a source of assistance," not in the normal course of trade, but "in the last resort,"[4] with a provision, left rather flexible in its wording, about the scope of its intervention.

Still there was an element of ambiguity in these principles, given the contradictory nature of the Bank's duties (to assist the public and to maintain the currency at par in the foreign-exchange market), and given also the necessity to provide for the dividend, because proprietors' funds had reached £17 million by 1832, some 60% of the English capital invested in banking.[5] Sooner or later it was bound to revise the balance that was kept between its public duties and its private operations. The question, however, did not come to the fore in the 1830s, such matters being the concern of the senior members of the court, who had made the reform and were still responsible for its application. From about 1826 they expanded the Bank's services to the government, opened up branches in the country to diffuse its notes and to supply safe remittances between places, and used the discretionary power that had been left with them to enlarge discounts in periods of monetary tension. But with the passage of time a younger generation of directors was to enter the various executive committees, chiefly between October 1838 and April 1842. And with this change in personnel a major reversal of policy was implemented. At the request of the new members, the protection of the market, which had been basic to the 1832 rule, was discontinued. After a period of discussion and experiment, the task of issuing the Bank's notes was entrusted to a separate department and made automatic, notes being exchanged henceforward, pound for pound, against gold, beyond a fiduciary minimum; the scheme, which was to relieve the institution of all further duties to the currency, received the sanction of Parliament in the Bank Acts of 1844 and 1845.[6] In addition, under a new regulation made public in 1858, the discount brokers were denied the privilege, dating back to Palmer's days, of having their bills discounted at the Bank; the market could no longer rely on its unlimited assistance. In addition, all concern for the public interest that had loomed so large in the court's statements was officially and repeatedly repudiated, the institution being presented by its directors as having no more responsibility to the public in a crisis than that of any other bank to its customers.[7] Central banking functions were thus excluded from the Bank of England for most of the free-trade era.

Two explanations have been offered for this change of attitude. The first takes into account long-term factors, the abundance of loanable funds that pressed on the London market in the post-Napoleonic period, and the necessity for the banks to restrict credit facilities. So long as interest rates were falling (because of the greater safety and speed that peace had brought back to trade operations, and of the major contraction in government borrowings and agricultural investments), the danger for bankers, more particularly for those in the city, was to lend to excess and to be caught during a panic with money loaned out or with the obligation to assist their country correspondents. It was those bankers who were instrumental (1) in developing the London discount market to refinance trade and let money rates find their own level and (2) in enforcing at the Bank the policy of restraint that had been embodied in Palmer's law. If it was made more stringent at a later date, it was simply because speculative excesses, similar to those of 1825, had created the impression that the Bank could still abuse its power of issue and endanger convertibility by departing from the rule of constant securities.[8] Secondly, in a more practical way, the record of the Bank in the 1830s had been somewhat disappointing. Starting from a reserve position of £11 million, it had suffered three major drains: in 1834, again in 1836–37 (most of the gold export being registered in the spring of 1836, and from December 1838 to September 1839, when bullion was to fall down to a level of £2,406,000, the lowest figure since the crisis of 1825 (Fig. 4.1). In all these instances, even though the ceiling on interest rates had been taken off by an act in 1833 (to make its interventions more effective), the court did not react firmly to the situation; it waited from three to five months before taking action,[9] and later, when its rates of discount and advances were finally unified and stepped up, the move was made so abruptly that the credit contraction had damaging effects. In the fall of 1836 it brought about an internal panic, owing to a failure of confidence in Ireland and in the northern industrial districts. And during the summer of 1839 it caused an impairment of the pound in the foreign exchanges. If it had not been for the cooperation of bankers in Paris, Amsterdam, and Hamburg, who made available a total of £2.9 million credits to London with the assistance of the Bank of France, the flight from the pound that developed would have compelled the British government to publish a suspension act, an outcome that was discussed in earnest, for the Bank seemed unable to stem the withdrawal of funds by merchants from the Continent in the early part of August 1839.[10] As a matter of fact, it was the object of the Bank Charter Act of 1844 to solve both the problem of the notes solvency and that of the credit contraction: It legalized the 100% gold backing for new notes (to prevent overissues), and it did not make the explicit requirement of an extra reserve against deposits (on the assumption that an earlier curtailment of credit would then be forced on the Bank in case of a drain).

But, in a broader historical perspective, was the final reform well conceived? Was it right to abandon the 1832 rule, with its flexible provisions,

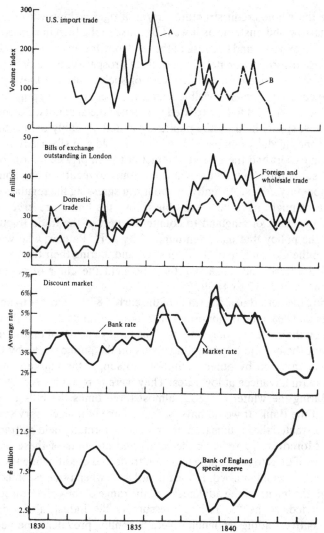

Figure 4.1. U.S. foreign trade and the London money market, 1830–44, quarterly averages. *Sources:* The two volume indices of U.S. imports (basis: 1833) are (A) dry-goods imports into New York, from the *New York Journal of Commerce,* and (B) Le Havre exports to the United States, from documents in the Basle economic history archives; both are seasonally adjusted from monthly data. The London bills series (quarterly value of inland bills of exchange created in England and Wales) is from documents collected in the preparation of a book by A. D. Gayer, W. W. Rostow, and A. J. Schwartz, *The Growth and Fluctuation of the British Economy, 1790–1850* (Oxford, 1953), quoted by courtesy of the authors. Discount rates and the Bank's statistics are from D. B. Chapman. *Select Committee on Banks Acts,* 1857, session 2, p. 463, and official returns.

and make the whole credit structure vary in a rigid fashion with the Bank's reserve, narrow and unstable as it was? Because of the high import content of major British exports, and because of the tendency for inventories and import prices to rise disproportionately in periods of prosperity, trade deficits in the early part of the nineteenth century were of such scale that they could not always be covered by such invisible sources of income as shipping and trade profits. Gold, then, had to be exported to balance the accounts. Furthermore, in the 1830s, specie held by the public amounted probably to less than £35 million[11] (one-third, by comparison, of French gold and silver holdings), and any bullion export had therefore to be met not from private hoards but from the Bank, submitting thereby the whole economy to recurrent and sometimes useless monetary crises. Actually, without transgressing the regulation of the note issue, it might have been possible to use the bullion reserve (and the credit) of the Bank of England to counteract part of the trade fluctuations. This was the policy that had been pursued by J. H. Palmer, who was still a member of the Committee of the Treasury, and, during their terms of office, by James Pattison and T. A. Curtis, who held the chair of governor, in succession, from 1835 to 1839.

1. During the period of slack trade of the early 1830s, in order to neutralize the effects that seasonal or abnormal absorption of funds into the Bank might have had on the currency, they had used the large deposits of funds left by the government (before the quarterly payments on the public debt), by the East India Company, and by other institutions to supply the market with short-term collateral advances at low rates: They were to reach an average of £8.7 million during the winter of 1835, almost three times the bills then under discount at the Bank. It would have been a source of unnecessary stringency to have abstracted these sums from the balances normally held by traders and bankers. Moreover, by revising the terms and amounts of these loans, the same group of directors was able to act on trade and credit, while keeping the Bank's discounts undisturbed. In the fall of 1835, when prices seemed unduly depressed, the length of the advances and the range of the collateral securities were extended, so as "to relieve pressure in the industrial districts." In contrast, as overtrading tendencies were becoming prevalent one year later, the loans were restricted in the fall of 1836 and finally called in.[12] Eventually, in March 1838, at T. A. Curtis's initiative, the Bank took the further step of shipping £1 million gold to America "to hasten the restoration of trade." That shipment was equivalent to twice the amount of specie held by the New York City banks. The objective, often stated, was "to prevent undue fluctuations of the currency."

2. While accepting the necessity to restrict discounts when the fall of the foreign exchanges resulted from a major disparity between domestic and foreign prices, these directors maintained that temporary deficits caused by

harvest failures and by other noncommercial accidents should be offset without contracting credit – on the assumption that a contraction would hinder exports (and not merely imports) and adversely affect the foreign position. Thus, in 1832, in 1836, and during the winter of 1838 (when payments for some £6 million or £7 million of corn imports had to be made), with the agreement of the Committee of the Treasury, the governors authorized the house of Rothschild to negotiate uncovered bills on the Continent (from £0.6 to £1 million at a time) to be met at maturity by shipments of silver or to be renewed, after three months, so that the economy would have time to adjust.[13] As J. H. Palmer was to comment, during a meeting of the court held in October 1839, just after the international panic against the pound (which, he felt, had been caused "artificially" by an unnecessary increase of the Bank rate): "In the absence of speculation on prices, when specific payments have to be made to foreign countries, the most advantageous means to liquidate such amounts is by the general export trade," to the exclusion of credit contraction or any measure that might disturb trade and create a panic.[14]

Briefly stated, these are the two sides of a debate that went on endlessly during the nineteenth century whenever new commercial crises were to raise the issue of central banking. Because the need to provide for a reliable currency, readily convertible into metallic coins, had been met by the act of 1844, was it still the duty of the Bank of England to keep an extra reserve, available at all times, and to stand ready as a lender of last resort to reduce the shock of monetary crises? As already stated, the Bank's response was negative. In reaction against its former position, it maintained a course of "steady and undeviating" contraction when specie was abstracted from the reserve, on the assumption that the pressure would lessen in a crisis if curtailment of credit was brought into play at an early stage, and in conformity with a fixed rule that could be followed by the 450 or 500 country banks still issuing notes in England and Wales.[15] But a smaller group of the Bank's directors, made up chiefly of merchant bankers, and so more attentive to the international environment, went on asking for some years that "no hasty or unnecessary action be taken, that would affect prices and credit at home, but also in foreign countries," that the Bank's reserves be increased in order to gain time and protect the money market, until the foreign exchanges would improve, etc.[16] One may wonder whether the nineteenth century might not have been spared some of its instability, given the Bank's financial power, if discretionary management of the currency had been preserved. Would greater credit facilities have been useful to limit the intensity of international monetary crises? It is this alternative that is to be examined here, on the basis of the 1830s experience (the only period when an active policy of this kind was applied) and from the single point of view of Anglo-American trade and finance, because of their major influence in the debate. Two points will be considered in succession: What were the risks that the Bank of England had assumed when acting as a central bank, and on what grounds was the policy changed? What were the immediate determinants that caused the Bank to sacrifice its functions?

I. The panic of 1837

The 1830s trade cycle was one of the very first that was synchronized on both sides of the Atlantic. This pattern was due to demographic and other factors making for mounting consumer demand and production, but even more so to the key role of the United States as the best customer for western European industries (the country received, on the average, 12%–13% of the total exports of Britain and France) and to its position as chief supplier of raw materials. Any deficiencies in cotton, tobacco, and even grains in the mid-1830s reacted on the U.S. price level – with greater amplitude than in Europe (Fig. 4.2) – and after a lag of two or three years on their production. American exports, therefore, surged forward (in volume) during the 1833–42 period at a rate of 8% per annum, almost twice the increase registered for the country's commodity output, bringing thereby, once the balance had been restored between supply and demand, overproduction, price regression (the fall, from peak to trough, for corn and cotton, was of the order of 65% – 75%, and for all countries concerned a slower pace of industrialization.

These movements common to most nineteenth-century cycles need not be examined here in detail, except for three aspects. First, the cotton boom that culminated in 1835–36, when sales for the first time provided more than half of the American foreign-exchange earnings, was based on solid foundations. There had been major reductions of inventories from the late 1820s, both in the ports and at the mills, because importers and manufacturers, trying to restore their former position, had been frustrated by restocking operations in the intermediary stages of industry. Even though new lands had been brought into cultivation by planters in the Mississippi and other gulf states, the ratio of cotton stocks to mills' consumption kept falling; stocks in Liverpool amounted to 14 weeks' consumption in 1835–36 (against 43 weeks' supply in 1827), and prices remained at a high level for almost three years, 40% above the 1833 average. As a consequence, U. S. cotton exports in 1836 doubled to $70 million.[17] But, second point, given the high income elasticity of the country's demand for imports, any increase in prices and incomes was bound to have two opposite effects: positive in Europe (25% of Britain's domestic exports and 18% from France were shipped to America in 1836) and negative in the American market, because the fluctuations in imports were of greater amplitude than those of exports (both moved with the same

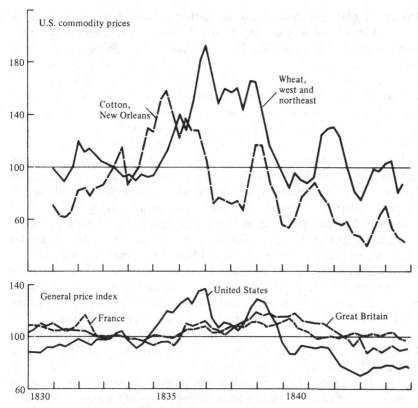

Figure 4.2. Wholesale prices quarterly index, 1830–44 (basis: 1833 = 100).
Sources: Prices for the United States are those of A. H. Cole, partially used in
Fluctuations in American Business (Cambridge, Mass., 1935), p. 170; for the U.K.,
the series is that of A. D. Gayer, W. W. Rostow, and A. J. Schwartz, *The Growth
and Fluctuations of the British Economy, 1790–1850* (Oxford, 1953).

timing and direction, but at respectively 20.3% and 11.3% per annum, in
value terms, during the years of prosperity). Hence the worsening of the
balance on current account: The American deficit in 1836 reached a total of
$56 million, almost twice the average balance of the preceding three years. A
final point is worth mentioning. The closing of its branches and the partial
liquidation of the assets of the Second Bank of the United States, after its
conflict with President Jackson in 1832–34, and the loss of its federal charter
in March 1836 had brought caution in monetary matters. New state banks
were founded (some 225, half the number in operation in 1833), but they
were planned and managed on more conservative lines than in the past, and
the public itself was more inclined to hold metallic coins rather than notes or

deposits.[18] This attitude imposed one further constraint on foreign trade: A total of $36 million in coins and bullion had to be imported (40% for the banks and 60% for the public) during the same 1833–36 period. In a very short time the United States had accumulated an aggregate deficit, on all accounts (merchandise, services, and bullion), that exceeded probably $125 million, the equivalent to the planters' debts in the gulf states, or to the capital invested in the new state banks, or even to the sum of the federal income receipts: perhaps one month of gross national product.

In the absence of a substantial flow of foreign investment,[19] this balance had to be covered from abroad out of commercial bank credits: £10 million and even £15 million (some $75 million) of short-term debts, according the London press, were said to be running against American merchants by October 1836. This should have made the country highly vulnerable to changes in the money market, but for a time it proved remarkably resistant. In the early part of the year, after the period of harvesting and crop sales when bills and notes were being remitted from New Orleans and the interior for their annual settlements by country merchants to the Atlantic cities and by importers to Europe – the foreign exchanges tended to rise, on a seasonal basis, each year in March, April, and May – even though large imports were still entering the port of New York (Figure 4.1), there was no weakening of the currency. London bills in the exchange market remained at a discount, at 1.4% under real par, lower than in the same period of 1835, and they were to stay at 1.26% discount in the next 10 months, preventing any outflow of gold. In July 1836 the specie circular was published, an executive order for federal agents to accept only lawful money in payment for public lands. But, here again, it did not provoke a significant increase in hand-to-hand circulation; no excess demand for specie was reported until October, at the time of the "autumnal drain," when movements of coins out of cities to pay for the crops had always put pressure on the banks.[20] Further, the demand for cash abated somewhat with the shipment of the new crops during the winter. Then, suddenly, the whole debt structure gave way, with the collapse of cotton prices in Liverpool and the consequent downfall late in March 1837 of the New Orleans factors who had financed the crops. A run for cash developed throughout the United States, breaking the entire trading community, which had been standing between country merchants and New York foreign houses; it continued for two months up to May 1837, when the banks' suspension of specie payments brought the panic to an end. More than 300 firms had stopped in the single port of New York, and estimates of capital losses were of the order of $125 million, or, on the basis of recent figures, two-fifths of the country's commercial capital.[21]

Actually, given the size of the debts, domestic and foreign, and the high level of short interest rates, which had trebled through the year, it is not so much the end of the boom that raises a problem, for it was overdue, but its long deferment. In most American cities the break in commodity prices had come in April 1836, one full year before the crash; domestic markets were overstocked with European goods, at least from June 1836.[22] And at the very moment when the downturn should have called for some credit contraction, the country was given new assistance from abroad. As Figure 4.1 shows, sterling bills of exchange, created for wholesale and foreign-trade operations, and so in part to finance American imports, increased between July 1836 and March 1837 by £10 million to an average of £42.9 million per quarter, against £32.3 million in the first six months of 1836. Leaving aside economic factors that brought the boom to its end, the problem is really one of financial responsibility: What was the institutional framework that made possible the accumulation and renewal of such large credit facilities? And how did the Bank of England adapt its policy to counteract the movement?

The Anglo-American merchant-bankers. The major part of American foreign-trade operations in the 1830s were financed from London and Liverpool by a group of seven banking houses (and a few minor ones) still operating as merchants and shipowners, with branches and agencies overseas, and endowed with substantial means. The leader in those days, the house of Baring, was to reach in 1836 £1.1 million capital, including the partners' accounts with the firm, and a total of £6.1 million assets. This situation was a legacy dating back from postcolonial days, when American merchants had access to England's manufactured goods and long-term credits, and so were running large commercial debts in sterling (U.S. imports from England amounted to three times their sales in British territories) that they had to cover with the proceeds of their exports and shipping operations in third countries. To fill the gap, but also to protect themselves against the monetary and political insecurity that existed on the Continent during the French wars, they tended to collect and transfer to their London correspondents the funds and properties they could dispose of in Europe and overseas and to finance all their foreign operations from that place. After the return to peace, this tradition was maintained, first, because trade had expanded between the two countries (40%–43% of American imports were still coming from England under acceptance credits opened by the new generation of bankers who had taken over existing firms or entered new partnerships in the late 1820s) and, second, because Londoners extended the same credit facilities throughout the world, but more particularly in those regions east of the Cape of Good Hope and in the Pacific where American supercargoes had not regularly had outward freights in the past, except specie. They were allowed from about 1827 to buy homebound cargoes with bills of exchange drawn on their London bankers.[23] Hence, in spite of the rapid development of staple

Table 4.1. *United States foreign trade: regional structure, 1833–42, annual averages (in $ million) and dispersion (%)*

	N. British colonies	North Europe	France	Great Britain	Asia	South America & others	Total
Merchandize ($ million)							
1. Exports	+3.99	+10.04	+16.92	+47.03	+1.65	+27.18	+106.81
2. Imports	−1.35	− 8.94	−20.03	−46.41	−9.80	−33.95	−120.48
Balances ($ million)							
3. Trade	+2.64	+ 1.10	− 3.12	+ 0.62	− 8.14	− 6.77	− 13.67
4. Shipping	+0.81	+ 0.25	+ 0.80	+ 1.74	+1.45	+ 4.07	+ 9.42
5. Specie	−0.26	+ 0.07	− 0.02	− 0.44	+1.61	− 5.17	− 4.21
Total (3–5)	+3.19	+ 1.42	− 2.30	+ 1.92	−5.08	− 7.87	− 8.46
Dispersion							
6. Imports (%)[a]	26.9%	25.2%	32.8%	31.0%	11.4%	13.8%	23.5%
7. Exports (%)	29.2%	19.3%	13.0%	26.7%	8.7%	8.9%	10.2%
8. Ratio (6:7)	0.69	1.31	2.51	1.85	1.32	1.55	2.3

[a]The coefficients of variation, that is, the standard deviations as percentages of the average values of imports and exports (lines 6 and 7), have been used as a rough measure of import fluctuations; they refer (column 6) to South America only, not to "other countries." An independent estimate, based on T. S. Berry, *Revised Estimate of American Gross National Product* (Richmond: Bostwick, 1978), shows that the income elasticity of demand for imports in the 1833–36 period was 1.87 for total imports but 2.1 for those coming from England and 2.7 for those from France.

Sources: Annual Reports on Commerce and Navigation of the U.S., 1833–43; D. C. North, "The United States Balance of Payments, 1790–1860," in *Trends in the American Economy in the Nineteenth Century*, edited by W. N. Parker (Princeton: Princeton University Press, 1960), Table B-5, p. 621.

exports and of a substantial reduction in the bilateral trade gap (Table 4.1), American importing firms were still in debt to London, first for the rather long credits their agents received when purchasing manufactured goods in England or France (they were sold on a 4-months basis, while cotton shipments to Liverpool were bought with 60 days-sight bills) and second for the new facility of having at their disposal in distant seas the surplus balances British merchants accumulated out of the export of manufactured goods in Canton, in "the Country trade" between India and China, and in Valparaiso and the west coast of South America.[24] These services contributed to the growth of foreign trade. They were beneficial to all parties: American merchants could buy on cheaper terms (sterling drafts being equivalent to cash), while keeping for the home market silver coins and bullion that were previously received from South America, for reexport to the Far East. They were useful to importers in third countries for the reason that they were no longer limited, when receiving British goods, by the necessity to remit specie; shipments of local produce, to be sold in New York, Amsterdam or any other port, were used thenceforward to cover the balance. And the London merchant-bankers were able to expand steadily the area in which sterling bills could be utilized: England accounted for probably 26% of world imports in the late 1830s if goods entering British ports are made the basis of the estimate, but as much as 46% if all imports financed through London credits, in and out of the country, are taken into account.[25] The position assumed later by London as the pivot of international trade was already taking shape.

At first this system seemed to be safe, in spite of the greater centralization of credits and payments, both for the bankers and merchants, who transmitted the bills of exchange, once issued in Manchester or some distant place overseas, or retained them as a cash reserve or as a short-term investment, and for the acceptance houses, which were normally supplied with funds in time to pay for the bills at maturity. Formerly, it had been devised at the initiative of British manufacturers and merchants because they had been exporting on their own account during the early part of the Industrial Revolution and they were trying ways to limit the effects that dumping, falling prices, and profits had on their operations during the post-Napoleonic depression. Their aim had been to reduce their financial involvement, or at least to share risks, to shorten credits, and to substitute commission business for outright purchase and sales, so that new intermediaries would stand between them and foreign markets. And they had been partly successful, because American importers' agents were now active in Europe and overseas, taking charge of the actual transmission and sale of goods; and their operations were being financed by chains of foreign merchants who held the debt instruments, the length of the bills being made equal to the time needed for shipment, sale, and remittance of the proceeds.

Basically, however, the risks involved were still there: Overdrafts were always possible, specifically during a boom; foreign bills could be remitted before maturity and converted into cash through the London discount market, shifting the burden of financing sizable transactions on English investors, and any delay or interruption in the flow of remittances was to leave the acceptance houses unprotected. In practice, perhaps because of the new bankers' wrong estimates of market potentials, or because of some structural imbalance in American trade, the transfer of commercial risks from British merchants to the American importer and his bankers made the London market much more vulnerable to international monetary crises than it formerly had been.

1. Initially, the new Anglo-American houses had applied strict rules in their operations to prevent excess lending: All had partners or agents on the other side of the Atlantic, generally in Boston, New York, or Baltimore, to select customers, evaluate their credit standing, and control their payments. They limited credit facilities to only part of each transaction, advances

amounting generally to one-third of the goods consigned, and they reserved for themselves or for their agents either the sale of the goods or the shipping documents, to be delivered abroad in exchange for remittance on London. But in the early part of the 1830s, during the period of high prices and activity, competition between banks brought a loosening of controls. Credits were opened, more frequently, without the usual insurance and shipping documents, these being sent directly to the American importers. The percentage of credits advanced on consignments was increased, sometimes to full costs, and correspondents were permitted not to cover the bills drawn at maturity.[26] Of course, cash advances were not the rule. A few houses maintained or even reinforced their older regulations; the Barings, for instance, improved their cash position from £1.3 million to £1.8 million in the course of 1836, that is, from 64% to 81% of the acceptances running against them. But most of the London firms had much lower reserves and were to find themselves in great difficulties on that score in the latter part of that year.

2. Foreign pressure on the London money market had been somewhat offset in the past for the reason that the British balance of payments had what has been termed "contrasting movements vis-à-vis Europe and the U.S."[27] Britain tended to have a passive balance with the Continent during periods of prosperity, when high incomes and prices raised the demand for imports, and an active balance during periods of depression, because of the low supply elasticity of such imports as grains from the Baltic, silks and fancy goods from France, etc. The worsening of British terms of trade with Europe in the upswing and their improvement in the downswing were the main factors in the anticyclical behavior of those regional payments. On the contrary, the balance improved cyclically with America during a boom on account of the synchronization of the two economies and the greater impact that income fluctuation had on the U.S. imports. As shown in Table 4.1 (lines 4–6), cyclical variations in the value of British exports to America, measured over the 1833–42 period, were twice as great as those of British imports from that country. As a result, the balance tended to move favorably for Britain in the early 1830s and unfavorably in the latter part of the period, making up for the inverse relationship with Europe. Once the Anglo-American houses had assumed a greater share of the U.S. financial operations, however, such compensatory movements were hardly significant. The coverage of the U.S. deficit in England could be delayed. And London had to provide for payments in third countries: A supplement (in net terms) of £2.25 million in 1836 (probably the equivalent of its own deficit) was required to settle the American balance with France, for that country also improved its position cyclically with the United States (actually in a greater degree than England); £1.4 million went to the Baltic in 1836 and 1837 to

cover grain imports, because harvests had failed in the American West and in upper Canada; some £2 million to £3 million went to the Far East in 1837, the equivalent to the 1836 deficit, distance making it impossible to revoke orders once they had been dispatched, etc.[28]

Thus, it was not simply that remittances had been allowed to be delayed, leaving American accounts overdrawn in London; the accumulation of negative balances in almost all foreign markets in the course of 1836 and the necessity to provide thereafter for extra imports from northern Europe and China and to offset the shortfall of current sales in American markets were responsible for a steep increase in London bankers' acceptances up to the end of 1836 and for their relative stability in the following months. British foreign earnings had to cover the country's own payments abroad, as well as those of the United States.

The Bank of England's first policy. These problems had been the concern of the directors at the Bank from the spring of 1836 because of the mounting pressure in the money market and the loss of some £2.6 million specie, one-third of the reserve, which was exported, to a great extent, to pay for American debts on the Continent. English bullion statistics are defective and cannot indicate precisely the geographic distribution of exports (before 1837). Nevertheless, indirect evidence does exist: Anglo-American acceptances were remitted in great numbers during the summer of 1836, from New York, but also from Paris, to be cashed through the London discount market and to draw specie away. Weekly controls were set up at the Committee of the Treasury's initiative, the Bank holding already £1.72 million of this paper by August 1836, probably as collateral for its special advances. Moreover, the pound sterling lost in value against most Continental currencies in Hamburg, Amsterdam, Antwerp, and Paris – in this last place, the rate of exchange for one-month bills fell steadily over the year from 25.65 to 25.10 francs per pound. But strange as it may seem, the new position assumed by the London merchant-bankers and its effect on foreign payments were not immediately perceived, attention being focused on the bilateral trade with the United States that was still active and favorable "without any evidence having then existed of a derangement in prices."[29] The general attitude in London was not to relate the drain to American overtrading but to blame it on special circumstances, such as the rediscounting operations of newly formed joint-stock banks, speculative investments in foreign securities, President Jackson's efforts to substitute gold for silver in the American circulation (the silver price of gold had been raised by an act of 1834) and his insistence on forcing specie imports into the country. Writing early in 1837, just after the end of the external drain, J. H. Palmer was still under the impression that £2.3 million of the Bank's reserves

Table 4.2. *United States trade and specie balances by regions, 1832–42*
($ million per year)[a]

	1832–5		1836		1837		1838–42	
	Trade	Specie	Trade	Specie	Trade	Specie	Trade	Specie
British N. Am.	+ 2.51	−0.13	+ 0.70	−0.48	− 0.90	−0.04	+3.44	−0.29
Baltic	− 1.66	+0.02	− 2.37	+0.02	− 4.57	+0.03	−0.74	+0.02
France	− 0.32	−0.19	−10.94	−4.74	− 2.66	+0.27	−3.59	+0.99
United Kingdom	− 4.63	−1.30	−18.46	−2.31	+ 7.36	+2.34	+7.30	+0.06
Far East	− 8.52	+1.89	−11.20	+1.86	−13.61	+0.62	−6.12	+1.53
South America	− 2.14	−6.75	−10.47	−3.43	− 5.40	−7.76	−6.60	−3.96
Total	−13.76	−6.80	−52.24	−9.08	−19.03	−4.54	−4.83	−1.15

[a]One pound sterling is equivalent to $4.85.
Source: See Table 4.1.

(the equivalent of $11 million) had gone to America, a "fact" disproved by bankers during the crisis[30] and in contradiction with the U.S. statistics (Table 4.2).

Hence the undecisiveness of the court, its tardiness in raising the Bank rate to stop the gold outflow, and its tendency to react to the situation by taking discriminatory measures. There had only limited results, for the decisions were either countermanded forthwith (in August 1836, when the Liverpool agent of the Bank was instructed to abstain from discounting any more American paper) or left in abeyance (when members of the leading Anglo-American houses were asked in October to close all uncovered accounts and to abstain from endorsing bills for the market). It was only in February 1837 that a sharp credit contraction took place, and then at the initiative of the leading discount brokers, who temporarily discontinued handling American paper. The repayment by the Bank of England of the special deposits left by the East India Company and the publication of poor returns (bullion was down at £4 million, whereas securities had not yet been reduced) were clear indications that the court, at last, was about to apply stern measures of retrenchment.[31] But after almost one year of slow erosion of its reserves, it can be stated in fairness that the Bank's delays and uncertainties, far from having helped the market, had deepened the crisis by giving added strength to the two underlying forces that had intensified the panic: the internal drain in both countries and the growing imbalance between the supply of and demand for loanable funds.

First, domestic movements of coin, which were then customary at harvest time, acted as the main determinant of the final crash. This was due in the two countries to the rise in interest rates and to the tendency for bankers in distant regions to lock up funds when the pressure for money created apprehension and alarm. In England, no less than £0.93 million of gold was shipped to Ireland in the course of 1836 and some £0.40 million to the northern district, while many bankers were reported as storing up cash resources far above their ordinary needs. In America, independent forces were at work: the high price of corn, new farm settlements, and the fact that a great number of unit banks in the northern rural districts (some 410 out of a total of 645) had to operate for the first time without the assistance of the Bank of the United States (BUS). This contributed to the aggravation of the withdrawals of idle balances from the East Coast to meet farmers' demands; in New York City, bank reserves fell by one-fourth in the last quarter of 1836.[32] Furthermore, under the strain caused by gloomy reports from London and the transfer of public moneys in compliance with the Surplus Revenue Act, funds were not sent back to New York, once the crops had been paid for; there was a constant drift of coin into circulation, notes being returned to issuing banks and deposits withdrawn, compelling the banks to call in resources. Specie balances in the hands of the public, almost nonexistent in the past, were to reach $35 million in December 1836, and perhaps $50 million, or 48% and 70% of the total stock (Table 4.3). From the point of view of Anglo-American relations, the situation offered something of a paradox. Banks in Ohio and the Northwest were amply supplied with funds (they held 19.3% of the state banks' reserves in December 1836 and 23.6% in May 1837, as well as the highest cash ratios), whereas the stringency had grown more acute at the shipping points from which London bankers might have expected specie remittances (the Boston banks were left with only $0.93 million in April 1937 and those in New York City with $2.6 million, or, for the two cities, 16.6% of all the state banks' cash holdings, less than 5% of the stock existing in the country).

Second, the same factors (increasing prices and interest rates) were responsible for the sudden accumulation of bills that developed in England during the second part of 1836 to fill the gap caused by the contraction in the money supply (Figure 4.1). They represented three categories of debts: (1) new drawings on the Anglo-American houses accompanying Britain's record exports of June–August 1836 and those of January 1837 (both explain the seasonal increase in payments registered with a lag of three months in Table 4.4); (2) substitutes for money, because inland bills were always readily expanded in response to higher discount rates, both by country bankers and in many lines of trade by merchants; (3) to a large extent in the last months of 1836, finance bills, that is, a category of paper, generally issued within the country to raise money on fictitious transactions, but used this time to lend capital on short term in America on the basis of the difference in discount rates (money was borrowed at 5.5% in London and

Table 4.3. *Components of the stock of money, 1833–7 ($ million)*

	Specie held by			Note issues	Deposits	Money stock		Cash ratio (%)[a]	
	Public	Banks	Total			Current	Deflated	A	B
Dec. 1833	15.8	27.0	42.8	72.7	63.5	152.0	152.0	36.9	19.8
Dec. 1835	25.0	40.0	65.0	108.2	84.6	217.8	198.7	38.5	20.7
Dec. 1836	35.0	27.9	72.9	112.7	77.0	224.4	187.3	48.0	20.0
May 1837	(50.0)	21.8	(71.8)	72.3	45.2	168.5	163.8	(69.6)	18.6
Dec. 1837	52.0	35.2	87.2	91.2	78.0	221.1	185.0	59.6	20.8
Dec. 1838	42.0	45.1	87.1	107.8	81.3	231.1	241.5	47.1	23.9
Dec. 1839	50.0	33.1	83.1	86.2	68.1	204.3	209.8	60.2	21.5
Dec. 1842	56.0	33.5	90.0	45.3	47.9	152.5	207.9	62.2	35.9

[a]The cash ratios refer to the public's specie holdings, as percentages of total stock (A), and to those of the banks, compared with their demand liabilities (B). Public deposits, after an increase from $7.9 million in 1834 to $45.1 million in 1836, were only $5.8 million in December 1837.

Sources: M. Friedman and A. J. Schwartz, *Monetary Statistics of the U.S. Estimates, Sources, Methods* (New York: NBER, 1970), Table 13; P. Temin, *The Jacksonian Economy* (New York: W. W. Norton, 1969), Table 3.3, p. 71; for May 1837, *Annual Report of the Comptroller of the Currency*, 1876, pp. 111–15, and *Hunt's Merchants Magazine*, 1841, 2:139, 270–1.

Table 4.4. Anglo-American payments position and trade movements, 1833–7

	American acceptances in London, bills outstanding (£1,000)					New York imports indices			New Orleans indices	
	Baring	Wildes	Wiggin	Wilson	Total	volume	prices		volume	prices
	A	B	C	D	E	F	G	H	I	J
Dec. 1833	2288	861	680	813	8080	125	103	102	90	117
Dec. 1834	1882	753	560	731	6830	99	106	118	73	129
Dec. 1835	2078	1070	1147	1504	10100	251	128	119	104	134
Dec. 1836	2187	1539	1922	2112	13625	305	111	149	70	129
Mar. 1837	1571	1385	1162	(1812)	10320	90	109	139	76	113
May 1837	1261	505	675	936	6170	234	105	122	72	72
Dec. 1837	986	—	—	—	—	63	80	99	113	77

Sources: (A–E) *B.E. mss.* (for the May 1837 accounts); *Baring mss.* and R. W. Hidy, *The House of Baring in American Trade and Finance* (Cambridge, Mass.: Harvard University Press, 1949), p. 232; *Edinburgh Review* 65(July 1837):231–7. The total (E) has been estimated on the assumption that these four firms and W. & J. Brown of Liverpool, who had £1.56 million acceptances in May 1837, accounted for 80% of the acceptance credits. (F–J) all the index series have been calculated from the monthly data to show the seasonal payment position in London (taking into account actual movements of trade and prices, but also credit length) for dry-goods imports in New York (F), prices of Manchester goods (G) and Lyon silks (H), and cotton exports in New Orleans (I–J). Data are from *France, Rapports consulaires*, Liverpool, 15 October 1842; *New Orleans Price Current* and *New York Journal of Commerce.*

lent on first-class commercial paper, for two or three months, at 24%–30% in New York and Boston).[33]

Thus the difficulties experienced by brokers in the course of the winter of 1836–37 were coming at the same time from an increase in the volume of bills pressing on the market (as Table 4.4 shows, there had been only a slight reduction in the amount of American paper outstanding) and from the risks involved in endorsing it to English investors (£2 million to £2.5 million out of a total of £10 million was accommodation paper revolving between New York and London). To limit the pressure of demand, various devices had been used at first, loans, in particular, being substituted for outright purchases.[34] But because cotton shipments were bringing in a fresh supply of remittances that were immediately presented for discount, the interruption in brokers' operations brought about a general curtailment of credit throughout the country and forced the Anglo-American houses to apply to the Bank of England for new facilities in order to meet their acceptances at maturity. George Wildes was the first banker to submit a demand, on February 27, 1837.

The problem at that stage was to prevent a complete breakdown of the system and possibly a denunciation of American debts, if the flow of acceptances and payments were interrupted. The course of events from then on is well known. After two weeks of discussion, and very much at the urgent request of J. H. Palmer, the Bank chose to assume a more central position in the market: On March 10, three houses in London (remembered as "the three W's") and that of the Browns in Liverpool were permitted to discount at the Bank specified quotas of bills, amounting in all to £1.25 million; and later in the month the BUS was offered a substantial credit of £2 million, to be drawn from Philadelphia, half against a shipment of gold and half against bills endorsed to the Bank of England. These were major departures from the conventional rules, but unrealistic ones. With the fall in the price of securities and produce (cotton lost 30%–35% of its value in February–March 1837) a great many bills were returned under protest or were refused acceptance. Very soon the London bankers found that no paper of any sort was remitted for fear it would be dishonored. Thus the three W's, among others, had to suspend payments on June 1, having exhausted practically all bills and cash assets, and being therefore unable to meet a total of £2.3 million immediate liabilities.[35] Further, no specie could be shipped from the United States so long as hoarding prevented gold from flowing back into the banks; in April the BUS declined the Bank of England's credit – it was holding at that time less than $1.5 million of reserve (about £0.3 million), in spite of the successful issue in the same month of $5 million worth of sterling bonds to meet the reflux of its own notes. The Bank of England, though, maintained the same course: Discount facilities (including a special credit of £1.95

million for the house of W. & J. Brown) were granted in May and June to Liverpool merchants through the local branch of the Bank and the head office, as well as short-term loans to London merchants on the security of American bills under protest. Actually, with the news of the suspension of specie payments in the United States, the pressure eased in the money market; bullion was back at £7.7 million at the Bank in October 1837, its precrisis level, and the market rate of discount was at 3.75% in November.

But the Bank's action, its passivity in the first part of the drain, the feeling of alarm that had developed, and the consequent abstraction of funds from the banks and the market were hailed with criticism.[36] Retrospectively, it seems fair to say that the contraction had been overdue. American debts had increased excessively after April 1836; there were still £6 million to £8 million bills and book debts unpaid 14 months later. The panic itself had been destructive of capital, all firms having still to cover besides their current liabilities the dishonored paper they had been compelled to endorse to the market when the search for liquid funds had been most acute. To take the case of a banker who was to clear all his debts, William Brown in Liverpool had at one time £650,000 due from failed houses in the United States and £850,000 in bills on suspended banks in Britain, the greater part in circulation with his signature. From a review of ledgers and papers that have been preserved for the six main Anglo-American houses, their suspended debt at the end of May 1837 amounted to a total of £3 million, out of £13.4 million assets; and if losses, according to their own estimates, were really equal to £770,000, their capital had to be scaled down from £3.9 million to £3.1 million, and probably to some lower figures, as litigation and depreciation of assets were bound to occur.[37] The Bank of England, on its part, found itself with £3.74 million claims on the same houses, and the court took the unprecedented decision of sending two agents over to America with the mission of collecting £1.6 million bills left under protest for non-acceptance or nonpayment.

II. The change in the Bank's policy

There had been a panic, but to all appearances no crisis. Within 12 to 18 months American banks had resumed specie payments on the East coast, confidence being restored with the reflux of gold from the interior and from abroad. Some $14 million of bullion and coin entered the country early in 1838, to which the Bank of England contributed one-third. In New York, to mention one case, city banks' reserves were back to normal at $4.7 million, against sharply reduced liabilities, because notes in circulation had been halved to $2.3 million during the period of suspension. And within another 12 months, thanks to deficient crops in American cotton and European grain, prices revived, and the country experienced a rebound in foreign trade from the near stoppage in imports of 1837. Exports reached a level equivalent to that of 1835–36, whereas imports surged forward once more in response to higher prices and incomes. A new deficit of $40 million to $45 million on trade and specie accounts was registered in 1839, coming this time not so much from operations with Britain as with continental Europe (the balance, equivalent to £4.7 million, was twice higher than in 1836 and represented 44.7% of the trade deficit). With the accumulation of negative balances for nine years in succession from 1831 to 1839, the debt charges of $12 million to $15 million due annually to foreigners were for the first time in excess of all other invisible income.[38] The country's external debt increased, therefore, by some $45 million to $50 million in 1838–39, the equivalent to £10 million, which had to be borrowed again from (or through) London.

But the general conditions of trade had altered, and the foreign position of the United States could not be maintained or financed as it formerly was: (1) Market demand was not sustained. Wheat prices rose all through Europe, but most conspicuously in England (to 81 shillings per quarter in January 1839, against 53 shillings one year earlier and 39 shillings in April 1835). Four years of bad harvests, from 1838 to 1841, were to act as a general tax levied on all consumers. By transferring incomes to farmers, whose propensity to consume manufactured articles had always been lower than that of urban workers, they brought about a break in the growth of industrial production and a sharp accumulation of stocks (especially in the cotton industry[39]), both detrimental to the U.S. staple exports. (2) On both sides of the Atlantic, investments in railroads, shipbuilding, and capital equipment induced by the need for increased capacities and more extended transport facilities rose steeply in 1838, accompanied by similar movements in long-term interest rates. On the economic side, these activities were positive; they caused incomes to decline less than might have been the case after the boom had passed its peak. But they required a greater share of domestic savings, making the sale of overseas stocks, American and others, more difficult in London, more particularly from December 1838, when a run on Belgian banks temporarily stopped railway construction on the Continent, creating a greater awareness among investors of the risks of foreign ventures. (3) Britain had lost much of its financial capacity; exports were facing increased difficulties from renewed protection on the Continent and from the gap in commercial facilites that the 1837 crisis had left in the trade with the United States. British exports to that market did not regain their former level, whereas the French were still improving their position. Thus the gains Britain realized in third countries were not a sufficient offset to the rise in cotton and other raw materials imports owing to crop shortages and to the extra imports of wheat coming chiefly from France and the Baltic, at an average of £8.7

million per annum between 1839 and 1842, the greater part of which had to be covered by bullion taken from the Bank's reserve (Table 4.5).

In addition, repayment on past American debts proved unexpectedly slow after the panic,[40] except for a few houses like those of William Brown and the Barings. The group of London bankers, acting as intermediaries between U.S. and foreign markets, had therefore fewer members in the latter part of the 1830s, even if China and East India merchants were to enter the field in 1839 at the time of the Opium War. And all were more cautious in allocating credit: The highest figure, for acceptances per firm, that of £1.7 million in 1839 at the Barings', was lower by 20% to 25% than those of 1835–36, and its liabilities (net of capital) had been reduced from £5.3 million to £3.8 million.[41] If the U.S. economy recovered rapidly (the index of the volume of trade, domestic and foreign, in 1839 was within 5% of the levels reached in 1835–36), it was due to a great extent to the artificial ease of credit on both sides of the Atlantic (the Bank of England maintaining its advances and discounts at 3.5% to 4% from February–March 1838 to April 1839) and to a decentralization of trade. New commission houses, using local facilities, entered the cotton trade in Liverpool for the account of New Orleans shippers, and new French and Swiss firms opened up branches in New York to handle imports from the Continent. Moreover, a great number of agents were sent to London by American banks, chiefly during the winter of 1837. They had been appointed in the first place to take up the maturing obligations of their principals. Given the success that all American securities had in the postcrisis period, when remittances were urgently needed to replace the commercial paper then under protest or in discredit, these bank officers became the agents at large of states, corporations, and insurance and finance companies that had stocks to dispose of and were attracted to London by the high prices they realized for a time in the stock exchange. It is difficult to assess the amounts actually transferred. It was said that $60 million of American public securities had been sold in Europe in 1837 and 1838, some $30 million more in the next four years, whereas perhaps $35 million to $40 million of private shares were exported, but precision may be deceptive in these matters.[42] At any rate, together with the London merchant-bankers who took part in these issues, the American agents abstracted funds on a scale that had never been reached before, and they were able to counteract the rise in long-term interest rates and the slower disposal of bonds by pledging them as collateral for loans or, together with cotton, as cover for the issue of accommodation paper that was sold in increasing quantities to the market during the winter of 1838 and the early part of 1839.

It is on that score that these activities could lead to excess. The BUS, to take one instance, had embarked on a policy of reckless investments on the grounds that it was assuming some of its past functions as a federal agency,

Table 4.5. *United Kingdom regional structure of exports, 1833–42* (£ million)

	Domestic exports, current values			Gold and silver exports, current values						Shares (%) goods		specie
	1833–5	1836	1837–42	1837	1838	1839	1840	1841	1842	1833–6	1837–42	1837–42
North Europe[a]	8.6	8.4	10.1	0.3	0.5	3.3	1.3	1.8	0.9	19	20	24
France	1.1	1.6	2.5	3.1	3.6	2.6	4.3	2.4	2.3	3	5	56
B. colonies	4.8	6.5	5.8	0.2	0.1	0.2	—	—	—	11	12	2
United States	8.3	12.4	6.2	0.1	1.5	—	0.2	0.1	0.5	20	13	6
Far East	4.9	6.8	7.5	0.9	0.4	0.8	0.3	0.1	0.9	12	15	10
Others	15.1	17.7	17.2	—	0.1	0.2	0.3	0.1	0.1	35	35	2
Total	42.9	53.4	49.3	4.6	6.1	7.0	6.4	4.4	4.6	100	100	100

[a]North Europe comprises here the Low Countries, Scandinavia, Germany, and Russia; the British North American colonies and West Indies have been added together; the Far East includes Australia and the Pacific settlements.
Sources: The trade figures are adapted from B. R. Mitchell and P. Deane, *Abstract of British Historical Statistics* (Cambridge University Press, 1962), p. 313; those for specie are from *Accounts and Papers* (I), 1843, XXX, pp. 441–6.

buying first (for the account of a group of directors) "internal improvement stocks" during the downslide of Wall Street from October 1836 to March 1837 and then turning to cotton and Southern funds in the fall of 1837, and again in January–October 1838, partly to secure foreign exchange and partly to assist some of the gulf states in resuming payments.[43] The first shipments were disposed of easily in Liverpool and London during the period of low interest rates; £3 million to £4 million were realized between November 1837 and March 1839 to meet installments on the bank's foreign debt. But when the British public became distrustful of the large volume of American bonds pressing on the market, the greater part of the securities the BUS held (some £4.7 million in April 1839) tended to concentrate with S. Jaudon, its London agent. He found himself rapidly in debt on account of the BUS's drafts in advance of sales and of his own borrowing. Although he had no capital of his own, his liabilities were equivalent to those of an Anglo-American house; they were to reach £1.65 million in July 1839 and £3.18 million by mid-August, 65% in acceptances and 35% by means of short-term bonds and bankers' loans.[44]

This is an extreme case, but it helps to explain the difficulties the Bank of England met in the course of 1839. There were fewer American acceptances being discounted to the market, owing to the setback of British trade and perhaps to the greater use of local bank credit, and so less concern at the court than in 1836 (Table 4.6). But the use of stock loans was much greater, "five or six million pounds, beyond the ordinary amounts invested," according to Joshua Bates, a partner of Baring.[45] If the Bank chose to remain passive (and for many months it did not modify its discount rate), the gold outflow would continue unabated. Some £6.3 million, 75% of the reserve, was lost during the first seven months of the year. If, however, the Bank rate were raised, as from May 1839, the move would lead to an increase of real and accommodation bills in response to higher rates – inland bills created were actually raised from £74.0 million to £82.1 million between the second quarter and the third quarter (Figure 4.1). And the volume of loans would remain unaffected, the advances being simply renewed at a lower price for the stocks pledged as collateral, and on stricter conditions of time and rate. Jaudon's last loan in 1839 was made on a two-month basis, at 6% per annum and a commission of 2% plus a penalty rate of 1% per month, if the advance was not paid at maturity.

Hence the inconsistencies of the Bank's decisions and its reversals of policy: (1) In the earlier part of 1839 there was no discussion at the Bank of the change in the foreign debt structure or of general policy and no curtailment of credits. On February 28, and again on March 24, "a proposition to raise the rate on its quarterly advances [from 3.5% to 4%] was negatived," although this made money cheaper at the Bank than in the

Table 4.6 Bank of England: changes in the sectorial allocation of discounts (£1,000)[a]

	Merchants according to regions			Bankers	Bill brokers	Manufacturers and others	Total change	Average holdings
	N. America	Europe	W. & E. Indies					
1836	+232.8	+260.2	+ 69.4	+177.6	+131.2	+345.4	+1216.6	2069.6
1837	+337.2	+364.6	+ 46.8	+ 96.6	−209.0	− 13.8	+ 622.4	2692.0
1838	−598.8	−879.6	−114.8	−295.0	− 43.8	−493.2	−2425.0	267.0
1839	+ 59.2	+814.0	+115.4	+ 21.8	+502.0	+729.2	+2241.6	2508.0

[a]The table presents year-by-year differences in the average holdings of bills, by sectors, at the London head office.
Source: B.E. mss., court books, 20 February 1840.

market. The gold drain was therefore left to develop, except for the Rothschilds' foreign-exchange operations, which have already been mentioned.[46] (2) In the spring, with the seasonal increase in discounts due to the movements of foreign crops entering British ports, the court changed its course, as it had become clear that the £4 million reserve would not be maintained. In May and even more in June a sharp credit contraction was enforced at the initiative of the newly elected governors. The funds still in New York were called back, and all foreign-exchange operations were cancelled, while new and stricter criteria were applied to commercial discounts, the rates being raised to 5% on May 13 and then to 5.5% on June 20. At that time the court even refused discounts on exchequer bills. But no immediate relief could be expected from these measures, because the market had always responded to higher rates by a greater use of bills as money substitutes or as a means of raising working capital. (3) Because the international drain had intensified (the bullion reserve was then heading for £2.5 million), the court again reversed its course and approved a new exchange operation, identical to that of the Rothschilds, but left to the Barings, and of greater scope. The drain was halted, thanks to the £2-million loan negotiated in Paris by T. A. Curtis, the former governor of the Bank, the more easily as Continental markets were oversupplied with gold and idle funds after the 1838 run on Belgian banks and the pause in railway construction.

But the court's former decision to contract its note issues then was not revoked. The Bank rate was raised to 6% on August 1, and in the closing months of the year new regulations were applied refusing admission to new categories of bills and bank drafts, whereas stocks were sold and commercial paper was rediscounted to the market, this time with positive results (e.g., in the case of F. Huth, the London banker of the BUS, whose balance of acceptances and payments on American account was then immediately reversed) (Table 4.7). In October 1840 the same rules were reenacted, with discounts restricted to bills of less than 65 days, etc. Actually, it was not until the spring of 1842 that the Bank rate was set back to 4%, and the governor authorized after three years of retrenchment to invest excess balances in railway debentures and other securities. In the meantime, the separation of the issue and banking departments, used first as an accounting device, had been ratified by March 1840, and the key executive offices transferred in April–May 1841 to the authors of the reform.

During these three years there had been at the same time a sharp break away from Palmer's ideas and principles (on the basis of the beneficial results curtailment immediately had had on the foreign exchanges, and partly on the basis of increasing free-trade sentiments) and a new assessment of the functions and services the public could expect from the Bank. It was this

Table 4.7. *Frederick Huth & Co. acceptances and bills receivable on American account (quarterly amounts, £1,000)*

Quarters	1837		1838		1839		1840		1841	
	Accept.	Bills	Accept.	Bills	Accept.	Bills	Accept.	Bills	Accept.	Bills
First	97.4	61.5	23.1	14.8	69.1	37.4	239.7	348.2	14.8	6.8
Second	170.1	57.0	56.9	66.0	229.1	48.5	142.0	95.2	11.6	62.8
Third	223.4	12.5	169.5	13.7	315.8	63.3	59.0	42.4	17.1	3.6
Fourth	30.0	6.2	89.9	20.9	256.6	216.3	11.9	10.1	10.9	13.0

Source: F. Huth mss.; see also J. R. Freedman, *A London Merchant Banker in Anglo-American Trade and Finance* (University of London, Ph.D. thesis, 1969).

change of attitude that made the abandonment of central banking functions definitive.

1. The whole policy of the Bank during the crisis came under severe criticism. Departures from the rule of 1832 had already been discussed after the panic of 1837, but in an abstract fashion, from the quarterly accounts the Bank had been made to publish. In 1839, however, two of its initiatives were specifically discussed in a negative way. First, the foreign-exchange operations that had been kept secret from the court during most of the drain were condemned by its members in November 1839, when reviewing the past procedure, (1) for the discredit they had caused to the Bank when they were made public and (2) for their ill results. It was held that "by artificially supporting the exchanges, they had destroyed the only indication of the state of the currency, and created a liability that was to retard the Bank's return to a position of safety." In fact, owing to the depressed state of foreign trade (which was in part the result of the necessity to maintain credit restricted so long as the reserve had not been restored), the French loan was not repaid until April 1840, and the loss in bullion was not made up until May 1842, when the precrisis level was regained. Second, the Bank's assistance to American firms in 1837–38 and its passivity during the early part of the 1839 drain were made partly responsible, in Manchester in particular, for the attempt by the BUS and a group of Mississippi banks at controlling the cotton market in Europe. There never was a corner. But because the channels through which cotton was normally handled had been destroyed, this group was able to concentrate a large part of the shipments (27% of Liverpool imports in 1838, 16% in 1839) and, by withdrawing from the market, to force prices to levels that were not justified by the state of the trade.[47] These abuses were remedied in the course of the year – in May by short-time working at the mills in Lancashire and France and in September by concerted action of Boston and New York merchants to start a panic in Wall Street against the BUS, on the eve of its second suspension.[48] But the Bank of England's lack of reaction during the greater part of 1839 was an important factor in reviving the distrust that had long been prevalent among merchants and bankers, both in the United States and in England, against the monopoly and the management of the currency that had been claimed by the Bank in 1832, and by the BUS at the time of the Bank War in America. There was a general concern for the necessity to neutralize money lenders and preserve the free functioning of markets: The feeling expressed by Manchester representatives in Parliament and in the press during the summer of 1839 when they asked for a national bank was that discretionary management of the currency was a dangerous instrument with which the Bank should no longer be trusted.[49]

2. The depression in America was the result of the land boom of the mid-

1830s. But by holding temporarily in check the price fall, the 1837–39 recovery increased its effects, for it resulted in a considerable expansion of output: newly opened lands in the Southwest were brought under cultivation, and the completion of waterways in the Northwest gave access to larger and more populated markets for new farm settlement. Hence the violence and widespread character of the fall in prices from 1839, the sharp deterioration of the terms of trade, but, in reverse, the progressive improvement of the British trade balance and export prices (Figure 4.3) and from a financial point of view the growing inability of planters and farmers to meet their debt charges to the banks. Loans and discounts in the West had increased by 40% after the first crash, against 6% in the rest of the country (Table 4.8). In February 1839, after an attempt at resuming specie payments had failed in Mississippi, banks became discredited all through the West, and a new panic set in that was to cost $60 million to $65 million in notes, three-fifths of the circulation, and $30 million of deposits in four years (Table 4.3). This sharp curtailment need not be detailed here, except for the incidence of the debt-deflation process in the various regions: Banks in Boston and New York were able to withstand the reflux of their notes in the latter part of 1839, but the BUS and other firms in Baltimore and New York, heavily in debt to Europe, were compelled first to sacrifice the property they still held in London, to consolidate their short-term position during the winter of 1838–40, and so could not resist the domestic drain; they closed generally in 1841 at a great loss for their shareholders,[50] whereas some 80 Western banks out of a total of 129 active banks were sent to receivership when they were forced by law to meet their own issues with specie. The contraction therefore had different impacts in the three regions according to the degree of inflation: From the fall in the regional terms of trade (Figure 4.3) it was worst in the Middle Atlantic states and in the West, where 70% of bank liabilities (including the post-notes and interbank balances) were destroyed. This gave added strength to the prejudices of bankers and merchants against paper money (which A. Gallatin wanted to limit to less than five weeks of national product), to their fear that the money supply would not conform to "the operation of a metallic currency," and, probably because of the cheapness of land and the low requirement of fixed capital in industry, to their desire to limit the supply of bank credit and prevent the use of "cheap capital and premature investments that keep production ahead of demand."[51]

  3. British exports to the United States did not regain their former level; they remained at an average of £12.2 million for 10 years up to 1846, or at 12.6% of domestic exports during the depression and at 11.7% in the mid-1840s, against 20.4% earlier in the 1830s. This was in part an effect of the losses made by bankers in London. The panic had left them with unpaid debts dating back to 1837 and with frozen assets – the stocks that were

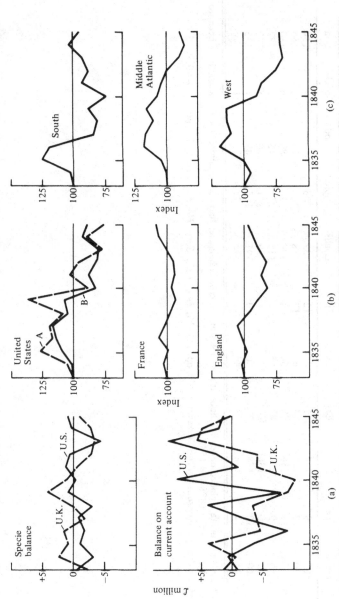

Figure 4.3. Terms of trade and balances of payments, 1833–45; (a) foreign balances; (b) foreign terms of trade; (c) domestic terms of trade. *Sources:* The balance-of-payments figures are those of A. H. Imlah, *Economic Elements in the Pax Britannica* (Cambridge, Mass., 1958), pp. 70–5, for the United Kindgom, and D. C. North, "The U.S. Balance of Payments, 1790–1860," *Trends in the American Economy in the XIXth Century* (Princeton, 1966), pp. 605 and 621. In both cases, interest on foreign debts is not included. The terms-of-trade series are from the same authors for England and the United States (variant A); variant B is the ratio of the U.S. general commodity prices to the average of English and French price indices. The U.S. price relatives are the domestic terms of trade (local prices relative to other U.S. and foreign prices) from A. H. Cole. *Wholesale Commodity Prices in the U.S., 1790–1861* (Cambridge, Mass., 1938); prices are those of New Orleans, Philadelphia, and Cincinnati.

Table 4.8. *American state banks, end-of-year position, by regions, 1838–42 ($ million)*[a]

	New York and New England				Middle and South Atlantic				West (North and South)			
	Capital	Liabil.	Specie	Loans	Capital	Liabil.	Specie	Loans	Capital	Liabil.	Specie	Loans
1836	99	103	9	178	71	85	12	132	86	82	14	154
1837	103	70	7	155	74	60	12	118	105	70	13	165
1838	95	77	11	156	78	64	14	120	118	80	16	180
1839	99	56	9	134	82	55	11	112	121	73	12	182
1840	97	61	10	136	80	52	12	99	111	50	11	140
1841	105	60	10	138	77	50	10	91	105	49	11	133
1842	104	55	12	128	72	40	12	75	72	29	11	76

[a]Only notes and private deposits are included under liabilities; if post-notes and interbank balances had been included, the fall would have been from $115 million to $36 million between 1838 and 1842.
Sources: Annual Report of the Comptroller of the Currency, 1876, pp. 111–15; 29 *Cong. 1 Sess., Ho. Exec. Doc.* 226, pp. 1234–49.

pledged by the BUS and other firms or bought immediately after crisis. The Barings held £310,000 of American securities by the end of 1840, 80% bought in 1839 and 1840, and other bankers, Hope, Rothschild (in Paris), Magniac, Morrison, Palmer, etc., were in a similar position. Some of these stocks were eventually written off; others were sent back to New York from the fall of 1842 as new capital was becoming available for investment in Wall Street, etc. But the process was slow, and in early 1840s American acceptance facilities in London were to remain depressed; they were at 62% of their 1839 level at the house of Baring, at 24% with F. Huth, etc. In the meantime, the economy had recovered in the United States. The trade balance had turned around as a consequence of the fall in imports, and so without delay and irrespective of prices and terms of trade. Further the domestic market had proved resistant to the crisis, because farmers' real incomes improved during these years, with the rise in production, the improvement in transport facilities, and the benefit of lower costs, the frontier entering regions of superior productivity. Wheat, for instance, in the Northwest was sold at two-fifths of the prices realized in the Atlantic markets. The gap left by Britain was therefore taken up by domestic manufactured goods, coming chiefly from New England, distributed by country shops, and financed by small-size banks (not unlike the farms they served) centered in Boston and New York, tied in with local communities, but spreading the risks by holding seasonally commercial paper acquired through New York dealers or placed directly with them.[52] Thus the protracted state of the depression, accompanied as it was by the 1842 tariff and the opening of short-haul railroads from Boston to the Northwest, contributed to developing new commercial structures to compete more effectively with foreign industry. From this point of view the new banking regulations in London, even if their effect was to create greater instability, assisted British merchants in two ways: By restricting credit early in a crisis they tended to limit overproduction and the risks of stocks accumulation, and by protecting the reserve at the Bank they helped to shorten the periods of credit stringency and to hold off the process of import substitution in foreign countries.

III. The nineteenth-century perspective

It would not be fully justified from this review of the 1830s experience to conclude that nineteenth-century crises, together with free trade, were the products of a deliberate choice. Nonetheless, the Bank Charter Act of 1844 and free trade had the same objectives: markets were narrow, easily oversupplied, and rapidly cut off, given the great fragility of commercial credit institutions; thus the problem for bankers and merchants in the 1840s was not to maintain stability to protect long-term investments but to promote the expansion of foreign markets and so to keep prices, incomes, and imports in what were mostly agrarian economies from too wide fluctuations. J. H. Palmer had been conscious of these problems, but his views were not realistic. Gold drains left unchecked were a cause for alarm and internal panics; debts, short and long, tended to accumulate; and, contrary to his impression, prices and exports were not responsive to changes in the discount rates, when they were moderate, whereas the 1839 measures (a 6% interest rate, a partial sale of securities and some rationing of discounts) had an immediate impact on stock holding, new transactions, short-term capital movements, etc.[53] In addition, the depression was severe and called for a radical change in policy: 34% of the total money supply had been wiped out in the United States between 1839 and 1842; commodity prices and import values fell by 45% in many industrial regions, overcapacity and unemployment reached unprecedented levels (25%–30% of the labor force was out of work in Lancashire during the winter of 1841, and similar cases of distress were reported on the Continent in regions where production was still based on domestic out-work). Of course, the new banking procedure under the acts of 1844 and 1845 could not solve all problems; it did not prevent the recurrence of monetary panic, because the division of work among small operating units and imperfections of the transport and communications systems made "miscalculations in commercial matters" unavoidable. Because of the widening of interest margins in periods of stringency when New York discount rates were at 24% to 36% as in the fall of 1837 or 1857, London bankers could also not resist the temptation to provide new facilities for their American correspondents and postpone debt settlements.[54] But the new banking legislation had at least one result, to use Lord Overstone's expression: "to compel both the public and the Bank to form a more definite estimate of the true limits of the resources of the Bank," and to accept its policy of nonassistance in a crisis.[55] This explains that all later attempts to increase the bullion reserve or to insert a relaxing clause in the statutes were strongly resisted. No fundamental changes were to modify the regulation of the money market until the end of the century. In spite of the development of the credit structure (bank deposits and bills outstanding were multiplied by eight, to reach £1,800 million in 1913, against £225 million in the late 1830s[56]), the Bank of England kept to the identical rules: It economized on its bullion reserve, which amounted to £30 million to £35 million in 1900–13, only twice the midcentury figure, and in counterpart it relied steadily on the variations of the discount rate as its most useful weapon for the protection of the currency.

Under these circumstances, how can we account for the smooth functioning of the money market in the pre-1914 period? In contrast with the intense monetary crises of the midcentury decades, stability then was to

Table 4.9. *British international position (yearly averages, £1,000)*

	1836–40	1876–80	1881–90	1890–1900	1901–10	1911–13
World trade[a]	618	2686	2990	3521	5428	7858
U.K. trade	124	527	566	625	853	1221
U.K. other earnings	35	205	231	254	338	434
U.K. total	159	732	797	879	1191	1655
Sterling bills	352	1317	1272	1202	1384	1730
Inland bills	284	697	—	512	535	614
Foreign bills	68	620	—	690	849	1116

[a]Trade figures include exports and imports; other earnings refer to reexports and indivisible earnings. The distinction between inland and foreign bills is based on the domiciliation of the drawer, so that many inland bills were issued for export purposes.
Sources: British Consular Reports, 1836–40; F. Hilgerdt, *Industrialization and Foreign Trade* (Geneva: League of Nations, 1945), pp. 157 et seq.; S. Nishimura, *The Decline of Inland Bills of Exchange in the London Money Market, 1855–1913* (Cambridge University Press, 1971).

prevail: The amplitude of the short-term fluctuations, measured in each cycle by the dispersion of wholesale commodity prices and market rates of discount, fell steadily after the 1880s; the Bank rate remained at a moderate level during the same period, at an average of 3.43% with a standard deviation of only 0.69, half the range of market-rate fluctuations. And this was not the result of a shrinking of the British financial position. In spite of the country's declining share of world exports and imports, there was a widening of the geographic area in which sterling bills of exchange were utilized and a major increase of the bills drawn on London from abroad. These bills reached £1,203 million in 1913, 60% of the total amount that had been issued in that year, in contrast with earlier periods, when inland bills had constituted the bulk of the drawings (Table 4.9).

Actually, a continuous flow of new acceptance houses had joined the London merchant-bankers: correspondents of Boston and New York railroad promoters in the 1840s, agents of German bankers from New York and Frankfurt during the Civil War, imperial banks, etc.[57] New functions also were added, London credits being still used to finance bilateral transactions for resident merchants, but even more so to facilitate shipments of goods between places in third countries. The opening of new territories, the displacement of Britain's export trade to distant markets beyond the Suez Canal, and the consolidation of its surplus with primary producing countries – all these developments made London bankers' acceptances not simply interest-yielding assets, discountable in the bill market and thus readily convertible into gold, but the basis of an expanding system of multilateral payments.[58] What had been experimental during the 1830s when American firms were able to cover their Far Eastern deficit through London with the balances English merchants held in China was made the general practice. From the 1860s, London acted as a clearing center and its merchant-bankers as intermediaries between industrializing countries (which used their export surplus with England to pay for their deficit overseas) and the new producers of food and raw materials (having to make payments in England, on current and capital accounts, that were met with the balance of their sales in the United States and in Continental Europe).

This new pattern tied together more closely the different money markets around London. Given the increase in demand for remittances by all parties, British and foreign, the accumulation of working balances held in sterling by trading and banking firms, overseas and in north Europe, and their use as partial substitutes for gold by central banks, the influence of the Bank of England could hardly be resisted. Earlier in the century there had been room for competing discount policies: Money rates had been forced up at times, in the 1850s and in the early 1860s, by the Bank of France to attract short-term balances and gold to Paris. From the 1890s, however, any increase of London interest rates met with a totally different response. Banks in most places, overseas and on the Continent, reacted to the increasing cost of securing new reserves by shifting to more liquid assets, and so to sterling.[59] This neutralized the two factors that had led formerly to monetary stringencies during the prosperity stages in the trade cycle. The domestic outflow of gold to meet demands for cash balances was partly offset, because the depletion in the banks' reserves and the consequent appreciation of the cost of money brought about countervailing movements of short-term capital and gold into England. Imports from abroad made up for the internal drain. Of course, the second factor was still operative. American booms continued to absorb gold from London, because of the violent movements of short-term interest rates in New York. But they had lost some of their drive for the reason that, given the power of the Bank rate, the specie shipped by the Bank of England came from a temporary diversion of the flow of newly mined gold being accumulated in the reserves of the major banks on the Continent, and in extreme conditions from those reserves.[60] In short, the position of London, as the pivot of international trade, made it possible, first, for the Bank of England to step up its rate of discount, not in order to act on prices and production but to influence effectively international movements of short-term capital, banks overseas being induced to strengthen the balances they held in London, and, second, for the major Continental banks to respond to higher rates in London not by restricting credit to force a reduction of domestic prices but by releasing capital and gold to be used in London. The Bank of France, in particular, moved to a policy of assistance, lending gold during the 1890 crisis and buying sterling bills from 1902 to moderate the rise of interest rates in London, for fear it would react on the Continent.[61] Instead of two rival markets, London and Paris worked in concert: the first setting the Bank rate in conformity with its traditional rules, and the second, with its vast specie holdings, keeping for the Bank of England the reserve that under the constraint of the 1844 act the latter had been disinclined to accumulate. Cooperation made the international monetary system more tightly bound and safer.

It should also be mentioned that, beyond the changes in the institutional framework, trade relations were based on much sounder foundations. In the 1830s, when London had assumed the financing and clearing of American foreign payments, the two countries encountered the same difficulties. These came from the financial strain caused by the rapid growth of their foreign-trade operations and from the deficit and adverse terms of trade that developed during the upswing in both countries. They were partly remedied in the 1839–42 depression, once credit had been curtailed, because the burden of the price adjustment had been shifted to America and to weaker countries overseas. Similar transfers of cycles were repeated throughout the century, because England fared better than primary producing countries in recession on account of the low supply elasticity of unprocessed goods compared with that of manufactures.[62] But from the 1890s, new deflationary measures had lost their economic justification. First, Britain's trade balance and terms of trade improved during prosperity, so that the country's foreign position no longer required corrective action. This was probably due to the role of new industrial exports, metal and capital goods, that had wider fluctuations in production and costs than other internationally traded articles. In addition, the United States, still a large supplier of crude and semifinished products, had a moderating influence on European import prices. The greater dependence of its production on the domestic market (exports took a smaller share of production than in other countries) made American prices less susceptible to the international cycle; their sales abroad varied more in quantity than in price and tended to stabilize prices in primary-goods markets.[63] Second, from a financial point of view, the emergence of large-scale banks, overseas and in Europe, made domestic markets more autonomous and more resilient to economic setbacks. Hence the new structure of international credits: Bills drawn on London, after the 1890s, included a greater portion of finance bills issued by American and overseas banks to borrow money on short term (with stocks as collateral) in the cheapest European market. They amounted in London to £210 million in 1913, out of the £350 million in prime bank acceptances then outstanding.[64] Monetary pressure thus could not reach the same intensity as in the past. Formerly the demand for cash tended to accumulate in the last stages of an upswing, in spite of the Bank's restrictive action, because trade bills increased in volume with prices and activity, without regard to the cost of money. But the new financial drafts, being negatively correlated with interest rates, were automatically reduced or even transferred to the Continent when interest differentials made London more expensive as compared with other places. A statistical analysis shows that the total volume of bills (trade and finance) and differences in discount rates (between London and Paris) moved in a parallel fashion and so were positively correlated for the major part of the century, but moved inversely from the 1890s to 1913.[65]

This means that although the Bank of England was still following the identical rules, these rules applied to altogether different worlds. Formerly, in each monetary crisis, commercial bills, with their rigid geographic and time constraints, were pressing in great number on the London money market, whereas bullion was drained away, making it necessary for the Bank to contract credit drastically. However, in the 20 years before the war, when the second industrialization was resettling the structure of foreign trade in the northwestern part of Europe, the Bank could remain more passive, acting through the discount market, as it usually did, but relying also on the financial assistance of the major central banks on the Continent and on the greater restraint of overseas banks' demands. In a sense, even though international payments had been centralized into one single market, the regulatory influence of the Bank was already something of the past.

Notes

1   Newmarch, W. 1851. "An Attempt to Ascertain the Amount of Bills of Exchange in Great Britain." *Journal of the Statistical Society* 14:604; *Select Committee on the Bank of England Charter*, 1831–1832 (henceforth *BPP 1832*), J. H. Palmer, Q. 26.

2   W. Newmarch, Note 1, pp. 599 et seq.; King, W. T. C. 1935. "The Extent of the London Discount Market in the Middle of the XIXth Century." *Economica* 2:321–6.

3   *BPP 1832*, J. H. Palmer, Q. 198; see also Morgan E. V. 1942. *The Theory and Practice of Central Banking, 1797–1913.* Cambridge University Press; Horsfield, J. K. 1949. "The Opinion of Horsley Palmer." *Economica* 16:143–58; Fetter, F. W. 1965. *Development of British Monetary Orthodoxy, 1797–1875.* Cambridge, Mass.: Harvard University Press, pp. 152–6.

4   *Secret Committee (Lords) on the Causes of the Distress*, 1848, G. W. Norman, Q. 2746; see *BPP 1832*, J. H. Palmer, QQ. 72–89, and Wood, E. 1939. *English Theories of Central Banking Control, 1819–1858.* Cambridge, Mass.: Harvard University Press, pp. 102–3, F. W. Fetter, Note 3, pp. 259–62.

5   Cameron, R. 1967. *Banking in the Early Stages of Industrialization.* New York: Oxford University Press, p. 33.

6   The creation of an issue department as a "self-operating machinery," to exonerate the Bank from the responsibility for the currency and to give it more freedom of action, was submitted to the court in July 1838 and put into operation in March 1840: Bank of England records (henceforth *B.E. mss.*), court books, 26 July 1838, 13 February, 26 March, 2 April 1840, etc.; see E. Wood, *Central*

Banking (Note 4), p. 132, F. W. Fetter, *Monetary Orthodoxy* (Note 3), pp. 144–97. The new regulation determined once and for all the amount of fixed securities that were kept constant under the 1832 rule, and so was not opposed by J. H. Palmer. But he remained critical, because he, as well as other bankers, brokers, and merchants, kept asking that the Bank deposits be also regulated: see O'Brien, D. P. 1971. *The Correspondence of Lord Overstone*, Vol. 1. Cambridge University Press, pp. 85–6.

7 F. W. Fetter, *Monetary Orthodoxy* (Note 3), pp. 267 et seq.

8 King, W. T. C. 1936. *History of the Discount Market*. London: Routledge, pp. 20, 120; Dixon, K. F. 1962. *The Development of the London Discount Market, 1790–1830*. University of London, Ph.D. thesis, pp. 165 et seq.; see also Loyd, S. J. 1837. *Reflections Suggested by Mr. J. Horsley Palmer's Pamphlet*. London: P. Richardson, pp. 45–8, and Loyd, S. J. 1837. *Further Reflections*. London: P. Richardson, pp. 33–4, 44.

9 Arbitrage operations between exchequer bills (to be sold first) and commercial bills (to discount, without exceeding the limits set by the 1832 rule) were in part responsible for the delay; see E. Wood, *Central Banking* (Note 4), pp. 70, 80–9.

10 Chauduri, P. F. 1963. *Foreign Trade and Economic Growth: The Balance of Payments as a Factor Limiting the Expansion in the British Economy, 1819–1875*. Cambridge University, Ph.D. thesis.

11 Bank of the United States records (henceforth *BUS mss.*), J. H. Palmer, letter to C. A. Davis, 28 February 1839.

12 Special advances were increased up to August 3, 1836, and called back in October–November of the same year, whereas quarterly advances were still being offered, the collateral securities remaining unchanged until March 1837; *B.E. mss.*, Committee of the Treasury (22), 5 October to 31 November 1836. On all these questions, see Matthews R. C. O. 1954. *A Study in Trade Cycle History. Economic Fluctuations in Great Britain, 1833–1842*. Cambridge University Press, pp. 165–201, and Collins, M. 1972. *The Bank of England and the Liverpool Money Market, 1825–1850*. University of London, Ph.D. thesis, pp. 92 et seq.

13 *B.E. mss.*, court books, 6, 20 June 1839; *Select Committee on Banks of Issues*, 1840, J. H. Palmer, QQ. 1368–9, 1426–52, 1524; G. Gore, QQ. 1625 et seq.; *Secret Committee (Lords) on Commercial Distress*, 1848, J. H. Palmer, QQ. 838–48, 1045; *BPP (Commons) 1848*, QQ. 2007, 2043, 4431–2.

14 *B.E. mss.*, court books, Lb, 24 October 1839.

15 The necessity of a fixed rule is expressed by, among others, S. J. Loyd (Lord Overstone). 1837. *Thoughts on the Separation of the Departments of the Bank of England*. London: P. Richardson, pp. 28–32, 34 et seq, and *Select Committee on Bank Acts*, 1857, QQ. 3650–5.

16 Palmer, J. H. 1837. *The Causes and Consequences of the Pressure upon the Money Market*. London: P. Richardson, p. 23. The idea that the Bank should act "gradually" in order to prevent an internal panic was also decisive in the late 1820s and again during the mid-nineteenth-century crises; hoarding, for instance, took £4 million to £5 million out of the £21 million notes in circulation in 1847; see *BPP (Lords) 1848*, T. Tooke, QQ. 3086–107; J. H. Palmer, 730–54, 868–84, 1010–18; S. Gurney, 1123, 1143.

17 Stock depletion and the absence of speculation were noted in the conference held about the crisis by the governor of the Bank and London bankers in the fall of 1836; *Baring mss.*, J. Bates to J. Pattison, 18 October 1836; see R. C. O.

Matthews, *Trade Cycle History* (Note 12), pp. 43–69. According to a Liverpool broker's account (S. Pilkington, 1884), the annual movements and stocks of cotton at the year ends (in 1,000 bales of 400 lb) were as follows in Britain:

	Imports (net)	Consumption	Sales to trade	Stocks		Stocks in weeks of consumption
				Ports	Mills	
1828	506	545	71	282	86	37
1832	675	692	72	191	68	23
1834	740	759	187	158	48	14
1835	822	795	120	183	41	15
1836	948	869	130	230	61	19
1840	1362	1147	209	407	110	24

18   Sushka, M. E. 1976. "The Antebellum Money Market and the Economic Impact of the Bank War." *Journal of Economic History* 36:809–35, and, earlier, see Gatell, F. O. 1966. "Sober Second Thoughts on Van Buren, the Albany Presidency and the Wall Street Conspiracy." *Journal of American History* 52:19–40; Rockoff, H. 1971. "Money, Prices and Banks in the Jacksonian Era." In *The Reinterpretation of American Economic History*, edited by R. W. Fogel and S. L. Engerman. New York: Harper & Row, pp. 448 et seq.

19   The refunding of the U.S. federal debt, the Bank War (in 1833–4), and a boom in Spanish and Portuguese stocks (in 1834–5) closed the London market to American securities; some Louisiana bank stocks, issued at that time by Baring, had to be sent back to New York. In 1836, according to the *Course of the Exchange* (London, 1833–43), transactions were sparse – each stock was quoted only five or six times per month, on the average, with a maximum of 13 to 14 times in April–May 1836, when a £1.5 million BUS two-year loan was issued in London and Paris, to prepare for its operations under a Pennsylvania charter. Further, American stocks, when issued in London, were often bought by foreigners, whereas English people tended to invest in English railroad and other stocks; see Gérard, M. 1968. *M. M. Hottinguer, banquiers à Paris*. Paris: Draeger Frères, pp. 458–9; Freedman, J. R. 1969. *A London Merchant-Banker in Anglo-American Trade and Finance: F. Huth & Co.* University of London, Ph.D. thesis, pp. 28–38; Platt, D. C. M. 1980. "British Portfolio Investment Overseas before 1870." *Economic History Review* 33:1–16.

20   The weakening of sterling in the early part of 1836 may have been due in part to the payment of £6.5 million out of the total £15 million indemnities due to West Indian claimants under the Emancipation Act; sterling bills were brought back then in number to New York from the Caribbean and Nova Scotia by American ships; see *New York Journal of Commerce;* Davis, L. and Hughes, J. R. 1960. "A Dollar-Sterling Exchange, 1803–1895." *Economic History Review* 13:65. See also Timberlake, R. J. 1965. "The Specie Circular and Sales of Public Lands." *Journal of Economic History* 25:414–16; Temin, P. 1969. *The Jacksonian Economy*. New York: W. W. Norton, pp. 120 et seq. The after-crop peak in internal payments is confirmed in monetary series available in *22d Con. 1st sess., Sen Rep. 98*, p. 4, for the bank drafts and notes out of the BUS and discount operations of the state bank of Indiana and the New Orleans banks. On

seasonal aspects, see Lainer, J. F. D. 1877. *Sketch of the Life of J. Lanier.* New York; Cole, A. H. 1929. "Seasonal Variations in Sterling Exchanges." *Journal of Economic and Business History* 2:203; Kemmerer, E. W. 1910. *Seasonal Variations in the Relative Demand for Money and Capital in the U.S.* Washington: U.S. Government Printing Office, Sen. Doc. 61st Cong. Vol. 39; Lander, J. E. 1972. *Operations in the London Money Market, 1858–1867.* University of London, Ph.D. thesis, pp. 11–14.

21 *Circular to Bankers*, 15 June 1837; the estimates of U.S. commercial capital are those of Marburg, T. F. 1960. "Income Originating in Trade, 1799–1869. In *Trends in the American Economy in the XIXth Century* edited by W. Parker. Princeton University Press, Princeton, p. 319. On the commercial crisis, see *France, Rapports consulaires*, New York, 2 April to 16 June 1837.

22 The extent of the recession was concealed at first by dumping (dry-goods imports into New York during the first quarter of 1837 were equal to those of the same period in 1836) and by the rise of wheat prices after the failure of the bread crops in the Northwest and in upper Canada; see Cole, A. H. 1938. *Wholesale Commodity Prices in the U.S., 1700–1861.* Cambridge, Mass.: Harvard University Press; Ouellet, F. 1976. *Le Bas Canada, 1871–1840.* Ottawa: Editions de l'Université d'Ottawa, pp. 424–8.

23 The extension of credits is reflected in the Anglo-American accounts, registered in *B.E. mss.*, court books; Th. Wiggin & Co. and W. & J. Brown & Co., still with £2 million to £3.5 million assets in 1837, allocated 70% of their credits to dry goods, 20% to staples, and 10% to operations between third countries and America; Th. Wilson & Co., also with £2.5 million assets, gave 35%, 40%, and 15% to the same three sectors and 15% to exchange and stock operations; their capital, but for doubtful debts, would have been of £300,000 to £400,000. On international trade balances, see Baring, A. 1808. *An Inquiry into the Orders in Council: the Conduct of Great Britain toward the Neutral Commerce of America.* London: J. M. Richardson; Pitkin, T. 1835. *A Statistical View of the Commerce of the U.S.* New Haven: Yale University Press, etc.; Lévy-Leboyer, 1965. *Le dollar et la zone sterling: N. Biddle, 1836–1842.* Paris: thèse, pp. 79–83.

24 In China, specie brought in by U.S. ships fell from an average of $5.3 million per annum in 1820–6 to $1.5 million in 1827–32 and $0.7 million in 1833, whereas London bills were covering in the last two periods $0.62 million and $4.8 million of American purchases; see Green, M., and Cheon, W. E. 1962. *Some Aspects of British Trade and Finance in Canton, 1784–1834.* University of London, Ph.D. thesis.

25 A survey made from British consular reports in the 1830s brings world imports to £322 million (of which £230 million was seaborne), whereas U.K. imports reached only £83 million, and imports financed through British credits may be estimated at £145 million to £150 million; see Lévy-Leboyer, M. 1964. *Les banques européennes et l'industrialisation internationale dans la première moitié du XIXe siècle.* Paris: Presses Universitaires de France, pp. 241–5.

26 Buck, N. S. 1925. *The Development of the Organization of Anglo-American Trade, 1800–1850.* New Haven: Yale University Press; Williams, D. M. 1963. *The Function of the Merchant in Specific Liverpool Trades, 1820–1850.* University of Liverpool, M.A. thesis; Killick, J. 1974. "Risk, Specialization and Profit in the XIXth Century Cotton Trade: Alexander Brown & Sons. 1820–1880." *Business History Review* 16:1–16.

106   M. Lévy-Leboyer

27   R. C. O. Matthews, *Trade Cycle History* (Note 12), pp. 95–101. See also Trotter, A. 1839. *Observations on the Financial Position and Credits of Such States of the North American Union as Have Contracted Public Debts.* London: Longman, Orme, Browne, Green, and Longman, 46–9.

28   Some $4.3 million of grain (almost 4 million bushels) entered the United States in 1837 against an average of $0.2 million in the five preceding years, besides $6 million of tea imports from the Far East; see M. Lévy-Leboyer, *Les banques européenes* (Note 25), pp. 521 et seq.

29   J. H. Palmer, *Reply to the Reflections* (Note 8), p. 15.

30   *B.E. mss.*, Committee of the Treasury (22), Wm. Brown, letter to the governor, 5 September 1836. The letter contained a detailed analysis of gold shipment costs to demonstrate that the only specie movements from England to the United States for the account of government depository banks in New York and Baltimore had been at a loss. See also J. H. Palmer, *Causes and Consequences* (Note 16), pp. 29–32; *Circular to Bankers*, 8–29 April 1836; P. Temin, *The Jacksonian Economy* (Note 20), p. 167

31   The reduction in its securities by the Bank came from the sale of bills to the market (£1 million in January 1837), a limit to the operations of two brokers, a reduction in quarterly loans (from £3.2 million in November 1836 to £0.6 million, and only on bills of exchange, in March 1837): *B.E. mss.*, Hb, 12 January to 2 March 1837, and the records to the Committee of the Treasury in the same period; *Baring mss.*, J. Bates, letters to S. Jaudon, 21 January to March 1837; *Journal of Commerce*, 4 April 1837.

32   On the drain in England, see J. H. Palmer, *Causes and Consequences* (Note 16), pp. 37–40; Cramp, A. B. 1959. "Horsley Palmer on Bank Rate." *Economica* 26:341; M. Collins, *Liverpool Money Market* (Note 12), pp. 109 et seq. In the United States, see *Reports of the Bank Commissioners of the State of New York*, 1835, pp. 15–16, and 1836, pp. 7–8; *24 Cong. 2d. sess., Ho. Doc. 65*, pp. 67, 71–72; Scheiber, J. 1959. "The Pet Banks in Jacksonian Politics and Finance, 1833–1841." *Journal of Economic History* 23:196–214.

33   A close correlation exists between market rates of discount and the creation of large inland bills for wholesale and foreign trade (for the quarterly data over the years 1833–42 the coefficient is 0.85, against 0.68 for the other bills). But it is not possible to differentiate further between bona fide commercial bills and finance paper. See *France, Rapports consulaires,* Liverpool, 15 May 1838; W. Newmarch (Note 1) pp. 586–8; R. C. O. Matthews, *Trade Cycle History* (Note 12), pp. 46, 185–7; M. Collins, *Liverpool Money Market* (Note 12), pp. 106, et seq.; J. R. Freedman, *A London Merchange Banker* (Note 19), pp. 28–36 (which retraces the circulation accounts maintained by F. Huth from October 1836 to February 1837 with 28 American correspondents). Similar short-term lending had been done in 1833–4; see Cole, A. H. 1935. *Fluctuations in American Business, 1790–1860.* Cambridge, Mass.: Harvard University Press, p. 177; F. Hidy, *The House of Baring* (Table 4.4), pp. 177.

34   As early as 16 November 1836, Overend, Gurney & Co. had advanced directly to the Anglo-American houses £1.55 million, leaving £6 million for current discounts; see K. F. Dixon, *London Discount Market* (Note 8), p 196; M. Collins, *Liverpool Money Market* (Note 12), p. 112.

35   Besides *B.E. mss.*, court books, see *Baring mss.*, letters to T. Ward and S. Jaudon, 31 January to 3 May 1837. Firms with low cash reserves had to take the risk of cotton-bill remittances, whereas a house like Baring prevented its correspondents from using them as early as January 1837.

36   S. J. Loyd, *Reflections* (Note 8), pp. 6–7 (the pamphlet was written in February 1837).

37   The six firms are G. Wildes, T. Wiggin, and Th. Wilson (the "three W's") (with £0.87 million combined suspended accounts and £4.77 million assets), J. & W. Brown (£1.5 million out of £2.24 million), F. de Lizardi (£0.12 million out of £0.89 million, and the Barings (with £0.52 million debts unpaid in May 1837 and £3.93 million assets at the end of the year); the position of the Bank of England is detailed in *B.E. mss.*, Ib, 16 September 1837, 15 February and 1 March 1838. The general position, on the American side, is best summarized by T. W. Ward (*Baring mss.*); on 1 July 1837, once £2.5 million paid in April–June are deducted, he believed that there were still due £3.8 million to the three W's, £2.5 million to other London firms (including £2 million to Baring and J. Morrison, Cryder & Co.), £2.6 million to Manchester (of which £1.6 million were due to Brown and Lizardi), and £1.5 million to France. After deducting 10% losses, he concluded that the balance of £9 million due to Europe would not prevent an early resumption, because £3.5 million of cotton and other staples were to be shipped by the end of 1837 and £20 million before 1 July 1839 (including £2 million of specie and £2 million of American stocks).

38   The charge on the foreign debt was currently estimated at $12 million to $14 million per annum: Van Buren, in Richardson J. D. 1910. *Messages and Papers*, Vol. 3. Washington, D.C.: U.S. Government Printing Office, p. 553; *France, Rapports consulaires*, Liverpool, 30 January 1840, New York, 1 March 1842; D.C. North, "Balance of Payments" (Table 4.1), p. 621.

39   Growth rates were 6% per annum in 1832–8, 4% in 1838–43 (less if the latter year is excluded); see R. C. O. Matthews, *Trade Cycle History* (Note 12), p. 127. This is confirmed by the British cotton trade statistics (in 1,000 bales of 400 lb):

	Consumption	Imports		Stocks	
	Total	Total	U.S.	Total	U.S.
1836	869	949	654	19	9
1837	914	921	733	19	11
1838	1042	1176	984	20	18
1839	954	875	709	17	15
1840	1147	1362	1129	24	21
1841	1095	1131	855	27	20
1842	1087	1208	969	30	22
1843	1306	1569	1060	35	28

Stocks are presented in "consumption-weeks". Reexports are included in the U.S. imports and deducted from total imports.

40   Brown paid off £0.6 million of the £1.95 million due in 1837 and the rest by December 1838; Baring's overdue account was at £0.17 million in March 1838. But the three W's and Lizardi were still in debt by £1.03 million in December 1838 and £0.34 million in March 1845, when the sum was written off.

41   By comparison, F. Huth, a member of the court at the Bank of England and the most active London banker of the BUS in 1837–9, had a total of £1.3 million liabilities, including £0.16 million for this capital and £0.56 million for his acceptances, one-third the level of the Barings: *Huth mss.*

42   Sales of American stocks to Europe were £40 million in the 1830s (D.C. North,

Table 4.1), compared with £22 million issued for the West Indies and Brazil and £16 million for European governments. But the difficulty is to specify the 1837–9 American issues. From the Johnston report of 1843 it appears that $82.4 million were effectively issued (against $21.4 million in 1840–1), of which only 56% to 63% (using the sample of defaulted states in 1841–2) were held in Europe; this would make a total sale or shipment of £10 million, in keeping with the estimate (£5–£10 million) of the Chamber of Commerce of Manchester for 1837–8. The proportion for private securities was not higher (52% in January 1837); this would make £4 million of private stocks and no more than £15 million of stocks sold abroad: Flagg, A. C. 1840. "Report on State Debts," *American Almanac*, pp. 105–10; *27 Cong. 3d sess.*, *Ho. Doc. 296*, pp. 50–101; *France, Rapports consulaires*, Philadelphia, 3 February 1842; Green. G. D. 1972. *Finance and Economic Development in the Old South: Louisiana Banking, 1804–1861*. Stanford: Stanford University Press, p. 80.

43   The 1836–7 operations of E. R. Biddle (of the Morris Canal) and N. Biddle (of the BUS) are detailed in *BUS mss.*, Vol. 65, N. Biddle, letters of 27 January to 24 March 1837; J. R. Freedman, *F. Huth* (Note 19), p. 183. For the later operations, see Gallatin, A. 1841. *Suggestions on the Banks and the Currency of the U.S.* New York: Wiley & Pulman, pp. 42–4; Williams, E. 1949. *The Animating Pursuits of Speculation*. New York: Columbia University Press, pp. 105 et seq.; Smith, W. B. 1953. *Economic Aspects of the Second Bank of the U.S.* Cambridge, Mass.: Harvard University Press, pp. 178 et seq.; M. Lévy-Leboyer, *N. Biddle* (Note 23), pp. 173–84; R. C. O. Matthews, *Trade Cycle History* (Note 12), pp. 61–9.

44   *29 Cong. 1 sess.*, *Ho. Exec. Doc. 226*, pp. 478–9; *Baring mss.*, letter to Prime, Ward & King, 23 August 1839; *New York Morning Courier* and *Enquirer*, 31 March 1840.

45   *Baring mss.*, J. Bates, letter to C. A. Davis, 18 October 1839.

46   Drawings on the Continent amounted to £0.4 million in December 1838 and £0.6 million in April 1839, the latter drawing did contribute to the gold outflow of August when it came up for repayment: *B.E. mss.*, 20, 27 June, 21 November 1839. Discounts at the Bank were £3.2 million in the first quarter of 1839, against £11.0 million and £3.4 million in the same periods of 1837 and 1838.

47   Market conditions were abnormal in 1838 and 1839; there were fewer firms in Liverpool (the three first importers handled 26% and 17% of the total receipts), and, among them, the American agents had greater facilities (the Southern banks and the BUS issuing post-notes in the United States and their agents raising credits from the Liverpool banks on their stocks). The BUS realized a gross profit of £0.27 million out of a total sale of £1.47 million in 1838–9, but a net loss of $0.63 million the next year; see *BUS mss.*, M. Humphreys' letters; D. M. Williams, *The Merchant in Liverpool* (Note 26), pp. 29 et seq.

48   *Baring mss.*, T. Ward, letters, 21 September, 14 October 1839; *New York Morning Courier*, 16–19 September, 20 December 1839; *New York American*, 25–28 March 1840; Gregory, F. W. 1949. *Nathan Appleton, Yankee Merchant, 1779–1861*. Radcliffe College, Ph.D. thesis; Hammond, B. 1947. "The Chestnut Street Raid on Wall Street." *Quarterly Journal of Economics* 61:605–18.

49   F. W. Fetter, *Monetary Orthodoxy* (Note 3), pp. 175–6; Chamber of Commerce of Manchester, records, 4 July, 26 December 1839. For the United States, see Lawrence, A. 1837. *Letter on the Subject of the Currency*. Boston: C. Little, pp. 6–9; Appleton, N. 1841. *Remarks on the Currency and Banking*.

Boston: J. Brown, pp. 22–4; *22 Cong. 1 sess., Ho. Rep. 460,* C. Cambreleng, pp. 334 et seq; Wilburn, J. A. 1969. *Biddle's Bank. The Crucial Years.* New York: Columbia University Press, pp. 66 et seq.; Sharp, J. 1970. *The Jacksonians versus the Banks. Politics in the States after the Panic of 1837* New York: Columbia University Press, Chapter 2.

50 Only one-third of the $35 million capital of the BUS was left; it had lost 50% to 60% of the $4.3 million of Southern monies accumulated before February 1839, 30% of the $14.45 million of American securities used to issue at a large discount £2.3 million of bonds in London, Paris, and Amsterdam between October 1839 and July 1840, etc. Other cases are studied by Redlich, 1947–51. *The Molding of American Banking. Men and Ideas.* New York: Hafner.

51 *BPP 1832,* J. B. Smith, Q. 4198; Gallatin, A. 1831. *Considerations on the Currency and the Banking System of the U.S.* Philadelphia: Carey & Lea, pp. 9, 14–16, and *Suggestions* (Note 43), pp. 12–13; N. Appleton, *Remarks* (Note 49), pp. 19–20.

52 Greef, A. O. 1938. *The Commercial Paper House in the U.S.* Cambridge: Harvard University Press; Federal Bank of Boston. 1960. *Commercial Banking in New England, 1784–1958.* Boston.

53 *BPP 1840,* G. W. Norman, Q. 1948; E. Wood, *Central Banking* (Note 4), pp. 46–9, 109; Cramp, A. B. 1961. *Opinion on Bank Rate, 1822–1860.* University of London, Ph.D. thesis, p. 58.

54 Lord Overstone (S. J. Loyd), *Thoughts on the Separation* (Note 15), pp. 4–7; *BPP 1857–8 (Bank Acts),* Report on the Committee, pp. 15–21.

55 *BPP 1857 (Bank Acts),* Lord Overstone, Q. 3646.

56 Higonnet, R. P. 1957. "Bank Deposits in the U.K., 1870–1914." *Quarterly Journal of Economics* 71:329–67.

57 Chandler, A. D., Jr. 1954. "Patterns of American Railroad Finance, 1830–1850." *Review of Business History* 28:248–63; Madden, J. J. 1958. *British Investment in the U.S., 1860–1880.* Cambridge University, thesis, pp. 98, 130 et seq.; Scammel, W. 1965. "The Working of the Gold Standard." *Yorkshire Bulletin of Economic and Social Research* 17:38.

58 Tew, B. 1948. "Sterling as an International Currency." *The Economic Record* 24:42–55; S. B. Saul, 1960. *Studies in British Overseas Trade, 1870–1914.* Liverpool: Liverpool University Press.

59 Bloomfield, A. I. 1963. "Short-Term Capital Movements under the Pre-1914 Gold Standard." *Princeton Studies in International Finance,* No. 11; Lindert, P. H. 1969. "Key Currencies and Gold, 1900–1913." *Princeton Studies* No. 24; Oppenheimer, P. M. 1966. "Monetary Movements and the International Position of Sterling." *Scottish Journal of Political Economy* 13:91.

60 Beach, W. E. 1935. *British International Gold Movements and Banking Policy, 1881–1913.* Cambridge, Mass.: Harvard University Press, pp. 170–80; Sayers, R. S. 1972. "From Note Issue to Central Banking, 1800–1930." In *Credit, Banks and Investments, XII-XX c.* Prato: Institute Francesco Datini.

61 R. S. Sayers, "From Note Issue" (Note 60); Sayers, R. S. 1953. "The Bank in the Gold Market, 1890–1914," In *Papers in English Monetary History,* edited by T. S. Ashton and R. S. Sayers. Oxford: Claredon Press; Billoret, J. L. 1969. *Systèm bancaire et dynamique économique dans un pays à monnaie stable: France, 1816–1914.* Nancy: thèses

62 Triffin, R. 1947. "National Central Banking and the International Economy." In *International Monetary Policies.* Postwar Economic Studies No. 7. Washington, D. C.: Federal Reserve System, pp.46–81; MacBean, A.I. 1966. *Export*

Instability and Economic Development. London: Allen & Unwin.

63   Martin, K., and Thackeray, F. G. 1948. "The Terms of Trade of Selected Countries, 1870–1918." *Bulletin of the Oxford Institute of Statistics* 10:373 et seq.; Martin, K. 1949. "Capital Movements, the Terms of Trade and the Balance of Payments." *Bulletin of the Oxford Institute of Statistics* 11:357 et seq.; Mintz, I. 1959. "Trade Balances during Business Cycles: U.S. and Britain since 1880." *NBER Occasional Papers No. 67;* Mintz, I. 1967. *Cyclical Fluctuations in the Export of the U.S. since 1879.* New York: National Bureau of Economic Research.

64   American banks were still using London for their foreign operations (they had about £650–£100 million in bills outstanding in London and Paris in 1902–6), in part because their own financial paper was not acceptable in Europe, being mostly single-name promissory paper; see York, T. 1923. *International Exchange.* New York: *Wall Street Journal*; Goodhart, C. A. E.1969. *The New York Money Market and the Finance of Trade, 1900–1913.* Cambridge, Mass.: Harvard University Press, pp. 28 et seq.

65   Oppenheimer, P. M. "The Position of Sterling" (Note 59), pp. 96–7; Nishimura, S. 1971. *The Decline of Inland Bills of Exchange in the London Money Market, 1855–1913.* Cambridge University Press, pp. 68 et seq.

Comment

R. C. O. MATTHEWS

Maurice Lévy-Leboyer's extremely interesting and scholarly chapter is an important contribution. I have learned a great deal new from it. I shall not attempt to offer critical comments on his interpretation of the events of the 1830s. Instead, I shall make a few remarks on some of the more general issues he has raised about central banking policy in England in the nineteenth century.

He asks: What were the circumstances that led the Bank of England to move away from the discretionary policies of the 1830s to the more mechanical and rigorous policy enshrined in the Bank Charter Act of 1844? And how was it that the latter policy did not lead to more instability than it did? Was it because the discipline of the act worked, through rational expectations, to prevent crises from occurring, even though it admittedly made it more difficult to cope with a crisis if one did occur? Or was it that the environment became more favorable, for reasons independent of the policy of the Bank?

To take the latter point first, Levy-Leboyer describes some of the changes in the environment that made matters easier after 1890. Diminished financial instability was in fact apparent well before 1890: The Overend-Gurney crisis of 1866 was the last true financial crisis of the pre-1914 era, and even it was due to the failure of a single major firm rather than to general financial collapse. Some favorable changes in the environment, compared with the troubled days of the 1830s, occurred quite early and can be added to Lévy-Leboyer's list. The peculiarities of the old Corn Law sliding scale had the effect of amplifying fluctuations in corn imports and hence in the balance of trade. This had been a very important factor in 1839, more important, indeed, than disturbances in financial relations with the United States: The failure of the harvest of 1838 added over 10% to the value of Britain's total imports in a single year, an amount equivalent to about the whole of the Bank of England's bullion reserve. This early Victorian OPEC-effect did not recur with the same force after the repeal of the Corn Laws, which increased corn imports on average but at the same time made them less variable from year to year. Another stabilizing factor was the speeding up of communications: The commercial overshooting in the American market in the 1830s would surely not have gone so far if there had been a trans-Atlantic telegraph (that did not happen until 1866).

Notwithstanding these and other stabilizing factors, the questions can still be asked why the Bank of England's rigorous new policy did not make for greater difficulties after 1844 than it did. My doubt is whether the policy was really either so rigorous or so new. Was there not a good deal of pragmatism in the Bank's policy throughout the century? Theorists like Lord Overstone and Bank spokesmen appearing in times of tranquillity before Parliamentary inquiries might speak of strict principles and deny that the Bank had public obligations; but, after all, "chancellor's letters" indemnifying the Bank against breaches of the act of 1844 were issued when it came to the point in each of the crises of 1847, 1858, and 1866. Pragmatism was a natural consequence of the part-time status of the Bank's directors and governor before 1914. No governor was likely to experience more than one commercial crisis during his two-year tenure, and although experience built up in the Bank's Committee of the Treasury, differences of opinion existed among its members. In some cases, too, they had other matters on their mind: In the crisis of 1847 the governor and two directors had to resign because of the bankruptcies of their own private firms.

I was rather surprised that Lévy-Leboyer saw such a sharp change in the policy of the Bank at the beginning of the 1840s, because that had not been the impression I had formed when I worked on the subject. As a quick and crude test of both the novelty and the rigor of the policy, I have done a simple regression of the annual movements of the Bank's liabilities, that is, its note circulation (C) plus its deposits (D), against the annual movements of its holding bullion (B).[1] If the pre-1844 policy was discretionary and the post-1844 policy was mechanical, one would expect to find an increase after 1844 in the correlation and regression coefficients. These are the results:

$$(1826\text{--}43) \quad \Delta(C + D) = 0.25 + 0.52\Delta B \quad (R^2 = 0.46)$$
$$(1844\text{--}90) \quad \Delta(C + D) = 0.37 + 0.62\Delta B \quad (R^2 = 0.56)$$

The changes between the two periods are in the predicted direction, but they are very moderate. The correlation in the earlier period would admittedly be less good if the break were made in 1840 rather than at the date of the actual passage of the act, but some of the main irregularities in the 1830s were due to unusual fluctuations in the deposits of the government and the East India Company rather than to the exercise of central banking discretion of the type here at issue. Moreover, the regression coefficient after 1844 remained well below the value of unity that it ought in theory to have had if the Bank had really followed the policy of "steady and undeviating" contraction when its reserves fell. I do not deny that there was some change in policy, but it was not a revolution. Insofar as there was a change, the regularity of its effect was probably diminished by the fact that the Bank Charter Act in one respect took a backward step intellectually from the previous Palmer rule. The Palmer rule was that the securities should be held constant (apart from certain discretionary exceptions), which amounted to saying that the Bank of England should undertake zero domestic credit expansion in the face of changes in its reserves; the 1844 act, by contrast, prescribed different policies according to whether the drain on the reserves fell on the note circulation or on the deposits, because the authors of the act were obsessed by the idea that notes were money and deposits were only means of economizing money (no need to labor present-day parallels).

It is arguable that the Bank Charter Act to some extent was successful because expectations were not fully rational. The threat that the Bank would decline to act as lender of last resort was believed, even though in the event it was not always carried out. The let-out provided by a chancellor's letter could never be relied on in advance, and speculative excesses may have been curbed by the fear that the rigorous announcement embodied in the act would be carried out. Then, when a crisis came, the Bank relented to some extent; so it was not quite so bad after all.

It is perhaps inappropriate to press too hard the question whether or not the Bank was conscious of public obligations as lender of last resort after 1844. If a financial crisis threatens, it is in the self-interest of all large banks to take steps to prevent the collapse of confidence. There is an element of self-interest in procuring the common interest. The position of the Bank of England was different only in degree from that of the other leading houses in the city. As the premier institution, it was in the best position to give a lead. This was so even before the Bank came to be more self-conscious about the moral obligations of the leader and the followers, as expressed in the language of muscular Christianity by the energetic Governor Lidderdale after the Baring crisis of 1890: "It would be for the common advantage of bankers and the country if the rowers would take their time a little better from the stroke oar.[2]

Notes

1 Data from Mitchell, B. R. 1962. *Abstract of British Historical Statistics.* Cambridge: University Press, pp. 443–5.
2 Clapham, Sir John. 1944. *The Bank of England: A History, Vol. II.* Cambridge University Press, p. 346.

Comment

PETER TEMIN

Lévy-Leboyer has treated us to a detailed and fascinating account of the 1830s that exposes his intimate knowledge and understanding of the contemporary materials. His exposition is organized around three questions, posed at different points in the narrative, and it can best be understood by reference to them.

First, Lévy-Leboyer asks at the beginning of his chapter why the Bank of England abandoned the Palmer rule in favor of a more passive stance. The answer, he proposes, is that the Bank was burned by the ill-effects of active intervention in the financial markets in the 1830s. It tried to react to the credit expansion of the 1830s in a continuing, supervisory way. But it was blamed for making things worse. The financial edifice constructed in the mid-1830s fell apart, taking with it the Palmer rule.

Second, how was it possible for credit to expand so extensively during the boom? Implicit in this question are the assumptions that the expansion of credit was extraordinary and that it made a contraction inevitable. Lévy-Leboyer answers that the permissiveness of the Bank allowed credit to expand and that the Bank was as much to blame for its policies during the expansion as for its policies during the subsequent contraction.

Third, does it follow that the comparative quiet in the financial markets after 1840 was the result of the Bank's passivity? Lévy-Leboyer draws back from this implied causality, preferring instead to emphasize the growing breadth of the international financial markets and cooperation among central (or at least national) banks.

These views are well presented and persuasive as they stand. But one cannot help feeling that Lévy-Leboyer has accepted history as it happened as too inevitable. In other words, he seems to suggest that changes in the Bank's actions could have reduced the severity of the depression starting in the late 1830s but that they could not have avoided it. Could the depression have been avoided? At what point did it become inevitable? We can understand Lévy-Leboyer's chapter better if we can approach such questions.

Table 4.10. *Annual average balance on current account*

	United Kingdom (£ million)	United States ($ million)
1815–20	7.22	NA
1821–5	10.34	1.3
1826–30	2.58	1.1
1831–5	6.38	−16.5
1836–40	2.62	−21.7
1841–5	5.90	5.9
1846–50	4.70	3.4
1851–5	7.98	−24.1
1856–60	26.22	− 4.6

Sources: Imlah, A. H. 1958. *Economic Elements in the Pax Britannica.* Cambridge: Harvard University Press, pp. 70–1; North, D. C. 1960. "The United States Balance of Payments, 1790–1860." In *Trends in the American Economy in the Nineteenth Century, Studies in Income and Wealth, Vol. 24.* Princeton: Princeton University Press, p. 581.

The problem in the 1830s, according to Lévy-Leboyer, was excessive lending. He does not talk of the money supply, but rather of the total lending from England to the United States. He departs, therefore, from a strict definition of the Bank's responsibility. It is instructive to place this lending in context to evaluate the claim that the Bank was responsible for the magnitude of the capital flows. We do not have data on British lending to the United States, but we do have independent data on British lending and American borrowing. They are shown in Table 4.10.

It is clear from the first column that British lending in the early 1830s, although larger than that in the immediately surrounding quinquennia, was hardly out of the range of contemporary experience. The rise in lending in the 1830s was, for example, markedly lower and of shorter duration than the rise in the previous decade, the 1820s. The Bank of England cannot be faulted for allowing this lending to take place.

An entirely different story is revealed in the second column. American borrowing in the 1830s stands out from the favorable balances of trade in the surrounding decades. The capital inflow surrounding the American boom was unusual, but it is not clear that the Bank of England is to be held responsible for it. Whereas one could say that no central bank should be held responsible for events outside its country, Charles Kindleberger has shown, at least for the 1930s, that a consideration of international connections is needed to assess accurately the effects of central-bank activities.[1] A closer look is needed.

Looking at the Anglo-American connection, we find that the peak of American borrowing in the 1830s came after 1836, when the rate of British lending had already declined. It was also after the Bank of England's actions restricting credit to the United States in 1836. If there was a connection between the Bank's actions in 1836–37 and the subsequent American borrowing, then it is fair to hold the Bank responsible for the lending.

A connection there is, but one not emphasized by Lévy-Leboyer. The Bank of England's actions precipitated the dramatic fall in the price of cotton in late 1836 that led in turn to the financial crises of the late 1830s. The contractionary actions of the Bank of England raised its discount rate in response to a loss of gold. This was contractionary. The Bank also restricted its discounting of bills arising from the Anglo-American trade. This aimed at the contraction of only a part of the British economy. And, slightly later, the Bank acted as a lender of last resort to the three W's. This was expansionary, but (like the Bank of England's loan to Austria in 1930) it was too little and too late.[2]

Why did the Bank of England embark on this course? Because it was losing specie and because it thought it was losing it to the United States. As I pointed out, and as Lévy-Leboyer now says that contemporary observers other than Palmer knew, the gold was not going to the United States.[3] Lévy-Leboyer does not help us with the mystery of where the gold went, but further research along the lines of his chapter may solve that particular puzzle. The Bank of England's policy can justly be faulted as being too aggressive on the basis of limited information.

Once the price of cotton fell, the United States found itself with sharply reduced export earnings. Its imports did not fall as quickly, and commitments made during the boom years continued to exert their influence. It is possible, therefore, to argue that the high American capital imports after 1836 were at least in part the result of the Bank of England's actions that precipitated the panic.

There are, however, two problems with this easy argument. First, the quinquennial averages in Table 4.10 hide a remarkable annual diversity in the American balance of payments of the late 1830s. The merchandise balance of trade was actually in surplus during two of the five years in which average borrowing was at its local peak. It is not appropriate here to detail the events of those years, but any argument that said the American borrowing was the result of the Bank of England's actions would have to relate the tumultuous events of those years to the panic of 1837.[4] Second, the American borrowing in the late 1830s exceeded British lending in those years. The Americans borrowed on average approximately £4 million whereas the British loaned on average less than £3 million. To the mystery of the 1836 gold flows we can add the mystery of the capital flows in the following years. Who was lending to the United States in the late 1830s?

In any case, the Bank of England cannot be faulted for encouraging American excess early in the 1830s, that is, at the time Lévy-Leboyer says the Bank was too permissive. But if the Bank had acted differently in 1836 and 1837, we might have seen a relatively smooth adjustment of the cotton and financial markets to changing conditions in the United States and Britain. If the price of cotton had not fluctuated so widely, perhaps the financial crisis would not have developed. Without the panic, perhaps Anglo-American trade would not have been so disrupted. American borrowing might well have been smaller in the late 1830s. The Bank of England certainly would have come in for less criticism.

Consequently, I agree with Lévy-Leboyer's main point. The Bank of England retired from active interventionism because it got itself into hot water in the 1830s. I also agree that this change in policy was probably less important for the stability of the international financial system than many other changes going on at roughly the same time. But I suggest that the Bank of England should not have been faulted, then or now, for its looseness in the early 1830s, but rather for its tightness later in that decade. Instead of seeing the alternative to the actual past as a smaller depression, can we not envisage a smooth transition from the boom of the mid-1830s to a quieter period in the 1840s? Perhaps Lévy-Leboyer can be urged to use his considerable talents to explore this question in a future report.

Notes

1   Kindleberger, C. P. 1973. *The World in Depression.* London: Allen Lane.
2   *Ibid.*, p. 151.
3   Temin, P. 1969. *The Jacksonian Economy.* New York: W. W. Norton, p. 137.
4   *Ibid.;* Chapter 5 contains an account.

5. Domestic and foreign expectations and the demand for money during the German inflation 1920–1923

CARL L. HOLTFRERICH

I. Introduction

In the 1950s Milton Friedman counterattacked the Keynesian doctrine that aggregate expenditure rather than money supply *eo ipso* determines the levels of real income, employment, and prices. He reformulated the quantity theory of money, discarding the traditional but unrealistic assumption of a stable relationship between quantity of money and prices and relied instead on a stable demand function for money, proof of which constitutes the empirical cornerstone of the new monetarism (Johnson, 1972:62). This approach allows for fluctuations in the relationship between the volume of money and prices without reducing the importance of the money supply for the price level. In terms of capital theory, money is regarded as one among several ways of holding wealth. The demand for real cash balances is seen as a function of the expected rate of return on money, as well as of the yields of alternative forms of wealth, assuming that individual wealth holders mix their portfolios in such a way as to maximize their utility (Friedman, 1956:4–5). If such a functional relationship between the demand for money and other economic variables can be identified as stable, notwithstanding large and obvious fluctuations in real cash balances over time, then the control of the money supply remains an effective tool of economic policy, provided that the factors affecting the demand for and the supply of money are not wholly identical. This approach excludes destabilizing expectations such as those that have been generated in the history of financial crises, for instance, by political events (Kindleberger, 1978:41–3).

In his pioneering econometric study of hyperinflation, Phillip Cagan (1956) analyzed the demand for money under conditions of extreme depreciation. He regarded the demand for real cash balances as a function of expected price changes, assuming that the rate of depreciation in the value of money constitutes the only cost of holding cash balances that fluctuates widely enough to account for the drastic changes in real cash balances during hyperinflation. He found the equation

117

(1) $\log_e \dfrac{M}{P} = -\alpha E - \gamma$

suitable "to account for most of the changes in real cash balances in seven hyperinflations" (Cagan, 1956:35). M represents the quantity of money in circulation, P the wholesale price index, and E the expected rate of change in prices; α and γ are constants. The development of E is seen as a function of the cumulated differences between expected (based on past experience) and actual price changes (i.e., adaptive expectations are assumed). The correlation coefficients between the two variables of equation (1) and the graphs of estimated and actual data for real cash balances during the seven hyperinflations (Cagan, 1956:43) show that Cagan's functions fit actual developments rather closely.[1]

Cagan himself, however, pointed out one of his model's weaknesses, namely, that before the onset of hyperinflation there must have been a change in expectations for which his model did not account. "The expected duration of inflation apparently underwent a sudden rise. The sharp decline in balances following their long rise in the months preceding hyperinflation seems to reflect a sudden realization by the public that greater price increases lay ahead. The precise timing of such shifts in expectations appears incapable of prediction by economic variables ... But when the shifts are absent, expectations of price changes depend closely on past events" (Cagan, 1956:77).

It is almost a question of taste (*de gustibus non est disputandum*) whether these findings should be treated as exceptions to or refutations of the rule of a stable demand function for money. In my view, a model that fails to account for the great shift in expectations that paved the way for the transition from inflation to hyperinflation might serve descriptive purposes well, but it does not explain the most decisive change in such developments.

The main purpose of this chapter is to offer an explanation for the shift in expectations at the starting point of hyperinflation. To criticize Cagan's model means to question its assumptions. If a factor that is important in reality is excluded from the analysis, the model can give only insufficient explanations of real developments. Cagan's study is based on the premise "that domestic monetary factors alone explain hyperinflations" (Cagan, 1956:90). However, evidence on post-World-War-I inflations, especially the German case, demonstrates the importance of foreign demand for domestic money as a determinant of inflationary developments. Cagan's assumption would be valid only if this foreign demand for money had responded to domestic factors in the same way as the home demand. It can be shown, at least in the German inflation, that this was not the case. I shall therefore attempt to improve Cagan's specification of a demand function for real cash balances by adding a factor that should mainly explain the variance of the nondomestic demand as distinct from the domestic demand. In other words, I shall extend Cagan's approach from a closed economy to an open-economy model.[2]

Section II will provide some general evidence of the impact that the foreign demand for domestic money exerted on inflationary developments in the post-World-War-I period. Section III will present empirical findings on the development of foreign holdings of mark balances during the German inflation of 1918–23. Section IV will deal with factors that influenced the foreign demand as distinct from the home demand for German money. Finally, Section V will integrate the swap rate as an index for changes in the foreign demand for German funds into Cagan's model, which is regarded as representative for the development of the domestic demand for real cash balances.

II. The role of foreign demand for domestic money in post-World-War-I inflations

In his comparative study of post-World-War-I inflations, R. Nurkse (1946) pointed out that these were heavily influenced and determined by international transactions. He argued that even if no new money had been created, exchange depreciation could still have occurred, "as the need for imports was so great that people were prepared to spend out of accumulated money savings and to reduce their cash balances in relation to current incomes" (Nurkse, 1946:44). Here he attributed part of the early inflationary developments to a shift in demand patterns toward import goods combined with a reduction of the domestic demand for real cash balances. Nurkse argued further that the development of the foreign demand for domestic money, as distinct from home demand, played an important role in post-World-War-I inflations, specifically with regard to exchange-rate depreciation. Nurkse distinguished two phases of inflation: the "moderate" phase and the "runaway" phase (Nurkse, 1946:8, 43), the crucial variable being a shift in the expectations of the public from bull to bear with regard to the future value of the currency in question (Nurkse, 1946:7).

As to the moderate phase, Nurkse (1946:44) noted that "there was a strong belief that the depreciation of European currencies was a purely temporary phenomenon due to temporary post-war needs and adjustments, and that these currencies would sooner or later return to their pre-war gold parities." People with more sophisticated attitudes, who knew the practical impossibility of returning to prewar par in the inflation-torn countries of central Europe, nevertheless also behaved bullishly with regard to depreciated currencies. As Einzig (1937:290) pointed out, they based their expectations on the purchasing-power-parity doctrine: Whenever the external value of the currency fell below its internal value (and there were, at times, large divergences[3]), foreigners expected an upward adjustment of the exchange rate. "Given this state of anticipations, any fall in a currency's exchange value created an inducement for foreigners to acquire bank notes, deposits and other assets expressed in that currency. In response to this inducement, foreign funds in fact entered many European countries in considerable volume . . . Part of the money newly-created, or released by the public from pre-existing cash balances, came to be held by foreigners and was thus withdrawn from the domestic circulation. The foreign holdings were of course essentially speculative; but so long as they were held, they were inactive" (Nurkse, 1946:44–5). This foreign demand for domestic currency during the moderate phase of inflation also compensated in part for the reduction of domestic demand for home currency associated with the early transfer of domestic funds into "hard" currencies ("flight of capital") as a safeguard against future depreciation.

The runaway phase of exchange depreciation is the equivalent of what Cagan (1956:25) defined as hyperinflation, namely, the period during which the monthly price rise exceeds 50%. Nurkse (1946:47) saw it begin "when the balance of market opinion swung over from expectations of eventual recovery to expectations of further decline. The precise point at which this swing-over occurred was determined often by psychological and political factors . . . At that point foreign balances began to be withdrawn."

III. Foreign holdings of mark balances

Prior to World War I, Berlin had already developed into a financial center, along with London and Paris. German currency was used for private international transactions abroad and was held officially by governments or central banks as foreign exchange reserves. Official foreign holdings of mark exchange have been estimated rather reliably at $152.3 million (640 million marks) for the end of 1913 (Lindert, 1969:19). Total foreign short-term debts of German banks just prior to the war have been put more vaguely at about 1 billion marks (Bloomfield, 1963:78). This amounts to slightly under 20% of the deposits of the seven great Berlin banks that totaled 5.1 billion marks on December 31, 1913 (Whale, 1930:216). There were probably additional private foreign debts on commercial account and official foreign debts because of short-term government issues placed abroad, although the value of these has not been calculated. An increase of Germany's mark indebtedness to foreigners financed part of Germany's import surplus during the war, which totaled 15.1 billion (gold) marks. This increase was estimated at about 7 to 8 billion (gold) marks by Glasenapp (1922:29), vice-president of the Reichsbank.

During the postwar years of inflation, 1919–23, Germany again ran high deficits on current account, according to the McKenna Committee findings (Moulton, 1924:Appendix) an import surplus of 6.4 to 7.4 billion (gold) marks (at prewar gold parities) and cash payments under the Versailles Treaty of 2.6 billion (gold) marks, thus a total deficit of 9 to 10 billion (gold) marks. This deficit again was mainly covered by an increase in Germany's mark indebtedness to foreigners who were demanding and willing to hold marks in expectation of a future recovery of the low mark quotations on the foreign-exchange markets. Foreigners accumulated their mark claims in the form of direct delivery credits, German bank notes, mark deposits with German banks, and mark bonds (Graham, 1930:255). Even the foreign holdings of mark bonds can be regarded here as a short-term credit, because in most cases the motive was speculation on the exchange-rate profit rather than on the interest rate of return. When the overall expectations of foreign mark holders as to the future value of the mark exchange turned from bull to bear, and this in turn reduced the demand for German currency abroad, foreigners contributed to the decline in the value of the mark as they attempted to protect themselves by selling the depreciating currency.

The impact of changes in such nondomestic elements of the demand for German cash on the value of the German currency (in other words, the foreigners' contribution to the depreciation of the mark) depended on their share in the total holdings of domestic monetary assets. For a monetary analysis, the foreign demand for and holdings of German bank notes and deposits with German banks are of prime importance. I shall therefore focus on these two items.

During World War I the German government and the Reichsbank not only had expanded the money supply (mainly through deficit spending for war purposes) but also had enlarged the demand for money by introducing German currency in the occupied territories of Belgium and northern France in lieu of the indigenous currencies. After the war, the French and Belgian governments exchanged the German currency circulating in their countries back into domestic money. The German money thus withdrawn was held by the French and Belgian governments as an open claim against the Reichsbank. These claims amounted to about 8 billion marks in bank notes.[4] In addition, German bank notes continued for some years to circulate abroad in ceded territories such as Alsace-Lorraine and parts of Upper Silesia. In addition, with the end of the war the wider public in foreign countries started speculating in German currency. Inasmuch as it was nonprofessional, this speculation was done in bank notes. Based on estimates by the Reichsbank,

Table 5.1. *Nondomestic creditors of the seven great Berlin banks 1918–23*

	I. Total deposits			II. Nondomestic deposits			
	Paper mark (billion)	Gold mark (billion)		Percentage of I	Paper mark (billion)	Gold mark (billion)	
		a	b			a	b
31 Dec 1913	(5.1)						
31 Dec 1918	19.7	9.8	8.0	20	3.9	2.0	1.6
31 Dec 1919	39.1	3.3	4.9	35	13.7	1.2	1.7
31 Dec 1920	62.6	3.6	4.4	36	22.5	1.3	1.6
31 Dec 1921	115.6	2.6	3.3	36	41.6	0.9	1.2
31 Dec 1922	1,618.2	0.9	1.1	11	178.0	0.1	0.1
31 Dec 1923	1.1×10^{12}	1.1	0.9	2	220×10^9	0.02	0.02

Note: The seven great Berlin banks were Deutsche Bank, Dresdner Bank, Disconto-Gesellschaft, Darmstädter und Nationalbank, Commerz- und Privatbank, Berliner Handelsgesellschaft, Mitteldeutsche Creditbank. According to an inquiry of the McKenna Committee, they transacted about 75% of Germany's total foreign-exchange business. (*a*) Deflated by the dollar exchange rate (1913 = 1). (b) Deflated by the German wholesale price index (1913 = 1). *Sources:* I: Whale (1930: 216). II: Holtfrerich (1977: 282). Deflators for *a* and *b* in Statistiches Reichsamt (1925: 6, 16–17).

the share of foreign holdings in the total circulation of German bank notes in 1919–20 was approximately 50% (June 1919: 15 billion marks out of a total of 30 billion marks; June 1920: 25 billion marks out of a total of 54 billion marks) (Holtfrerich, 1977:285). However, in the later stages of the inflation, foreign holdings of German bank notes did not rise very much, and thus its share in the total issue fell.

Foreign deposits in German banks played an even more important role during the 1919–23 period. According to an investigation of the McKenna Committee into the seven great German banks, more than a million accounts had been kept for foreign clients. This demonstrates the broad base of the foreign engagement in the German money market. The proportion of foreign deposits to domestic deposits had developed as shown in Table 5.1. This shows the following:

1   With a maximum share of 36% of total deposits in the big German banks, the foreign demand for this domestic monetary asset was considerable.

2   Foreign demand for German currency was influenced by factors different from those that affected the domestic demand, which accounts for the movement in the percentages.

3   The period of moderate inflation until the summer of 1922 coincided with a high and rising share of foreign deposits in total deposits; the period of runaway inflation from mid-1922 to the end of 1923, in contrast, coincided with a drastic fall in the foreign share.

This indicates that fluctuations in the foreign demand for German monetary assets played an important role in stimulating changes in both the total demand for nominal monetary balances and the price level, or, in other words, in real cash balances. It challenges Cagan's assumption "that domestic monetary factors alone explain hyperinflations" for the German case.

IV. Factors influencing foreign and domestic demand for money

Although the domestic demand for money during hyperinflations may depend (as Cagan assumed) primarily on the expected rate of change in prices, the foreign demand for domestic money in this situation can be regarded as primarily dependent on the expected future course of the exchange rate. However, fluctuations in the internal value and the external value of a currency do not necessarily coincide in the short run. In the German case there had been large divergences.[3] For this reason it was possible that rising domestic prices created expectations that reduced the domestic demand for real cash balances, while at the same time exchange rates falling at an even faster rate created anticipations among foreigners of a recovery of this currency on the exchange market; and this in turn led to an increase in the foreign demand for domestic monetary assets. This could happen because the purchasing power-parity theory led foreigners to believe that divergences between the internal and external values would not last and would be adjusted at least partly by a movement in the exchange rate. For the German case, Friedrich Hesse (1938:354) described this two-tier phenomenon as follows: "The speculative expectations are not unambiguous. On the German side, they undoubtedly reckon with a depreciation of the mark, abroad, however, with an appreciation."[5] Heilperin (1945:94) noted: "Bearish speculation against the mark started earliest in Germany itself, while the outside world still maintained a belief in the eventual rehabilitation of the currency." Therefore, it seems reasonable in a money-demand function to separate the influence of foreigners' expectations about the future exchange value of the German mark from that of domestic expectations about the future price development. These were not independent of each other, certainly not in the long run. But in the short run the divergences were important and have to be taken into account for the explanation of a short-run phenomenon such as the turning point in Germany from inflation to hyperinflation in July 1922.

Anticipations of the future course of a currency's exchange rate are reflected in the forward exchange rate. Data on the forward exchange rate of the mark on the London market are available from May 1920 to August 1923. In May 1920 the Reichsbank had started official dealings in forward

Table 5.2 *Covered interest arbitrage between London and Berlin 1920–3 (% per annum)*

	I	II	III	IV	V
	Swap rate between Reichsmark and £ sterling	Rate of discount on 3-month bank bills		Difference	Covered interest arbitrage
		Berlin	London	II − III	(I + IV)
May 1920	5.5	3.55	6.74	−3.19	2.3
June	8.0	3.53	6.70	−3.17	4.8
July	4.0	3.57	6.63	−3.06	0.9
Aug.	7.5	3.50	6.69	−3.19	4.3
Sept.	3.4	3.50	6.73	−3.23	0.2
Oct.	5.6	3.45	6.66	−3.21	2.4
Nov.	2.3	3.43	6.67	−3.24	− 0.9
Dec.	5.0	3.37	6.71	−3.34	1.7
Jan. 1921	11.1	3.40	6.61	−3.21	7.9
Feb.	8.2	3.46	6.69	−3.23	5.0
March	9.9	3.43	6.37	−2.94	7.0
April	7.6	3.45	6.03	−2.58	5.0
May	7.1	3.33	5.62	−2.29	4.8
June	6.0	3.35	5.48	−2.13	3.9
July	4.1	3.38	4.93	−1.55	2.6
Aug.	5.6	3.38	4.71	−1.33	4.3
Sept.	3.8	3.38	4.21	−0.83	3.0
Oct.	4.2	3.56	4.00	−0.44	3.8
Nov.	2.6	3.58	3.99	−0.41	2.2
Dec.	3.4	4.18	3.33	+0.85	4.3
Jan. 1922	4.3	4.37	3.60	0.77	5.1
Feb.	3.0	4.00	3.25	0.75	3.8
March	0.8	4.24	3.27	0.97	1.8
April	0.2	4.36	2.61	1.75	2.0
May	0.6	4.55	2.35	2.20	2.8

exchange. The data in Table 5.2 show that the forward mark fluctuated widely but that it was traded at a premium (higher than 11% per annum at one point) until the spring of 1922. Not until July 1922 did it fall to a discount, which from September 1922 onward grew much larger than the premia before.

Figure 5.1 shows the development of the swap rate on a per annum basis between the pound sterling and the mark from 1920 to 1922, as well as the interest rate differential between bankers acceptances in London and Berlin. The third curve represents the summation of the other two and indicates the development of opportunities for covered interest arbitrage between London and Berlin. It shows that except for one month in 1920 the premium on the forward mark much more than compensated for the initially negative interest-rate differential. There thus remained a considerable inducement for foreign

Table 5.2 *(continued)*

	I	II	III	IV	V
	Swap rate between Reichsmark and £ sterling	Rate of discount on 3-month bank bills		Difference II − III	Covered interest arbitrage (I + IV)
		Berlin	London		
June	0.3	4.58	2.38	2.20	2.5
July	−3.3	4.85	1.96	2.89	− 0.4
Aug.	− 12.5	6.12	2.26	3.86	− 8.6
Sept.	− 43.3	7.32	2.51	4.81	− 38.5
Oct.	− 92.3	8.15	2.40	5.75	− 86.6
Nov.	−163.6	8.92	2.53	6.39	−157.2
Dec.	− 92.9	9.77	2.53	7.24	− 85.7
Jan. 1923	−104.1				
Feb.	−285.2				
March	− 77.6				
April	− 89.4				
May	−143.6				
June	−141.3				
July	−452.8				
Aug.	−658.5				

Note: Column I: A positive number indicates a premium for Reichsmark on the forward exchange market in London.
Sources: May–Dec. 1920 computed from the one-month forward rate for the first day of the month (Keynes, 1922:14); Jan. 1921 to Aug. 1923 computed as monthly mean of weekly quotations (until Dec. 1922 from the three-month forward rate; Jan.–Aug. 1923 from the one-month forward rate) (Einzig, 1937:450–5).
Note: Column II: So-called *Privatdiskont.*
Source: Statistisches Jahrbuch (1923:269).
Note: Column III: Mean of monthly maximum and minimum of 3-month bank bills.
Source: Statistical Abstracts (1931:205).

banks to place funds in Berlin instead of in London until mid-1922. After June 1922 the situation was reversed. These opportunities for arbitrage operations were created by foreigners who before mid-1922 held the (erroneous) belief that the mark exchange would tend to recover and thus held long positions in the mark. Thereafter foreigners predominantly anticipated a decline of the mark and thus turned to short positions in marks.

The following political events might explain the changeover from optimism to pessimism with regard to the mark exchange rate:

1   The reparations and reconstruction conferences of Cannes and Genoa early in 1922 failed to achieve the breakthrough in the reparations issue that financial circles, even in Allied countries, considered to be necessary for a solution to the German monetary problems.

2   On June 10, 1922, an international bankers' committee under the leadership of J. P. Morgan reported to the reparations commission that long-

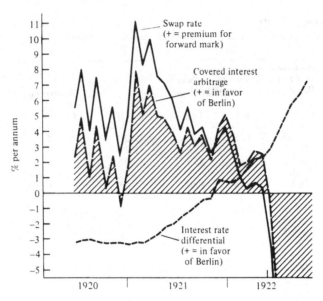

Figure 5.1. Covered interest arbitrage between London and Berlin, 1920–2.

term loans to Germany could not be recommended under the currently existing reparations schedule.

3   On June 22, 1922, the murder of the German foreign minister, W. Rathenau, who was highly esteemed in Allied countries for his cooperative attitude in reparations negotiations, frightened foreign investors about the future political stability of Germany.

A domestic liquidity crisis as a result of the drain of foreign funds (as happened, for example, in Germany in July 1931) did not take place in 1922, because the Reichsbank reacted to the credit shortage by discounting commercial bills on a large scale and thus opened its credit potential to the private sector from July 1922 onward. Before than, it had almost exclusively served the government's financial needs (Graham, 1930:62).

Of course, the hyperinflation would have been impossible without the additional money creation, which constituted the necessary condition for such a development. Without an augmentation in the money supply the depreciation of the German exchange (because of the crumbling demand for German money abroad) and the increase in German domestic prices would have reached limits. But monetary policy is more than juggling with one ball. Besides price and/or exchange-rate stability, other economic policy goals were at stake. Should the German monetary authorities have risked a liquidity crisis with its well-known consequences on employment and growth and further on the political stability of the young republic to prevent the hyperinflation at no matter what cost? Or would the cost have been less than the benefits of avoiding hyperinflation? The answers to these questions will vary according to individual preferences. But there should be agreement that when foreigners ceased to demand additional German cash, the social cost of restricting the inflation in Germany increased. To this the monetary authorities at the Reichsbank reacted with additional money supply. Why they opened the floodgate for hyperinflation precisely in June 1922 can thus be explained by the preceding change in expectations among foreigners speculating in German marks. These expectations, however, were not solely dependent on domestic monetary factors, but on the international political factors and developments as well.

V. An econometric test

As a first econometric test of the significance of differentiating between foreign and domestic expectations and the demand for money during the German hyperinflation, I have taken Cagan's demand function for real cash balances as representative of the domestic element of money demand and have extended it in the following way to take into account the foreign element:[6]

$$(2) \qquad \log_e \frac{M}{P} = -\alpha E - \gamma + \beta X_f$$

where X_f represents the forward exchange rate of the mark converted to a swap rate per annum. A positive swap rate indicates a premium on forward mark in foreign currency, indicating foreign anticipations of a future revaluation of the mark. The coefficient β has to be positive, because the foreign demand for a country's monetary assets correlates positively with anticipations of a revaluation of this currency.

To stabilize the variance (i.e., to dampen the effect of the high negative swap rates after the onset of hyperinflation in mid-1922 on the outcome of the regression and to increase the relative importance of the swap-rate variance in the earlier stages of the inflation), I have used the cubic root of the per annum swap-rate figures for X_f. This procedure offers the advantage over the use of logarithms that problems with the sign of the original data do not arise.

To ease the problem of strong multicollinearity between the variables due to their trend behavior over the hyperinflationary period as a whole, I have regressed the first differences of the variables, as represented in Table 5.3. The results are given in Table 5.4.

The regression of changes in the demand for real cash balances on Cagan's expectation variable E alone (although yielding an R^2 of 0.88) leaves out an

Table 5.3. *Variables: real cash balances, domestic price expectations, foreign-exchange-rate expectations 1920–3*

	$\text{Log}_e\ M/P$ (1913 = 0)	E (β = 0.2)	X_f (swap rate)$^{1/3}$
Sept. 1920	−0.2035	2.02	1.50
Oct.	−0.1501	1.48	1.78
Nov.	−0.1681	1.44	1.32
Dec.	−0.0944	0.81	1.71
Jan. 1921	−0.0852	0.65	2.23
Feb.	−0.0506	0.18	2.02
March	−0.0129	−0.07	2.15
April	0.0039	−0.13	1.97
May	0.0263	−0.21	1.92
June	0.0051	0.17	1.82
July	−0.0099	0.48	1.60
Aug.	−0.2821	2.71	1.78
Sept.	−0.3111	2.81	1.56
Oct.	−0.4271	3.67	1.61
Nov.	−0.6850	5.59	1.38
Dec.	−0.6005	4.73	1.50
Jan. 1922	−0.5871	4.27	1.63
Feb.	−0.6756	4.38	1.44
March	−0.8948	5.79	0.93
April	−0.9742	5.97	0.58
May	−0.9171	5.01	0.84
June	−0.9107	4.76	0.67
July	−1.1568	6.71	−1.49
Aug.	−1.6311	10.58	−2.32
Sept.	−1.7838	11.83	−3.51
Oct.	−2.1292	15.03	−4.52
Nov.	−2.4133	17.92	−5.47
Dec.	−2.1600	16.61	−4.53
Jan. 1923	−2.1748	16.40	−4.70
Feb.	−2.4764	20.49	−6.58
March	−1.9022	15.71	−4.27
April	−1.6293	13.15	−4.47
May	−1.7919	13.56	−5.24
June	−2.2722	17.97	−5.21
July	−2.6026	23.49	−7.68
Aug.	−3.6190	39.87	−8.70
N = 36			

Note: $\text{Log}_e\ M/P$ was computed and E was taken from Cagan's work (1956:102); X_f is the cube root of the swap rate as presented in Table 5.2.

important element of the statistical explanation of money-demand changes, because, as the low Durbin-Watson statistic (1.30) shows, the unexplained residuals of the regression function have a systematic bias.[7] In other words, the regression function may be misspecified.

Table 5.4. *Regression analysis of first differences of monthly data for real cash balances, domestic price expectations, and foreign-exchange-rate expectations during the German inflation, October 1920 to August 1923*

Constant	ΔE Domestic price expectations	ΔX_f Foreign-exchange-rate expectations	Standard error of estimate	R^2 Coefficient of determination[a]	Durbin-Watson statistic
0.010 (0.015)[b]	− 0.067 (0.005)	0.054 (0.021)	0.085	0.897	1.64
− 0.017 (0.016)	− 0.074 (0.005)		0.092	0.880	1.30
− 0.039 (0.036)		0.202 (0.041)	0.203	0.410	1.97

[a]Corrected for the number of variables.
[b]Standard errors in parentheses.

Yet, adding X_f to the regression function improves R^2 slightly; the coefficients of both independent variables come out significantly, the standard error of estimation is reduced considerably, and the Durbin-Watson statistic (1.64) shows that systematic bias in the residuals has been eliminated by adding the second variable.

Approximately 90% of the variance of *changes* in real cash balances has thus been statistically explained by the two independent variables. With an R^2 of only 0.327 between them, the problem of multicollinearity is not grave.

In conclusion, this first approximation to differentiating between formations of domestic and foreign expectations and their impacts on the demand for real cash balances has turned out to be statistically significant. An important difference between the two independent expectation variables lies in their predictive power for the development of the demand for real cash balances, and thus in their contribution to the stability of the money-demand function. Given the nominal money supply, this also affects the predictability of price developments. In Cagan's model, price expectations and their impact on the demand for cash are taken as dependent on past experience. They are predictable inasmuch as they depend on past price developments. This explains why the great "shifts in expectations" (Cagan, 1956:77) eluded Cagan's model. Expectations as measured by the swap rate, however, are taken as independent of past events. They determine changes in the demand for cash that are unpredictable by past events. Inasmuch as the demand for cash depends not on Cagan's adaptive-expectations variable (which endogenously summarizes past experience of actual and anticipated price developments) but on expectations formed exogenously (e.g., by current political events), it is unstable and unpredictable to the same extent as the political process. During the German inflation of 1919–23, foreign speculative demand for cash constituted the bulk of this unpredictable critical mass that initiated the great shifts in expectations. Domestic demand, on the other hand, constituted mainly transactions demand for cash, which was also subject to contractual and institutional requirements and therefore changed more slowly than the speculative demand.[8]

Acknowledgments

I owe thanks to my colleagues H. S. Buscher, B. Fritzsche, and P. Kuhbier for advice on statistical problems. In revising this chapter, which first circulated under the title "Domestic and International Factors in a Case of Hyperinflation" (1976), I have benefited from suggestions by C. S. Maier, M. J. M. Neumann, P. Temin, and, of course, the participants in the conference on which this volume is based.

Notes

1   This is partly a consequence of regressing the trends: Rising actual and expected rates of price increases coincide with falling real cash balances, or a higher velocity of circulation.

2   Abel and associates (1979) have also moved in this direction recently and have treated domestic money as a substitute not only for goods but for foreign monies as well. They differentiated, accordingly, between expectations on future price developments and expectations on future exchange-rate developments as two arguments in their money-demand function for the German hyperinflation without taking into account the historical evidence that substitution between domestic money and goods constituted the main option for domestic money holders, whereas substitution between domestic and foreign monies was an option primarily open to and exploited by foreigners.

3   Tables and diagrams with information on this point can be found in the work of Bresciani-Turroni (1937:23–39); see also the work of Hawtrey (1923:409).

4   Six billion marks in Belgium, 2 billion marks in France (Keynes, 1920:112).

5   My translation from the German original.

6   The mere substitution of Cagan's expectation variable by another based on the forward exchange rate, as undertaken by Frenkel (1977), although a step forward toward an independent measure of the expectation variable, suffers from the same shortcomings as Cagan's approach, namely, the lack of differentiation between formations of domestic price expectations on the one hand and foreign exchange-rate expectations on the other.

7   This is even more true for Cagan's regression of his original data series: The Durbin-Watson statistic is as low as 0.38.

8   Laursen and Pedersen (1964:68–9) calculated the export of paper marks on the basis of assumptions corresponding to these. They assumed that the domestic circulation of bank notes during the German inflation varied approximately in direct proportion to the wage-rate level multiplied by the index of employment. The expansion of the supply of bank notes beyond that was assumed to represent the amount of notes exported.

References

Abel, A., Dornbusch, R., Huizinga, J., and Marcus, A. 1979. "Money Demand during Hyperinflation." *Journal of Monetary Economics* 5:97–104.

Bloomfield, A. J. 1963. *Short-Term Capital Movements under the Pre-1914 Gold Standard.* Princeton Studies in International Finance No. 11. Princeton: Princeton University Press.

Bresciani-Turroni, C. 1937. *The Economics of Inflation. A Study of Currency Depreciation in Post-War Germany.* London: Allen & Unwin.

Cagan, P. 1956. "The Monetary Dynamics of Hyperinflation." In *Studies in the Quantity Theory of Money,* edited by M. Friedman, pp. 25–117. Chicago: University of Chicago Press.

Einzig, P. 1937. *The Theory of Forward Exchange.* London: Macmillan.

Frenkel, J. A. 1977. "The Forward Exchange Rate, Expectations and the Demand for Money: The German Hyperinflation." *American Economic Review* 67:653–70.

Friedman, M. 1956. "The Quantity Theory of Money – A Restatement. *Studies in* the *Quantity Theory of Money,* edited by M. Friedman, pp. 3–21. Chicago: University of Chicago Press.

Glasenapp, O. von 1922. "Germany's Balance of Payments with Other Countries." *Manchester Guardian* (commercial supplement: Reconstruction in Europe, 20 April, pp. 28–9).

Graham, F. D. 1930. *Exchange, Prices, and Production in Hyperinflation: Germany 1920–1923.* Princeton: Princeton University Press.

Hawtrey, R. G. 1923. *Currency and Credit.* London: Longmans & Green.

Heilperin, M. A. 1945. *Postwar European Inflations, World War I. A Study of Selected Cases.* New York: National Bureau of Economic Research.

Hesse, F. 1938. *Die deutsche Wirtschaftslage von 1914 bis 1923. Krieg, Geldblähe und Wechsellagen.* Jena: G. Fischer.

Holtfrerich, C. L. 1977. "Internationale Verteilungsfolgen der deutschen Inflation 1918–1923." *Kyklos* 30:271–92.

Johnson, H. G. 1972. "The Keynesian Revolution and the Monetarist Counter-Revolution." *Further Essays in Monetary Economics,* edited by H. G. Johnson, pp. 50–87. London: Allen & Unwin.

Keynes, J. M. 1920. *The Economic Consequences of the Peace.* London: Macmillan.
 1922. "The Forward Market in Foreign Exchanges." *Manchester Guardian* (commercial supplement: Reconstruction in Europe, 20 April, pp. 11–14).

Kindleberger, C. P. 1978. *Manias, Panics, and Crashes. A History of Financial Crises.* New York: Basic Books.

Laursen, K., and Pedersen, J. 1964. *The German Inflation 1918–1923.* Amsterdam: North Holland.

Lindert, P. H. 1969. *Key Currencies and Gold, 1900–1913.* Princeton Studies in International Finance No. 24. Princeton: Princeton University Press.

Moulton, H. G. 1924. *The Reparation Plan.* New York: McGraw-Hill.

Nurske, R. 1946. *The Course and Control of Inflation. A Review of Monetary Experience in Europe after World War I.* League of Nations publication, 1946, II. A. 6.

Statistical Abstracts for the United Kingdom 1913–1929. 1931. London.

Statistisches Jahrbuch für das deutsche Reich. 1923. Berlin.

Statistisches Reichsamt. 1925. *Zahlen zur Geldentwertung in Deutschland 1914 bis 1923.* Sonderheft 1 zu Wirtschaft and Statistik. Berlin: Hobbing.

Whale, P. B. 1930. *Joint Stock Banking in Germany.* London: Macmillan.

Comment

JEAN-CLAUDE DEBEIR

Holtfrerich's approach consisting in locating the crisis of the mark in 1920–3 within the international financial context seems to me quite relevant; indeed, to consider the hyperinflation of the mark as a phenomenon limited only to the German economic area would be groundless, because it did involve in its own consequences – both complete havoc and super profit – Europe and the United States. However, despite the converging figures of his

Tables 5.2 and 5.3 that, respectively, display premiums for the Reichsmark on the forward-exchange and foreign expectations, I would offer Holtfrerich a few methodological remarks.

His method, based on discrimination between domestic and foreign expectations, does not enable one either to know who the actors were or to determine the volume of their operations. Indeed, the discrimination between national and foreign operators is not significant insofar as foreign expectations take into account the behavior of agencies and affiliated firms of German banks abroad as well as that of foreign banks. In the same way, domestic expectations take in those of affiliated firms of foreign banks in Germany and those of German banks. How can we distinguish among those expectations, the active ones from those that are only adapting to the movement on the domestic level as well as on the foreign level? The expectations of the great bankers who may intervene in money policy through their agents duly accredited to the central bank, or with discrete injunctions to the finance minister, are certainly not the same as exporting manufacturers' expectations, which do not correspond to the raw-material-importing manufacturers' nor to those of the wage earners, consuming and/or saving. The fact that there was in Germany a widespread determination to protect against depreciation of the mark in 1922–3 and at the same time a consensus among the leaders of different economic sectors in favor of inflation appears as a phenomenon exceptional enough to ask oneself when it started, from which circles, and with what purposes.

Holtfrerich says: "the foreigners' contribution to the depreciation of the mark . . . depended on their share in the total holdings of domestic monetary assets," and he shows the extent of foreign assets in Germany, thereby suggesting that a great deal of responsibility for the rapid depreciation of the mark that took place during the summer of 1922 lay with foreign operators, in which case the Reichsbank's agreement to inflation could only be a response to the withdrawal of foreign assets.[1] But the figures backing up that study would deserve a closer examination when one considers that bankers always stress their reservations when disclosing this kind of information. One could also ask oneself to what extent those foreign mark deposits were covered by foreign exchange held by German banks. The second committee of experts presided over by McKenna at the end of 1923 estimated that German assets abroad and foreign exchange owned in Germany amounted to 8 billion gold marks. In 1922, some countries such as Switzerland and Holland were virtually invaded by capital coming from Germany.[2]

Whereas Holtfrerich is certainly right in insisting on speculation from abroad, stimulated by the hope that the mark would recover, he is not convincing when he connects the withdrawal of foreign capital only to a change in foreigners' expectations for the mark based on the German situation. Indeed, the speculators' attitude on the London market (the only one studied) depended more on the economic and financial situation in Great Britain than on the German one. The excess of capital noted by English bankers in 1920–1 and early 1922,[3] arising from British economic depression, was directed toward foreign investment, partly toward Germany. But the economic recovery reflected in May 1922 by the halt to falling wholesale prices and the turnaround in prices and other indexes from June onward gave rise to capital demand at home that had nothing to do with German problems. The change in the behavior on the London market about the mark is not "psychological" at all but the result of causes directly linked with the English economic position.

What is striking in the great movements of speculation in the twenties is that speculation is always presented as foreign; if speculation is geographically international, it is essentially supplied by all national institutions. Besides, at that time, how could one have borrowed marks without asking German banks?

The argumentation drawn from the high percentage (36%) of foreign deposits in German banks should be qualified by two types of considerations: (1) Compared with the whole amount of money, the proportion of foreign assets falls to 15% to 18%. (2) Deposits converted to gold marks slumped so much between 1918 and 1922 that the figures are not representative of foreign holdings. No amount of short-term debt in foreign hands can justify a model in which German difficulties from 1922 onward stem mainly from abroad. Inflation was resorted to by the Reichsbank and the German government in order to solve foreign problems as well as domestic ones. That ruling circles justified giving in to inflation with arguments about foreign policy must not hide the fact that for domestic reasons an important part of German big industry considered inflation as early as 1919–20 as the means to boost a declining business and to solve an extremely tense social situation. The center-left government shrank from applying a monetary policy that would have alienated the labor electorate, which would have turned to the Communist Party because of the crisis and unemployment linked to deflation. It would be interesting to know if there was at one moment or another a debate about inflation within the German ruling class. Does not the policy recommended by such a personality as Erzberger in 1919–20 express a more traditional attitude in money matters?

The liquidity crisis experienced by the German economy in 1922 seems to me much more due to the flight of German capital; with the depreciation of the mark, German managers of industry were incited both to exports (because of the gap between German and foreign prices) and to maintaining abroad the proceeds of their sales. In order to prevent a collapse of German banking, which would be a result of this capital export, the Reichsbank discounted bills of exchange on a large scale until it became practically the only agent issuing money.[4]

Last, it seems to me that the monetary crises of the twenties can provide the analysis of the functions of the lender of last resort with further arguments. In this respect I shall enlarge my comment by taking as an example the French situation at the same period.

First, the lender of last resort does not differ in his activities and strategies from other financial institutions; he behaves neither better nor worse. In the case of speculation against the franc from December 1923 to March 1924 we find among the banks going bearish the banks of the Morgan group in Europe (the Equitable Trust and the Guaranty Trust), as well as French banks. The lender of last resort in March 1924 did not behave differently from the other banks. This fact, confirmed by sources as surprising as convincing in their accuracy as reports of banks' bugging would be,[5] should not be astonishing. Indeed, in the face of large possibilities of profit in foreign-exchange speculation, why would foreign banks, even friendly ones, behave "better" than French banks?

Second, with the harsh conditions demanded by the lender of last resort, its rescue actions did not appear as a philanthropic operation but rather as a police operation. Holtfrerich shows that the Morgan bank in June 1922 cut credits to Germany and recommended making no more long-term loans so long as the German government had not settled a schedule for the payment of reparations. Credits would be granted only when the German government undertook to respect the Dawes requirements, that is to say, to balance its budget and to pay reparations.

In March 1924, during the negotiations for the Morgan loan that was to halt the depreciation of the franc, J. P. Morgan demanded that the French government should engage explicitly not only to increase taxes and to achieve budget balance but also to slow down the reconstruction of wasted regions and to avoid new expenses.[6]

Those conditions limiting French political sovereignty that caused Poincaré's defeat at the elections were renewed on the occasion of the subscription to the long-term loan issued in November 1924 at the expiration of the March loan, as the correspondence between Clementel and J. P. Morgan reveals.[7] Yet the American market pictured on November 8, 1924, by J. P. Morgan as unable to supply the $100 million asked if the budget were not balanced proved to be quite capable on November 26 to supply $350 million! In the interval there had been a secret letter in which the minister engaged to balance the French budget and a speech at the French parliament on the same topic; but above all there were much more stimulating offers from a rival bank, Dillon, Read.

To conclude this comment I will point out that the study of inflation and the speculation generated with it should be conducted not only at the macroeconomical level but also at the level of the financial groups involved in order to understand the strategies of the actors and thus the characteristic reversals of the phenomena. That speculation is an activity almost without first-hand records must not excuse us from making the history of it.

Notes

1 Holtfrerich, C. L. 1977. "Internationale Verteilungsfolgen der deutschen Inflation, 1918–1923." *Kyklos* 30: 271–92.
2 *Die Bank,* January 1922.
3 Bank profit and shares, *Statist,* February 17, 1923.
4 Orlean, A. 1979. "Une nouvelle interprétation de l'hyperinflation allemande." *Revue Economique* 30:518–39.
5 Debeir, J.-C. 1978. "La crise du franc de 1924. Un exemple de spéculation 'internationale'," *Relations Internationales* 13:29–49.
6 Archives de la Banque de France. Procès-verbaux du comité des Régents, March 13, 1923.
7 Archives Clementel, correspondance avec Lamont, Harjès, et J. P. Morgan, August–December 1924.

Comment

JACOB A. FRENKEL[1]

In his interesting chapter Carl Holtfrerich deals with two basic issues. First, he analyzes the determinants of the demand for marks by distinguishing between domestic and foreign demands; second, he determines that the turning point from inflation to hyperinflation occurred by the middle of 1922. The key argument underlying the distinction between domestic and foreign demands rests on the supposition that the holdings of marks by domestic residents depend on different factors than the holdings of marks by foreigners. Specifically, Holtfrerich assumes that the only factor determining domestic holding of marks is the expected depreciation of marks in terms of goods (i.e., the expected rate of inflation), whereas the only factor determining foreign holdings is the expected depreciation of marks in terms of foreign exchange. Because expectations are unobservable, they need to be proxied. In estimating the expected rate of inflation Holtfrerich follows Cagan's procedure (1956), and in estimating the expected rate of depreciation he follows Frenkel's procedure (1977). Employing a regression analysis, he shows that both measures of expectations have played a significant role in explaining the holdings of marks. These results are then interpreted as providing support to the hypothesis that domestic and foreign holders of marks played distinct roles in influencing the evolution of the inflationary process in Germany.

My comments are divided into three parts. In the first part, I compare Holtfrerich's hypothesis with an alternative one. In the second part, I deal with some issues related to the empirical analysis. In the third part, I discuss the question of when the hyperinflation began.

I. Holtfrerich's hypothesis and an alternative hypothesis

The key hypothesis underlying Holtfrerich's discussion is that domestic and foreign holders of marks have been influenced by considerations that are fundamentally distinct from each other. In order to evaluate this proposition it is useful to contrast it with an alternative hypothesis according to which both domestic and foreign holders of marks have responded to the same set of considerations. The alternative hypothesis states that the demand for money depends (negatively) on the expected cost of holding money and that the expected cost can be expressed in terms of goods as well as in terms of foreign exchange. To the extent that there are short-run deviations from purchasing-power parity, reasonable asset holders (of whatever nationality) will take account of both margins of substitution (as well as of other margins). It thus follows that the fact that expected inflation and expected depreciation both "help" to explain the aggregate holdings of marks need not indicate necessarily that domestic and foreign holders have responded to different sets of expectations. Rather, this empirical finding may indicate that both groups have responded to both sets of expectations. On this question, see the work of Abel and associates (1979) and Frenkel (1979). My purpose in posing the alternative hypothesis is not to refute Holtfrerich's hypothesis but rather to emphasize the fact that his test is not powerful enough to discriminate between the two alternative interpretations.

Whereas the empirical results do not necessarily support the asymmetric treatment of domestic and foreign holders of marks, the historical record might indeed provide some support for the hypothesis. But it should be emphasized that such support would stem from factual circumstances associated with institutional and legal constraints on domestic holdings of foreign exchange, as well as from different information sets possessed by domestic and foreign asset holders, rather than from theoretical reasons concerning differences in the margins of substitution that are relevant for the decisions of domestic and foreign asset holders. As a matter of fact, there is ample evidence that domestic asset holders did view foreign exchange as an important substitute for the mark. For example, the evidence of Young (1925:402, 538) indicates that the value of foreign bank notes held in Germany at the end of 1923 amounted to about 1,200,000,000 gold marks, whereas the gold value of total Reichsbank circulation amounted to only 112,100,000 marks. Furthermore, it would be very difficult to rationalize the German authorities' numerous attempts to protect the mark by legislating various controls on foreign exchange if it were not for the potentially massive substitution of foreign exchange for marks by domestic asset holders. These domestic attempts at substitution were frequently successful, and, indeed, in discussing the role of foreign demand, Holtfrerich himself states that "this foreign demand for domestic currency during the moderate phase of inflation also compensated in part for the reduction of domestic demand for home currency associated with the early *transfer of domestic funds into 'hard' currencies ('flight of capital') as a safeguard against future depreciation*" (italics added). In addition to this substitution of foreign exchange for marks, the evolution of the exchange rate played a key role in domestic wage-setting behavior (Bresciani-Turroni, 1937:310). The concern with foreign exchange as a substitute for marks led to the famous quotation from the *Daily Mail* of August 1923: "The mark is becoming the slave of the dollar. We have marks in our pockets but dollars in our heads." All this suggests that as theoretical and factual matters the hypothesis that the domestic demand for marks depended exclusively on the expected rate of inflation and not on the expected depreciation of the currency in terms of foreign exchange does not seem to correspond fully to the reality of the period of the German hyperinflation.

Although I have argued that holders of marks (domestic and foreign) did not ignore its expected depreciation in terms of goods and foreign exchange, it is conceivable that because of different sets of information and perception, domestic and foreign behaviors differed. This difference led Bresciani-Turroni (1937) to conclude that, by and large, foreign speculators were more confident than the Germans themselves of the future of the mark. This evaluation was also shared by Hjalmar Schacht, the president of the Reichsbank at the time. In analyzing the ultimatum of London of May 1921, which required Germany to institute a tax reform intended to generate tax revenue that would finance the reparations payments, Schacht argued: "The London Ultimatum of May 5, 1921, was accepted by Germany only for political reasons, although it was clear enough that the payments demanded could not be made. It could only be hoped that our adversaries would develop clearer perceptions when once it became clear that all the earnest efforts of Germany to make the payments imposed were doomed to be shattered on the hard fact of economic impossibility" (Schacht, 1927:54).

This and other evidence indicating that the expectations held by Germans did not coincide with those held by foreigners might have stimulated Holtfrerich's hypothesis. It should be emphasized, however, that the fact that domestic and foreign expectations did not coincide does not imply that the margins of substitution over which domestic and foreign asset holders form expectations are not the same. I conclude this section with the suggestion that instead of interpreting the results as indicating the difference between the domestic demand and foreign demand for marks, one could interpret them as indicating the different roles played by expectations concerning the internal and external rates of depreciation in determining the global demand for marks. Thus, in contrast with Holtfrerich's assertion, the factual circumstances *do not* imply a systematic difference between the determinants of domestic and foreign demand.

II. Comments on the empirical analysis

Holtfrerich argues convincingly that the ultimate support for his hypothesis comes from the fact that it passes the empirical test, that is, both measures of expectations play (statistically) significant roles in accounting for variations in the demand for marks. My discussion in the previous section took the empirical evidence as given but suggested an alternative interpretation. In this section I shall argue that the empirical evidence should be viewed with great caution because of difficulties with the quality of the data and the econometric procedures.

Quality of the data. Holtfrerich's analysis of the opportunities for covered-interest arbitrage between London and Berlin implies that until the middle of 1922 there was "a considerable inducement for foreign banks to place funds in Berlin instead of in London." This analysis of covered-interest arbitrage assumes that the arbitrage is between securities that are identical in all respects except for the currency of denomination and that the data on the rates of interest and the forward premium on foreign exchange correspond to the same point in time. It is noteworthy that the German rate of interest is the *Privatdiskont,* whereas the London rate is the mean of monthly maximum and minimum 3-month bank bills. In addition to this difference, the German rate (particularly for the later part of the period) seems extremely low relative to any reasonable standards. For example, the per annum discount rates for the last three months of 1922 are 8.15%, 8.92%, and 9.77%, respectively, whereas the rates of inflation during these months (measured in terms of the wholesale price index) are 814.9%, 854.9%, and 294.5% respectively. The implied extraordinary magnitudes of the negative real rates of interest raise the question whether the reported German rates of interest were actual market rates at which everyone could borrow or were just "list prices."

The forward premium on foreign exchange is derived by different methods for the different time periods. For the period May 1920 to December 1920 the premium is computed using data from Keynes that correspond to the first day of the month. For the period January 1921 to December 1922 the data are based on monthly means of weekly quotations of three-month premia, whereas for the period January 1923 to August 1923 the data are based on monthly mean of weekly quotations of one-month premia; in all cases the monthly data were annualized without compounding. The data from January 1921 onward are taken from Einzig (1937), with the primary source being the weekly circular published by the Anglo-Portuguese Colonial and Overseas Bank, Ltd. (originally the London branch of the Banco Nacional Ultramarino of Lisbon). As far as I know, this is the only easily available source of data on the forward exchange rate. Because a study of this kind requires data of the highest quality, it is very much hoped that more effort will be directed at obtaining alternative data sources that are most probably available in archives in East Germany.

Econometric procedures. In estimating the demand for marks, Holtfrerich uses as explanatory variables measures of the expected rates of inflation and depreciation. In what follows, I comment on the use of both measures.

The series of expected inflation is taken from Cagan (1956), who hypothesized that expectations were formed adaptively according to an error-learning process. Cagan estimated the adaptive coefficent to be 0.2. This estimate was obtained by maximizing the fit of the (semilogarithmic) demand for money conditional on the assumption that the only argument in the demand for money is the expected rate of inflation and that expectations are formed adaptively. It is most likely that the estimated adaptive coefficient would be different for a different specification of the demand for money such as, for example, the specification that includes the forward premium on foreign exchange. Yet Holtfrerich's analysis assumes that the estimate remains at 0.2.

Instead of using the forward premium on foreign exchange, Holtfrerich decided to use the cubic root of the premia in order to mitigate its variance. This decision is puzzling, because it is precisely the large variability of the premium that enables a relatively tight estimate of its effect on the demand for money. The transformation results in a waste of information. To illustrate the point, consider an alternative transformation that multiplies the forward premium by its inverse; clearly in this case all the numbers will be unity, the variance in the series will be reduced (in fact, eliminated), but the transformed series will contain no useful information. Furthermore, because Holtfrerich's transformations was applied only to the forward premium and not to the expected rate of inflation, it changed the functional form in an asymmetric way (this is in addition to the fact that expected inflation is measured per month, whereas the expected depreciation is measured per year).

To illustrate the sensitivity of the estimates to this transformation, I have reestimated the (first difference of the) demand for money using an alternative transformation of the type employed by Holtfrerich and using his

Table 5.5. *Demand for money, expected inflation, and expected depreciation: first differences of monthly data, September 1920 to August 1923*

C	Δ Expected inflation ΔE	Δ Expected depreciation Δπ*	(Δπ*)^{1/3}	S.E.	R^2	D.W.
− 0.017 (0.017)[a]	− 0.075 (0.007)	0.124 × 10^{−4} (0.029 × 10^{−4})		0.093	0.88	1.31
0.010 (0.015)	− 0.067 (0.005)		− 0.054 (0.021)	0.084	0.90	1.64

Note: The dependent variable is $\Delta \ln M/P$, where M is the nominal money stock and P the wholesale price index. E denotes the (monthly) expected rate of inflation generated by an adaptive expectations process with an adaptive coefficient of 0.2. π^* is the (annualized) forward premium on foreign exchange (on pound sterling). S.E. is the standard error of the regression, R^2 the coefficient of determination, and D.W. the Durbin-Watson statistic. All the data are from C. L. Holtfrerich's chapter.
[a]Standard errors in parentheses.

own data. The results are reported in Table 5.5. The first equation used Holtfrerich's data without any transformation, and, as is apparent, in this case the forward premium enters significantly with the wrong sign. The second equation uses the cubic root of the forward premium and thus replicates Holtfrerich's results (note that I have defined the forward premium in the conventional way, and thus it corresponds to minus the swap rate defined by Holtfrerich). These results illustrate the sensitivity of the estimates to the transformation of the data. They suggest, therefore, that the results of the regression analysis need to be interpreted with great care and caution. While functional forms are not always implied by theory, one could determine the functional form through a maximum-likelihood method as in Frenkel (1977).

III. When did the hyperinflation begin?

One fascinating question that comes up in an analysis of the German hyperinflation concerns the determination of the date of the turning point from a controllable inflation into an uncontrollable runaway hyperinflation. An analysis of this question should be of interest to economic historians as well as more general macroeconomists. The answer to this question might also provide for the material relevant for a counter-factual exercise in economic history and might yield useful lessons about what could have been done to prevent the hyperinflation.

In his classic study, Cagan (1956) dated the start of a hyperinflation according to the month during which the rise in prices exceeded 50%. By this criterion, Cagan determined the start of the German hyperinflation at August 1922. In contrast, Holtfrerich determined the start of the hyperinflation according to the date at which expectations showed a drastic change. Measuring expectations in terms of the forward premium on foreign exchange, he concluded that the turning point occurred in July 1922, the month in which the mark was traded at discount in the forward market.

An alternative criterion would put more emphasis on the analysis of the budget and on the relationship between spending and their means of finance. Thus, for example, in February 1921 only about half of the government budget was financed by floating debt (most of which was absorbed by the private sector), whereas the other half was financed by taxes. This budgetary structure could in principle be sustained for a while without resulting in a complete collapse. The budgetary burden became much more severe with the occupation of the Ruhr in early 1923 and the loss of important sources of tax income. The large deficits induced by the massive relief payments to Ruhr workers were associated with a significant deterioration of the fiscal system and an acceleration of the hyperinflation. By this criterion the turning point occurred with the occupation of the Ruhr.

The virtue of both Cagan's and Holtfrerich's criteria is that they provide for a relatively precise and unambiguous answer, because both are based on objective quantitative measures: in Cagan's case the actual rate of inflation, and in Holtfrerich's case the date at which expectations (as measured by the forward premium) have turned around. This virtue, however, is also the main limitation of the criteria: Both judge the turning point according to the manifestations of processes in a specific time series and thereby pay less attention to the details of the economic forces and processes that underlie the rise in prices and the shift of expectations. A less objective criterion that emphasizes underlying factors will, of course, be less precise but may be useful for carrying out counter-factual exercise. In this context it is of interest to note that Schacht blamed the hyperinflation on the tight pressure put on Germany by the reparations: "From first to last it was the perpetual compulsion to make foreign payments which was the origin of the mark's collapse. If the reparation screw had only been left for a while in peace, Germany could undoubtedly have arrested the mark in its downward course" (Schacht, 1927:57–8). In analyzing the role played by Poincaré (the French head of the state), Schacht claimed that "his post-war period of office and his policy in the treatment of Germany coincide in time, and is in direct causal connection with the complete collapse of German currency" (Schacht, 1927:48). Thus it seems that Schacht would have argued that the hyperinflation started (or, more precisely, that the process from which the hyperinflation became inevitable started) with the treatment of Germany by Poincaré or even earlier with the reparations imposed by the Treaty of

Versailles. There were even views that attributed the cause for the great inflation to the method by which Germany financed World War I, thus implicitly dating the start of the process at about 1916. For example, the British chancellor of the exchequer, Mr. McKenna, predicted in an interview with the *New York World* (in November 1916) that the method used by Germany to finance the war would result in unparalleled difficulties in Germany's exchanges. Likewise, in early August 1917 the London *Economist* described the German war finance as "a policy of inflation" (Schacht, 1927:32–3).

These examples illustrate the fundamental differences between two approaches to the dating of historical episodes. One approach defines a turning point in terms of the occurrences of a specific change in a specific time series, whereas the other emphasizes the role of the basic mechanisms and processes that underlie the manifestation of the specific change in the time series. As such, the second approach is necessarily less objective and less precise, but nevertheless it seems to be a very useful complement to the more precise but less insightful information obtained by the first approach.

Note

1 I am indebted to Craig S. Hakkio for comments and research assistance. Financial support was provided by the National Science Foundation (Grant SOC 78-14480). The research reported here is part of NBER's research program in international studies. Any opinions expressed are those of the author, not those of the NBER.

References

Abel, A., Dornbusch, R., Huizinga, J., and Marcus, A. 1979. "Money Demand during Hyperinflation." *Journal of Monetary Economics* 5:97–104.
Bresciani-Turroni, C. 1937. *The Economics of Inflation.* London: Allen & Unwin.
Cagan, P. 1956. "The Monetary Dynamics of Hyperinflation." in *Studies in the Quantity Theory of Money,* edited by M. Friedman, pp. 25–117. Chicago: University of Chicago Press.
Einzig, P. 1937. *The Theory of Forward Exchange.* London: Macmillan.
Frenkel, J. A. 1977. "The Forward Exchange Rate, Expectations and the Demand For Money: The German Hyperinflation." *American Economic Review* 67:653–70.
  1979. "Further Evidence on Expectations and the Demand for Money during the German Hyperinflation." *Journal of Monetary Economics* 5:81–96.
Holtfrerich, C. L. 1982. "Domestic and Foreign Expectations and the Demand for Money during the German Inflation 1920–3." (This volume).
Schacht, H. 1927. *The Stabilization of the Mark.* New York: Adelphi Co.
Young, J.P. 1925. *European Currency and Finance, Vol. I.* Washington, D.C.: U.S. Government Printing Office.

Rejoinder

CARL L. HOLTFRERICH

I start with a general remark concerning Frenkel's understanding of the relationship between "factual circumstances" and "theoretical reasons," in other words, between the respective roles played by theory and empirical evidence. Should empirical findings that do not fit the prevailing patterns of theoretical analysis be ignored in order to be able to uphold a certain theory? This seems to be the attitude Frenkel takes in his comment. Or should theory rather be the interpretive tool of *factual* findings and be adjusted when empirical evidence is found that demonstrates that assumptions underlying the prevailing set of theory do not conform to reality? This is the approach I have chosen for my chapter.

Not only can we find in the literature numerous references to the fact that during Germany's post-World-War-I inflation the expectations held by Germans did not coincide with those held by foreigners, but also Table 5.1 of my chapter shows that the development of foreign holdings of marks differed from that of domestic holdings. This indicates that it is useful to discriminate between expectations held by foreigners and those held by Germans as to the future value of the mark. Under the then-existing legal restrictions on convertibility of the mark, domestic citizens and firms were allowed to buy on the foreign-exchange markets only for financing imports and were forced to convert export earnings into domestic money (Kuehne, 1970). The development of the trade balance and the foreign-exchange dealings connected with it on the German side can be regarded as relatively "sticky" (Keynes, 1929:6). The foreign demand for marks, in contrast, presumably was more "liquid" and volatile, because it primarily reflected financial investments for speculative purposes and was unhampered by legal convertibility restrictions. Therefore, the swap-rate development, in my view, can well be assumed to indicate primarily the development of foreigners' expectations concerning the future value of the mark.

In my opinion there can be no doubt that foreigners holding German money regarded these assets as a close substitute for foreign exchange (monies of their own countries), whereas Germans regarded their mark balances in the first place as substitutes for goods and real assets available on the domestic market. Not only do the then-existing legal convertibility restrictions for domestic citizens and firms (with no restrictions for foreigners) support this assumption; there is also the fact that domestic residents, in relation to foreigners, generally enjoy the benefit of lower information, transportation, and transactions costs in regard to purchases and investments on the domestic-goods and real-assets markets. This does not exclude the possibility that domestic money holders viewed foreign exchange as a secondary substitute for marks during the hyperinflation.

I do not argue that the only (or *exclusive*) factor determining domestic holdings of marks was the expected depreciation of marks in terms of goods and that the only factor determining foreign holdings was the expected depreciation of marks in terms of foreign exchange. I do assume, however, that the domestic demand for money depended primarily on the expected rate of price changes and the foreign demand for domestic money primarily on the expected future development of the exchange rate. I am well aware that there were domestic money holders who, in spite of convertibility restrictions, could and did indeed sell some of their mark positions in exchange for foreign exchange, as well as that there were foreigners who exchanged their mark balances for German goods or real assets.

Anyone who has experience in working with historical statistics will readily concede that the data basis for statistical analysis or econometric testing is the less "ideal" the further one goes back into history. The interest-rate data I have used for calculating the interest-rate differential between London and Berlin might not be ideal in an absolute sense. I wish to point out, however, that commercial and financial bills traded in Germany on the money market at the *Privatdiskont* rate corresponded closely to the English three-month bank bills as regards the credit quality of the debtor as well as the technicalities of the credit instrument. Because daily fluctuations in the discount rates were relatively small, results are not significantly distorted by using monthly averages.

Furthermore, it is a well-known fact, already regarded as a scandal by some contemporaries, that the interest rates in Germany remained relatively low until the last stages of the hyperinflation (Hirsch, 1924:14–16). Whereas not everybody after the summer of 1922, the period of runaway inflation, had access to credit at the negative real interest rates (because of credit rationing by the Reichsbank and the private banks), there is no evidence for the assumption that more than the quoted rates could be earned on funds placed on the German money market.

As to the swap-rate data, as long as more detailed and consistent data are not available,[1] one should not, in my view, hesitate to work with the existing material. From early 1921 to the end of 1922 (the period of most importance as regards the transition of price developments from relative stability before May–June 1921 first to moderate inflation until June 1922 and then to hyperinflation thereafter) the swap-rate data are of a consistent quality. That the annualized swap rates do not differ, whether calculated from the three-month or one-month premia or discounts (except for rounding errors), can be seen from Einzig's data for the period January 1921 to December 1922, for which Einzig (1937:450–3) presents the one-month as well as the three-month quotations. The annualization of the rates with compounding would tendentially increase the annual swap rates – slightly as long as they were relatively low, more so when they became higher after the onset of hyper-inflation in the summer of 1922. Therefore, compounding would basically strengthen rather than weaken my assertion concerning the important role of exchange-rate expectations for the onset of the hyperinflation. On the other hand, the data basis of forward exchange rates for 1920 is indeed weaker than for the period thereafter. Therefore, a choice had to be made between shortening the period of statistical analysis at the danger of less significant results or extending the period with less reliable data to improve the probability of the findings. I have chosen the latter alternative, because the swap-rate data for the months before 1921 seem to fit fairly well with what can be expected from the interest-rate differential and from the development of the swap-rate and the interest-rate differential thereafter.

Frenkel argues that Cagan's adaptive coefficient (0.2) might well turn out to be different when estimated for demand-for-money function that specifies a forward-exchange-rate variable as a second argument besides the price-expectations variable. This point is well taken, and the issue has to be tested empirically.

Frenkel accuses me of wasting information by using the cubic root of the swap rate as a determinant of the demand for real cash balances. As a demonstration of his point he argues that a transformation of the data through multiplication of the forward premium by its inverse results in the destruction of the variance in the series. I accept the result of his demonstration case, but it is false analogy to apply it to my case. Using the cubic root does not destroy, but rather stabilizes, the variance in the series. It implies that the functional relationship between the independent variable in its original form and the dependent variable is not linear and can be linearized by the chosen transformation method. Frenkel (1977:657) himself has applied various more complicated procedures (among them the Box-Cox procedure) to produce a transformed variable that he enters in his money-demand function.

There has been general agreement among economic historians and economists that hyperinflation or runaway inflation started in Germany in the summer of 1922. This has been determined on the basis of inflation symptoms like price and exchange-rate developments. Frenkel proposes instead to look for criteria on the causal side, namely in public finance. There can be no doubt that deficit-spending behavior of governments can be one of the fundamental sources of inflationary processes. Yet the short-term changes in inflationary developments are mostly not determined by changes in government spending (or money supply), which create more or less inflationary potential, but by changes in expectations and mass behavior that governments or central banks are unable to predict or control. It is noteworthy that the relative share of the German government's budget that was financed by taxes rose in the first half of 1922 and reached its highest proportion (90%) in July 1922 (*Germany's Economy* 1924:30–2), precisely when inflation and depreciation accelerated. Reichsbank money supply between 1916 and 1922 rose fairly steadily, whereas the short-term trend movements of prices (or exchange rates) changed several times during that period (Holtfrerich, 1980:95). Changes in expectations and in money demand provide the explanatory link, especially for the transition from inflation to hyperinflation.

In medical science one approach is to search for underlying causes of a disease, for instance in eating habits. But it is also important to analyze why, with the same diet, some people catch the disease and others do not, and among those who catch it, at what stage they do and why at that stage. Let us look at economic troubles from both sides also.

Note

1   Better data might be contained in the Reichsbank files in East Germany (Metschies, 1968), but they have been unaccessible to Western scholars so far.

References

Einzig, P. 1937. *The Theory of Forward Exchange.* London: Macmillan.
Frenkel, J. A. 1977. "The Forward Exchange Rate, Expectations and the Demand for Money: The German Hyperinflation," *American Economic Review* 67:653–70.
Germany's Economy, Currency, and Finance. 1924. Berlin: Zentral.
Hirsch, J. 1924. *Die deutsche Währungsfrage.* Jena: G. Fischer.
Holtfrerich, C. L. 1980. *Die deutsche Inflation 1914–1923. Ursachen und Folgen in internationaler Perspektive.* Berlin: de Gruyter.
Keynes, J. M. 1929. "The German Transfer Problem." *Economic Journal* 34:1–7; reprinted in *Readings in the Theory of International Trade,* selected by a committee of the American Economic Association, Philadelphia: Blakiston, 1949, pp. 161–9.
Kuehne, R. 1970. *Die Devisenzwangswirtschaft im deutschen Reich während der Jahre 1916 bis 1926. Eine währungspolitische Reminiszenz.* Frankfurt/Main: Selbstverlag.
Metschies, K. 1968. Der Bestand "Deutsche Reichsbank," Volkswirtschaftliche und statistische Abteilung, im Deutschen Zentralarchiv Potsdam, Historische Abteilung I, *Jahrbuch für Wirtschaftsgeschichte,* Heft III, pp. 387–91.

6. The sterling system and financial crises before 1914

L. S. PRESSNELL

I. The sterling system

This is a preliminary survey of a set of problems that can easily slip from view the further we move back from the 1930s. To summarize in a single question: What has been the significance in international monetary experience of financial developments in dependent economies? The study of the pre-1914 gold standard tends to concentrate, in the case of British economic history, on the London money market and on the British monetary system. The London money market was, however, the financial center for numerous monetary systems, especially within the British Empire. This function is of special significance in considering the evolution of financial strains and financial crises; in the operation of its economy, Britain was something of an odd man out compared with important areas of the British Empire. Britain to 1914 had essentially a private-enterprise economy, with limited government involvement. In contrast, there was something almost resembling guided development in some empire countries, for instance Australia, New Zealand, India, and Malaya. In those territories, governments fostered notably the construction of railways, roads, and public utilities and were responsible for substantial proportions of investment.

Much of this investment the governments financed by borrowing in the London capital market. Such governments therefore had a debt-service problem. India's link with the London short-term money market was of special importance. The India Council needed sterling to pay in England the "home charges" of debt service and pensions for retired Indian civil servants. To secure sterling against rupees available in India, the India Council normally sold council bills in the London market. It maintained cash in England, where also were held by the late nineteenth century the Paper Currency Reserve and the Gold Standard Reserve (in gold, in British government securities, and in the money market). Outside India and the colonies of white settlement, the governors of colonies had a general responsibility to uphold the stability and convertibility of the local currency.

The economic and financial systems of empire countries were closely linked to those of Britain. New Zealand has been described as a British dairy farm in the Pacific. These links were not only those flowing from the international specialization that outflows of capital and labor fostered. There were also strong, indeed quite striking, financial links, which, like the economic ones, reached beyond the imperial territories. Empire banks were largely British-controlled, and in any case they looked to Britain for capital, bank deposits, and facilities to sustain liquidity.

Numerous British-owned international banks were active in Latin America and elsewhere. There was a boom in the founding of these banks in the mid-nineteenth century (Baster, 1929, 1935). They used sterling as their main currency. Further, particularly from the late 1890s, they frequently depended significantly on fixed-term deposits raised in Great Britain. Such funds might come from the London money market or, in very substantial amounts, from Scotland. Edinburgh had many agencies for banks and other financial institutions seeking funds (Bailey, 1959). Scottish investment trusts and solicitors put funds into various financial companies. How far these were invested with an eye on, say, Australian, Latin American, or Indian development, or were simply invested in London-based firms that happened to offer higher interest rates than were available on shorter-term deposits, is a question to which the answers are missing.

By no means the least important financial activities in London were those of empire governments. India has already been mentioned. The state governments of Australia borrowed in London, as did the governments of New Zealand and South Africa. They maintained resources in London, and their securities became regular constituents of British portfolios. The Bank of England came to manage new issues for them and to act as registrar. The Colonial Trustee Stocks Acts provided a further *cachet* for British investors (Cairncross, 1953:89; Sayers, 1976:I, 26).

II. Local economic fluctuations and local flexibility

One may reasonably describe this as a sterling system. Capital moved freely, in markedly preferential channels. During the second quarter of the nineteenth century the Treasury had more or less succeeded in stabilizing local currencies in relation to sterling and hence, at one remove, to the gold standard (Pressnell, 1978:67). Later, starting with Ceylon in 1884, there were to be currency boards and the like in colonies to provide virtually automatic links between the supply of sterling and that of local currencies (Greaves, 1953). Yet there was some flexibility. A little of this might be provided by the operation of currency boards. A good deal came with the growth of bank credit. By no means least, it seems possible, there was a degree of flexibility (and perhaps of danger) in the subsystems beneath the imperial sterling umbrella. There was something like an Indian Ocean economy that looked to India and its rupee; Australia, New Zealand, and South Pacific islands formed another grouping.

In the sterling system, economic fluctuations and crises were likely to be contagious, but there were also likely to be quite special local features within or possibly independent of the major trends, and there were local features in the treatment adopted for crises. At first glance, some crises, especially before the mid-nineteenth century, may seem indeed to have been predominantly local. Certainly the distance from Britain and the relatively small scale of early colonial economies might in varying ways have allowed considerable divergence from broad international trends. Against that, there must be considered two aspects. First, the colonies and India did depend very heavily on a flow of resources from Britain and on trade. Their responses to general trends did come, but perhaps with a lag. Australia in the early 1840s responding to British contraction commencing in the late 1830s is a case in point. Second, events at the periphery frequently stimulated the center country's action in expanding or contracting the flow of capital; Australia around 1840 again provides an illustration (Butlin, 1953:Chapter 10).

III. Local monetary management

The increasingly close currency and institutional links with Britain from the mid-nineteenth century did not bring an entire loss of control by dependent economies over their financial systems. Indeed, a critical question arises: How far did their local management affect that of sterling in London? How far did the Bank of England and other London financial institutions learn to accommodate themselves to the development of monetary management by other countries? In general, and in the longer run, it may be the case that economic influences predominated in the demand for and supply of funds flowing overseas from Britain. Such influences were, however, dampened imperially in two ways. Governmental, and therefore political, decisions greatly affected the demand for capital. Further, empire governments had (or claimed, and certainly appear to have been granted) a degree of privileged access to London funds. It may be said that the substantial volume of British investment in nonempire countries before 1914 underlines its primarily economic nature. It is the case, however, that whereas there seems to be a strong relationship between the flow of British investment and economic profitability in Argentina, such relationships appear to be much weaker for Australia and New Zealand (Capie and Tucker, 1976; Ford, 1971; Richardson, 1974). There was some expectation by empire countries that they could borrow in London when necessary, particularly during their own financial difficulties. Institutional links and the preferences of investors helped, as did the trustee legislation, in popularizing securities of Indian railways and those of colonial governments.

IV. Financial instability and crises: Queensland, India, Ceylon, and Mauritius

In dependent economies, financial instability and financial crises could come from two sources: external influences, particularly from the center country, and from their own domestic weaknesses. Did this mean double the danger or less than the danger to which the center country's economy was exposed? For perhaps the first two-thirds of the nineteenth century the former may have been the general tendency. Then the learning process that made the 1866 crisis the last financial catastrophe in Britain led to a strengthening of the center. This probably overshadowed and, because of its greater importance, obscured and may have delayed the strengthening of the financial arrangements of overseas countries, which were able to enjoy (should one even say exploit?) British financial resources. To illustrate these developments we can look at three aspects: reactions to particular local difficulties; policies that seemed to evolve and to operate over a period; experience of crises of a more or less general character.

Queensland, then a relatively young Australian colony, responded to the worldwide cotton shortage during the U.S. Civil War by expanding cotton production in the 1860s. With the end of the war and the collapse of cotton prices, Queensland was already facing difficulties when the Overend Gurney crisis occurred in May 1866. Initially, the shock was more than the immediate pain, when the London crisis and numerous overseas weaknesses also brought down the London bank through which the Queensland government had been raising capital to build railways. Despite the telegraph, full news of the crisis reached Queensland only with the mail steamer in July 1866. There was immediate panic, with fear of unemployment and of social disorder, for the government, it seemed, would be deprived of the funds it had intended to spend on railway construction. There was also an immediate political crisis, as the governor of the colony resisted pressure to issue inconvertible paper currency. He stood defiantly by his official instructions when appointed, to protect the currency. He insisted on raising money instead of creating it, and he sold Treasury bills in Melbourne, the chief Australian financial center, and elsewhere. Thereby sufficient funds became available to maintain the railway construction work. The price was high – some 10% on the Treasury bills against some 7% on the money to be raised in London. Moreover, the governor had aroused considerable enmity in his local politicians and was shortly after replaced, but he had provided lender-of-last-resort facilities successfully (PRO, CO 234/15–16).

British India suffered badly in the 1866 crisis. There had been over-expansion of banking and heavy speculation on cotton. There was advance warning of trouble a year or so earlier when leading banks began to be more cautious in lending. It was a sign of the weakness of monetary arrangements that whereas there had been 46 exchange banks in Bombay and Calcutta before the crisis, afterward only 7 banks were left. Thereafter, as in England, there was to be greater concern for monetary prudence; this was probably reinforced by the opening of a direct cable between Bombay and England, which ended the speculative shipping of commodities (Mackenzie, 1954:35–40).

The crisis of 1873 does not seem to have disarrayed outer sterling countries any more than it did the London market, with its vigorous manipulation of Bank Rate (there were 24 changes during 1873). Indeed, in the empire the long stretch from the Overend Gurney crisis of 1866 to the Baring crisis (which was not an "open" crisis as the earlier had been) was comparatively free of the major disasters of earlier years. For Aust:alia and New Zealand, borrowing heavily abroad, the 1870s and 1880s constituted virtually a long development boom. Crises tended to be institutional and local. India was worried from 1873 by the unprecedented decline in the value of silver and hence of her currency, but this had two positive results. One was the stimulus of depreciation at a time when the rest of the world was struggling with deflation. The other, to be discussed shortly, was the enhanced concern of the Indian government to ensure monetary stability of a sort.

What could have led to a wider financial crisis, but for the accumulation of caution from earlier experience, was the collapse of a major international bank with many branches in Southeast Asia and in Australia. This was the Oriental Banking Corporation, which closed in May 1884. This is of particular interest because it led in Ceylon to the establishment of what was to be a familiar feature of British colonies: a currency board or commission. Ceylon used the Indian silver rupee, and it was something of a currency entrepôt in which there was considerable activity in gold from Australia, sterling bills, and silver. On the Oriental's collapse, the colony's governor and the banks acted promptly. The governor guaranteed its substantial note issues. The other banks imported silver rupees from India. Within a fortnight confidence had been restored.

Such discretionary action commended itself to the Colonial Office, but not to the British Treasury, which then tied the Ceylon currency more tightly to sterling. Currency commissioners were appointed to ensure that henceforth the note issue should be a public responsibility and that it should be adequately backed by reliable assets. There was, however, an element of flexibility: The commissioners could vary the proportions in which the two assets, coin and British or Indian securities, were held. This enabled the commissioners to have some direct influence on the external position, for instance, by buying or selling foreign exchange (Gunasekera, 1962:Chapter 4).

A final episodic illustration of lender-of-last-resort action in colonial economic difficulties comes from the small sugar island of Mauritius in 1898. The subcurrency area centering on the Indian rupee had been under some constraint since 1893. The prolonged depreciation of silver and hence of the rupee had then led at last to modification of their historical links, in favor of appreciation and eventual stability of the rupee–sterling exchange rate under a gold exchange standard (see the following section). A drought produced a miserable sugar crop for Mauritius in 1897–8 when world sugar prices were falling, while in India famine and plague increased the cost of food exports to the island and decreased the supply of credit on which its commerce normally depended. The weakness of the balance of payments led to an overflow of specie from Mauritius and anxiety over the impact on the monetary system. The governor of the colony then acted like a central bank governor. He suspended the local equivalent of Britain's 1844 Bank Charter Act; notes were temporarily not convertible into silver rupees and were backed by securities held by commissioners in London. Loans were made to a bank and to planters. The government undertook to try to maintain a supply of small change. To meet the shortfall of Indian credit, it offered to provide its own drafts on Bombay or on the crown agents in London. The success of these measures was reinforced by a record sugar crop in 1898–9 (BPP 1900 (3-2) LIV; PRO, CO 694/6 and CO 537/418–22, 424–9).

V. Fluctuations and stabilization policies: India

To take ad hoc action in a crisis was a step toward a stabilization policy, or at any rate a step away from allowing crises to boil dry. How far, before 1914, did more continuous stabilization policies evolve, to operate between crises in order to ensure their better control or even prevention? In England such a policy did emerge, although it was not known widely enough, nor adequately understood when known, nor generally accepted when understood (Pressnell, 1968). After its fright in 1866, by the last of the three fierce midcentury crises the Bank of England used Bank Rate and open-market operations to influence banking liquidity and lending, by what I have elsewhere described, after the Bank directors apparently responsible for evolving it, as the Greene-Gibbs policy (Pressnell, 1968). In the absence of legislative control of banks' asset ratios, and while the Bank remained a sometimes strong competitor in financing the private sector, commercial banks resented such a policy. After 1890, when the Bank presided over the containment of the crisis threatened by the illiquidity of Baring Brothers, a leading merchant bank, the principal banks accepted reluctantly and only provisionally the Bank's management of the country's gold reserves. The chaos of the money-market crisis on the outbreak of war in August 1914, when the Bank wildly raised the Bank Rate, and when commercial banks aggravated the panic, registered the still-raw condition of central banking even in its classical home (Morgan, 1952: Chapter 1; Sayers, 1976:Vol. I, 66–78, Vol. III, 31–45).

In the history of monetary management in the wider sterling system, the role of India may be the great uncut diamond. Some of the best British official brains were absorbed by problems on Indian currency and finance. The operations of the Indian government in London's capital and money markets were among the most substantial before 1914. Three phases in Indian monetary policy can be discerned, the division between them being blurred rather than a clear line (Keynes, 1913). Up to the 1860s a series of banking crises reflected in part a structural weakness. Banking disasters preceding and following London's Overend Gurney crisis of 1866 marked the coming of a second phase. This had domestic and external emphases. Already in 1862 the three major banks ("the presidency banks") had surrendered note issues to the government, and after the crisis of 1866 a leading bank official argued for their amalgamation into a single bank; this would have created an institution potentially so strong in relation to the government that the viceroy and the secretary of state opposed it. Financial officials eventually took a second-best route toward control of the banking system. The problem was viewed from the angle of the government's own banking needs. It had maintained balances at banks in compensation for their losses of note issues. This involved a risk familiar in banking history: that its funds might not be fully available when required, and might even be at hazard. But to insist that against such balances banks should hold specific securities ran up against the fundamental problem in the absence of central banking: that the banks might be able to realize them only at a loss. The government's solution was the establishment in 1876 of its "reserve treasury system." Under this, it made its resources beyond minimum balances available as advances at interest. Such lending appears to have been normal until the 1890s, when it became infrequent after the turning point of 1893.

The external aspect of this second phase of nineteenth-century Indian monetary management seems clear from the statistics (which may merit econometric treatment) and the literary record (BPP for financial measures, financial reports, financial statements, statistical abstracts relating to British India, and other financial papers). A favorable trade balance and planned long-term borrowing in England (e.g., to finance railway construction) could be expected to provide adequate overseas resources in normal times. The obsessive concern tended to be with problems of appropriate techniques .o provide sterling in London to meet "home charges." The favored and usual method of remittance was by sale in London of India Council bills ("Councils"); exchange banks might purchase them to secure rupees in India to pay for imports. The extent to which the Indian government met its obligations in England by sale of Councils, or by other means, and therefore the impact of its operations on London monetary conditions, depended on several considerations. Chief of these were the rising costs of sterling with the remorseless fall of silver and the rupee from 1873. Others were the desired absolute and relative levels of cash balances in India and in England (where balances had been maintained at the Bank of England since 1838), the relative attractiveness to exchange banks of the cheaper Councils compared with the costlier alternative of telegraphic transfer (given the delay in receiving the proceeds of the former, and the Indian interest rates that could be secured with the latter), and the relative costs of borrowing short on Councils or long in other ways.

Indian governments regarded the London capital and money markets broadly as lenders of last resort. Before the 1830s the choice between sterling and rupee borrowing was a matter of cheapness. Then the secretary of state of India in London directed that sterling debt be reduced by conversion into local rupee debt. The aim was to reduce sterling debt in good times "in order that, in times of emergency, the Government may fall back on the London money market" (BPP 1881 (203) LXVIII:Paragraph 62). In practice, policy seems to have changed little. Moreover, a run of losses on short-term borrowing in London, against a background of a falling rupee, relatively high money-market rates in London, and a banking crisis, was relieved by a switch during 1884–6 to long-term borrowing in England (the increases in "permanent debt" being entered in the financial accounts for 1885–6 and 1887) (BPP 1884–5 (151) LVIII; BPP1886 (172) XLIX) (Table 6.1).

A third phase in the Indian government's monetary mangement opened in 1893. Between 1888–9 and 1890–1 it had borrowed steadily in London on long term. After the Baring crisis of November 1890, such borrowing was more difficult for several years. The Indian government nevertheless resorted to substantial borrowing in 1893–4. It had initiated a fundamental change in an attempt to raise and then to stabilize the sterling value of the rupee following the closure of the mints to the free coinage of silver (BPP 1894 (92) LVIII). Hitherto, the exchange rate had borne much of the burden of adjustment (though not all, as has been seen). Now, if exchange rates were to be stabilized, strains would have to be borne to a greater extent by borrowing in London (hence the increase in 1893) as well as by domestic measures: Thus in 1893 the Indian government withheld advances from a presidency bank that by lending rupees to an exchange bank had contributed to the reduction of demand for Councils and hence to the government's need to borrow

Table 6.1

	Financial years ending 31 March					
	1882	1883	1884	1885	1886	1887
Permanent debt						
£ million in England	68.1	68.6	68.1	69.3	73.8	84.2
£ million in India	88.7	90.1	93.2	93.2	92.7	92.7
Sums received in bills drawn on						
India (Councils) (£ million)	18.4	15.1	17.6	13.8	10.3	12.1
Cash in England (£ million)	2.6	3.4	4.1	2.2	4.7	5.3
Cash in India						
Rupees (in ten millions)	14.5	14.8	13.2	12.5	12.8	13.2
Rupees (in £ million equivalent)	1.5	1.5	1.3	1.3	1.3	1.3
Market rate of discount in London						
(weekly averages) (%)	3.23	3.11	2.96	2.58	1.71	2.42
Sterling rate (average) received on						
Councils (old pence)	19.90	19.53	19.54	19.31	18.25	17.44
Notional loss on exchange compared						
with rupee rate of 24 old pence						
(£ thousand)	3799	3465	4023	3343	3240	4564
Trade (sea): merchandise balance						
(£ million)	34.9	33.3	35.4	30.1	32.0	29.7
Treasure: net exports(−), net						
imports(+) (£ million)	10.2	12.5	11.9	11.9	14.4	9.4

Sources: BPP, 1890(6123)LXXVIII, and 1899(9519)CV, Statistical Abstracts relating to British India; Nishimura, 1971:112.

by other, more expensive, means (Baster, 1929:171). In fact, it took some five years, until 1898, to achieve and to sustain the desired exchange rate with sterling. The operation of this gold exchange standard meant constraint on government advances to banks, a readiness to use gold and other London resources (including borrowing) to sustain London cash balances or the rates or both, and from 1904 the development of a systematic stabilization mechanism. This last involved as a complement to ordinary Councils the readiness to sell "reverse councils" in Calcutta, that is, to sell drafts on London, thereby absorbing rupees and strengthening the rate (Keynes, 1913:75–6; Mackenzie, 1954:185).

For the present study, these developments have a dual interest. First, as Keynes pointed out, there was an echo of the American experience of dependence on the quasi-central banking functions of its Treasury. The government's monetary arrangements might conflict with those of the private sector, as when revenue inflows coincided with seasonal peaks in credit requirements. Much worse, such arrangements were destabilizing, for confidence that government gold would always be available in a crisis led banks to relax their own defenses against disaster. Not surprisingly, the desirability of a proper central bank for India was increasingly debated. The case was, however, strongly and successfully resisted until the 1930s. The Bank of England's central banking was regarded with much suspicion. Even the Baring crisis had not shifted sufficiently the opposition in England to increased fiduciary note issues. Keynes's own proposals for India were too radical for the times (Baster, 1929:169–95; Keynes, 1913:40–2 and Chapter 6; Pressnell, 1968:217–28). The second point of interest follows. In the absence of an Indian central bank, there was potentially an extra strain to be thrown on London in the event of an Indian monetary crisis, particularly if a fixed rupee rate of exchange were to be maintained. The first part of such a conjuncture was not to emerge before 1914; it threatened to do so during the 1920s and did in fact materialize during 1930–2 (Tomlinson, 1979).

VI. Fluctuations and stabilization policies: Australia

The monetary histories of Australia and New Zealand within the sterling system before 1914 have some resemblance to each other and to the Indian picture. Such stabilization as there was, however, came to a greater extent than in India from the banks, especially in Australia; governments were nevertheless of considerable economic weight through their responsibility for a high proportion of investment, particularly in New Zealand. The three main phases in the monetary history of the Australasian countries roughly corresponded with those of India in timing. In both countries external funds were at different times of considerable significance for the level of economic activity: British funds in Australia, British and Australian funds in New Zealand. Both countries provide illustrations of the variety and inadequacy of lender-of-last-resort action before 1914.

In the early Australian period up to the late 1870s, unhappy experiences in the 1840s and 1850s were reinforced by those of the 1866 crisis, to deter banks from regular dependence on London funds. The policy was to use them rather for short-term stabilization. Between adequate provision for emergencies and more permanent use of such resources was, however, an easily crossed line. Expansionists in this vigorously developing country pressed to jump it. From the late 1870s to the early 1890s during the second phase, even the better banks did just that (Butlin, 1961:224–5) (Table 6.2). During the 1880s there were heavy inflows of long-term capital to the private and government sectors alike. Low interest rates in Britain during the 1880s and the shock of the failure in 1878 of the City of Glasgow Bank encouraged investors, especially in Scotland, to look elsewhere. They wanted high-yielding long-term deposits, and Australian banks offered to take them, for instance in London and in Edinburgh, which, in a frequently quoted description, was "honeycombed with agencies for collecting money not for

Table 6.2. *Australia and Britain: capital flows, bank borrowing in Britain, interest rates, and security yields 1877–96*

| | Net capital inflow to Australia (£m) | Borrowing by Australian banks in Britain[a] | | Bill discount rates, London (April–March year) (%) | Bank deposit rates in Australia (%) | | | Redemption yields (%) | | | |
| | | Gross (£m) | Net (£m) | | 3 mo. | 6 mo. | 12 mo. | Britain | | New South Wales | |
								Consols	Met. bd. of wks.	Existing	New issues
	(1)	(2)	(3)	(4)	(5)	(6)	(7)	(8)	(9)	(10)	(11)
1877	3.3	12.4	– 0.6	2.46	3	4	5	3.17	3.46	3.94	
										–4.46	
1878	6.6	14.2	+ 0.6	3.42	4	5	6	3.17	3.56	4.12	
										–4.48	
1879	14.1	14.4	– 0.4	1.66	4	5	6	3.07	3.43	4.12	4.12
1880	7.3	15.5	– 6.0	2.41	3	4	5	3.04	3.32	3.74	
1881	7.7	18.3	– 3.4	3.23	2	2½	3	3.01	3.28	3.73	3.92
1882	15.9	19.4	+ 3.0	3.11	2	3	4	2.97	3.31	3.75	
1883	13.3	23.2	+ 3.8	2.96	4	5	6	2.98	3.31	3.84	4.00
1884	16.8	26.1	+ 4.8	2.58	3–4	4–5	5–6	3.02	3.22	3.71	3.81
1885	19.6	31.2	+ 7.8	1.71	3	4	5	3.01	3.17	3.75	3.85
										–3.82	

1886	22.1	32.7	+ 9.7	2.42	3–4	4–5	5–6	2.94	3.20	3.81	3.72
1887	16.2	34.7	+ 9.2	2.07	2–3	3–4	4–5	2.94	3.11	3.63	
1888	19.5	41.1	+14.3	2.62	2–3	3–4	4–5	2.82	3.06	3.38	3.43
1889	20.8	44.3	+17.2	3.01				2.83	3.00	3.35	3.43
1890	18.9	50.2	+20.2	3.37	2	3	4	2.87	3.16	3.48	
1891	14.2	50.3	+21.8	2.41	3	4	5	2.88	3.07	3.81	3.68
1892	9.1	48.7	+24.2	1.39	2½	3½	4½	2.80	2.98	3.78	
1893	3.9	40.0	+24.2	2.22	2–3	3–4	4–5	2.79	2.91	3.84	4.08
1894	2.6	37.3	+19.7	0.84	2–2½	1½–3½	3–4½	2.67	2.73	3.54	
1895	1.9	31.3	+11.7	0.81				2.57	2.66	3.26	3.10
1896	8.8	31.2	+10.8	1.78	1½	3	3	2.48	2.64	3.21	

a"Net" borrowing is liabilities in Britain minus assets in Britain; minus indicates net assets in Britain; plus indicates net liabilities due in Britain.
Sources: Col. 1: 1877–80 (Butlin, 1962:Table 251); 1881–96 (Boehm, 1971:15). Cols. 2 & 3 (Reserve Bank of Australia, 1971:Table 4(ii), p. 126). Col. 4 (Nishimura, 1971:112). Cols. 5, 6, & 7: 1877–8 (Butlin, 1961:238); 1884–96 (Boehm, 1971:212). Cols. 8, 9, 10, & 11 (Hall, 1963:Table III, p. 208).

use in Australia alone, but for India, Canada, South America—everywhere, almost and for all purposes, on the security of pastoral and agricultural lands in Texas, California, Queensland and Mexico" (Bailey, 1959:272). Nor was such investment necessarily misguided: Australia's gross domestic product advanced more than twice as fast as that of Great Britain during the 1880s (Butlin, 1962:33; Feinstein, 1972:T24). What did prove to be misguided was the confidence of the banks. There was virtually a long, not seriously interrupted, boom from the late 1860s to the late 1880s. The banks successfully contained bank crises in 1879 and 1884. They seemed to be in control. By late 1888, however, the boom had clearly peaked. A fascinating counterfactual beckons in contemplation of the possible avoidance of over-investment in Argentina and of the Baring crisis of 1890, if the early collapse of the Australian boom had shaken London's money and capital markets in 1889. The full crisis and collapse were in fact postponed to May 1893; meanwhile, its causes were being transformed (Boehm, 1971; Butlin, 1961).

Although leading banks began to retrench in 1888 (their liquidity ratios were low and their advances ratios high), an inflow of British funds sustained companies financing urban development and speculation. Although the land boom had really broken by then, these funds deferred the collapse. By the time that materialized in mid-1891, the chance that the boom might in fact be prolonged had tempted a number of banks into aiding companies deep in land troubles. With the slackening of British capital exports in 1890, the first serious failures were not far away. They came with failures of urban finance companies in 1890–1 and of banks in early 1892. A year later there was a general banking crisis. The failure of leading banks collectively to halt the disintegration simply accelerated it. It then fell to governments to act. That of New South Wales had already acted in 1891, thereby helping to delay the adjustment. It used its own resources and those supplied by Australian banks and the Bank of England. In 1893 the Victorian state government was first to act, with the declaration of five consecutive bank holidays to ease the panic. In New South Wales the state government took two bites at legislation to assist bank depositors and note holders (Boehm, 1971:176–7, 307–10, 314–15). These measures eased the crisis, but drastic reconstructions of surviving banks and a shrinkage in the money supply followed.

In all this, what had been the role of borrowed sterling? The boom and the crisis were largely Australian in origin. They had, however, been fed by rises and falls, respectively, in British long-term capital export. But it was the withdrawal of Australian deposits, not the withdrawal of those borrowed from Britain, that caused bank failures. The fallen banks were, nevertheless, those possessing extremely high proportions of British deposits; some did not have to be repaid at once, and others could not be repaid because of bank suspensions, and British depositors then began to recall when they could.

Above all, leading banks began to run down such liabilities by the end of the decade to one-half of what they had been at the beginning. The third phase in Australia's pre-1914 monetary history had opened. Banks were afterward to be much more cautious. Overseas borrowing shrank, indeed became negative until the last two or three years before the 1914–18 war. Dissatisfaction with monetary arrangements encouraged talk of the need for a central bank. This became entangled with the wish of some for a government commercial bank, which in fact emerged in 1913 with the establishment of the Commonwealth Bank of Australia. For some years yet, with persisting hostility between the new bank and the trading banks, the latter were to continue to dominate Australia's monetary management.

VII. Fluctuations and stabilization policies: New Zealand

New Zealand's economic history cannot be considered in isolation from Australia's, but New Zealand is distinctive in its monetary history. Again, there were three broad phases before 1914, not entirely parallel with those of Australia. Perhaps the first phase came in the 1860s, with a slackening of attachment to Australian facilities and closer direct links to London, including a steamer connection to Panama for mail. The small young colony was by no means a strong candidate for London borrowing; moreover, it was badly affected by Maori wars and by the depression brought by the 1866 crisis. In the 1870s, however, it shared for a decade the Australian boom, but with its own special flavor. This was the second phase, in which ambitious government policies fostered fast growth, with borrowing in Britain. The banks joined in by borrowing British deposits to finance rapid land and farming development. Bankers apparently regarded British funds as being readily available at their attractive rates of interest. This second phase stuttered to a close between 1880 and 1885. The economy was supported by government long-term and bank borrowing in Britain. Meanwhile, the collapse of land and export prices foreshadowed the depression that persisted until 1895. A series of banking troubles accompanied the prolonged reduction in bank lending from 1886 to 1891. Lender-of-last-resort action came in 1893. The Australian banking crisis threatened to close a leading New Zealand bank. The government responded with emergency legislation to enable it to help the bank and to make bank notes legal tender. The government aided the bank again in 1895; there was to be no central bank, however, for another 40 years, the banks and the government continuing to share responsibility for the monetary position.

There then began New Zealand's third phase. This proved to be predominantly an export-led boom from 1895 to 1914. In the first dozen years its monetary history was that of the Australasian subcurrency area. Neither

Australia nor New Zealand was a net borrower in Britain, but the former did lend to the latter. The position was reversed after 1907: Until shortly before 1914, Australian bank activity in New Zealand eased, when for two or three years its revival accompanied a greater resort of both countries to the London market (Simkin, 1951).

VIII. Crises and the sterling system: 1893 and 1907

Sterling relationships, in the sense of currency links and flows of short and long-term funds, were clearly significant for a number of economies and in the crises that affected them. Although none of the crises has been adequately investigated, two that appear to hold particular interest for a study of the sterling system are those of 1893 and 1907. The earlier crisis was one of cyclical fluctuations in income, investment, and trade, but it was also a peculiarly financial one. Changes in American and Indian silver policies colored the crisis.Unlike Australia, India, with better access to the London market at the time, was spared the worst of the crisis (BPP 1899 (C.9519) CV; BPP 1894 (92) LVIII). In the next crisis both countries experienced its aftereffects of depression but not major financial crises in their own systems. This reflected a combination of chance and experience. The chance was India's. Failure of the monsoon in 1907 worsened trade and contracted currency. This released gold. There was also a demand for gold for hoarding when a weakened trade balance strained the rupee rate, and also when panic-hit America attracted a golden flood by offering a premium. To check the fall in the rupee, the Indian authorities virtually stopped selling Councils and released gold (which helped to ease the strain of American demand on London's international gold market), but they also borrowed very substantially on long term. Moreover, under their incomplete gold-standard system they were able to limit the outflow of gold from India to the United States (Keynes, 1913:97–100; BPP 1908 (170) LXXIV). The Australian position was different, being that of frightened remembrance of the 1893 crisis. Bank lending had recently picked up, but net London resources were higher than they had ever been. The banks were much less vulnerable.

A matter of chance as well as of experience: Suppose that the Indian monsoon had not failed, that India had required more sterling funds, that France and Germany had not cooperated in releasing gold. To ask these and other questions (e.g., about the apparent responsiveness of foreign deposits to the rise in the Bank of England's bank rate) is to indicate the potential fragility of international monetary relationships before 1914. There were already discussions about some minimal form of international cooperation (Bloomfield, 1963:33). During the 1914–18 war an unorthodox scheme, which appalled the Treasury and the Bank of England, to create some kind of imperial monetary authority attracted some influential support (Pressnell, 1978:77–8). All this underlines the limited development before 1914 of the theory and practice of the lender of last resort.

References

Bailey, J. D. 1959. "Australian Borrowing in Scotland in the Nineteenth Century." *Economic History Review* (Second Series) 12:268–79.
Baster, A. S. J. 1929. *The Imperial Banks*. London:King.
1935. *The International Banks*. London:King.
Bloomfield, A. I. 1963. *Short-Term Capital Movements under the Pre-1914 Gold Standard*. Princeton Studies in International Finance No. 11. Princeton: Princeton University Press.
Boehm, E. A. 1971. *Prosperity and Depression in Australia 1887–1897*. Oxford: Clarendon Press.
BPP (British Parliamentary Papers) 1881. (203) LXVIII, Financial Statement of the Government of India for 1881–2. London: HMSO.
BPP 1884–5. (151) LVIII, Indian Financial Statement for 1885–6. London: HMSO.
BPP 1886. (172) XLIX, Indian Financial Statement for 1886–87. London: HMSO.
BPP 1890. (6123)LXXVIII. Statistical Abstract relating to British India, 1879/80–1888/9.
BPP 1894. (92) LVIII, Financial Statement of the Government of India for 1893–4. London: HMSO.
BPP 1899. (9519) CV, Statistical Abstract relating to British India, 1888/9–1897/8. London:HMSO.
BPP 1900. (3-2) LIV, Mauritius and Rodrigues. Reports for 1898. London: HMSO.
BPP 1908. (170) LXXIV, Government of India, Financial Statement for 1908–1909. London: HMSO.
Butlin, N. G. 1962. *Australian Domestic Product, Investment and Foreign Borrowing 1861–1938/9*. Cambridge University Press.
Butlin, S. J. 1953. *Foundations of the Australian Monetary System 1788–1851*. Melbourne University Press (reprinted 1961, Sydney University Press).
Butlin, S.J. 1961. *Australia and New Zealand Bank*. London: Longman.
Capie, F., and Tucker, K. A. 1976. "Foreign Investment in New Zealand, 1870–1914." Unpublished report, Institute of Commonwealth Studies, London.
Cairncross, A. K. 1953. *Home and Foreign Investment, 1870–1913*. Cambridge University Press.
Feinstein, C. H. 1972. *National Income, Expenditure and Output of the United Kingdom 1855–1865*. Cambridge University Press.
Ford, A. G. 1971. "British Investment in Argentina and Long Swings, 1880–1914." *Journal of Economic History* 30–1:650–63; reprinted 1973. *Essays in Quantitative Economic History*, edited by R. C. Floud. Oxford: Clarendon Press.
Greaves, I. 1953. *Colonial Monetary Conditions*. London: HMSO.
Gunasekera, H. A. de S. 1962. *From Dependent Currency to Central Banking in Ceylon*. London: London School of Economics and Political Science.
Hall, A. R. 1963. *The London Capital Market and Australia 1870–1914*. Canberra: Australian National University.

Keynes, J. M. 1913. *Indian Currency and Finance*. London: Macmillan; reprinted 1971. *The Collected Writings of J. M. Keynes, Vol. 1*. London: Macmillan.

Mackenzie, Sir C. 1954. *Realms of Silver*. London: Routledge & Kegan Paul.

Morgan, E. V. 1952. *Studies in British Financial Policy, 1914–25*. London: Macmillan.

Nishimura, S. 1971. *The Decline of Inland Bills of Exchange in the London Money Market 1855–1913*. Cambridge University Press.

Pressnell, L. S. 1968. "Gold Reserves, Banking Reserves and the Baring Crisis of 1890." In *Essays in Money and Banking in Honour of R. S. Sayers*, edited by C. R. Whittlesey and J. S. G. Wilson, pp. 167–228. Oxford: Clarendon Press.

1978. "1925: The Burden of Sterling." *Economic History Review* (Second Series) 31:67–88.

PRO (Public Record Office). CO (Colonial Office) records.

Reserve Bank of Australia. 1971. *Australian Banking and Monetary Statistics 1817–1914*, edited by S. J. Butlin, A. R. Hall, and R. C. White. Occasional Paper No. 4A. Sydney: Reserve Bank of Australia.

Richardson, H. W. 1974. "British Emigration and Overseas Investment 1870–1914." *Economic History Review* 27:980–1007.

Sayers, R. S. 1976. *The Bank of England 1891–1944, Vols. I and III*. Cambridge University Press.

Simkin, C. G. F. 1951. *The Instability of a Dependent Economy*. Oxford: Oxford University Press.

Tomlinson, B. R. 1979. "Britain and the Indian Currency Crisis, 1930–2." *Economic History Review* 32:88–99.

Comment

ARTHUR I. BLOOMFIELD

Few, if any, studies have ever been made of the pre-1914 sterling area (or sterling system, as Pressnell more aptly calls it), perhaps in large part because it had no formal basis whatever and comprised a large number of countries or territories with widely differing and rapidly changing monetary arrangements. Although much has been written about the financial relations, including capital movements and banking connections, between the center country, Great Britain, and many of the more important individual peripheral countries, such as India, Australia, South Africa, and New Zealand, there has been no study of the pre-1914 sterling system as a whole. There is also a lack of histories of financial crises in the peripheral countries. Largely unexplored, too, are the causal relations between business cycles and financial crises in the center and those in the periphery.

Pressnell's chapter is of much interest because it tries, in a preliminary way, to fill some of these gaps by assembling and analyzing some illuminating material bearing on these matters. It examines some of the main features of the pre-1914 sterling system, although it focuses mainly on the financial experience of India, Australia, and New Zealand rather than on the system as a whole. It surveys some of the financial crises that actually occurred and how they were handled, but it directs even more attention to the evolution of monetary management in these countries designed to ensure better control of their crises. It raises a number of important questions, even if it does not answer all of them. It is clear, however, that the topic is a large and complex one in which much basic research has still to be done.

Pressnell does not make entirely clear which countries he would include in the sterling system. For example, he refers to the close financial links between London and various Latin American countries, such as Argentina. He also notes that large-scale borrowings from Britain and the influx of British-based banks were distinguishing features of the overseas sterling countries. Argentina, as it so happens, was characterized by both. Are we to infer from these observations that he regards Argentina as a part of the system? I can only presume that he does not. He also uses the term *empire countries* from time to time in referring to sterling countries. But he cannot be including Canada, which, despite its heavy long-term borrowing from Britain, was clearly on a U.S dollar (not sterling) exchange standard.

In none of the peripheral sterling countries was there a central bank before 1914. As a result, the role of lender of last resort, when needed, had to be performed by the governmental authority of the country or territory concerned or by some foreign lender. Pressnell shows that in some cases the local authority did in fact perform this function, at times on the basis of funds borrowed abroad. He implies, without specifically saying so, that in other cases the London-based head offices of banks operating in these countries came to the rescue of their branches when in financial difficulties. But a significant fraction of the banking business in many of these countries was in the hands of purely local banks that did not have access to head offices abroad. For example, the Bank of New Zealand, a local bank, did half of the banking business in New Zealand. In times of crisis such banks had to turn to the local government for help or simply had to fend for themselves. Indeed, a large number of these banks were forced to suspend payments, write off a large part of their capital and reserves, or go into bankruptcy during financial crises and the depressions that followed when a large part of their loans went sour and/or when they faced runs.

In his discussion of various financial crises that occurred, Pressnell draws his illustrations from the experiences of Australia, India, New Zealand, Ceylon, and Mauritius. There are other fairly well documented cases that he could have cited. I have in mind, for example, some of the financial crises that occurred in South Africa, such as the so-called diamond crisis of 1881, which was followed by the most severe depression that South Africa had in the nineteenth century, and the so-called gold crisis of 1889–90. But most of the information on financial crises in the peripheral sterling countries and on the methods taken to meet them undoubtedly lies buried in the London Public

Record Office and in British parliamentary papers still waiting to be unearthed.

Pressnell seems to use the term *lender of last resort* rather loosely to embrace all actions taken by the governmental authority to meet or prevent emerging financial crises. Some of the specific actions that he mentions in his various illustrations, such as the declaration of a bank holiday, the making of bank notes legal tender, and the guarantee by the state of bank-note issues, can hardly be described as last-resort lending. It seems better to treat expedients such as these separately from the act of issuing money through a lender of last resort.

Comment

WOLFRAM FISCHER

Pressnell's learned chapter confirms the view that the international monetary system before World War I was much more fragile than the generations after the war thought when they compared their own difficulties with the apparently smooth functioning of the system under the uncontested leadership of the pound sterling. Pressnell confines himself to the sterling system itself and traces some of the problems those countries had that were directly tied to it. Therefore, the question arises: What about the rest of the world? Was London indeed the lender of last resort for everybody, or did there exist other financial centers that operated similarly for other parts of the world? And, if so, how were these centers linked together, and how did they cooperate? It has been noted before that whenever the Bank of England ran its remarkably small gold reserves down to a dangerously low level it had to turn to other central banks, mainly to Paris, but also to Amsterdam or Berlin, and that, even within the sterling region, the Canadian banks more and more relied on New York if they needed a lender of last resort.

It seems that even before World War I the international monetary system was not just an extension of the sterling area, but that several subcenters existed that acted as lenders of last resort for certain regions. Paris certainly was the most important one, not only for the countries of the Latin monetary union but for many parts of Continental Europe, including Russia, who tried, because of political reasons, not to become too dependent on Berlin. Regional trade and finance in Continental Europe could do most of the time without reliance on London. But overseas trade in many countries dealt in sterling, and it was the international commercial centers, like Hamburg in Germany, that pressed toward the adoption of a gold currency or at least a quasi gold currency to peg the internal money in some calculable way to the world leader, the pound sterling. Silver and bimetallist traditions became weaker, but did not vanish altogether. Thus, theoretically London may have been the lender of last resort for the world; in practical terms, business and banks in some regions, like Continental Europe and North America, turned to other lenders of last resort, be it national central banks or a leading bank or banking group. And usually this was enough. If the Bank of England had been used as a real central bank for the world, it would have broken down fairly often.

This brings me to a question that, I think, ought to be explored much more thoroughly, namely: Were there some "lenders of next-to-last resort," and how did they function? The international monetary system before 1914 can best be understood as a multitier system in which the uppermost tier, the pound sterling, was known to exist but was not needed in many cases because lower tiers sufficed to do the job of a lender of last resort. In the United States there was the house of Morgan and the New York banking community to serve as a lender of next-to-last resort, and the Treasury might be regarded as the real lender of last resort for internal transactions, confining the Bank of England to the task of acting as lender of last resort for the relatively small international sector of the American economy. In Europe, several central banks in Paris, Berlin, Rome, etc., were strong enough to act if need arose. But even before some of them existed, financial centers like Frankfurt, Zürich, and Amsterdam, and banking houses like the Rothschilds, with their roots in several countries, did the job in smaller and medium-size crises. If real panic broke out, they may have been too weak, but so was the Bank of England. Governments had to step in and did step in. Even in England the Bank alone could not weather real storms alone but had to cooperate closely with government and Parliament. Therefore, one could say that the real lenders of last resort were the politically organized leading economies of the world, whereas the central banks and some leading private banks can be classified as lenders of next-to-last resort.

Part III. Policy

7. Policy in the crises of 1920 and 1929[1]

D. E. MOGGRIDGE

I. Introduction

Professor Kindleberger's discussion (1978) of the role of the lender of last resort in the international economy in *Manias, Panics, and Crashes* is, in many respects, a distillation of an established tradition in the literature. The locus classicus for modern discussions, which itself turned a conventional interwar view into a traditional view, was W. A. Brown's monumental *The International Gold Standard Reinterpreted 1914–1934* (1940). In his two volumes, Brown argued that the pre-1914 international monetary system worked relatively smoothly because it was dominated by one center that was the main clearinghouse for credit and commodity transactions, as well as the major source of international lending at both long and short term. He then went on to suggest that one of the major reasons for the fragility and ultimate breakdown of the interwar gold standard was the fragmentation of central functions between London and New York, and to a lesser extent Paris, without any compensating coordination of policy.

In the course of the 1960s, in his writings on the international monetary system, Professor Kindleberger came to something approaching the Brown position when discussing the role of the United States in the postwar system (1970:Chapters 13 and 14). In the years following, he made his affinity to Brown's position quite clear, notably in *The World in Depression* (Kindleberger, 1973:291–2), where he argued:

The explanation of this book is that the 1929 depression was so wide, so deep and so long because the international economic system was rendered unstable by British inability and United States unwillingness to assume responsibility for stabilizing it in three particulars: (a) maintaining a relatively open market for distress goods; (b) providing counter-cyclical long-term lending and (c) discounting in crisis . . . The world economic system was unstable unless some country stabilised it, as Britain had done in the nineteenth century and up to 1913. In 1929, the British couldn't and the United States wouldn't.

Although this view went somewhat beyond that of Brown,[2] Kindleberger has now taken it even further. He has taken over from the domestic central banking literature the idea of the lender of last resort and added it to his

171

conception of the usefulness, in an imperfect world, of hegemonic international monetary arrangements. As well, he has argued that in three international crises, those associated with the years 1873, 1920, and 1929, the absence of an international lender of last resort made the crises and their associated slumps more severe than they might otherwise have been (Kindleberger, 1978:188, 192, 194).

In what follows, I have largely ignored 1873. This omission is not a reflection of Kindleberger's uncertainty as to his case for this crisis (1978:213–14). Rather, it reflects my inability in the time available to marshal the relevant material in a useful manner, as well as a historical problem. For 1873 sits oddly with its successor crisis in that, as Frank Fetter (1965:255–6) has pointed out, there was no recognition that any organization or any country had any particular responsibility for the stability of the international economic system. By contrast, in 1920 and 1929, the recognition of responsibility, not to mention the willingness to accept it, may not have been as widespread as some think desirable, but at least it existed in influential circles.[3] Moreover, in regard to 1873 it is arguable that in many of the relevant countries there was no agreement on the usefulness or desirability of a national lender of last resort; so it was hardly likely that an international lender of last resort would exist or operate effectively except as an outcome of market forces or a series of fortunate accidents. I should add, though, that my ignoring of 1873 has its compensations in the form of Professor März's comments that follow.

Even leaving 1873 to one side for purposes of the present discussion, there is still another problem that rears its head several times during this discussion: What exactly is an international lender of last resort to do in particular cases? In the case of a domestic lender of last resort, although one might dress the function up with phrases such as maintaining the stability of the financial system, practice historically has usually boiled down to maintaining one-to-one convertibility across a fairly narrow range of financial assets, notably bank deposits and national currency, with some proviso as to allowing unsound concerns to go under. Internationally, however, there may, as in 1873, 1920, or 1974–9, be no analogue, no pattern of fixed exchange rates the maintenance of which, as Kindleberger seems to suggest, might be the object of a successful lender's policy. Internationally, the freedom of exchange rates to move will provide some insulation from international events for national economies; this could, in theory at least, make an international lender of last resort less necessary. Exchange-rate fluctuations, it is true, might produce other problems for economic actors, but they might also allow the levels of output, employment, and prices in individual national markets to remain more stable than they might otherwise be and so reduce the need for a lender of last resort. Indeed, it might be argued that exchange-rate flexibility might actually be preferable to a lender of last resort. Of course, as the events of recent years have indicated, even flexible exchange rates may need supportive international lending on a large scale if the shocks to the system are large and the relevant learning processes of market participants are relatively slow. And even in a fixed-exchange-rate regime, international suport could be conditional on exchange-rate alterations. Moreover, in the aftermath of major wars the disequilibrium may be so large as to require large amounts of reconstruction lending before either fixed- or flexible-exchange-rate systems can work effectively. In any event, all I am trying to suggest is that simple analogies between domestic and international lending of last resort may often be misleading.

Lest these remarks seem to be taking me too far away from my topic, I would suggest that they are relevant to both interwar crises discussed by Professor Kindleberger. To tie them in, let me examine economic events and policies in each of the crises.

II. The crisis of 1920

Although many of the external trappings of the pre-1914 gold standard survived World War I and most of the important countries ended the war with exchange rates relatively close to their prewar parities, the events of the war years had destroyed many of the elements underlying the prewar pattern of exchange rates. The war brought marked disparities in inflationary experiences, which in many cases became even greater in the immediate postwar period. In addition, at the end of the war, government finances in the core countries of the international economy were in varying degrees of disarray. By themselves, these factors would have made an early return to exchange stability (not to mention the prewar pattern of exchange rates desired by many policy makers and expected by many other economic actors) extremely difficult, especially in the early postwar social turmoil and revolutionary threats to the existing order (Gilbert, 1970:17–18, 25–8, 35–6; Maier, 1975:Part I). As well, the war had altered many of the "fundamentals" underlying the old regime. It disrupted prewar patterns of trade, to the longer-term disadvantage of such large prewar traders as Britain and Germany. Along with the Russian Revolution, it had markedly changed the invisible income positions of many countries as a result of inflation, wartime liquidations, borrowing, seizures, and shipping losses. Also, the peace settlement had left the defeated stripped of many remaining assets and liable for a stream of reparations payments the magnitude of which was still unknown a year after the end of hostilities. Finally, the collapse of old empires and shifting frontiers, not to mention four years of destruction and neglected wear and tear, had left many countries financially and economically devastated. These problems were most acute in central and eastern Europe.

If anything was necessary in this situation, it was an international program for postwar relief and reconstruction. Beyond some relief in the form of food supplies, much of which was available only on a cash or credit basis, the governments in a position to provide aid made no provision. Several ambitious schemes were in the air in the spring of 1919 and later, but they came to nothing. What Allied (and neutral) governments were unwilling to agree to, the private sector could hardly replicate; so the issue went by default, and governments and private individuals made the best arrangements they could in the circumstances. Given that the major international creditors immediately after the war were the United States and other non-European countries – Britain was in current-account deficit in 1919 (Morgan, 1951:341) – Europe covered her immediate postwar deficit by running down existing balances, short- and long-term borrowing, and sales of securities, as well as by moving to eliminate the deficit through exchange depreciation, in the process attracting short-term capital (Aliber, 1962:187–8).

Against this backcloth, after a brief postwar breathing space, a short, sharp postwar boom occurred lasting roughly a year. Its origin lay in postwar shortages and supply disruptions in the context of a restocking boom, which coincided with the end of wartime controls in most potential supplying countries. In Britain and the United States, as elsewhere, the boom was initially fueled by large government deficits financed by credit creation and easy credit conditions. In countries outside the United States, such as Britain, exchange depreciation also gave the price level an upward twist during the boom, especially given wage indexation, and some of the Anglo-American differences in price experience during the boom reflect this depreciation (Aliber, 1962:197). As well, in Britain a sharp upward twist in labor costs came very early in the boom (Dowie, 1975), but elsewhere (and later in Britain) money wages followed prices upward.

As the boom gathered momentum, generating and fulfilling inflationary expectations, the stance of policy began to change, notably in Britain and the United States. In both countries, when the boom began in the spring of 1919 the central government's budget had been heavily in deficit. Sharply falling expenditures coupled with rising revenues brought both budgets into surplus in the last quarter of 1919.[4] These swings into surplus, which continued in 1920, exerted a marked deflationary pressure on aggregate demand. They reflected not only the process of demobilization but also the beginnings of attempts by the governments concerned to return to budgetary "normalcy" and to cope with the debts left over from the war. At the same time, the monetary authorities in the two countries were struggling to gain their independence (or regain it, in the case of Britain) and their control over events, most often by argument but on occasion by stealth (Howson, 1974:96, 98). By the end of 1919 discount rates had started to move upward in response to deteriorating central-bank reserve positions, which, despite government desires for cheap finance, made some action imperative in both countries (Howson, 1974:98–100; Wicker, 1967:45). In the early stages the rise in rates was larger in Britain, as was the slowdown in the rate of growth of the monetary aggregates (Friedman and Schwartz, 1963:229–30; Howson, 1975:17–18). Thus, by the end of 1919, policy had changed markedly from its earlier relative ease. Moreover, Britain and the United States were not the only countries cutting back in 1919.

The postwar boom, which had carried wholesale prices up by 46% in England in 13 months and 39% in America in 15 months, broke in the early part of 1920. In the United States, if we are to believe the National Bureau of Economic Research, the break came in January and coincided with a sharp rise in Federal Reserve discount rates, which, coupled with a refusal by American banks to continue advances to exporters holding sales proceeds in foreign currencies, produced a sharp fall in European exchange rates (Hawtrey, 1923:71). In Britain the turning point came in March,[5] with other countries following. In both Britain and the United States the origins of the slump lay in the domestic economy; in Britain, export markets did not become unfavorable until later in the year (Lary, 1943:142; Pigou, 1947:185–6). In both countries, the upper turning point was followed by a further turn of the monetary screw that carried the bank rate and the New York Federal Reserve discount rate to 7% on 15 April and 1 June, respectively. Both rises reflected further reserve stringency (Chandler, 1958:183–5; Howson, 1975:23). In Britain, the possibility of another rise in rates was discussed during the summer of 1920 but was vetoed by the chancellor (Sayers, 1976:123). On both sides of the Atlantic the high rates of the spring of 1920 were to remain in force for a year.

In late 1919 and 1920 some deflation was a deliberate policy goal of the authorities in both Britain and the United States. In Britain, some of the desire for deflation was a reflection of the policy goal of a return to gold at prewar par, which became official policy in December 1919, for such a goal required a measure of relative British deflation. However, some of the impetus toward the deliberate use of monetary measures to break the boom came from the view that the consequences of a rate of inflation of 1919–20 proportions (which was higher than that of 1973–5) were in themselves undesirable for society (Howson, 1973, 1974:100–5). As well, both the British and American authorities believed that once deflation had started, it was desirable to maintain deflationary monetary pressure until the system came to rest at a new equilibrium with lower prices (Chandler, 1958:69–74; Howson, 1975:28–9; Wicker, 1967:Chapter 3).

The sharp decline in activity that began in 1920 was fairly general internationally, as was the fall in prices. True, some of the countries that were to fall into hyperinflation were to prove exceptions to the rule, as were countries such as Australia, The Netherlands, and Sweden (Maddison, 1977:Table A5). Although exchange rates were flexible, with little direct official intervention even to smooth trends, and did move in some countries to provide some insulation from international deflationary pressures (Palyi, 1972: Table II–4),[6] the range of movement was often constrained by official policies that more often than not were directed at clearing away the financial debris of the war and preparing the ground for fixed parities. In this regard, the situation was similar to that of 1873, when, although Britain was the only country on a full gold standard, exchange-rate fluctuations were very small. Deflationary pressures were therefore more easily transmitted through current accounts and capital movement than would otherwise have been the case, notably in the sharp fall in imports into the United States between 1920 and 1921 and the sharp rise in gold movements to the United States.

Despite all that happened during the recession that began early in 1920, it is not clear that a lender of last resort would have had an important role to play. For one thing, the upper turning point was not followed by or accompanied by a financial crisis, although the difficulties of the Japanese silk market have played a role in some accounts of the turning point. Moreover, it is doubtful that any lender could have encouraged exchange stabilizations at or around 1920 levels – the lure of prewar par was too strong, as it was to remain later,[7] and even the Genoa resolutions on currency with their let-outs for severely depreciated currencies were two years away. Nor can one really blame the absence of such a lender and the resulting exchange depreciation for the German hyperinflation, as Kindleberger seems to do (1978:192). The mark exchange rate with the dollar was roughly the same in May 1921 as it had been in April 1920; German domestic prices remained relatively stable over the year, and with the fall in import prices the general price level actually *fell* (Bresciani-Turroni, 1937:30; League of Nations, 1946:104). True, despite the Erzberger reforms, the budgetary position was far from ideal, and the balance-of-trade position remained weak, but a lender of last resort would hardly have improved matters. In fact, it might be argued that rather than a lender of last resort in 1920–1, what the world could have done with was an international relief and reconstruction program in 1918–19, a more orderly process of decontrol and conversion after the war, and a Federal Reserve system that understood its business better during 1919–21.

III. The crisis of 1929

The 1929 recession and its succession of financial crises took place in the context of a disintegrating regime of fixed exchange rates. The years prior to 1929 had seen a painful reconstruction of the international monetary system and the return of all major economies (except in Japan) to fixed exchange rates. The reconstructed system of the late 1920s was, however, hardly an equilibrium system, even before the slump perturbed it. The exchange rates chosen in the series of national stabilization decisions in the 1920s had left a significant number of substantial overvaluations and undervaluations among the currencies of the industrial countries, but no common perceptions as to how the adjustments necessary to remove the resulting stock or flow imbalances would occur. Subsequent events had done little to remove the initial imbalances in the system and in some cases (such as that of Germany) had added problems, so that some countries entered the recession with inappropriate exchange rates. At the same time, although global supplies of international liquidity were probably adequate, they were badly distributed: From 1928, when France began to acumulate gold on a large scale (as well as worry about the composition of her reserves) and the United States experienced a stock-exchange boom, most countries in the system felt the pressure of undesired reserve losses.[8] As well, many countries other than France were already unhappy with the composition of their international reserves. The gold exchange standard, reborn at Genoa as a gold-economizing device and a possible means of stabilizing the purchasing power of gold and adopted by a number of countries, often as a part of a League of Nations stabilization scheme, was now less popular. This decline in popularity was the product of several factors: the rise of France, contemptuous of British pretensions in the face of weakness and looking for her place in the sun; the belief that the gold exchange standard was a second-class regime; the post-1925 weakness of sterling, the major reserve currency. This unpopularity produced added strains in the system as France altered her pattern of asset accruals and other countries became less willing holders of sterling. Finally, French and American monetary policies had ensured that even such little adjustment as occurred during the upswing did so against a slightly falling price level.

At the center of the international economy, the downturn in economic activity came in the course of 1929 (except in the case of France, where it came in 1930). At the periphery, in many cases the downturn came earlier.[9] During 1928–9 primary producers faced a variety of problems: Prices were weak, stocks were rising, capacity levels often were excessive, levels of borrowing had been high for some years, and debt service loomed large.

Exacerbating these problems were various attempts to raise producers' prices through schemes designed to restrict output and/or hold stocks from the market. Overseas borrowing often played an important role in financing these schemes. During 1928–9, borrowing for these and other purposes became more difficult as a result of the sharp decline in American overseas lending and the repercussions of this and the Wall Street boom on European capital markets (Fleisig, 1972:151–7; Williams, 1963b:92, 96, 98). The upshot of output restrictions, weakening prices, and reduced overseas borrowing often was balance-of-payments difficulties. Peripheral countries met those difficulties in part by financing (by the use of official reserves and short-term borrowing), although they also turned to other measures (additional deflation, protection, and exchange depreciation). These problems and policies had repercussions at the center of the system, because falling investment, falling incomes, and increased protection and exchange depreciation reduced the demand for exports of manufactures from the industrialized center and had, for example, an important role in initiating the British recession (Corner, 1956). So, too, did their methods of financing balance-of-payments deficits: For example, the large gold movements from the periphery eased London's position in 1930, whereas the reduction of sterling balances by proto-sterling-area countries, plus their demands for short-term accommodation, made her position more difficult (Pressnell, 1978:81–2; Williams, 1963 a:518–19).

Although economic activity in many peripheral countries, as well as in Britain and Germany, had turned down before the United States moved into recession in the summer of 1929, American events made the situation more difficult. The relative impacts of the various proximate causes of the American recession remain matters of controversy, as do the factors that turned a severe recession into a great depression (Mayer, 1978). However, falling incomes and industrial production at the center resulted in a sharp decline in international trade and a decline in the demand for primary products, which, with the large stock overhangs of the late 1920s and borrowing difficulties, led to a fall in prices, the collapse of many restriction schemes, further falls in prices, and further difficulties for producers, which, of course, fed back into the system (Lary, 1943:170–1).

The collapse on Wall Street brought a cautious easing of monetary policy at the center (Chandler, 1971:149–52; Sayers, 1976:229–32; Wicker, 1967:144–51). By June 1930, discount rates in New York and Paris were down to 2.5%, and in London and Berlin they stood at 3% and 4%. However, the reductions in discount rates probably exaggerated the easing of the monetary situation. In Britain, interest rates on long-term government securities remained at the level of early 1929, whereas both high-powered money and the money stock fell in the first half of 1930 (Howson, 1975:68). In the United States, as well, bond yields remained high (and probably rose slightly if one allows for reclassifications), whereas the money stock declined from its preslump level (Friedman and Schwartz, 1963:307–8; Temin, 1976:104, 107). True, in both countries there was some revival in overseas lending from 1929 levels. But in London, except for an Austrian government loan, the Young loan (which did not result in any flow of funds overseas), and a last loan for Brazilian coffee valorization, controls prevented any lending to governments outside the empire (Moggridge, 1972:212–13); in New York, beyond the Young and Austrian government loans, the major borrowers were Canada and Argentina (Lary, 1943:100). Even at this stage, some overseas debtors were experiencing financial difficulties and were finding their access to financial markets barred (Schedvin, 1970:Chapters 6 and 7; Tomlinson, 1979:89–93). There was also an expansion of lending from Paris and Amsterdam, but total lending remained below the 1925–8 level (RIIA, 1937:282), and French lending sometimes had unfavorable repercussions on London (Clarke, 1967:171). In the second half of the year, long-term lending dropped sharply, and defaults increased. After the year's end there were to be proposals for an international institution to expand the volume of lending, particularly to ease the German situation, but these foundered on American and French opposition (Clarke, 1967:179–80).

The lack of longer-term accommodation was, to some extent, offset by short-term lending from the United States and some stronger Continental centers, but not by enough to avoid balance-of-payments problems in a number of countries, which added to the widespread deflationary pressures already present in the system. In the second half of 1930, both Britain and Germany came under increased balance-of-payments pressure, thus joining much of the periphery, as gold flows to the United States resumed and those to France accelerated (Lary, 1943:133; Wolfe, 1951:Appendix III). The gold flows to countries in surplus, which also included stronger European countries such as Switzerland and The Netherlands, exceeded new supplies of monetary gold by a large margin, with the result that most countries experienced a further fall in reserves. The typical responses followed with added twists of retaliation for the sharply increased American tariff. Toward the end of the year, the Bank for International Settlements, the Federal Reserve, and the Bank of France provided a modicum of assistance to the Reichsbank and the Bank of England, but the prospects of further central-bank cooperation were not bright (Clarke, 1967:173–6; Sayers, 1976:233).

As 1930 progressed, many of the problems that were to preoccupy central bankers and governments in 1931 became evident. In November, a series of bank failures and a scandal in Paris brought a large movement of French balances from London and forced the Bank of France to intervene in the exchange market to stabilize the situation. During November and December the slump in the United States took a more serious turn as 608 banks, including the infamous Bank of United States, closed their doors, causing precautionary changes in the deposit/currency and deposit/reserve ratios (Friedman and Schwartz, 1963:308–12; Temin, 1976:91–3). Even Britain had her banking difficulties (Sayers, 1976:Chapter 10B). Moreover, on the international scene the outlook was hardly encouraging. The Young loan, issued in June 1930, remained well below par, standing at a discount of almost 30% by year's end, a reflection of the growing uncertainty about Germany's ability to maintain reparations payments in a slump and the increasing power of domestic political opponents of the reparations settlement (Davis, 1975:245–6).

Following a brief respite in the early part of the year, the difficulties of 1930 became more acute in 1931. For a time, even the mark and the pound sterling enjoyed a reduction in the pressures of earlier months, although in these countries, informed, inner opinion was hardly optimistic (Clarke, 1967:177–8; Clay, 1957:371; Howson, 1975:69–71; Howson and Winch, 1977:82, 86–7). Between March and June another wave of bank failures in the United States occurred. In the months following 11 May, four days after the governor of the Bank of England first heard of the difficulties of the Creditanstalt and three days before the last internationally concerted reduction in discount rates of the period, the system fell apart. The spark that set off the 1931 explosion could have come from any number of places, for banking difficulties were widespread, reaching London at the height of the crisis (Sayers, 1976: Chapter 10D, pp. 530–3). With the collapse of the Creditanstalt, the largest bank in Austria, events took a more serious turn. The Austrian authorities and the international central banking community moved to pick up the pieces and limit the repercussions of the collapse. But the international community moved slowly, constrained by caution, domestic worries, political considerations (more prominent, given recent Austro-German behavior), and lack of awareness of the real magnitude of the problem (Bennett, 1962; Clarke, 1967:183–9; Clay, 1957:375–7). In the meantime, foreign creditors and residents ran down their Austrian assets until standstill arrangements, later backed by exchange controls, made this impossible.

The Austrian crisis also led bankers to attempt to improve the average quality of their assets by withdrawing funds from other weak centers. Hungary experienced an almost immediate run, as did many of the other small countries of eastern Europe, but from the end of May the important country in difficulties was Germany, whose bankers were known to be involved in Austria and whose overseas short-term liabilities were huge. Again the resulting support operations were subject to delays caused by lengthy negotiations at every turn, largely the result of French attempts to use the crisis to win political concessions from Germany, but also the result of

British attempts to use the crisis to make more far-reaching changes in the international economic order (Bennett, 1962:Chapters 6–8; Clarke, 1967:189–201; Clay, 1957:377–83). The delays meant that at each stage the assistance, when granted, was probably too little, as the situation had deteriorated sharply in the interim, culminating in the failure of the Danatbank on 13 July, bank holidays, and the beginnings of exchange control.

From 13 July the crisis switched to London, the third largest short-term creditor to Germany and the premier international money market in Europe (RIIA, 1937:238). By this time, sterling had been under a cloud for some months, given the by-then-widespread acceptance that it was overvalued at $4.86 and the existence of continuing budget deficits in the home of the high priests of sound finance (Sayers, 1976:390–1), but, as yet, the authorities had done nothing beyond appointing expert committees on the unemployment insurance system and the budgetary problem and making alarmist noises about the situation. It was the conjuncture of these circumstances with a very weak underlying balance-of-payments situation (vide infra), the freezing of substantial British short-term assets in central Europe, and the publication of the Macmillan report (which revealed, albeit incompletely, the magnitude of Britain's net foreign short-term debtor positions) that made the British crisis so difficult to deal with (Clarke, 1967:185, 202; Sayers, 1976:390).

As in the previous cases on the Continent, international financial cooperation came into play as the Bank of England and the government raised credits totaling $650 million in New York and Paris, initially to hold the exchange rate while preparing a program of financial retrenchment and then to put into operation a program acceptable to the financial community. The assistance came relatively promptly, despite the difficulties of making a public issue for the second credit in the liquidity-conscious New York market (Moggridge, 1970:839; Moggridge, 1972:196). In this case, however, the ample assistance merely prolonged the crisis, whereas a number of misunderstandings and tactical mistakes probably shortened it. Reports of unrest in the Royal Navy over pay cuts resulting from the retrenchment program, election uncertainties in Britain after the fall of the Labour government and the appointment of a national government, fresh financial difficulties on the Continent (this time in Holland), and the impossibility of obtaining any further financial support led the authorities to decide on 18 September to suspend gold convertibility on 21 September (Moggridge, 1972:194–6; Sayers, 1976:404–10).

The repercussions of Britain's decision to suspend gold convertibility were immense. It led to further crises elsewhere that took other countries from the gold standard and engendered another wave of exchange controls in central and eastern Europe. It led to attempts to liquidate the remaining remnants of the gold exchange standard, which resulted in large gold outflows from the United States, a sharp orthodox tightening of American monetary policy, and another even more spectacular wave of bank failures in the United States. Moreover, the new wave of exchange depreciations, exchange controls banking crises, tariffs, and retaliating trade controls that followed 21 September put still more deflationary pressure on the countries remaining on gold and on the gold price level, even if it somewhat eased the pressure among the depreciating countries. In these circumstances, it is, of course, worth asking if more short-term accommodation (a lender of last resort) might have improved matters.

Before attempting to answer that question, we should realize that the 1931 financial crisis did involve a large amount of supportive lending. The sum of such lending between May and September amounted to roughly $1 billion or 10% of international short-term indebtedness or just under 5% of the (slump-diminished) value of world imports (BIS, 1932:12–13; Maddison, 1962:Table 23). Such a sum compares favorably with the relationship between total IMF quotas and world imports in 1976 and 1977 (IMF, 1977:40), which hardly suggests an inadequate volume of assistance, especially if one were to compare it with the amounts that had gone before. One might argue that the sums involved were dissipated unwisely, but to take that tack is to change the basis of the argument.

Moreover, to evaluate the experience of 1931 as it finally turned out, one must have some idea as to what would have happened in the alternative situation. Even without the international liquidity crisis, many underlying balance-of-payments positions were in substantial disarray. The British case is perhaps the most important here, for any alternative scenario that failed to keep Britain on gold probably would have produced results similar in kind to those that actually occurred. Between 1929 and September 1931, despite the decline in the volume and value of Britain's exports, the deterioration in her balance of trade was minimal, of the order of £5 million. However, over the same period, the slump reduced the invisible surplus by 30% to 40% as income from overseas investment, shipping, and short interest and commissions declined sharply. Yet by September 1931 the invisible deterioration by itself implied a current-account deficit for Britain of the order of £90 million for 1931, even leaving aside any J-curve effects of the post-21-September depreciation and shipments of goods anticipating protection after the national government's electoral landslide in October (Howson and Winch, 1977:243–54; Moggridge, 1970:832–6). And this deficit ignores any net new overseas lending that Britain might undertake. To finance successfully a deficit on current and long-term capital account in the circumstances of 1931, Britain could not, as she had in the case of a similar deficit in 1926, depend on (1) French and Continental refugee capital or (2) reserve accumulations of the overseas proto-sterling-area countries; the former was falling as the French government drew on its London balances to meet a budget deficit, as French banks drew down their sterling secondary assets to increase their cash reserves and allow for deposit and currency expansion, and as foreigners tended to reduce their London balances in the face of low interest rates, whereas the latter were themselves in difficulties. Even without the liquidity crisis of 1931, Britain faced a serious balance-of-payments problem that entailed a substantial measure of additional deflation if the authorities were to avoid depreciation.[10] Whether or not Britain or the international economy could have coped with such additional deflation is arguable. But in a world where devaluations of the sort that have characterized the Bretton-Woods system were almost unthinkable, it is likely that any additional assistance to meet Britain's underlying balance-of-payments problem would have carried such deflationary conditions, as, of course, did the second round of lending to Britain during the liquidity crisis.

Britain, moreover, was not the only country with underlying balance-of-payments difficulties. Among the countries at the center, Germany had seen her international competitive position decline since 1929, despite acceptance of international deflationary forces and reinforcement of them through domestic policies (Moggridge, 1972:Tables 8 and 9). Despite the marked improvement in her current-account position between 1928 and 1931, Germany's position had been precarious even before the crisis, given the domestic repercussions of deflation, which affected short-term capital flows. and the need to make substantial reparations payments. No wonder international opinion was doubtful as to Germany's future in 1930! Perhaps Clay was right to suggest that if "a chance of checking the slide into insolvency existed, it was offered by the Hoover proposal" (1957:380). Perhaps it might have been if it had come earlier, but again this is hardly a lender-of-last-resort operation.

IV. Conclusion

I conclude that the international-lender-of-last-resort arguments put foward by Professor Kindleberger for 1920 and 1929 are rather incomplete and unconvincing. With respect to 1920, Professor Kindleberger seems to beg the underlying rationale of the doctrine of the lender of last resort, given that, whatever else happened, there was hardly a financial crisis during the recession and that the real need was for an international reconstruction and rehabilitation program in 1919–20. This is not to deny that there were mistakes in policy formulation and execution that brought with them great costs; it is merely an attempt to avoid confusing the issue. As for the period after 1929, the situation is more complex. In this case there was a substantial amount of emergency assistance, even if it came at the wrong times and in the wrong places. Events might have turned out differently if the $1 billion actually raised had found use earlier in Austria and Germany rather than later in Britain. However, even if the available assistance had been used more effectively, there remained the underlying sources of disequilibrium in the international economy: American economic policy, French gold accumulations, and the weakness of the British balance of payments at the post-1925 exchange rate in an international recession. As a result, I am inclined to the view that emphasis on and further investigation of these areas probably will be more fruitful than bringing in the absence of an international lender of last resort so early in the argument.

Notes

1 I should like to thank Susan Howson and participants at the colloquium and at the May 1979 meeting of the U.K. Social Science Research Council's Monetary History Group for comments on an earlier draft. The Social Sciences and Humanities Research Council of Canada provided financial support to enable me to attend the colloquium.

2 Other discussions of the same theme include those of Strange (1971) and Rowland (1976).

3 In 1931 the recognition of the need was primarily English, in both the Bank of England and elsewhere. Even there, though, it was better articulated after the event (Kindleberger, 1978:195–7).

4 Nor were the magnitudes involved unimportant for the final result. In the United States, between the fiscal year ending 30 June 1919 and that ending 30 June 1920, federal expenditures fell from $18.4 billion to $6.4 billion (American billion), whereas revenues rose from $5.1 billion to $6.6 billion. In Britain, comparing calendar 1918 with calendar 1919, central government expenditures fell from £2.2 billion to £1.4 billion, whereas revenues rose from £981 million to £1,019 million (Feinstein, 1972:Table T12; U.S. Department of commerce, 1975:Series Y335–6).

5 However, the outlook had been uncertain for some months before the turn (Howson, 1975:10).

6 An examination of monthly averages of exchange rates on New York for the period suggests that exchange-rate movements provided a significant element of insulation in countries pegged to silver, such as China and Mexico, and in Argentina, Brazil, Chile, India, Italy, Norway, Portugal, and Spain (Federal Reserve System, 1943:Table 173).

7 As it was to be in France in 1922, when the authorities flatly rejected an American stabilization proposal (Schuker, 1976:37).

8 The continuous pressure on London in the 1920s had its parallels in the years surrounding 1873, when the gold-accumulation policies of France, Germany, and the United States were a source of difficulty (Hawtrey, 1938:47–8).

9 As, for example, in Canada and Australia (Safarian, 1959:Chapter 3; Schedvin, 1970:Chapters 4 and 6).

10 Ignoring international repercussions, a £60 million reduction in imports would have required a fall in national income of something like £200 million. Given

output per man at the time, such a fall in national income would have entailed a 10% fall in employment – this at a time when unemployment already exceeded 20%.

References

Aliber, R. Z. 1962. "Speculation in the Foreign Exchanges: The European Experience, 1919–1926." *Yale Economic Essays* 2:171–245.
Bank for International Settlements (BIS). 1932. Annual report for the year ended 31 March, 1932. Basle.
Bennett, E. W. 1962. *Germany and the Diplomacy of the Financial Crisis, 1931.* Cambridge, Mass.: Harvard University Press.
Bresciani-Turroni, C. 1937. *The Economic of Inflation: A Study of Currency Depreciation in Post-War Germany.* London: Allen & Unwin.
Brown, W. A., Jr. 1940. *The International Gold Standard Reinterpreted, 1914– 1934* (2 vols.). New York: National Bureau of Economic Research.
Chandler, L. V. 1958. *Benjamin Strong: Central Banker.* Washington: Brookings Institution.
  1971. *American Monetary Policy 1928–1941.* New York: Harper & Row.
Clarke, S. V. O. 1967. *Central Bank Cooperation 1924–1931.* New York: Federal Reserve Bank of New York.
Clay, Sir H. 1957. *Lord Norman.* London: Mamillan.
Corner, D. C. 1956. "Exports and the British Trade Cycle." *Manchester School* 24:124–50.
Davis, J. S. 1975. *The World between the Wars, 1919–1939: An Economist's View.* Baltimore: Johns Hopkins University Press.
Dowie, J. A. 1975. "1919–20 Is in Need of Attention." *Economic History Review* (Second Series) 28:429–50.
Federal Reserve System, Board of Governors. 1943. *Banking and Monetary Statistics 1914–1941.* Washingon, D.C.: Federal Reserve Board.
Feinstein, C. H. 1972. *National Income, Expenditure and Output of the United Kingdom, 1855–1965.* Cambridge University Press.
Fetter, F. W. 1965. *Development of British Monetary Orthodoxy, 1797–1875.* Cambridge, Mass.: Harvard University Press.
Fleisig, H. 1972. "The United States and the Non-European Periphery during the Early Years of the Great Depression." In *The Great Depression Revisited,* edited by H. Van der Wee, pp. 145–81. The Hague: Montinus Nijhoff.
Friedman, M., and Schwartz, A. J. 1963. *A Monetary History of the United States, 1867–1960.* Princeton: Princeton University Press.
Gilbert, B. B. 1970. *British Social Policy, 1914–1939.* London: Batsford.
Hawtrey, R. G. 1923. *Monetary Reconstruction.* London: Longmans.
  1938. *A Century of Bank Rate.* London: Longmans.
Howson, S. 1973. " 'A dear money man'? Keynes on Monetary Policy, 1920." *Economic Journal* 83:456–64.
  1974. "The Origins of Dear Money, 1919–20." *Economic History Review* (Second Series) 27:88–107.
  1975. *Domestic Monetary Management in Britain, 1919–38.* Cambridge University press.
  and Winch A. 1977. *The Economic Advisory Council, 1930–1939: A Study of Economic Advice during Depression and Recovery.* Cambridge Univerisity Press.

International Monetary Fund (IMF). 1977. *Annual Report*. Washington.

Kindleberger, C. P. 1970. *Power and Money: The Economics of International Politics and the Politics of International Economics*. London: Macmillan.

 1973. *The World in Depression, 1929–1939*. London: Allen Lane.

 1978. *Manias, Panics, and Crashes: A History of Financial Crises*. New York: Basic Books.

Lary, H. G., et al. 1943. *The United States in the World Economy: The International Transactions of the United States during the Interwar Period*. Washington, D.C.: U.S. Department of Commerce.

League of Nations. 1946. *The Course and Control of Inflation: A Review of Experience in Europe after World War I*. New York.

Maddison, A. 1962. "Growth and Fluctuations in the World Economy 1870–1960" *Banca Nazionale del Lavoro Quarterly Review* No. 61, pp. 127–95.

 1977. "Phases of Capitalist Development." *Banca Nazionale del Lavoro Quarterly Review* No. 121, pp. 103–38.

Maier, C. S. 1975. *Recasting Bourgeois Europe: Stabilization in France, Germany and Italy in the Decade after World War I*. Princeton: Princeton University Press.

Mayer, T. 1978. "Money and the Great Depression: A Critique of Professor Temin's Thesis." *Exploration in Economic History* 15:127–45.

Moggridge, D. E. 1970. "The 1931 Crisis: A New View." *The Banker* 120 (No. 534):832–40.

 1972. *British Monetary Policy, 1924–1931: The Norman Conquest of 4.86*. Cambridge University Press.

Morgan, E. V. 1951. *Studies in British Financial Policy 1914–1925*. London: Macmillan.

Palyi, M. 1972. *The Twilight of Gold, 1914–1936: Myths and Realities*. Chicago: Regnery.

Pigou, A. C. 1947. *Aspects of English Economic History 1918–1925*. London: Macmillan.

Pressnell, L. S. 1978. "1925: The Burden of Sterling." *Economic History Review* (Second Series) 31:67–88.

Rowland, B. M., editor. 1976. *Balance of Power or Hegemony: The Interwar Monetary System*. New York: New York University Press.

Royal Institute of International Affairs (RIIA). 1937. *The Problem of International Investment*. London: Oxford University Press.

Safarian, A. E. 1959. *The Canadian Economy in the Great Depression*. Toronto: University of Toronto Press.

Sayers, R. S. 1976. *The Bank of England, 1891–1944* (3 vols). Cambridge University Press.

Schedvin, C. B. 1970. *Australia and the Great Depression: A Study of Economic Development and Policy in the 1920s and 1930s*. Sydney: Sydney University Press.

Schuker, S. A. 1976. *The End of French Predominance in Europe: The Financial Crisis of 1924 and the Adoption of the Dawes Plan*. Chapel Hill: University of North Carolina Press.

Strange, S. 1971. *Sterling and British Policy: A Political Study of an International Currency in Decline*. London: Oxford University Press.

Temin, P. 1976. *Did Monetary Forces Cause the Great Depression?* New York: W. W. Norton.

Tomlinson, B. R. 1979. "Britain and the Indian Currency Crisis, 1930–32." *Economic History Review* (Second Series) 32:88–99.
United States Department of Commerce. 1975. *Historical Statistics of the United States: Colonial Times to 1970* (2 vols). Washington, D.C.: Bureau of the Census.
Wicker, E. R. 1967. *Federal Reserve Monetary Policy 1917–1933.* New York: Random House.
Williams, D. 1963a. "London and the 1931 Financial Crisis." *Economic History Review* (Second Series) 15:513–28.
    1963b. "The 1931 Financial Crisis." *Yorkshire Bulletin of Economic and Social Research* 15:92–110.
Wolfe, M. 1951. *The French Franc between the Wars.* New York: Columbia University Press.

Comment

EDUARD MÄRZ

Contrary perhaps to Moggridge, I believe that the lender of last resort is as common in European financial history as the deus ex machina in the Greek tragedy. He differs, however, from the Greek gods, who are introduced to straighten out the tangled skein of the tragedy, in two important respects: First, the lender of last resort is a sort of protean being who appears in strikingly different guises – in the shape of the central bank of a country, or as a government agency like the treasury, sometimes as a consortium of banks, and not infrequently as an international body or group of bodies. Second, the lender of last resort, in contrast to the Greek gods, does not always succeed in putting matters right again, but leaves behind a rather messy and sometimes even ominous situation. Moggridge is probably right in implying that the lender-of-last-resort strategems worked out in the early twenties were in no way adequate to the multidimensional problems they were supposed to deal with.

There is, however, one aspect of the lender-of-last-resort phenomenon that is only fleetingly referred to in Kindleberger's book and, if I am not mistaken, is completely ignored in Moggridge's chapter. I have in mind the simple fact that the lender of last resort is not an ethereal or neutral agency, divorced from any sectional or class interest, but as a rule comes up with solutions beneficial to certain privileged groups or institutions of society. If rescue operations are undertaken aimed at bailing out a certain country or group of countries, conditions are usually imposed that have a distinctly conservative bias. This, at least, is the impression one gains if one takes a closer look at the rescue operations in central Europe, to which I now turn.

I. The crash of 1873

The panic of 1873, which ushered in a long drawn-out depression in central Europe, shattered mass confidence in the ideological and institutional foundations of Western capitalism. A convincing case can be made, I believe, that the specters of chauvinism, militarism, and fascism that came to haunt Europe in the first half of this century had their roots in the first spectacular breakdown of the capitalist order of things.

The speculative mania that had taken possession of the great financial centers of central Europe in the early 1870s collapsed in May 1873 soon after the opening of the world exhibition in Vienna. The crash of 1873 had been preceded by a number of storm signals, especially by a noticeable weakening of the long upswing in the previous year, but the speculative fever had in characteristic fashion completely divorced itself from the underlying economic reality and drew its nourishment in the last stages of the mania from rumors, slogans, and illusionary hopes. The crash was by far the heaviest that had been experienced in this part of the world, involving almost the entire business community and vast strata of the population. It is obvious, therefore, that the Austrian government was compelled almost from the outset to organize rescue operations. (I shall from now on restrict my remarks to the Austrian scene of the financial debacle.)

Although the government acted promptly, it left the working out of a plan and its subsequent execution to a consortium of eminent banking houses headed by the central-bank authorities. The only positive action taken by the government itself was the suspension of the Banking Act of 1862. This action was meant to assist the mobilization of central-bank funds in case a liquidity shortage should make itself felt. To the suprise of some contemporary observers, no such shortage occurred, despite the severity of the financial crisis. Again, the activities of the rescue committee (Aushilfs-Comité) were surprisingly limited, if one considers the swelling number of insolvencies and bankruptcies that involved even some of the oldest Viennese banking houses. At the end of the year the committee reported that its total turnover amounted to no more than 88 million gulden, the greater part of which had been used for advances on securities and for discounting short-term commercial paper (88 million was but a tiny fraction of the astronomical losses endured by the Viennese stock market and its main protagonists in the year 1873).

The government emerged from its self-imposed inactivity only a half year after the great crash. The reasons for its sudden intervention are indeed illuminating. On November 2 it became known that one of the mightiest bastions of Austrian capitalism, the Bodencredit-Anstalt, the mortgage bonds of which had the same standing abroad as Austrian treasury certificates, was facing imminent collapse as a result of its risky stock-exchange operations. The shutdown of such an illustrious institution, whose board of directors was composed of some of the best-known public figures, had to be prevented at all cost, because nobody could foresee the economic and political consequences of a disaster of this dimension. Thus the government approached the banking house of Rothschild, its close ally, the renowned Creditanstalt, and two other financially solvent houses to bail out the endangered Bodencredit-Anstalt by making use of the discount facilities of the central bank. In Solow's words, the situation was ripe for the emergence of a club of insiders, oldtimers, gentlemen, and for the exclusion of newcomers and unknowns. The government, whose leading figures belonged to the bourgeois-liberal party of Austria, had at first done little to stem the rising tide of business failures, convinced no doubt that every financial crisis ought to be permitted to run its course and to cleanse thereby the economy of all its morbid excrescences. This complacent philosophy had to be abandoned when the crisis took an unexpected turn and threatened to sweep away one of the pillars of the financial establishment. The collapse of the Bodencredit-Anstalt was prevented by the united efforts of the mightiest of the mighty, the central bank, the Rothschilds, and the Creditanstalt, but the cumulative forces of deflation were otherwise allowed to wreak havoc almost unchecked, ushering in thereby a period of extreme entrepreneurial caution and of more than the ordinary aversion of banking toward new and untried business ventures. The financial-instability hypothesis of Minsky can, perhaps, be successfully tested when applied to the central European scene in 1873 and the subsequent depression period.

II. Financial crises and stabilization, 1922–4

My thesis that the lender-of-last-resort concept becomes operative only under certain conditions, when social interests are at stake that are of special force and dominance, holds true for the national as well as the international stage. This can be demonstrated by the example of the international financial rescue operations of the twenties and the early thirties. Again, I shall confine myself to the Austrian scene.

The year 1920–1 was marked in Austria by an acceleration of the postwar inflation, but contrary to western European experience, unemployment was light, and industrial activity was on the rise because of easier access to raw materials and export markets. Throughout the early years of the republic, however, the balance-of-payments deficit proved intractable and provoked toward the end of 1922 the intervention of the major powers of the League of

Nations with the intent of providing sufficient credit until measures could take hold to balance the budget and to stop the continuous hemorrhage of gold and foreign exchange.

Because Kindleberger might object that an international stabilization scheme is not a lender-of-last-resort operation, I shall skip the so-called Geneva reform except for saying that it provided foreign credit at a stiff interest rate for the sole purpose of covering the budget deficit and for enabling the Austrian government to take remedial measures until a new equilibrium position could be found. It was tacitly assumed that "sound" fiscal policies would eventually restore the balance of foreign accounts. It should also be noted that the soundness of the fiscal policy to be adopted by the Austrian government was to be determined by a foreign commissioner appointed by the great powers that guaranteed the international loan. It is hardly surprising that the bulk of the loan was earmarked for purely financial purposes and released in piecemeal fashion with the explicit approval of the commissioner. A quarter century later, another international stabilization scheme, known under the name of Marshall Plan, put the emphasis on investment rather than on budgetary requirements and thus created a suitable foundation for the reconstruction of the economy and its remarkable recovery after the depression of the thirties and the ravages of World War II.

In the wake of the stabilization scheme of 1922, a boom at the Viennese stock exchange got under way whose only raison d'être was the commonly held belief that Austrian stock was strikingly undervalued as a result of the war and postwar inflation. The boom was bound to sputter out soon, for it lacked any conceivable material basis. Yet its collapse in the spring of 1924 was hastened by the misconceived bear speculation against the French franc in which almost the entire Austrian banking community participated. This episode was the opening shot of a series of bank failures culminating in the breakdown of the Creditanstalt in the spring of 1931.

The ill-fated speculation against the franc resulted in a severe drain of foreign exchange. Between March and July 1924 the Austrian national bank lost about one-third of its gold and foreign-exchange reserves; during the same time its bill portfolio increased almost threefold, and the presumption was that the greater part of the new bill material resulted from the urgent financial needs of the anti-franc speculation. In this predicament the national bank turned to the commissioner, who had up to that moment released hard currency for no other purpose than covering the budget deficit. The commissioner complied with the request, thereby putting at the disposal of the banking community considerable amounts of currency via the intermediary services of the bank. This episode affords us another glimpse into lender-of-last-resort mentality. The commissioner, who had steadfastly declined to earmark parts of the Geneva loan for investment purposes, had no hesitation to use these moneys in order to rescue drowning financial institutions that could exercise some political pull.

III. The crash of the Creditanstalt, 1931

I now turn to the third act of the tragedy, the crash of the famous Creditanstalt, which set into motion a chain reaction leading to the depreciation of the pound sterling in the fall of 1931. The Creditanstalt was one of the oldest credit-mobilier-type institutes in Europe, and it maintained from the very start the closest ties to the house of Rothschild. It is hardly necessary to mention that the credit-mobilier type of banking implies a heavy and enduring commitment to the promotion of industry through stock ownership and long-term credit operations. The Creditanstalt emerged from World War I in a greatly weakened position, because it had to relinquish a number of industrial holdings in the so-called succession states that had formed part of the Habsburg Empire prior to World War I. Yet very early in its postwar career the Creditanstalt leadership took a decision of the greatest consequence, namely, to carry on its operations on pretty much the same scale as before: American capitalists and to a lesser extent western European capitalists acquired substantial minority holdings in the Creditanstalt; moreover, in the course of the twenties, the bank borrowed increasing amounts of hard currency from Western banking houses for the purpose of channeling it into its eastern and southeastern European industrial dependencies. As time wore on, the prospects of recalling those funds at short notice became more and more unlikely.

The definitive story of the collapse of the Creditanstalt has not yet been written. We owe, however, to Walter Federn, a contemporary economic journalist of great eminence, several penetrating short studies on the financial crisis of 1931. After analyzing the erroneous and sometimes even frivolous decisions of the leading personalities of the Creditanstalt, he raises the question why these men could indulge in policies that were bound to lead them ever closer to the abyss. His answer is that they were certain that in a time of crisis they could count on help from above (Federn, 1932:415). And, indeed, when the moment of truth arrived, massive financial aid was soon forthcoming. Again, we cannot help noting that the lender of last resort is an "insurance scheme" of remarkable selectivity, accessible only to those whose interests are deemed more equal than others.

The Creditanstalt was by far more equal than other Austrian banking houses. Its volume of business in the critical year 1931 approximately equaled total public expenditures. It was multinational in its capital structure as well as in its banking activities. When it had to disclose enormous losses on May 14, 1931, an immediate run set in that could be staved off only by taking recourse to the lending facilities of the national bank. Because foreign creditors, too, began to withdraw their deposits, the crisis soon threatened to affect the precarious balance-of-payments position of Austria. The government faced a real dilemma. It could refuse to come to the rescue of the Creditanstalt and thereby maintain its imperiled balance on foreign account. The consequences of a refusal of help could, however, be formidable, for the openly declared bankruptcy of Austria's foremost bank was sure to be followed by numerous business failures and by a steep rise in the number of unemployed. Moreover, because the Creditanstalt counted among its foreign creditors some of the leading Western banking houses, such as the London house of Rothschild and the Chase National Bank of New York, a negative attitude on the part of the government could jeopardize future lending operations abroad that in view of Austria's shaky financial condition would have to be undertaken sooner or later, no matter whether or not the government intervened in the present crisis. On the other hand, if the government assumed the burden of salvaging the Creditanstalt, a burden the real size of which could hardly be assessed on the basis of the first disclosures of the bank, it exposed itself to an immediate colossal drain of its resources.

From the incomplete evidence at my disposal I can only conclude that the pressure, political and otherwise, of foreign creditors was such that after some initial hesitation the government decided to assume full responsibility for the liabilities, both domestic and foreign, of the Creditanstalt. It was aided in this decision by the Bank of England, which advanced, on short notice, a moderate amount of sterling to bolster the weakened position of Austria's central bank, whereas the French withheld even a modicum of help, in protest against the abortive custom-union negotiations between Germany and Austria. The reconstruction of the Creditanstalt proved a formidable task. In the end, the government emerged as the majority stockholder of the bank, and foreign banking interests partook of the rest of the shares. Almost all foreign assets of the bank had to be transferred into foreign hands. The remaining liabilities were paid off in installments that were pared down in the succeeding years. A stabilization scheme, the so-called Lausanne loan, which was closely modeled on its better-known predecessor, the Geneva reform loan, topped off the reconstruction efforts of the government.

IV. Conclusion

Lender-of-last-resort operations and stabilization schemes cannot be sorted out very neatly in the instances I have discussed at some length. Whenever large-scale loan operations were involved, they were proffered at what may be called penalty rates. Kindleberger is quite right in stressing in his book (p.

225) that the conditions imposed were such as to make sure that the creditor nations could receive in due course full interest and amortization payments. Moggridge implies that the measures taken in the twenties and thirties were hardly adequate considering the gravity of the situation. I would add that neither on the grounds of the scale of operations nor on those of "conditionality" were they designed to benefit primarily the receiving countries. One may go even further and maintain that some of the conditions attached to the various rescue schemes were liable to prolong the financial stress rather than to shorten it. And this may well apply, as Kindleberger intimates, to most of the present IMF operations. In the end, I refer, once again, to a stabilization scheme that was exclusively determined by the needs of the receiving nations and achieved its policy objectives beyond all hopes entertained at the time of its conception: I mean, of course, the Marshall Plan.

References

Bennett, E. W. 1962. *Germany and the Diplomacy of the Financial Crisis, 1931.* Cambridge, Mass.: Harvard University Press.
Born, K. E. 1967. *Die Deutsche Bankenkrise 1931.* München Piper.
Federn, W. 1925. "Die Kreditpolitik der Wiener Banken," In: *Geldentwertung und Stabilisierung in ihren Einflüssen auf die soziale Entwicklung in Österreich,* edited by J. Bunzel, pp. 54–74. München: Duncker & Humblot.
   1932. "Der Zusammenbruch de österreichischen Kreditanstalt." *Archiv für Sozialwissenschaft und Sozialpolitik* 67:403–35.
Kamitz, R. 1949. "Die österreicheische Geld- und Währungspolitik von 1848–1948." *Hundert Jahre Oesterreichischer Wirtschaftsentwicklung 1848–1948,* edited by H. Mayer, pp. 127–221. Wien: Springer-Verlag.
Kienböck, V. 1925. *Das österreichische Sanierungswerk.* Stuttgart: Ferdinand Enke.
März, E. 1968. *Oesterreichische Industrie- und Bankpolitik in der Zeit Franz Josephs I.* Wien: Europa Verlag.
   and Socher, K. 1973. "Währung und Banken in Cisleithanien." In: *Die Habsburgermonarchie 1848–1918, Die wirtschaftliche Entwicklung,* edited by A. Brusatti, pp. 323–68. Wien: Verlag der österreichischen Akademie der Wissenschaften.
Neuwirth, J. 1874. *Bank and Vuluta in Österreich, Vol. II: Die Spekulationskrisis von 1873.* Leipzig.
Pietri, N. 1970. *La Société des Nations et la reconstruction financière de l'Autriche.* New York: Carnegie Center for International Peace.
Rist, C. 1931. "Bericht über eine Mission in Wien, 31. Mai bis 24 Juni." *Archives économiques et financières* F 30/1847.
Schäffle, A. 1886. "Der 'grosse Börsenkrach' des Jahres 1873." In *Gesammelte Aufsätze, Band II,* pp. 67–131. Tübingen: Verlag der H. Laupp'schen Buchhandlung.

Stiefel, D. 1979. "The crisis of the Creditanstalt." Presented at the symposium "International Business and Central Europe, 1919–39," University of East Anglia.

van Walré de Bordes, J. 1924. *The Austrian Crown. Its Depreciation and Stabilization.* London: P. S. King.

8. Central banks and foreign-exchange crises today

PAUL COULBOIS

I. Introduction

Definitions. A foreign-exchange crisis may be defined as a period when the two following developments occur at the same time: (1) Expectations of a change in parity (if any) or in the spot exchange rate give rise to short-term capital flows, which may be called speculation in the broadest sense of the word (i.e., including pure speculation, leads and lags, or hedging). (2) One central bank (at least) believes that the market expectations are wrong and takes steps to keep the exchange rate within the fluctuation margins (under a regime of parities) or to control its evolution (when the currency is allowed to float). Whether this conviction is well- or ill-founded does not matter in the short run: As soon as a central bank supports the rate of its own currency against a speculative run, it has to face the situation described by the title of this chapter, whatever could be the final outcome of its policy.

As for the word *today*, I shall use it to mean since October 1964, the date at which began "the travail of the sterling," as Solomon (1977:86) put it, until the end of 1978. This period encompasses both adjustable parity and floating-rate regimes, but the importance of this change must not be over-estimated. The world has not suddenly shifted from one polar regime to the other. Even under the Bretton-Woods agreement some currencies have been floating, before and after 15 August 1971; fixed parities were in fact adjustable; floating is never clean, but dirty, controlled, or managed.

From the standpoint of a central bank facing a foreign-exchange crisis, only one significant difference appears between the two regimes: Floating gives the central bank more freedom of action, both for its internal monetary policy and for its interventions in the foreign-exchange market. Yet even this freedom has its limits, because a central bank cannot at the same time choose the exchange rate of its own currency and the degree of liquidity of the national banking system. "The danger to the stability of the floating-rate system," as Volcker (1977:34) said, "seems to me to lie in the presumption that it promises more autonomy than it can really deliver in an integrated world." The experience of Germany and Switzerland in 1978 is a case in point.

As the asset-market theory of foreign exchange shows, floating may bring about exchange-rate instability, even in a world of perfect markets. Grubel (1977b:135) contended that in such an ideal situation "exchange-rates must exhibit some variance" and that therefore "there exists the opportunity for governments to reduce this variance through stabilization policy," in order to get welfare gains. As to interventions in the foreign-exchange market, Grubel added that there can be no objection to a policy that aims at "leaning against the wind."

For a crisis period, Grubel's statement does not go far enough. Market imperfections in this case are of paramount importance, and a crisis is, by nature, a short-run phenomenon. Exchange rates must be viewed "as being determined entirely in the asset market" (Dornbusch, 1977b:128), whereas the purchasing-power parity obtains but in the long run. Practically, this means that a central bank facing a crisis may judge that the trend to which speculation gives rise, in the foreign-exchange market, is not in accordance with the fundamentals. Therefore, its intervention must go further than merely leaning against the wind.

In such circumstances it would not be advisable to infer the behavior of a central bank from its past policy, as it can be summarized in a so-called reaction function. History never repeats itself; the parameters in the reaction function are not stable, and the form of the function itself can be altered. Relationships established on the basis of previous-period policy are of little avail for present action. What is needed is some general theory of official counterspeculation, which cannot be built into a formal model with fixed coefficients, at least in the present state of our knowledge.

Alternative theories. The starting point of the theoretical thought in this field goes back as far as 55 years, with the proposals of Keynes in *A Tract on Monetary Reform* (1923), reformulated in *A Treatise on Money* (1930: Volume II, p. 327): "I would propose, therefore, to furnish Central Banks with a trident for the control of the rate of short-term foreign lending – their bank-rate, their forward-exchange rate, and their buying and selling rates for gold." Taking into account what has happened since 1930, the trident consists of the following: domestic monetary policy and interventions in the foreign-exchange market, both spot and forward. The following sections will indicate how these three instruments may be used today by a central bank facing a foreign-exchange crisis.

Of course, the three components of Keynes's trident are interdependent: The forward rate of one currency against another is the algebraic sum of the spot rate and the forward premium (discount), the latter being determined by the interest differential (ID) between these two currencies. This is the interest-parity theory (IPT), which may be interpreted in two ways.

The first view may be called, following Prissert (1972a, 1972b), the academic theory. It asserts (at least implicitly) that the spot rate and the forward rate are determined in two distinct markets, connected by the pure covered arbitrage function, the characteristics of which are such that the IPT is but a tendency.

For various reasons that are too well known to be restated here, pure arbitrage does not necessarily ensure a complete and permanent equality between the exchange agio (swap rate) and the ID. The forward rate is determined by the excess demand of forward contracts, and Dornbusch (1977b:129), for instance, assumes that "the forward rate is set by speculators." Likewise, a change in interest rates does not necessarily affect the exchange agio. Thus, intrinsic premiums (discounts) may appear and give rise to covered interest arbitrage, which tends to bring about a forward exchange rate close to, but not identical with, the rate corresponding to the ID. To quote Grubel (1966, 1977a:250–7), "inspection of actual data on covered arbitrage margin reveals that it is very rarely zero." This "observed persistence . . . has led to the development of the so-called modern theory of forward exchange," which explains why under "normal" conditions "the equilibrium forward exchange rate is not equal to the parity forward rate."

This first line of argument has an important consequence as regards the policy of a central bank having to fight a speculative run. By raising the rates of interest and/or by intervening in the forward exchange market, the central bank is able to have an intrinsic premium quoted on the national currency, which is then bought spot and sold forward by arbitrageurs. These covered arbitrages help the central bank support its own currency in the spot foreign-exchange market.

The second view may be called the cambist theory, after Spraos (1972:186). It stems from the observation of how foreign-exchange dealers (cambists) behave in practice. Put in a nutshell, the argument runs this way. When a speculator wants to sell one currency forward against another (and the same applies to every outright forward transaction), he has to deal with a bank. Assuming that the bank does not want to keep an open exchange position (if it wants to, it need not wait for a client's order), it has to cover itself in the interbank market, either spot or forward.

To close its position by an outright forward deal, the bank must find another one willing to act as a counterpart. This possibility cannot be ruled out (although outright forward transactions between banks are rather unusual, at least in Europe), but the argument along this line cannot proceed vary far. In a crisis situation, there is a one-way market, and forward counterparts are impossible to get. In "normal" times, the unwinding of clients' outright forward orders in the interbank outright forward market requires nothing less than general equilibrium in the forward market at the current rate, a dubious assumption indeed.

In practice, banks cover their clients' forward orders in the spot market. But because the forward contract will be unwound only on maturity, spot covering requires that the bank borrow the currency that the client sells forward and lend the currency he buys. In so doing, commercial banks act "like" the arbitrageurs depicted by the academic theory, but there is a fundamental difference. They set the forward rate by adding (substracting) to the current spot rate a premium (discount) computed on the basis of the ID between the relevant money and/or Euro-money markets. No intrinsic premium (discount) appears, and the IPT always obtains (Coulbois, 1979:Section 5.2; Coulbois and Prissert, 1974; Prissert, 1972c, 1977).

From the standpoint of a central bank having to face an exchange crisis, this argument has the following consequence: As the forward exchange rate is always at the level corresponding to the differential between the relevant interest rates, a positive covered arbitrage margin does not exist; therefore the central bank cannot rely on covered arbitrages to help it get the effect it is looking for in the spot exchange market.

The differences between these two interpretations of the IPT may not be as simple as they appear in such a short summary. During the colloquium on forward exchange held in Paris in 1972 (Coulbois, 1972), Spraos, Aliber, and some others strongly advocated the same thesis as that of Grubel, quoted earlier from his textbook of 1976, but already published in 1966. More recently, Schep and Smits (1976:483) contended that the cambist theory was "no more than a special case of the simplified version of the IPT" and opposed to it an "extended version of the IPT," which is exactly what Grubel calls the "modern" theory.

Nevertheless, the two interpretations have drawn nearer to each other in the past few years. After the pioneering article by Aliber (1973), Frenkel and Levich (1975, 1977) have shown that "unexploited profit opportunities for arbitrage" (intrinsic premiums or discounts) almost disappear when the computation of the ID satisfies the comparability criterion and when transactions costs are properly taken into account. In other words, the IPT always obtains because the relevant markets are highly efficient as regards the arbitrage activity.[1]

No doubt this view is more in accordance with what may be observed when looking at the practical working of the foreign-exchange market.[2] Nevertheless it leaves me unsatisfied for two reasons.

First, when remembering how foreign-exchange dealers actually quote forward rates (as previously explained), I cannot help thinking that the work by Frenkel and Levich demonstrates what is only a tautology. They write in a footnote to their 1977 paper (p. 1216): "There is some evidence that banks use the Euro-currency interest rates in making their quotations of the forward exchange rate. To this extent the interest-parity relation in the Euro-market will be extremely robust."

The same point is made by McKinnon (1977:21), who says he is indebted for it to "two foreign-exchange traders." After having made reference to "the standard model of covered interest arbitrage," McKinnon writes: "The real story may be simpler. It seems to be common knowledge that foreign-exchange traders actually use the Euro interest-rate quotations (LIBOR) on currencies to determine their forward bid offer quotations."

The words "some evidence" and "common knowledge" are cautious ways of saying that forward quotations are computed by dealers on the basis of the relevant ID. The IPT relation is "extremely robust" or "simpler" than the standard model asserts, not because of arbitrageurs' intervention but merely because dealers automatically determine the swap rate according to the interest rates that prevail in the money markets in which they are actually dealing. Calling this sort of "mechanics" an arbitrage is misleading: Arbitrageurs' profit is the positive covered arbitrage margin; cambists' profits stem from the bid–ask spread.

Second, even in efficient markets it may happen that the premium (discount) expressed in "points" does not correspond to the ID expressed in percent per annum. This gap may be due to imperfect information or lagged reaction, but it will not be closed by "standard" covered arbitrage. Actually, the dealer who takes notice of this gap will simply make an arbitrage between the deposit market and the swap market, an operation that is not the same as covered interest arbitrage because it does not imply any spot exchange transaction.

To sum up, acknowledging that unexploited profit opportunities for arbitrage do not exist (contrary to what the "modern" IPT asserts) does not allow one to contend that academic and cambist theories amount to the same thing. I remain convinced that the cambist view is more suitable than the academic one (even in its "new modern" form), both for explaining how the foreign-exchange market works and for studying how central banks can cope with foreign-exchange crises.

II. Domestic monetary policy

The naive view. Short-term capital flows giving rise to a foreign-exchange crisis may run for or against a given currency. I shall put the main emphasis on the second case (bear speculation), saying only a few words on the first one at the end of the present section.

The first reaction of a central bank, the money of which is sold in a one-way market, is twofold: It raises its interest rates and supports the spot exchange rate. Although both measures are used simultaneously most of the time, the second one will be dealt with in the following section.

The more available the national currency is, the easier the speculation will be. As Sohmen (1969:74) wittily put it: "Everybody with money in the bank or under his mattress is a potential currency speculator, and those without can borrow some." Therefore, the task of a central bank in a crisis period is to make its own currency more difficult and more costly to get.

Support intervention in the spot market may have this effect, as it reduces the amount of high-powered money. Nevertheless, this relation cannot be totally relied on, especially in so-called overdraft economies, where enterprises have unused lines of credit and the Treasury may float more securities within the banking system, whereas banks can get easy refinancing from the central bank. These offsetting reactions call for a central bank to pursue a deliberate policy designed to raise interest rates.[3] Some people view this policy as aiming at attracting foreign capital flows, but such a view must be considered a naive one.

Every time a foreign-exchange crisis affects a currency, expectations about it are bearish, which precludes uncovered inward arbitrage.[4] The only consequence that an interest-rate increase may have is to bring about inward covered arbitrages. But observation shows that dealers immediately adjust the premium they quote on foreign currencies to the relevant ID (i.e., the difference between the rate on the domestic money market for the national currency and the rates on the Eurocurrency markets for other monies). (See the most recent example of a practitioner's view in the report of Kubarych 1978:45.)

Consequently, covered arbitrage is not profitable, except when arbitrageurs liquidate a given asset (e.g., Treasury bills) in one currency, switch the proceeds to another currency, and invest them in a different kind of asset (e.g., time deposit). Because of the great diversity of financial assets in modern economies, such an operation may yield a positive covered margin, but it cannot be considered as equilibrating the foreign-exchange market, contrary to what the academic theory asserts, precisely because it is not determined by the interest rates that banks use to compute premiums (discounts).

Covered arbitrage has no effect. Furthermore, even if inward covered arbitrage occurs, the cambist analysis shows that it cannot support the spot exchange rate. Although this statement may appear at variance with the general theory of market adjustment, its demonstration is straightforward.

Let us assume, for instance, that there is a speculation against the French franc (FF). The Banque de France raises the whole structure of short-term interest rates, which will bring about inward covered arbitrage, coming, say, from the Deutsche Mark (DM).[5] Then a commercial bank may receive from some nonbanks (NB) the following arbitrage order: NB buy FF against DM spot and, at the same time, sell FF against DM forward. How will the bank deal with the forward part of the covered arbitrage order?

It may try to marry this forward operation to another one running the other way round, but this attempt will come to naught. As the FF is attacked, a bull speculator cannot be found,[6] and the bank has to cover itself in the spot market. Consequently, it sells FF against DM spot, and in so doing it exactly offsets the spot buying of the covered arbitrageur. Nothing happens in the spot exchange market.

Money markets for FF and DM remain also unaffected. NB have liquidated assets in DM to buy FF spot, whereas the bank invests the DM it has bought spot, so that the amount of loanable funds in DM remains unchanged. Likewise, whereas NB invest in the FF money market, the bank has to draw on this same market to pay for the DM it buys. Therefore, interest rates on FF and DM stay the same as previously, and so does the ID.

The same conclusion applies to the forward rate, because neither the spot rate nor the ID has changed. Covered interest arbitrage has no effect on the three relevant variables, contrary to the academic argument.

What is, then, the motive for raising domestic interest rates as a defensive step against a bear speculation? It is simply that such a rise broadens the ID and makes speculation more costly. Those who speculate in the spot market have to borrow FF at a higher cost (or incur a higher opportunity cost); those who act in the forward market must pay larger premiums on foreign currencies. It may even happen that such a rise brings about some purchases of FF, as NB shift their financing of international transactions away from the FF (one form of leads and lags) or sell foreign currencies forward to take advantage of a large premium.

Of course, raising interest rates to support the national currency in the spot market has its drawbacks. "Dear money" may hinder economic activity, and highly unfavorable expectations require an interest-rate level that may appear impracticable.

However, this second argument loses some of its strength in a floating-rate regime, as exchange-rate adjustments no longer proceed in an abrupt way. A 10% devaluation during a weekend gave the speculator who had taken a short position on Friday a profit of 3,600% per year, which could not be reduced to zero by an increase in the ID; a decline of 1% within a month is equivalent to a profit of 12% per year, a magnitude not so unrealistic for an ID.[7]

Two-tier money markets. Direct controls may be used against speculation. Among them, an interesting measure is to forbid residents to lend domestic currency to nonresidents. Such a regulation is applied in the United Kingdom and in France, with different modalities (Cachin, 1978). The French regulation, which is the more restrictive, has the following consequences: (1) A forward sale of FF by a nonresident obliges the foreign bank that has to carry out the transaction to borrow FF on the only market available to it (i.e., the Eurofranc market). Every time a bear speculation occurs against the FF, rates in the Eurofranc market rise, all the more because of the narrowness of this market.[8] Short positions in FF become more costly, which amounts to a "cost deterrent," as Prissert (1978) put it, for sales of FF by nonresidents, both spot and forward. (2) Yet such a consequence does not apply to residents, whose short positions cost only the ID between domestic and foreign rates of interest. To suppress this loophole (which is important for the determination of national leads and lags) without further exchange controls, two devices may be used: In the United Kingdom, banks have to keep their forward sales of domestic currency within the limits of their purchases. In France, some practitioners have suggested a two-tier domestic money market: One would work only for ordinary cash requirements from commercial banks; the other would apply to the demand for FF resulting from the spot covering of forward purchases of foreign currencies by residents.

The choice between these devices is open to discussion. The French solution, as currently applied, has two drawbacks: It does not affect domestic leads and lags, and it gives rise to the quotation of two different forward rates for the FF. The English solution avoids both of these inconveniences. A one-way market against the sterling obliges English banks to swap in Euro-sterling, so that domestic speculation as well as foreign becomes more expensive; the forward rate of sterling is unique. Consequently, the defense of the sterling spot rate is easier, and market distortions do not appear.

Besides, as J. F. Lepetit contends (Coulbois, 1979:Sections 6.121 to 6.124), present French regulation may be considered as giving some facilities to foreign speculation against the FF. He asserts that FF are made available in the Eurofranc market by the larger part of French exports invoiced in FF (almost two-thirds as against less than one-third for imports).

A final remark is in order. When a country is not inclined to use direct controls (Germany, for instance), or when its money is the vehicle currency for a large part of international transactions (United States), money markets cannot be split into two parts. There is no doubt that foreign dollar balances are so extensive that interest rates in the Eurodollar market depend more on the Fed's policy than on the foreign dollar borrowings due to speculation against the dollar. When a dollar crisis occurs, the U.S. monetary authorities must accept a dearer dollar within their own country.

Crisis induced by bull speculation. When a currency is massively bought in the exchange market, one may dispute whether the word *crisis* is appropriate. Emminger (1977) has laid stress on the dilemma Western Germany was facing until 1973: either letting the DM appreciate, to the detriment of German producers' competitivity, or buying foreign currencies spot, thereby creating an excess supply of domestic high-powered money. He considered the advent of floating in March 1973 "a fundamental turning point in German as well as international monetary policy." Since then, the Bundesbank is no longer "obliged" to purchase dollars, so that Germany has been "able to cut itself loose from the international inflation convoy."

The issue may not be that simple. In a fixed-exchange-rate system, as Holtrop (1972:365) has stressed, the purchase of foreign currencies by the central bank does not necessarily bring about a rise in the domestic income stream. It does so when a surplus arises on current account, but this effect is "less sure" when the surplus comes from "an accumulation of short term capital," which is precisely what happens as a consequence of a bull speculation. Prissert (1972c:302) is more precise on the point: "The real demand for goods and services will rise only to the extent that there exists a potential demand for liquidity and credit, which was previously reined in by a somewhat restrictive monetary policy and which can henceforth be satisfied at a lower price, thanks to central bank creating money as a counterpart of capital imports."

The compensation thesis (*vide supra*) may reinforce this assertion. In addition, the central bank may apply a sterilization policy, the efficacy of which, however, is disputed among authors. Be that as it may, one point must never be forgotten: Even if the sterilization policy could be perfect, it would affect only the liquidity of the banking system. The counterpart of capital imports in domestic money remains in every case at the command of the nonbank operator who has initiated it.

The injection of this purchasing power "into the income stream," to quote Holtrop again, depends on the following factors: (1) When initiated by a resident borrowing abroad because of an advantageous ID, capital imports give rise to a real expenditure only if they are not used to repay outstanding bank loans. (2) When initiated by a nonresident who is pure speculator, a capital import does not lead to an increase in the income stream if the proceeds are kept in an idle account. The rise in the quantity of money is then offset by a decrease in the income velocity of money.

The creation of the European Monetary System (EMS) has given rise to new discussions about inflationary consequences in Germany of spot interventions by the Bundesbank to support, when necessary, the other currencies belonging to the system. It seems that the Bundesbank, after having been opposed to the EMS because of its possible inflationary effects on the German economy, eventually gave in to Bonn pressures, not only for superordinate political reasons but also, perhaps, because some came to think that a little monetary impulse could help economic recovery.[9]

So much for what might be called "a reverse crisis," the effects of which are not symmetrical to those of a crisis proper (a situation faced by central banks when speculation is of the bearish type). But in both cases the additional degree of freedom that floating exchange rates give the central bank must not be overestimated. There is always some conflict between domestic monetary policy and spot intervention in the foreign-exchange market.

III. Spot intervention in the foreign-exchange market

Tactical considerations. A central bank that supports the spot exchange rate of its own currency aims at avoiding the so-called bandwagon effect, which may initiate a vicious circle. In a fixed-exchange-rate system, some authors were in the habit of saying that such a risk was not probable in "normal" times, for a currency quoted at its floor could be expected only to rise. Obviously, such a statement does not apply in a crisis atmosphere; on the contrary, speculators expect a change in the existing parity and act accordingly.

As previously noted, the main advantage of the floating-rate system is to enable the central bank to implement an elastic defense policy in the spot market, letting the rate fall in order to make the speculation more costly, both spot and forward. Of course, such a policy may give rise to the bandwagon effect when expectations are adaptive. But if the market knows that the central banks are ready to intervene with a sufficient amount of resources (*vide infra*), speculators will be less inclined to take short positions, for they will be aware of a possible bear squeeze.[10]

The policy must not be directed at maintaining a given rate, because experience shows that in that case speculators are rather more "excited." Therefore, official dealers have to avoid two snags: first, keeping too stable a rate, which boils down to get back to a parity system, and, second, allowing an excessive drop in the rate, which may initiate the bandwagon effect. Indeed, high skillfulness is required from central-bank dealers, and the risk of a mistaken action (or of a mistaken interpretation by the market) cannot be ruled out.[11]

The difficulties of an elastic defense policy in a managed floating system are aggravated by the existence of time zones. A central bank cannot itself regulate the exchange rate of its own currency outside its working hours. On this account, erratic fluctuations may appear in other places at such times. Market expectations are necessarily influenced by such movements, more especially as dealers ordinarily take as opening rates of one day the closing rates quoted the previous day on the last working place. To avoid this detrimental effect, central banks give instructions to another bank (central or commercial) to act on their behalf. This practice is now widespread, but some cases have been observed, even recently, in which it was not completely successful.[12]

The main intervention currency is the U.S. dollar, and the bulk of transactions between two currencies runs through it. From a pure arithmetical standpoint, this practice should not alter the average dollar rate. Nevertheless, when a crisis atmosphere against the dollar exists, a shift of funds between, say, the Italian lira and the Swiss franc is carried out via the dollar, which falls against the Swiss currency. Unfavorable expectations about the dollar may thus be strengthened.[13] The same applies every time the members of the EMS buy or sell dollars for unequal amounts to keep their currencies within the margins of the parity grid.

Outside such a system, multicurrency intervention may seem useless, because official dollar sales (purchases) spread their effects over all foreign currencies, thanks to arbitrage. Nevertheless, a more direct impact is obtained when a central bank buys (sells) the foreign currency it is mainly interested in. Except in the case of the snake or the EMS, however, a central bank may object to another one buying its currency or may be reluctant to deliver it to be sold in the market.

Foreign currency resources. In the present state of the international monetary "system," one important reserve asset cannot be easily used to get foreign currency. The United States has succeeded in forcing the whole Western world into demonetizing gold, at least officially, so that a central bank that needs foreign currencies against gold can only pledge it as a collateral for a borrowing from another central bank, at a price derived from the market price, but with a substantial discount. For this reason, a country not willing to resort to this cumbersome and somewhat humiliating procedure must rely as a first line of defense on what the IMF calls its "liquid reserves," that is, official foreign-exchange holdings and Fund-related assets (reserve positions and SDRs).

Beyond that, there are a lot of additional possibilities: use of credit tranche positions within the IMF, borrowing in the Eurocurrency markets (by official, semiofficial, or private entities), floating abroad securities denominated in foreign currencies (Roosa bonds, Carter bonds), activation of swap lines between central banks, regional support within the EEC.

This is not the place to compare these means with one another. Suffice it to say that they are not perfect substitutes. Rather, they may be viewed as complementary. When given access to Fund credit tranches, a country gets some financial respectability, which enables it to borrow in the international market, or at least to pay a lower spread over the LIBOR. Swaps between central banks have the advantage of being available within a very short time, but they are centered on the Fed, which is not always convenient for third countries. In most cases, swaps are the first line of defense, pending a drawing on the IMF or the floating of an international loan. In every case, the country that borrows abroad assumes the exchange risk. This is the price it has to pay to improve its gross reserves, but this price will be low if the crisis is overcome without a substantial drop in the spot rate.

Transactions between the central bank and the domestic banking system may also be used to prevent (or limit) variations in official reserves arising from spot interventions. Of course, these means are not capable of altering the aggregate external position of the country, but they enable the central bank to loosen the link between its spot interventions and the evolution of its apparent reserves. This may prove useful not only from a psychological standpoint but also for the availability of high-powered money. The device may be used both ways: When swapping in foreign currencies from commercial banks, the central bank raises its apparent reserves; when swapping out, it reduces the liquidity of the banking system.

First, assume that a central bank has bought foreign currencies (dollars) to prevent the spot exchange rate of its own money from rising to a level it deems unrealistic. Swapping dollars against the national currency with commercial banks of the country has two effects: (1) The amount of reserves appearing in the balance sheet of the central bank does not rise as much as official dollar purchases. (2) The central bank builds a nest egg that may subsequently be used if and when capital outflows occur.

In so doing, the central bank smoothes the variation of its reserves, thereby putting speculators in a state of greater uncertainty as regards the amount of "ammunition" at the disposal of the monetary authorities. Besides, commercial banks swapping in dollars have to swap domestic money to the central bank. To this extent, excess liquidity created by the spot interventions is mopped up.

Largely used by the Bundesbank in the 1960s, this device has been accused of having inflationary consequences at the international level and even of being self-defeating. Indeed, so the argument runs, commercial banks lend in the Euromarket the dollars they got from the central bank, another speculator borrows them and sells them against DM, and so forth, giving rise to the so-called merry-go-round effect. This is the reason why in 1971 the central banks of the "group of ten" plus Switzerland decided to refrain from depositing their dollar reserves in the Euromarket, either directly or by way of swaps with commercial banks.

After having been considered almost self-evident for years, this argument was recently disputed by Dufey and Giddy (1978*a*, 1978*b*). They contend that it is based on either one of two misleading assumptions. The first is that Eurobanks would "systematically lend more to foreign residents for the purpose of conversion into their domestic currencies than do U.S. banks." Dufey and Giddy assert that such a "geographic bias" does not exist and, moreover, that when a central bank liquidates U.S. Treasury bills to deposit funds in the Eurodollar market, interest-rate movements induce an offsetting reflow of funds toward the U.S. money market. The second assumption "is based on the contention that what really matters is the specific sector of the U.S. money market from which the funds are moved." Dufey and Giddy consider it also misleading, as "arbitrage tends to ensure a stable relationship between rates on different money market instruments." They conclude that "the 1971 G-10 agreement should be quietly forgotten" (1978*b*:16).

In a period of bear speculation, swaps between the central bank and commercial banks work the other way round. If the central bank has already swapped out dollars to commercial banks, it unwinds these swaps, thereby getting back the dollars it needs for supporting the spot rate. If there are no outstanding swaps, the tactics of the central bank must be somewhat different. First, it uses its reserves to support the spot rate at the level deemed appropriate. Second, because part of the demand for foreign currency by commercial banks is due to the spot covering of clients' (nonbanks) forward purchases, the central bank may judge it advisable to get back the foreign currencies it has sold to accommodate this demand, instead of letting commercial banks invest them in the Euromarkets pending their delivery at the maturity of the forward contracts.

Using swaps for this purpose is not without drawbacks, for the central bank, when swapping in foreign currencies, is at the same time swapping out domestic money to commercial banks. In so doing, it gives back to them the money that had been destroyed by its spot interventions, thereby avoiding the liquidity squeeze and the correlative rise in interest rates, the result of which would have been to raise the cost of speculation. The monetary authorities may therefore prefer to get foreign currencies from commercial banks, not by swaps but by simple borrowings (deposits), that is, without giving out national money.

The Banque de France had recourse to swaps in the last months of 1968, but in 1969, having taken notice of the aforementioned drawback, it made use of deposit borrowings, according to a regulation enforced on January 20, 1969 (the so-called 2PB).[14] Henceforth, support interventions of the FF in the spot market were partly offset as regards their effects on official reserves, this result being obtained without giving speculation new "ammunition." Opening short positions became more costly, both spot and forward.

It appears that a central bank making swaps (both ways), or "raking in" foreign currencies on deposit from commercial banks, uses simultaneously the three components of Keynes's trident: It tries to regulate the spot rate of its own currency, while influencing domestic interest rates (i.e., the ID for given foreign interest rates). In addition to its effect on internal liquidity, such a policy cannot leave unchanged the forward exchange rate. Therefore, all these devices may be considered substitutable to some extent for outright forward interventions.[15]

IV. Forward intervention in the foreign-exchange market

A historical issue or a current issue? So much has been written about official forward counterspeculation for the past 20 years that one can hardly conceive of anything both new and worth saying. Furthermore, forward support in a crisis period seems to be a thing of the past. Now, an acute foreign-exchange crisis is dealt with by external borrowing, and especially by "central-bank credit arrangements," which P. M. Oppenheimer (Chalmers, 1971) considered to be "the decisive factor" as early as 1966.

Some central banks are still dealing forward, however, but only marginally, for the main purpose of regulating the domestic money market, and they use swaps rather than outright transactions. Obviously, this has nothing to do with the topic assigned to me.

However, two reasons have led me not to discard the problem of outright forward counterspeculation. First, the past is not so remote (remember "the travail of the sterling"), and no one knows if in the future forward interventions might not make a comeback. Second, in that case, we need precise knowledge of what may be expected from such a policy. I do not feel convinced that this task has been thoroughly completed in the 1960s and 1970s: Those who have been participating in the discussions have been perhaps a trifle too controversially inclined, which is quite natural when one argues about topical events.

Two alternative interpretations. Everybody agrees that forward intervention minimizes spot support and the rise in interest rates when a currency is under attack. The central bank acts as a speculator in favor of its own currency, thereby reducing speculative spot sales: The forward rate being higher than it would have been had the market be left to take care of itself, speculators are induced to shift their sales into the forward market, where they are offset by official purchases.

However, the agreement does not extend further, as the spot impact of forward deals is apt to be analyzed in two different ways. According to the academic theory, this impact proceeds from interest arbitrage; the cambist interpretation views it as the mere result of commercial banks having no longer to cover the excess forward supply of domestic currency in the spot market.

This distinction is not a purely formal one. To Spraos (1959), "it is important to insist that the loss of reserves should be attributed to arbitrage and not speculation—not on semantic or taxonomic grounds, but for the intensely practical reason that adverse arbitrage is far more tractable than adverse speculation."

What Spraos and, as far as I known, every follower of this theory assert is that central-bank forward intervention aims at having the currency under attack quote an intrinsic premium, in order to induce inward arbitrage or, at least, to prevent the emergence of an intrinsic discount, which would give rise to outward arbitrage by the holders of the domestic currency.

The cambist interpretation simply contends that official intervention frees commercial banks from the necessity to cover excess forward sales of domestic currency in the spot market, for the central bank provides the counterpart of them in the forward market.[16] Because commercial banks maintain a strict equality between the ID and the swap rate, no intrinsic differential appears, and the spot effect of the forward intervention cannot be ascribed to inward arbitrage. The currency under attack does not fall in the spot market as much as it would otherwise have done (or the spot support need not be as great) because the central bank speculates against the market, and not because arbitrageurs purchase this currency spot.

Although the incentive to bear speculation is of less importance in the cambist view, it does exist in both cases. This is inescapable, for speculative sales cannot be deflected from the spot to the forward market unless the latter is made more attractive. The conclusion follows that forward interventions designed to fight a crisis must be larger than spot interventions. What, then, is the rationale of forward as against spot support?

Forward versus spot intervention. The impact of forward intervention on confidence has been keenly disputed, but the debate remains inconclusive. Nobody knows whether forward support is better for confidence in the future of the currency under attack than spot support (with the correlative loss of reserve) or a drop of the spot rate. It is not even possible to say whether forward support, when it is officially acknowledged, will be interpreted as meaning that the central bank is strongly willing to keep the current rate (or parity) unchanged or will be interpreted as a sign of distress. "Little more can be said," wrote P. M. Oppenheimer in 1966 (Chalmers, 1971:35); this statement is valid both in a regime of adjustable parities and when exchange rates are floating.[17]

As regards the ability of the central bank successfully to undertake forward commitments, two extreme arguments have to be put aside, one because it is overoptimistic, the other because it is both overpessimistic and inconsistent.

Spraos (1959:14) has expressed the first argument in a famous sentence: "There is thus no limit to the resistance potential of the authorities to a speculative attack of this kind, except the size of the books in which they enter their forward transactions." He considers that "speculative forward deals are mere book-keeping entries destined to be rubbed off," because he assumes that all forward speculators are selling short the domestic currency, so that they have to buy it spot on maturity. This is too general a statement:

1   Of course, it is true for pure speculators, by definition. One may add that the central bank is able to render this kind of speculation very expensive when it has the possibility of applying a bear squeeze, which requires a sufficient amount of foreign currencies available to be paid out at the time the forward contracts mature.

2   As to leads and lags, the case is different, but the conclusion is the same. A trader who has a long position in the currency under attack and makes haste to sell it forward cannot be said to be selling short. On maturity, he does not have to buy spot the currency he has sold forward, because he gets it from his customer. Nevertheless, the forward sale has been only a "lead," and the trader will not sell the currency twice; forward official intervention results in offsetting leads and lags operations over time.

3   When forward sales arise from hedging, it is not sure that the hedger has to buy spot the currency he has sold forward. On maturity, the hedger may deem it advisable to liquidate the asset the value of which he was hedging, especially if this asset consists of inventories.

4   As to the speculator who holds the currency under attack, it is reasonable to argue that he had better sell it spot, except if official intervention results in the domestic currency quoting an intrinsic premium; this assumption is not accepted by those who believe that the IPT obtains even in a speculative run.

A completely opposed argument has been put forward by Tsiang (1959:105), who asserts that the central bank must incur cumulative forward commitments. He contemplates the "imaginary case where the current pressure on the exchange rate is expected to continue for more than three months (say, a year), and is expected to disappear after a year but not to be reversed."

In that case, Tsiang contends that the central bank has to double its intervention effort during the second quarter, to treble it in the third quarter, and so on. The reason he gives is that monetary authorities must, at the same time, offset the pressure of the current period and that which has been shifted from the previous one. He concludes that the rise in the central-bank forward commitments "might cause more damage to confidence than the extra decline of reserves that would have occurred but for official intervention."

This is a fallacy. At the end of the first quarter, the speculators who want to roll over their short positions have to buy spot the domestic currency and sell it forward, thereby replacing their initial contract by another one; the central bank's commitments do not rise.[18]

Having disposed of these two extreme arguments, we have to look for a realistic conclusion, if there is any. Unfortunately, this is an impossible task. Let us assume that the central bank that has given its own currency forward support eventually cannot prevent a devaluation or a drop in the spot rate. The reserve loss it incurs should be estimated in comparison with what would have happened had the support been confined to the spot market. Three factors must be taken into account to measure the net loss: (1) The excess of official forward sales of foreign currencies over the spot sales that would have taken place. This excess is positive, because forward support encourages speculation. (2) The difference between the forward rate quoted by the central bank and the rate at which spot support would have been made. This gap is positive, as it is reasonable to assume that in a crisis period foreign currencies quote a premium. (3) The increase in value of the reserves the central bank holds when the speculative run comes to its end.

None of these three quantities can be estimated. No one knows to what extent forward support induces additional forward speculation as compared with the amount that would have been sold forward without official intervention. By the same token, one cannot evaluate the magnitude of the premium rate that is necessary to deflect speculation into the forward market. Finally, Spraos's assumption, according to which all forward speculation consists of short selling, cannot be accepted,[19] and nobody can say how much of the currency that has been sold forward will have to be purchased spot. As Einzig (1967:521) put it: "Nobody who has any knowledge of the practical working of the foreign exchange market could possibly be cocksure that the *ultimate* counterpart of official forward transactions is not represented by a buyer who will be able to pay for it in sterling on maturity without having to buy sterling." When counterspeculating forward instead of spot, "the authorities would remain in the dark ... about the extent of the adverse pressure" (Einzig, 1967:522).

If official forward support is eventually successful (i.e., if the rate of the currency under attack is not adjusted downward), "it is likely that official losses owing to exchange rate depreciations or appreciations will be less than they would have been if only the spot rate had been supported" (Day, 1976:162). This cautious statement does not seem open to discussion, but it cannot be reversed. This means that we cannot say whether the cost of an exclusive forward support is greater or lower than that of an exclusive spot support when the domestic currency eventually goes down.

Perhaps the debate on this point has been going on for so long only because those who took part in it implicitly gave the factors set forth earlier some values determined by their mere prejudices. They may be excused for that, because factual observation does not allow measurement of these factors, as I have tried to show.

V. Concluding remarks

The different steps a central bank can take to fight a foreign-exchange crisis, although strictly interdependent, must be divided into two categories according to their respective impacts on the adjustment process. A restrictive monetary policy is part and parcel of the adjustment process: Dear money is an antiinflationary device and may be interpreted as a sign that monetary authorities are really willing to maintain the existing parity or rate of exchange. Of course, such an attitude may not suffice to reverse unfavorable expectations, given the high volatility of the current opinion in the foreign-exchange market. Therefore, other means of economic policy may also be necessary, such as fiscal policy, incomes policy, and so on.

As for intervention in the foreign-exchange market, both spot and forward, it only tends to bring about a breathing space, which may be justified by one or the other of the following considerations.

First, the speculative run may be ill-founded. It may arise from expectations that completely disregard the fundamentals. In such a case, official intervention suffices to provide the time necessary for expectations to change. This applies, for instance, when expectations are formed on the basis of political rather than economic considerations, as for France during the first months of 1978.

Second, the run may arise from a realistic appraisal of the current economic situation, but the authorities are convinced that a change in policy can improve the state of affairs within a reasonable period and are willing to implement such a change. In this case, official intervention is advisable to avoid a fall in the exchange rate that would prove detrimental by bringing about a bandwagon effect, perhaps leading to a vicious circle.

The danger is that the authorities may mistake official intervention for a remedy dealing with fundamentals and go on supporting an exchange rate that is already unrealistic or that may be proved indefensible in the near future because of an ill-devised economic policy. Every time a government has fallen into this trap, it has simply postponed the inevitable adjustment of the exchange rate and incurred unnecessary reserves losses, whether the central bank intervened spot or forward.

One explanation of such an attitude is that governments may be foolishly attached to the existing parity of their currency. Another may be that they were deceiving themselves as to their ability to implement a successful policy change in due time. A third one may be the misplaced belief that in supporting the forward rate of its own currency, the central bank is capable of inducing unlimited inward arbitrages.

I would conclude that detecting the occurrence of a foreign-exchange crisis and fighting it with appropriate measures are far easier for someone speaking in a classroom or in a colloquium than for those who are in charge of the national currency. The task becomes even more difficult when the central-bank action is not fully supported by the government, a situation that history has shown to be not uncommon.

Notes

1 During the discussion in Bad Homburg, it appeared that most of the participants shared this view, to which I had made but a quick reference in a footnote to my first draft. That led me to extend the end of the present Introduction. The reason is not that I have changed my mind. On the contrary, I felt it necessary to be more explicit as regards the differences between the two interpretations of the IPT.

2 It also avoids the mistakes of many previous statistical works in which the relations established between spot rates, forward rates, and ID may be considered mere artifacts for one or more of the following reasons: comparisons between irrelevant rates of interest, such as those of Treasury bills; use of variables that have not been observed at the same moment or have been averaged over a period; misplaced reliance on quotations sometimes given as "nominal."

3 The structure of the banking system and the type of relations between commercial banks and the central bank may put a limit to the use of this device; see, for example, the differences between the behavior of the Bundesbank and that of the Banque de France.

4 Uncovered inward arbitrages may arise when the ID is large, but then they are made for very short periods, and their volatility does not allow us to view them as a solution to the crisis (e.g., foreign deposits on the French money market in January 1978, which were suddenly withdrawn on 1 February). Conversely, one may take notice of the statement made in Zurich on 28 November 1978 by Dr. H. Mast, economic adviser to the Crédit Suisse, who said that the improved stability of exchange rates, which may result from new monetary arrangements (the "Carter package" of 1 November), would mean that international money flows would again develop *more in line with interest differentials*.

5   This simplified example assumes away exchange controls and, for the sake of argument, supposes that dealers do not immediately adjust premiums (discounts) to the new ID (an unrealistic assumption, as previously stated).

6   When an inward arbitrage is made outside a crisis period (in "normal" times), a bull speculator can be found. But his operation is not brought about by the arbitrage, so that the impact on the spot rate must be ascribed to pure speculation. The same argument applies to leads and lags and to hedging. Of course, when two arbitrages are made simultaneously in opposite directions, the case is devoid of any interest, as the arbitrages offset one another.

7   At the time of writing (middle of December 1978) the one-year rates of interest on the Eurocurrency markets were 0.75% for the Swiss franc, 11.375% for the dollar, 13.5% for the pound, and 15.75% for the Italian lire.

8   On 10 February 1978, the one-month rate on the FF was 10.25 % per year in the domestic money market and 16.25% in the Eurofranc market.

9   See the cautious statement by O. Emminger in the lecture he delivered at LSE in December 1978 (*The Financial Times*, 8 December 1978).

10 Toward the end of the morning of 30 November 1978, the Dow-Jones ticker gave this significant statement by a Zurich dealer: Nobody is willing to be short in dollar because official interventions may render these positions costly; but, as nothing fundamental has changed within the U.S. economy, nobody wants to take long positions; therefore, we have "a dull market."

11 A significant, although still somewhat mysterious, example may be given by the Bank of England action on 4 March 1976. On the contrary, the Banque de France appears to have managed with great skills the (limited) crisis that happened at the beginning of February 1978.

12 It seems, for instance, that the Bank of Japan was late in discovering how important it was to monitor the yen market in London. Nor was it always obvious, to give another example, that the Fed was able or willing to relay the Bundesbank correctly (before 1 November 1978) as regards the dollar–DM rate.

13 No doubt, this process played a major part in the sequence of events that began on 22 January 1973 and eventually led to the second devaluation of the dollar.

14 P stands for external position and B stands for banks; 2 is a serial number. The principle was that the external position of banks in foreign currencies had to be evened out if it was positive on 31 January 1969 or, if it was negative at that date, had to be left at least at the same level.

15 This substitutability may be illustrated by the following example: On 2 April 1971 the Bundesbank replaced its swap policy (designed to swap out dollars) by outright forward transactions. As E. Blumenthal clearly put it (Coulbois, 1972:145), the bank had "strong doubts about the real effectiveness" of both instruments, but it wanted to demonstrate its willingness "to purchase foreign exchange forward at the official rates . . . , a task which a monetary authority no doubt has to perform for superordinate reasons within the framework of international cooperation."

16 The Bank of England could be considered interpreting in this way its own action in its March 1965 *Bulletin* (p. 4), were it not that in the following sentence of the text it states that "by supporting the forward rate the authorities also lessened the cost of forward cover on short-term funds placed in the UK." Clearly, this last sentence refers to the "standard" theory of covered interest arbitrage.

17 The argument according to which forward support enhances confidence because

the forward rate is a reliable predictor of the future spot rate seems rather old-fashioned now. A lot of evidence shows that the predictor is poor.

18 As a matter of fact, the speculator who rolls over a position is making a swap, and swaps do not affect the spot rate; only outright transactions do.

19 See the work of Kindleberger (1978:203): "A few observers believed that operations in the forward market could relieve central banks of the necessity to hold reserves: when the forward contracts matured, they could be rolled over and extended. But the experience of the British from 1964 to 1967 suggests limits to this dream, as to the hope of perpetual motion."

References

Aliber, R. Z. 1973. "The Interest-Rate-Parity Theorem: A Reinterpretation." *Journal of Political Economy* 81:1451–9.

Cachin, A. 1978. "Commentaire: pour ou contre un double marché des changes." *Banque* December, pp. 1401–4.

Chalmers, E. B., editor. 1971. *Forward Exchange Intervention, The British Experience 1964–67.* London: Hutchinson.

Coulbois, P., editor. 1972. *Le change à terme: technique, théorie, politique.* Paris: Cujas.

1979. *Finance internationale. I. Le change.* Paris: Cujas.

and Prissert, P. 1974. "Forward Exchange, Short Term Capital Flows and Monetary Policy." *De Economist* 122:283–308.

Day, W. H. L. 1976. "The Advantages of Exclusive Forward Exchange Rate Support." *IMF Staff Papers* 23:137–63.

Dornbusch, R. 1977a "Capital Mobility and Portfolio Balance." In: *The Political Economy of Monetary Reform*, edited by R. Z. Aliber, pp. 106–25. London: Macmillan.

1977b. "The Theory of Flexible Exchange Rate Regimes and Macroeconomic Policy." In: *Flexible Exchange Rates and Stabilization Policy*, edited by J. Herin, A. Lindbeck, and J. Myhrman, pp. 123–43. London: Macmillan.

Dufey, G., and Giddy, I. H. 1978a. *The International Money Market.* Englewood Cliffs, N. J.:Prentice-Hall.

1978b. *Eurodollars and International Liquidity: Central Bank Depositing Reconsidered.* SUERF Series 22A.

Einzig, P. 1967. *A Dynamic Theory of Forward Exchange* (second edition). London: Macmillan.

Emminger, O. 1977. *The D-Mark in the Conflict between Internal and External Equilibrium.* Essays in International Finance No. 122. Princeton: Princeton University Press.

Frenkel, J. A., and Levich, R. M. 1975. "Covered Interest Arbitrage: Unexploited Profits?" *Journal of Political Economy* 83:325–38.

1977. "Transactions Costs and Interest Arbitrage: Tranquil versus Turbulent Periods." *Journal of Political Economy* 85:1209–26.

Grubel, H. G. 1966. *Forward Exchange, Speculation and the International Flow of Capital.* Stanford: Stanford University Press.

1977a. *International Economics.* Homewood, Ill.: Irwin.

1977b. "How Important Is Control over International Reserves?" in: *The New International Monetary System*, edited by R. A. Mundell, and J. J. Polak, pp. 133–61. New York: Columbia University Press.

216   Comment by R. Dornbusch

Holtrop, W. M. 1972. *Money in an Open Economy*. Leiden: Stenfert Kroese.
Keynes, J. M. 1923. *A Tract on Monetary Reform*. London: Macmillan.
    1930. *A Treatise on Money*. London: Macmillan.
Kindleberger, C. P. 1978. *Manias, Panics and Crashes*. New York: Basic Books.
Kubarych, R. M. 1978. *Foreign Exchange Markets in the United States*. Federal
    Reserve Bank of New York.
McKinnon, R. I. 1977. *The Eurocurrency Market*. Essays in International Finance
    No. 125. Princeton: Princeton University Press.
Prissert, P. 1972*a*. "La théorie générale du marché des changes à terme: analyses
    académiques et réalités techniques." In *Monnaie et balance des paiements*
    (papers and proceedings of a colloquium held at the Banque de France in 1969),
    edited by A. De Lattre and P. Berger. Paris: A. Colin.
    1972*b*. "Vers une remise en question fondamentale de la théorie académique des
    changes à terme." *Banque* April, pp. 333–43. An English revised version of this
    text was published by the SUERF, 1974, under the title "A critical reexamina-
    tion of the forward exchange theory."
    1972*c*. "Capitaux à court terme, euro-dollar et politiques monétaires." *Economie
    appliquée* 25:299–323.
    1977. *Le marché des changes* (second edition). Paris: Sirey.
    1978. "La dissociation des taux de terme et des taux d'intérêt est-elle possible?"
    Banque, June, pp. 721–4.
Schep, B. J., and Smits, W. J. B. 1976. "Forward Exchange, Short Term Capital
    Flows and Monetary Policy: A Comment." *De Economist* 124:475–89.
Sohmen, E. 1969. *Flexible Exchange Rates* (revised edition). Chicago: University of
    Chicago Press.
Solomon, R. 1977. *The International Monetary System 1945–1976: An Insider's
    View*. New York: Harper & Row.
Spraos, J. 1959. "Speculation, Arbitrage and Sterling." *Economic Journal* 69:1–21.
    1972. "An Academic's View of the Reconcilable and Irreconcilable Differences
    between the Cambist and Academic Theories." In: *Le change à terme:
    technique, théorie, politique,* edited by P. Coulbois, pp. 185–92. Paris: Cujas.
Tsiang, S. C. 1959. "The Theory of Forward Exchange and the Effects of Govern-
    ment Intervention on the Foreign Exchange Market." *IMF Staff Papers* 7:75–
    106.
Volcker, P. A. 1977. "The Role of Monetary Policy Coordination to Attain
    Exchange-Rate Stability." In: *The New International Monetary System*, edited
    by R. A. Mundell and J. J. Polak, pp. 25–36. New York: Columbia University
    Press.

Comment

RUDIGER DORNBUSCH

Professor Coulbois's scholarly chapter suggests many comments, some
invited by his view of the foreign-exchange market, some pertaining to the
scope for monetary policy under external balance constraints. I shall limit my
remarks to two areas. First, I shall briefly discuss what I understand to be the

accepted theory of spot, forward, and expected future spot rate deter-
minations in the current literature. I shall spell out a minimal framework that
will be applied to the question of forward-market intervention. My second set
of remarks concerns more properly the topic of this volume: central banks
and foreign-exchange crises.

I. Of cambists and academics

Professor Coulbois makes the distinction between a cambist theory and an
academic theory. The former amounts to the observation that dealers quote
forward rates off the spot rate and the prevailing interest differential,
mechanically and without obvious thought. The academic theory, by contrast, makes the forward premium *in equilibrium* equal to the interest
differential, calls this an arbitrage equilibrium, and requires the actual or
incipient elimination of unexploited profit opportunities to achieve the
balance. Is there any conflict? The positive economist would simply observe
that dealers behave as if they were eliminating profit opportunities; their
trading rules are compatible with arbitrage equilibrium. There is, accordingly, no conflict whatsoever; the academic theory provides the rationale
for the observed behavior in the dealing room.

There are, however, a few subtleties that deserve notice. Kouri (1976)
showed that with risky forward contracts, interest parity need not hold; the
riskiness of the forward contract determines the spread. Here is a good theory
to explain events where markets transitorily dry up.

Another point, more central, concerns the distinction between forward
rates and expected future spot rates. This distinction would appear unimportant to Professor Coulbois, but it is central to much of the recent
theories of asset markets and exchange rates. In this theory, economic agents
form expectations about the future course of exchange rates, assets are
imperfect substitutes because their stochastic returns are not perfectly
correlated, and asset stocks determine equilibrium rates of return and levels
of exchange rates. Here interest differentials can differ from the anticipated
rate of depreciation because the forward rate can differ from the expected
future spot rate. The difference, or bias, is a return to holders of open
positions. The distinction between forward rates and expected future spot
rates is essential for an understanding of asset-market intervention under
flexible rates. Intervention typically affects two margins: the interest differential and the premium. I shall now briefly spell out a framework of
analysis that captures these distinctions.

Suppose the home country is small, so that the world interest rate, i^*, is
given. Suppose also that we can neglect details of the interaction between
goods and asset markets and focus simply on the determination of the interest

rate at home and the premium on foreign exchange. For our analysis, risk aversion is now essential. Now domestic and foreign securities, even on a covered basis, are not perfect substitutes. Our model is developed in terms of two markets, those for forward exchange and for domestic securities.

In the forward market the authorities supply a forward position $\bar{F}$. The private sector's demand for forward foreign exchange is an increasing function of the covered and the uncovered anticipated returns, θ and $\bar{\theta}$, respectively. These yield differentials are defined as

(1) $\theta \equiv i - i^* - p, \qquad \bar{\theta} \equiv i - i^* - \bar{p}$

where p and $\bar{p}$ are the forward premium and the anticipated rate of depreciation. With these definitions we can write the equilibrium condition in the forward market as follows:

(2) $\bar{F} = F(\theta, \bar{\theta}) \qquad (F_1, F_2 > 0)$

Consider next the home bond market. The supply of public debt is $\bar{B}$, and the private sector's excess demand, B, is an increasing function of the covered and anticipated returns:

(3) $\bar{B} = B(\theta, \bar{\theta}) \qquad (B_1, B_2 > 0)$

In Figure 8.1 we show the market equilibrium schedules for the forward market and the bond market. The position of the schedules is determined by asset supplies, foreign interest rates, and the anticipated rate of depreciation, $\bar{p}$, that is treated as a parameter. The relative slopes reflect the gross substitute assumption. Equilibrium obtains at point E and implies an interest rate and forward premium, i_0 and p_0, respectively.

Suppose the central bank widens the forward position, supplying now an increased stock of forward contracts. At the initial equilibrium there is excess supply. To induce the public to take up an increased position for future delivery, either the anticipated or the actual return on domestic assets must rise. Accordingly, the FF schedule shifts up and to the left, leading to a new equilibrium (not drawn) with a reduced interest rate at home and a reduced forward premium. The interest rate and the premium are simultaneously determined here. But, because assets are not perfect substitutes, the new equilibrium is one where the premium has declined more than the interest rate, because we move along BB that is at an angle less than 45 degrees from the horizontal.

What does all this have to say about forward premia and interest differential? The point is that they are determined simultaneously and that in the presence of assets that are not perfect substitutes there are no simple one-for-one rules that describe their relationship.

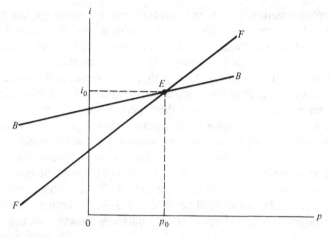

Figure 8.1.

II. Foreign-exchange crises: how to tell and what to do?

Central-bank locker-room talk abounds with foreign-exchange crises, ortho-doxy vindicated, and speculators battled and punished. Professor Coulbois's chapter tells us little about what makes a crisis, as opposed to run-of-the-mill intervention, nor does it tell us what to do except by appeal to Bagehot wisdom that high interest rates will bring money from the moon.

One of the interesting questions, from the point of view of theory, as much as and also from the viewpoint of exchange management, is whether an exchange crisis constitutes an unanticipated dramatic reversal of intervention requirements, an anticipated but dramatically enlarged intervention need, or a gradual but continuous buildup of pressure on the rate. The latter, I believe would not be commonly described as a crisis, and I shall therefore con-centrate on the former two possibilities, which admit of a jump in the rate of intervention but differ on the question of expectations. I shall draw here on the imaginative work of Krugman (1978) that models anticipated foreign-exchange crises. The point to be made is that crises are perfectly compatible with rational expectations; indeed, their timing may be predictable.

Consider now the Krugman model. Suppose our small country pursues a rate of domestic credit creation and that because the economy is stationary and prices are given under fixed rates there is a balance-of-payments deficit equal to the rate of credit creation. Thus the stock of reserves is falling over time, with domestic nominal and real balances remaining constant. Eco-nomic agents who watch the process realize (1) that one day the bank will run out of reserves, and on that day there will be flexible rates; and (2) that with ongoing credit creation the rate of depreciation of the exchange rate will then equal the rate of nominal money creation. The question left to answer is when and under what conditions the transition to flexible rates takes place. Krugman shows, and this is a general property of models with exhaustible stocks (Salant and Henderson, 1978), that there comes a day while stocks are still finite when capital flight wipes out the reserves all in one fell swoop.

What determines the transition? With perfect foresight there can be no anticipated jumps in the price level, because they would afford holders of foreign assets an infinite rate of return. Thus in the transition the price level must remain constant. Before the jump there is no inflation, and after the transition to flexible rates, induced by the cleaning out of the bank, there is inflation because of domestic credit creation. Thus in the transition the demand for real balances will fall because of the rise in nominal interest rates. But with prices given, a decline in real balances means that the nominal money stock must undergo a jump decline. This is precisely what happens, of course, when speculators clean out the central bank on transition day. Transition day is thus determined by the condition that the remaining stock of reserves be such that its loss reduces the nominal and real money stock precisely to the level desired under the inflationary flexible-rate regime. The properties of the demand for money determine that stock change and thus allow, for any current stock and rate of credit creation, the determination of transition day. What is so attractive about the rational-expectations formulation of a crisis is that it suggests that events that appear to the untutored eye as a crisis are in fact regularly predictable process in well-informed speculative economies.

How to cope with foreign-exchange crises? Reversal of the conditions of the crisis is, of course, essential. Those expectations that lead speculators to take the view that rates will be unsustainable must, of course, be reversed. But we certainly should expect that successful stabilization must go further. Those instances of success that stand out (Italy in 1964, the United Kingdom in 1976) suggest that quite dramatic acts are helpful. Surely the British example is the outstanding case of a reversal of expectations brought about by the very formal indenture of U.K. policy to IMF diktat. The failure of the U.S. stabilization of the fall of 1978, which early on was celebrated as a success, is by the same token due to the absence of any well-defined policy.

It would appear that there are two views of coping with crises that are quite different, although both will appear to solve the problem. One view is to think of the market as a bunch of nervous bandwagon speculators who can be turned around be a tightening of money, swap networks, and frightfully serious airs of commitment. The alternative view, more in line with the rational-expectations approach, views speculators as informed and able to see through gimmicks. In the latter view, nothing short of long-term macroeconomic programs will avoid ultimate crises. Runs here are natural transition phenomena, the timing of which is influenced by short-term stabilization policies, but not the fact of their ultimate occurrences. Recognition of such a group of speculators should make foreign-exchange authorities more wary in contemplating their apparent successes at coping with crises.

References

Kouri, P. 1976. "Essays on the Theory of Flexible Exchange Rates." Unpublished Ph.D. dissertation, Massachusetts Institute of Technology.
Krugman, P. 1979. "A Model of Balance-of-Payments Crises." *Journal of Money, Credit and Banking* 11:311–25.
Salant, S. W., and Henderson, D. 1978. "Market Anticipation of Government Policy and the Price of Gold." *Journal of Political Economy* 86:627–48.

Comment

PIERRE-MARIE LARNAC

Coming after Rudiger Dornbusch, I shall make a very short comment and shall not insist again on the overstating of the difference between the academic interpretation and the cambist interpretation, as long as the interest-parity equilibrium prevails. But I still wonder about the working, in a general-equilibrium framework, of those two "distinct" but "connected" markets. After all, the forward exchange market is nothing but one of the few instances of an actual Arrow-Debreu futures market.

Because I am not quite satisfied with such notions as "ill-founded" speculative runs, "realistic" appraisals of the situation, and "indefensible" exchange rates, I would have liked to have seen explicit models of the way anticipations are built (rationally or otherwise) and of the link between stocks and flows of financial assets (speed of adjustments to desired level, transaction costs, etc.). Besides, I do not see how we can dispense with reaction functions, however difficult to formalize they may be. If the statement "history never repeats itself" is to be taken seriously, what are we here for?

From a theoretical point of view, I think the framework recently provided by models of "overshooting" and a sharper distinction between "instability" and "variability" would be relevant to the problem of central-bank interventions.

My last remark is about the definition of crises. Is what happened in France in February 1978 a small crisis (Professor Coulbois called it a limited one) or hardly a crisis at all?

9. Less developed countries' rising indebtedness and the lender of last resort in international context

JOËL MÉTAIS

A 'sound' banker, alas! is not one who foresees danger and avoids it, but one who, when he is ruined, is ruined in a conventional and orthodox way along with his fellows, so that no one can really blame him.[1]

For some 8 to 10 years, now, the world of international finance has been experiencing its fifth wave of foreign lending to less developed countries (LDCs) since the beginning of the last century.[2] To some extent the situation today looks very much like that in the four previous periods of heavy LDC borrowing. Very often, the same names rank high on the list of borrowers, namely, Argentina, Brazil, Egypt, Mexico, Spain, and Turkey.[3] Once again these countries have tapped international capital markets on such an impressive scale as to awaken concern about their ability to meet their commitments. And although "it is comforting that for at least 100 years the debt problems of borrowing countries have always been thought to be increasing,"[4] indeed, some countries have already experienced serious difficulties during the last three years that breed fears that we are now on the eve of a worldwide financial crisis.

The first section of this chapter will provide some statistical evidence of LDCs' bank indebtedness since the beginning of this decade. The second will try to weigh the implications of this situation for the stability of the international financial system. The third section is more specifically devoted to an analysis of the means available to the international financial community to prevent the occurrence and consequences of widespread defaults, with particular attention paid to the problem of the would-be lender of last resort.

I. Third-world indebtedness: some statistical evidence

According to World Bank data, the external public (or publicly guaranteed) debt of 96 developing countries grew from U.S. $75 billion to U.S. $352 billion between December 1970 and December 1978. The portion owed to

222

private financial institutions (mainly banks) climbed faster, from U.S. $7.3 billion to U.S. $114 billion, so that its share in the total reached 32.4% in 1978 as against 9.7% in 1970.[5] When account is also taken of strictly private debt and of liabilities falling due within one year,[6] the records, however imprecise, appear even more impressive and the involvement of private banks much deeper.[7] And although figures for 1979 are not yet available, information about the borrowing activity of the LDCs on the international capital market suggests a reinforcement of this latter tendency. In particular, according to data from the BIS semiannual international banking survey, bank claims on LDCs amounted to U.S. $273 billion in December 1979, of which U.S. $104 billion had a remaining maturity of over one year.

If one allows for world inflation, however, the figure of LDC public external debt was only U.S. $161.5 billion in December 1978 at 1970 prices.[8] This corresponds to an annual average real growth rate of 10.1%. Related to export unit values of non-OPEC LDCs, the real value of this debt was U.S. $275 billion on 31 December 1978, against U.S. $139 billion on December 1970,[9] with an annual average growth rate of 8.9%. Whatever measures are taken, the size of bank lending to LDCs and its implications for the functioning of the international financial private system seem matters of concern.

Let us first call attention to some significant shifts that have taken place in the pattern of this bank financing. For some rapidly industrializing LDCs, traditional suppliers' and buyers' credits, although growing, had to be supplemented by large medium-term Eurocurrency credits granted by bank syndicates. Especially since 1974 these Eurocredits have proved one of the most efficient ways of financing the enlarged balance-of-payments deficits of these countries, which were thus enabled to pursue their development objectives. However, only a few countries were allowed to mobilize large gross amounts of such credits regularly. Table 9.1 reveals that during the years 1970–9, seven of them obtained U.S. $97 billion of U.S. $151 billion granted to LDCs (i.e., 64.1% of the total).

Bank portfolios (at least for the major institutions) have undoubtedly been altered by such a surge toward LDC financing. As early as 1976, fears were expressed in some official circles that some banks might soon be overloaded with claims on LDCs, probably unable to pay off their liabilities as a consequence of the lasting world economic slump. Until now a few countries have experienced difficulties, but no major default has been deplored.[10] Has the danger disappeared, or is the crisis still to come, particularly after the new oil shock of 1979? Before making a judgment on the situation today, a further look at available statistical material may provide a useful first step. Fortunately, the data published by international organizations (BIS, World Bank, IMF), by various national monetary authorities, and by some inter-

Table 9.1. *Eurocurrency bank credits to some major LDC borrowers, 1970–9, by World Bank income classificati* (*millions of dollars*)

High income		Upper middle income		Intermediate middle income		Low income	
Spain	14,080	Brazil	23,445	South Korea	8,771	Indonesia[a]	5,765
Venezuela[a]	12,259	Argentina	7,136	Mexico[b]	25,576		

[a]Oil exporter, member of OPEC.
[b]Oil exporter, not a member of OPEC.
Source: Computed from *World Financial Markets*, various issues, Morgan Guaranty Trust Company.

national banks have been considerably improved in recent years, as part of a deliberate move toward better coverage and understanding of international banking transactions, to help the bankers themselves in decision processes for lending abroad.[11] Table 9.2 presents BIS data broken down according to the World Bank's classification of non-OPEC LDCs in five groups, depending on annual income per capita. As already shown by data on medium-term Eurocurrency credits, banks seem to have been rather selective in their international lending policies. In December 1979,[12] only U.S $260 billion out of a total figure of roughly U.S. $665 billion corresponded to international assets owed by LDCs (i.e., only 39.2%).

American banks, which in the early seventies were the major suppliers of funds to LDCs, had only U.S. $89 billion of such assets in their books (i.e., 34.3% of all claims on LCDs). This last figure, though not fully comparable with the BIS data in Table 9.2 confirms their retreat, in relative terms, from such lending. According to estimates by the Morgan Guaranty Trust, at the end of June 1976 their share of bank claims on LDCs' borrowers had reached 65%.[13] More specifically, this movement means that during the last three years, which saw LDCs raise huge amounts of funds,[14] the corresponding assets were spread more evenly among lending banks. In particular, Japanese and European banks were able to support a much greater part of the burden than before, as they had by then acquired some experience and developed their skills in international financing and had ample liquidities to channel abroad.

Other details ought also to be emphasized:

1   Twenty-five percent of all international banks' assets on LDCs were owed by OPEC countries and another 36% by high-income and upper-middle-income countries, which in the long run appear to be good risks because they are "collateralized" by large reserves of mineral resources or diversified and fast-growing economies.
2   Conversely, low-income LDCs have only a 3.2% share in these assets.
3   Forty-three percent of all the assets that fall due within one year represent either (a) self-liquidating commercial credits or (b) balances held by foreign banks in some countries on a rollover basis. Except for upper-middle-income countries (for which it is lower), all groups show approximately the same ratio of short-term indebtedness, around 46%.
4   The separate groups, however, do not follow a uniform pattern as concerns medium- and long-term commitments. Once more, high-income, upper-middle-income, and intermediate-middle-income countries clearly experience higher ratios of long-term indebtedness than the other groups. This confirms the fact that they were the main recipients of the bulk of medium-term Eurocurrency credits, as shown in Table 9.1.

Finally the maturity structure of international claims of American banks always seems shorter than that of their competitors. At first glance, such a maturity structure of the banks' international claims on LDCs does not seem

Table 9.2. *Geographical breakdown and maturity distribution of banks' claims on LDCs, 31 December 1979 (millions of U.S. dollars and percent of total)*

	a	b	c	d	e	f	g
Total bank claims on LDCs	260,251 (100%)	64,606 (24.8%)	27,608 (10.6%)	65,557 (25.2%)	73,601 (28.3%)	20,573 (7.9%)	8,306 (3.2%)
of which total U.S. bank claims on LDCs	89,222 (100%)	19,952 (22.4%)	7,067 (7.9%)	21,325 (23.9%)	31,441 (35.2%)	7,887 (8.8%)	1,547 (1.7%)
Maturity under 1 year	111,797 (42.9%)	32,161 (49.8%)	12,611 (45.7%)	21,896 (33.4%)	31,644 (43.0%)	9,818 (47.7%)	3,667 (44.1%)
of which U.S. bank claims (% of total U.S. bank claims)	49,100 (55.0%)	11,732 (58.8%)	3,904 (55.2%)	9,632 (45.2%)	17,630 (56.1%)	5,146 (65.2%)	1,055 (68.2%)
Maturity between 1 and 2 years	21,787 (8.4%)	4,630 (7.2%)	2,271 (8.2%)	6,095 (9.3%)	6,964 (9.5%)	1,334 (6.5%)	493 (5.9%)
Maturity over 2 years	102,197 (39.3%)	22,156 (34.3%)	10,823 (39.2%)	31,405 (47.9%)	29,468 (40.0%)	6,326 (30.7%)	2,019 (24.3%)
Unallocated	24,470 (9.4%)	5,659 (8.8%)	1,903 (6.9%)	6,161 (9.4%)	5,525 (7.5%)	3,095 (15.0%)	2,127 (25.6%)
Total	260,251 (100%)	64,606 (100%)	27,608 (100%)	65,557 (100%)	73,601 (100%)	20,573 (100%)	8,306 (100%)

[a]Total figure.
[b]OPEC countries.
[c]High-income countries (over U.S. $2,500).
[d]Upper-middle-income countries (U.S. $1,136 to U.S. $2,500).
[e]Intermediate-middle-income countries (U.S. $551 to U.S. $1,135).
[f]Lower-middle-income countries (U.S. $281 to U.S. $550).
[g]Low-income countries (U.S. $280 or less).
Source: Computed from twice yearly reports on international banking, BIS, Basle, July 1980, and *Country Lending Exposure Survey,* Federal Reserve System, June 1980.

alarming. However, as Section II will go into in greater detail, the data may be misleading. In particular, one of the main questions to be answered is whether or not such financial resources, granted by banks to LDCs, in fact suit the particular needs of these countries.

More generally, aggregate records can give us no indication about either the spread of these claims among the banks in each lending country or their share in individual banks' portfolios. Nonetheless, annual reports of the bigger American banks[15] reveal that international lending to LDCs is highly concentrated among the leading ones. We may thus estimate that, on 31 December 1979, loans granted to LDCs by 13 major U.S. multinational banks amounted to U.S. $69.9 billion, not to mention their other claims on these countries.

Individual data also confirm that only a minor portion of these loans went to poorest countries. According to our own calculations, for the banks of this sample, the share of loans attributable to lower-middle-income and low-income countries ranged from 1.8% to 10.5% of their international loan portfolios. This latter share represents from 1.0% to 3.9% of their total loan portfolios.

To some extent, American banks thus appear rather more conservative in their lending policies to the poorest LDCs than suggested by the aggregate data from the Bank for International Settlements. This cautious attitude may be as much a consequence of their earlier experience in the international lending field as of the recommendations and warnings of their regulatory authorities, who are now jointly supervising their foreign activities.[16]

II. Bank lending to LDCs and the stability of the international financial system

The sudden breakthrough of private banks in the financing of LDCs is just one aspect of the global evolution experienced on the international monetary scene during the last decade, which saw the emergence of a strong international financial private system, led by a handful of big multinational banks, particularly the major American ones. In such fields as the daily management of the floating-exchange-rate system and the financing of payments imbalances, this system has progressively supplanted the official sector (central banks and IMF), particularly since 1973. Since the early seventies, the move from public sources of funds (bilateral and multilateral governmental aids and grants, loans from the World Bank group, etc.) in meeting the financial requirements of LDCs toward private ones appears as a logical outcome of a fundamental transformation in the international monetary system.

This growing involvement of private banks also represents a great change from the pattern of previous waves of international private financing referred to earlier. During the nineteenth century and the interwar period, public issues of shares and bonds were the principal means of raising funds for foreign borrowers. Today these have largely been displaced by bank credits, as LDCs have limited access to the highly selective international bond markets.[17] This obviously has important macro-economic consequences: Because investment in LDCs is no longer financed by accumulated savings but by bank credit, its relationship to and influence on the liquidity-creation process (in individual countries and at the international level) deserves more careful attention. But it also has other implications more directly relevant to our present purpose.

In particular, the risks associated with foreign lending are no longer shared and spread out among a large number of individual savers (and sometimes institutional investors) but are concentrated within a narrower group of large and middle-size international banks.[18] Because LDCs require very long-term funds and banks have mainly short-term resources, the latter must also face maturity-transformation risks that did not exist in the direct finance process of the last century.

Questions can thus be raised as to how banks can cope with these two types of risk and as to the consequences of the new pattern of financing on the stability and robustness of the international financial system.

Since the late sixties, international banks have increasingly relied on liability-management techniques that give strong impetus to the rapid growth of their international assets and to the accompanying maturity-transformation process.[19] At the same time, syndication of medium-term loans has enabled lenders to share and spread out the risk of debtor default more widely and more evenly. More recently, sophisticated procedures for assessing the "sovereign risk" of borrowing countries have been evolved by most international banks. Notwithstanding these improvements in international financial technology, which undoubtedly enlighten the decision process of lending to countries, we cannot ignore that the money markets on which banks fund their international assets remain highly sensitive to the least external or internal shock.[20] The spreading of internationl risks among the banking system of the main industrial countries still seems limited in scope, as many medium or small banks without significant international experience are not ready to commit funds in loans to borrowers whose credit ratings cannot be assessed. Finally, lending policies toward LDCs seem to obey the one absolute rule of credit rationing as banks strictly limit the sum granted to each individual country because of imperfect information about its true credit standing.[21] These last remarks will provide us with the general background to judge the current state and prospects of LDC indebtedness toward banks and their consequences for the international financial system.

Although today's global indebtedness of LDCs is not high by historical standards, because world inflation has largely eroded the nominal piling up of debts since the early seventies, some countries may experience difficulties in meeting payments of interest and/or principal. This is mainly a consequence of the short average maturity of private debt, as compared with the average amortization period of their investments.

Although the pattern of debt-service schedules during the years 1970–7[22] reveals that, except for a few countries (and contrary to a commonly widespread opinion), debt-service ratios[23] did not follow a clear rising trend,[24] nonetheless these ratios seem to have been sensitive to general economic conditions facing the borrowing countries and most of all to world prices for primary commodities and growth rates in the main industrial countries. This explains why problems appeared mainly among borrowers (like Zaire, Peru, and Chile) that are primarily exporters of such commodities, whereas countries with more diversified and stronger economic structures (like Brazil, Taiwan, and South Korea) showed a far better record.

On the other hand, as inflation and counteractive monetary policies produce rising and volatile interest rates, the actual cost of loans and the burden of debt service become more and more unpredictable for many borrowers.[25]

More precisely, because of the interdependence between Eurodollar deposit rates and those on money-market instruments in the United States, LDC borrowers (and others) on the international markets could be hard hit by the consequences of the decision, on October 6, 1979, of the Fed to emphasize the stabilization of monetary aggregates and to unpeg short-term interest rates. Should this new orientation of the U.S. monetary policy be confirmed, it might well lead to an increasing volatility of short-term interest rates on international money markets on which banks fund their foreign portfolios. The combination of rising and rather unpredictable debt service[26] with fluctuating foreign-exchange receipts undoubtedly enhances the risk of default among a larger group of debtors and accentuates the fragility of the international financial system (in Minsky's sense).

We must mention, however, that to prevent the eventual difficulties of a bunching up of repayments in 1979–80 of the huge Eurocurrency medium-term credits raised since 1974,[27] some borrowers (particularly in 1978) took the opportunity offered by the high liquidity of the Euromarkets and stiff competition among banks to restructure part of their privately owed debt. They seem to have succeeded well in this attempt, because according to data from Morgan Guaranty Trust, average final maturities on new Eurocurrency bank credits to governments and state enterprises in selected countries evolved as shown in Table 9.3.[28]

Very often, moreover, the proceeds of such loans helped a number of

Table 9.3. *Average final maturities (in years) on new Eurocurrency bank credits*

Quarters	1977				1978				1979		
	Q_1	Q_2	Q_3	Q_4	Q_1	Q_2	Q_3	Q_4	Q_1	Q_2	Q_3
Six non-oil LDCs	6.2	6.7	6.5	7.6	8.2	9.6	9.4	9.6	9.6	9.2	9.8
Four OPEC countries	6.9	7.0	7.1	7.0	8.9	8.4	8.2	8.2	5.8	8.3	6.1

Source: World Financial Markets, various issues.

heavy borrowers to rebuild their foreign-exchange reserves, which in June 1979 totaled U.S. $73.2 billion for non-OPEC LDCs. In the case of such a highly leveraged country as Brazil, these reserves amounted to U.S. $11.9 billion at the end of 1978, against U.S. $4.03 billion at the end of 1975.[29] For some countries, the gap between net and gross indebtedness has been also steadily widening. Last but not least, such loans were granted with much softer conditions as concerns the interest spread and various fees paid by borrowers.

This development, however, can give them only a short breathing space. All projections show that the bulk of repayments in the next five years combined with the effects of the recession spreading in industrial countries after oil price increases in 1979 and the effects of more costly energy imports will exacerbate debt-servicing problems for many LDCs. More generally, rather optimistic projections by Amex Bank in March 1977 had already stressed that over the whole of the 1977–85 period, amortization would average 55% of gross Euroborrowing needs for non-oil LDCs.[30] The latter, therefore, would appear to be more and more entangled in a process of "Ponzi finance," to use Minsky's term, and a crisis may soon be unavoidable. If such a crisis should occur, how could its spread be prevented?

III. LDC defaults and the
lender of last resort in international context

It is a paradox that the international financial community has already experienced over the last five years the main ingredients of a world-wide financial crisis. Fortunately, however, these came separately.

On the one hand, in the summer of 1974 the highly sensitive interbank markets of the Eurodollar system were disrupted by a confidence crisis that followed the failure of the Bankhaus Herstatt and a number of other incidents. Some consortia Eurobanks were hard hit, as they could not refund longer-term commitments because of a drying up of the money markets and had no other escape than to sell some of their assets at a loss.

On the other hand, since 1975 Peru, Zaire, Egypt, and, recently, Turkey[31] have nearly gone into default. In each case, however, rescheduling of debts was able to be arranged after the countries agreed with the IMF on a program for improving their economic performances; no bank suffered loss, confidence in the "soundness" of the international banking system was not questioned, and the mechanisms of various money markets continued to function smoothly. Here, in effect, lies the crux of the matter, for it could happen that if only a minor borrower went into default, and losses incurred by some banks were small, there would be devastating effects on highly intertwined international money markets all around the world that would lead to a major crash.

Moreover, banks, especially the bigger American ones, may have been made all the more sensitive to loan losses in LDCs because in spite of the huge sums charged off against operating revenues during the last four years, their balance sheets do not yet seem to have been netted out of all bad loans such as those to the real estate investment trusts (REITs) or to the very large crude-carrier shipowners, not to mention their municipal bond portfolios.

Rather than having to counter the consequences of a widespread financial crisis, it might seem wiser to prevent its occurrence. Debtors as well as creditors have diverging views on such a matter. For example, as early as 1976, nonaligned states had urged a major LDC debt rescheduling as part of the new international economic order. Until recently this solution had not been seriously considered by creditors, except for some (like Sweden, Canada, France, etc.) who went even further and canceled the public debt owed to them by the poorest LDCs.[32] Although, for various technical reasons, it seems that such a global scheme could only apply to this part of the debt owed to official creditors, there are some arguments in its favor. The first, often mentioned, concerns the relief given to LDCs hard hit by the consequences of the world economic disorders since 1974, and its positive effects on their demand for investment goods produced by the industrial countries. However, there are also strong arguments against such a general debt rescheduling: In particular, the relief for LDCs might prove short-lived if they continue to pile up debts against private creditors. This latter issue is all the more probable considering that banks might reappraise credit ratings of the borrowing countries and agree to extend new lines of credit to them, in view of the apparent improvement of their external-payments situation. Finally, after a few years, this latter might then prove severely worsened.

In fact, rescheduling ought to remain a case-by-case solution, applying to the whole external debt of a country and closely monitored by all lenders so as to avoid a quick resurgence of external-payments problems.

Aware of this growing fragility of the international financial system, the monetary authorities in many countries have recently expressed fears about the possibility of a major crash due to poorer countries' indebtedness. These authorities seem to be locked in a very complex situation. In the late sixties, some already wanted to lay down some prudential rules in the functioning of the Euromarkets, but since 1974 they have been split between this objective (aiming at "guiding" these markets) and the desire not to disrupt a mechanism that proved so efficient in recycling OPEC surpluses and without which the world economy would undoubtedly have experienced a much deeper recession than it actually did. It is not clear whether or not this contradiction in the position of central banks is the result of persistent misunderstandings about the true nature of the Euromarkets. Recently, however, more and more central banks (including the very liberal Bundesbank of Germany) have again worried about the Euromarkets, arguing that they had "overrecycled" the OPEC surplus and enabled some oil-importing countries to escape the inevitable adjustment policies required by higher energy prices.[33]

As a consequence, the big banks in the major industrial countries may soon reach the limit of their lending potential to the LDCs, according to the present size of their capital base. More precisely, fearing that assets/capital ratios have become too thin, monetary authorities in the United States, Switzerland, and Germany are now urging that banks be required to publish consolidated figures for their domestic and foreign operations and to conform to some regulatory ratios in both activities, not just the domestic ones.

If this prudential aspect of lender-of-last-resort activity has not yet fully developed,[34] some encouraging tendencies did emerge as early as September 1974, as concerns emergency interventions in times of crisis. At their meeting at the BIS, in Basle, central-bank governors agreed that they were ready to intervene as lenders of last resort on the Euromarkets if and when necessary, and they recognized that they had the means to do so. They did not, however, want to lay down detailed rules and procedures in advance. Each central bank felt responsible for providing liquidity to its own national banks; at the same time, the Bank of England urged shareholders of multibank consortia in London to specify the extent of their liabilities toward their affiliates, so as to prevent resurgence of the dramatic events of the summer of 1974.

Do these rather informal agreements provide a sufficient safety net? It is rather difficult to answer this crucial question, because, fortunately, they have not had to be put to the test since 1974.

As we have said, no country has yet been forced into default, and it remains doubtful that this could occur. First, the economic situation and its long-term prospects remain sound for many of the major borrowers, as long as foreign bank loans are productively invested in financing industrial or agricultural projects that will enhance the export capacity of the debtor country and raise its real GNP per capita. To a large extent, this inflow of foreign capital is acceptable as long as domestic savings fall short of domestic investment at the early stages of the development process. However, since 1974, some countries have also been incurring rising indebtedness toward private banks because they thought that their external-payments difficulties, increased by rising energy import bills, would be transitory and because the official sector (governments, IMF, World Bank) revealed itself unable to face the new situation.[35]

Although, on the one hand, the appreciation of the situation by some borrowers proved mistaken, on the other hand the official sector may now feel more or less committed to bail out private banks should problems occur. Understandably, precise rules cannot be set in such a field. Relationships between private banks and the IMF have already begun to evolve in such a direction. When a country comes near to default, the banks tie the rescheduling of debt to an agreement between the debtor and the IMF, as this is the only institution capable of forcing borrowing countries to pursue adjustment policies necessitated by their economic troubles. On the same occasion, the Fund provides the country with some credit, but this can give it only very short relief. The IMF cannot appear as a lender of last resort in the conventional sense, because it rescues the final debtor, not the lending institutions in trouble. Moreover, this latter procedure takes rather a long time to work out[36] and does not, therefore, seem appropriate for managing a situation of widespread difficulties for many huge borrowers.

Should difficulties occur, we can suppose that the banks will remain convinced that rescheduling is the lesser evil. In many instances, banks will feel that early refinancing is by far the surest and most convenient way to ward off difficulties that would threaten the stability of the whole international financial private system. The debtor itself will certainly look for such a solution, because this enables it to escape the formal and publicly unveiled procedures of the rescheduling that would durably injure its future credit rating in the international financial community.

But large-scale refinancing, probably with some lengthening of loan maturities (as occurred in 1978–9), implies that banks can easily attract new resources in such monies (dollar and DM, essentially) and in such amounts as to fund their foreign loan portfolios without major problems. Two situations are then possible:

In the first place, banking systems in the major lending countries may be flush with liquidity, as they have been during these two or three past years; free international capital movements are maintained so that multinational banks can rely on the smooth functioning of the highly sophisticated exchange and money markets to play the game of liabilities management and find the needed resources.

Second, however, due for example to stringent monetary policies (in these countries) to fight against reviving inflationary pressures,[37] banks may suffer some drying up of their funding sources. Their ensuing problems might quickly prove all the more intractable with the result that the debtors themselves, because of rising debt-service payments in a period of high interest rates, would not be able to meet their repayment commitments. If central banks then wanted to remove undue strains on their national banking systems, antiinflationary policy would have to be postponed. Moreover, because the dollar (and, eventually, the DM) remains the major currency of denomination for Eurocredits, the demand for resources by the banks would, finally, be a demand for dollars (DM), which would mean in such a case that the Federal Reserve System (and eventually the Bundesbank) incurs particular duties in providing the system with liquidity, directly for American (German) banks and their foreign branches and indirectly, through international money and exchange markets, for all other banks.

Finally, it is conceivable in such a situation that a sustained growth rate for the American (German) monetary base could be the means for ensuring banks of a "soft landing" as long as their portfolios remain overloaded with dubious assets on LDCs (not to speak of those on more conventional borrowers[38]). Economists know that money creation backed by bad-quality claims leads, sooner or later, to inflation.

Prolonged world inflation may thus appear as a consequence of the willingness of the authorities to avoid a major financial crisis prelude to a deep recession. In the long run, it could also prove an acceptable mechanism for forcing the transfer of real resources from industrial countries to LDCs, as long as it alleviates the real burden of their debt.

Notes

1 Keynes, J. M. 1963 (August 1931). "The Consequences to the Banks of the Collapse of Money Values." In: *Essays in Persuasion*. New York: W. W. Norton.
2 The four previous waves occurred in 1817–25, 1860–76, 1900–14, and during the twenties. Unfortunately, they all ended in widespread default crises. For a historical perspective on international lending waves, see Kindleberger, C. P. 1978. "Debt Situation of the Developing Countries in Historical Perspective." In: *Financing and Risk in Developing Countries,* edited by S. H. Goodman, pp. 3–11. New York: Praeger. See also "Financing the LDCs: The Role of the Euromarkets." *Euromoney* November 1977, pp. 76–83.
3 Unfortunately, this list is not exhaustive.

4 Hughes, H. 1979. "Debt and Development: The Role of Foreign Capital in Economic Growth." *World Development,* Vol 7; this special issue of *World Development* is devoted to LDCs' external debt problems.

5 Source: World Bank, 1980 Annual Report.

6 The latter figures are not regularly recorded by the World Bank in its debt-reporting system (DRS), but since January 8, 1979, this institution has provided, in a nonsystematic way, some information about the private nonguaranteed debts of some countries. A first survey was published in January 1979 (EC 167/78/S A). Others are expected.

7 For example, Brazil, which is one of the most indebted LDCs, had a disbursed public debt of U.S. $14.852 billion outstanding on 31 December 1976, of which U.S. $8.445 billion (57%) was owed to banks. At the same time, its disbursed private nonguaranteed debt reached U.S. $11.133 billion, of which U.S. $10.259 billion (92%) were private bank claims. Source: World debt tables and supplements, World Bank.

8 We use the world consumer price index computed and published in *International Financial Statistics* by the International Monetary Fund.

9 Base index 100 for 1975. Source: *International Financial Statistics.*

10 According to the 1979 annual report of the IMF, between 1974 and the end of 1978 the number of countries that experienced difficulties in the servicing of their external debt and had rescheduled it has risen from 3 to 18.

11 In particular, in assessing country credit risks.

12 This figure corresponds to the net size of the international bank credit market, as estimated by the Bank for International Settlements. In December 1979 the estimated gross size was U.S. $1,111 billion.

13 The gross figure of their claims was then U.S. $44 billion.

14 New medium-term Eurocurrency credits, on gross terms, granted to these countries reached U.S. $106 billion in 1977, 1978, and 1979, according to Morgan Guaranty Trust figures in *World Financial Markets.*

15 To our knowledge, American banks are the only ones required by their regulatory authorities to release to the public the information about the composition of their international loan portfolios.

16 Since 1977 the Comptroller of the Currency, the Federal Reserve System, and the FDIC have been jointly supervising the international activities of American commercial banks. These latter are required to file semiannual surveys of the geographic and maturity breakdowns of their foreign assets.

17 According to data compiled in *World Financial Markets,* LDCs raised only U.S. $14.728 billion in international bonds between 1970 and 1979. The share of OPEC countries in this total amounted to U.S. $3.226 billion.

18 Some risks are similar to those in every type of lending: for example, the risk of failure of the debtor. Other are specific: exchange risk and political risk.

19 The amount of maturity transformation performed by banks operating in the Euromarkets has substantially increased since 1973, as medium-term Eurocredits took a growing share in international bank lending activities. This is evidenced by a recent study: Little, J. S. 1979. "Liquidity Creation by Eurobanks: 1973–1978." *New England Economic Review* January-February 1979, pp. 62–72.

20 As the disruption of the interbank money-market mechanism, following the Bankhaus I. D. Herstatt failure in July 1974, clearly shows.

21   As evidenced by the statements of the lending officers of U.S. banks in their annual reports.

22   According to World Bank's annual reports.

23   This ratio is equal to interest plus amortization payments divided by the value of exports (all in annual terms).

24   More precisely, an article in *The Economist* (3 November 1979) shows that among a sample of 16 highly indebted LDSs between 1972 and 1978 this ratio rose for 8 (although very little for countries like Brazil and Venezuela) and fell for the others (in particular, South Korea and Iran).

25   Let us recall that Eurocredits are granted on a rollover basis, interest rates being generally revised every six months and indexed on the cost of resources for the lending banks, as represented by the LIBOR (London interbank offered rate).

26   For example, the six-month Eurodollar bid rate for deposits in London has been steadily rising from a low 5.44% in April 1977 to a high 12.31% in December 1978. After a brief decline to 10.56% in March 1979, it reached 12.71% in September 1979. Source: *World Financial Markets*.

27   These loans begin to fall due only now, because of grace periods.

28   Data compiled by the World Bank in its *Borrowing in International Capital Markets* confirm these results: in 1977, 72.6% of the amounts raised had initial maturities of more than 5 years; in 1978, 62.4% had initial maturities of more than 7 years; in 1976, 35.1% only had initial maturities of more than 5 years.

29   Source: *International Financial Statistics,* IMF. According to *The Economist* (November 3, 1979) this accumulation of reserves enabled non-oil LDCs of Latin America to pay 5.9 months of imports in 1978, against 2.4 months in 1975. For non-oil LDCs in Asia, the respective figures reached 3.6 and 2.8 months; for those in Africa, 2.0 and 1.8 months, respectively.

30   Amex Bank. "The Refinancing Effect." *Euromoney* October 1978, p. 219.

31   To take only a few well-known examples, alas.

32   For an overview of the problems attached to a major debt relief in favor of the LDCs, see Kenen, P. B. 1976. "Debt Relief as Development Assistance." In: *The New International Economic Order,* edited by Bhagwati, J. pp. 50–77. Cambridge, Mass.: MIT Press.

33   Deutsche Bundesbank, 1978 annual report, p. 52 of the English version.

34   However, commercial banks in the United States are already required to publish such consolidated data. More recently, Swiss banks, following the Dutch ones, have been asked by their supervisory authorities to file consolidated balance sheets (*Financial Times,* 2 August 1979).

35   To some extent, deficit countries favored bank borrowing because it is not conditional on the adoption of a particular economic policy program, as in the case of an IMF support.

36   Very often, discussions take a few months, at least. In the recent cases of Zaire and Turkey, while discussions were going on, banks had already prepared their rescheduling plans and were only awaiting the agreement with the IMF.

37   To our mind, this hypothesis is more sustainable than that of a strong economic expansion in industrial countries that would require banks to give priority to domestic financing. In the latter situation we can expect that LDCs' exports to industrial countries would grow and their debt-service problems would be alleviated.

38   Such as the Chrysler Corporation in the United States or steel-plant industry in some European countries.

10. On the lender of last resort

ROBERT M. SOLOW

I. Introduction

In this chapter I must try to walk a narrow line. My task is to discuss the role of the lender of last resort from the point of view of a theorist interested in economic policy. That seems to be the natural role for the theorist of last resort. Everyone at this conference knows more than I do about the historical and institutional texture of lenders of last resort, and most know more about the history of economic thought on the subject. That very fact suggests that no one at this conference wants to see real (or even nominal) theorist's theorizing, complete with hard mathematical models. So I shall aim for a compromise. My goal is to indicate in a general way what economic theory has to say on the two main analytical questions that generally arise in discussions of this subject.

The first question seems to be this: Is there a case for having a lender of last resort? In terms of the domestic economy, the only candidate in practice is the central bank. Should it stand ready, under well-defined circumstances, presumably including but not limited to situations of general credit stringency, to lend freely to private financial institutions, perhaps suspending the normal standards of credit-worthiness? In terms of the international economy, the same question can be asked, but if there is to be a lender of last resort it might have to be an institution yet to be created, and its potential borrowers might well include national central banks. In any case, because I owe to C. P. Kindleberger, the guiding spirit of this conference, the dictum that "We don't pay Solow to think about international economics," I shall think mostly about a national lender of last resort; but the issues I intend to take up are general enough so that the context is almost unimportant.

The second question to be discussed follows naturally: Does a serious problem of "moral hazard" arise whenever there is an effective lender of last resort? Does the existence of a credible commitment by the central bank to lend freely in time of trouble lead to the assumption of excessive risk by private banks in exactly the same way in which a family that is insured against theft may be excessively careless about locking up a house or a car before leaving it? The force of the term *excessive* here is not merely that banks or families may exercise less than socially optimal amounts of care because with insurance the net marginal social value of care exceeds its net marginal private value. In both the instances mentioned the existence of insurance may have the particularly perverse effect of increasing the incidence of the contingency being insured against – bank failures in one case and burglaries in the other. The answer to this second question is pretty obviously "Yes." The point of putting so easy a question is that the process of answering it will suggest what sorts of rules or devices might be expected to mitigate the consequences of moral hazard. I shall have a few words to say on that subject.

II. The need for a lender of last resort

Any fractional-reserve banking system is in principle vulnerable to runs. There is no guarantee that runs will occur, or occur often, but the possibility is there. If a run does occur, there is always a chance that it will cumulate, because any bank failure diminishes confidence in the whole system and brings stronger banks under increased pressure. The consequences of a banking crisis are likely to extend beyond the banking system into the "real" economy. Any developed capitalist economy supports a network of interrelated debtor–creditor relations. Inability of A to meet obligations to B may impair B's ability to meet obligations to C, and production may suffer as a result. The function of the lender of last resort is to stop such a chain reaction in its earliest stages, before it has a chance to cumulate, by visibly providing ample credit to keep the weaker links from giving way. This protection need not extend to the weakest links.

In the English-language literature the classic case for aggressive emergency use of its lending power by the central bank was, of course, Walter Bagehot's *Lombard Street* (1873). Actually, as early as 1802 the remarkable Henry Thornton argued quite forcefully that the Bank of England should use its reserves early and strongly to meet an internal drain of cash from the banks. Thornton understood clearly the role of the lender of last resort; witness this recent exegesis from *Paper Credit* (Reisman, 1971:82): "In Thornton's model the Bank should be at its freest in loans to the banks and the public precisely when risk and need are greatest and the Bank's gold is least, if only so that the total quantity of money in circulation does not decrease . . . . The Bank should not relieve those banks whose difficulties arise from 'improvidence' or 'misconduct' [although] the alternative to relief would be letting the bank fail, and this would shatter that very confidence in the credit system which is so necessary for the pyramiding of claims."

On the lender of last resort 239

John Hicks, in his essay on Thornton (1967:187), elaborates on what he describes as an "essential idea of Thornton's":

Every economy is liable to unexpected shocks – of which the harvest failures, that are Thornton's principal example, are of course no more than an example. One of the things which we should require of economic organization is that its institutions should be such that it can stand up to shocks; that it should have cushions against them, so that their secondary repercussions are minimized, not intensified by the fears and alarms that they so easily engender. But there are few cushions that will drop into place automatically; the most that is usually possible is that there should be reserves which can be used, if there are people who have the skill and courage to use them, at the right and not at the wrong time. A developed credit system . . . has the advantage over a pure hard money system, in that its reserves are in places where they can more readily be used, if there is the intelligence and the strength of will to use them. It is, of course, only too true that these essential qualities may not be there. But to fall back on rules, making the monetary system mechanical, is a confession of failure.

Bagehot, by the way, also commented that "the practical difficulties of life cannot be met by simple rules," and he would no doubt have applied this piece of wisdom to central banking. I mention this bit about rules only to remind everyone that there is another point of view. In *A Program for Monetary Stability* (1960:37–8), Milton Friedman takes the opposite position on central-bank emergency lending. At the beginning, "The Reserve System was to be a 'lender of last resort,' ready to provide liquidity in a time of crisis to satisfy a widespread demand for currency that otherwise would produce either suspension of payments or a substantial decline in the stock of money." After the passage of the Federal Deposit Insurance Act, however, depositors have no reason to fear that their deposits might become inconvertible into currency. "A liquidity crisis involving such runs on a widespread scale is now almost inconceivable. The need for rediscounting in order for the Reserve System to serve as 'a lender of last resort' has therefore become obsolete, not because the function has been taken over by someone else but because it no longer needs to be performed."

If Friedman is anti-Thornton, let me quote Harry Johnson as anti-Bagehot: "At least in the presence of a well-developed capital market, and on the assumption of intelligent and responsible monetary management by the central bank, the commercial banks should be able to manage their own reserve positions without the need for the central bank to function as 'lender of last resort'."

The proviso about intelligent and responsible monetary management is pretty sweeping. It comes close to saying that if central banks are smart enough to avoid liquidity crises they will not need to do the things they are supposed to do in liquidity crises. Both Johnson and Friedman seem to pay too little attention to nonbank financial institutions and their stability, and this failure is consistent with the normal monetarist fixation on M_1 as means of payment. Others would at least ask whether or not the central bank, or some other arm of the government, ought to be prepared to act as lender of last resort directly or indirectly to a wider class of financial institutions to avoid instability in the financial mechanism defined a little more broadly than currency and demand deposits. I do not think the answer is open-and-shut, but the question can be asked. It should be mentioned that Friedman has supported a 100% reserve requirement for checking accounts. This would sever the maintenance of the payments mechanism from any connection with the credit market. One might still want deposit insurance as protection against embezzlement, but there would be no way for bad debts to infect the payments mechanism or vice versa. Then, as Friedman could correctly point out, the lender of last resort would be a lot like the buyer of agricultural commodities of last resort, and the desirability of having one would be suddenly more problematical.

I am not sure that theory has much to contribute to this issue. There is, of course, an inevitable pure-externality aspect associated with the interlocking debt structure. My bank may go under, and I may suffer a loss, because we are at the far end of a chain reaction launched by the inability of some other debtor to pay a creditor who . . . . But one expects bank depositors, like other lenders, to look into the soundness of their banks. The capital market will and should offer a range of risk–yield combinations, and those who choose to live dangerously have to expect to take a tumble now and then. That does not call for a rescue operation. Lenders and depositors can legitimately be expected to know something about the asset structure they are buying into, but it may be asking too much to expect them to see through the thrice-removed financial interrelationships that might ultimately cause trouble. If that argument is accepted, there is clearly a case for intervention, and the lender of last resort seems like a good form for the intervention to take.

The cumulative chain reaction is an important part of this argument. My goose-down business may suffer because of some events involving labor relations in the industry manufacturing the cables that carry ski lifts, but hardly anyone would regard that complicated story as a case for indemnifying wholesalers of goose down. The difference appears to be that the Ski Lift Story is expected to damp quickly; the process is effectively stable, self-limiting. The financial panic is an unstable system; small differences in initial conditions lead to vast differences in the final outcome.

That, at least, seems to be the logic of the argument. Its empirical truth or falsity is another matter. How far would the waves and ripples have traveled if the Franklin National had simply been allowed to fail? Does anyone know? Did the rescue operation stage-managed by the Fed head off a panic, even a minipanic, or did it simply bail out a few big shots? One could argue that merely to count noses, after allowance for deposit insurance, is an inadequate measure of the potential damage, because any blow to confidence in the banking system may later prove highly destabilizing. On the other hand, it is inadequate to rest on the fact that financial panics do happen; the optimal flood-control system will not necessarily reduce the probability of overflow to zero. All the theorist can say is that there is a potentially sound argument that rests on the unstable propagation of disturbance through the financial system, beyond the bounds of what ordinary prudence can be expected to cope with. For the very same reason, private insurance cannot be expected to meet the system's needs, because what needs to be insured against is a crisis on a scale too large for any private lender. But it is not obvious, especially in the presence of deposit insurance, that the instability is really there.

Throughout its history the Federal Deposit Insurance Corporation has had an upper limit on the coverage provided any one account (that maximum is now $40,000). The logic of this limit presumably has been that the small depositor cannot be expected to judge the ultimate soundness of his bank. One consequence of this limit has been that the FDIC has been generally unwilling to let a major bank fail and trigger the payment of insurance, because a substantial fraction of aggregate deposits would go uncovered. In the case of the U.S. National Bank of San Diego in 1973, with almost a billion dollars in deposits, only about three-quarters of aggregate deposit liabilities would have been covered by deposit insurance. In this case of the Franklin National Bank, pretty clearly a case of poor management, only about half of the $1.7 billion in deposit liabilities would have been covered. The FDIC has generally tried, in such cases, to arrange a takeover of the weak bank by a solvent one, perhaps with the help of an infusion of FDIC funds. The argument has been that partial payoff of insurance would not be enough to maintain confidence in the banking system as a whole. On FDIC policy, see the work of Varvel (1976).

All this suggests a slightly different way to describe the role of the lender of last resort in terms of the categories of economic theory. One could argue, with some justice, that a confidence-worthy and confidence-inspiring monetary-financial system is a public good. Exactly like the standard textbook examples – national defense, the cop on the beat – it necessarily spreads its benefits over those who contribute to it and those who don't. The advantages of a well-functioning monetary-financial system are not divided up, like coffee, but shared, like peace. As with any public good, the problem of the free rider intrudes. It may profit any individual to do things that undermine the stability of the monetary-financial system, so long as everyone else plays the game. Everyone is then a potential free rider. If the stability of the monetary-financial system is not looked after by a public body, it will be inadequately looked after, perhaps not at all.

I think that is a sound argument. I have tried to call attention to the one important weakness in it by using the awkward phrase "the monetary-financial system." Reasonable people could differ about the size of the umbrella that should be provided. At the core, I suppose everyone would include the payments mechanism; a drift toward barter is bound to be inefficient. But 100% reserve banking or deposit insurance is probably enough to prevent a breakdown of the payments mechanism. At the other extreme, hardly anyone would wish the lender of last resort to provide backstop credit for even fundamentally solvent mutual funds. Somewhere there is a line to be drawn, and I tend to side with Thornton and Bagehot that it is better to rely on sometimes fallible judgment than to try to draw the line once for all times and occasions.

Neither mode of operation is without its problems, as pointed out by Fred Hirsch (1977). Any informal system that leaves a lot to the discretion of the central bank is open to refined corruption. The authorities will have to protect the system from exploitation by those who would naturally like to pocket the profits from successful ventures and pass the losses from unsuccessful ones to the lender of last resort. Some sort of code of good behavior is required; the central bank can extend the rescue net only to those who can be trusted not to abuse the privilege. You can trust only those whom you know. The situation is ripe for the emergence of a club of insiders, old-timers, gentlemen, and for the exclusion of newcomers, unknowns, and aggressively competitive upstarts.

The alternative is a system of objective criteria and formal rules. As Hirsch remarks, any such system is bound to provide more complete coverage for large banks than for small ones, and for defensible reasons: If the purpose of the system is to protect the monetary-financial system against socially destructive disturbance, then the failure of a large bank is clearly socially more costly than the failure of a small one. But this provides an incentive for risk-averse depositors to shift from small to large banks and confers a clear competitive advantage on large size. So a formal system can be expected to promote concentration in banking. This can perhaps be regarded as a manifestation of a species of increasing returns to scale; it will be reinforced by the normal advantage that the law of large numbers confers on any large pooler of risks.

It does not follow from this difficulty that the function of lender of last resort costs more than it is worth. If the analogy to increasing returns to scale is acceptable, then the corresponding element of natural monopoly needs to be offset or corrected by regulation. Obviously the regulatory process is itself vulnerable to corruption through the club of insiders, but that problem is common to all regulated industries, not special to the lender of last resort.

III. The problem of moral hazard

The existence of a credible lender of last resort must reduce the private cost of risk taking. It can hardly be doubted that, in consequence, more risk will be taken. The portfolios of insured financial institutions will be less conservative and their average yields will be higher.

All insurance schemes face this problem, and in that context it is called the problem of moral hazard. I have already mentioned the obvious examples: All of us would be more careful about fire prevention if our houses were not insured against damage from fires. Evidently, then, the availability of fire insurance probably increases the number of fires. The social advantage of fire insurance is that by reducing individual uncertainty in a risk-averse population, it creates benefits that presumably outweigh the extra fire damage that occurs because the insured are less careful than they would otherwise be.

Moral hazard, however, is not confined to ordinary insurance situations. It has been argued recently that the building of levees or dikes may increase the amount of flood damage. The mechanism is similar: In the absence of levees, no one would dare to build in the flood plain. There would be many floods, but little damage each time. When levees are built, people crowd closer to the river. Floods occur very rarely, but cause much more damage when they do occur. This case differs from fire insurance in one respect; there the availability of insurance can be expected to increase the incidence of fires, whereas here the physical incidence of floods decreases, but the damage per incident rises.

The effect of the lender of last resort is something of a mixture. The number of bad debts will rise, like the number of fires. But the number of financial crises will be reduced, like the number of floods. It might be possible, in principle, to build dikes so high and so strong that no flood will ever occur, and therefore no flood losses. But the cost of complete security could easily be so great that it would be preferable to limit the amount of building near the river, either by direct regulation or by other means to be discussed in due course. Financial crises do not have the nice statistical properties of flood crests; I take it for granted that a national (and perhaps an international) lender of last resort would be instructed to permit no panic that it was able to prevent.

Here I shall digress briefly. No one has a kind word to say in favor of fires and floods. There may, however, be something to be said for risky assets. One can imagine a situation in which it is felt that lenders are too conservative, perhaps because the private cost associated with default exceeds social cost. In that case, at least part of the moral hazard accompanying the introduction of an insurance scheme might be a good thing. The question would then turn on whether or not the increase in portfolio risk goes too far. Thus, for instance, when Governor Zolotas of the Bank in Greece proposes an international loan-insurance scheme (1979:34–46), his explicit purpose is to encourage the flow of international lending to developing countries despite its riskiness. The motivation in this case is primarily redistribution rather than efficiency, but the point is the same. I do not intend to consider this issue further. It may be important, but it is off the main theoretical track.

Where does the main theoretical track lead? The standard model is an abstraction of the fire-insurance situation; an excellent example is provided by Shavell (1979). A risk-averse consumer can buy an insurance policy against a contingency whose probability of occurrence is known, but it is known as a function of the amount of "care" taken by the customer himself. The customer pays a premium, which may perhaps be a function of the amount of care taken. If the adverse event happens, the consumer receives an indemnity that may also be a function of the amount of care taken. In the fire-insurance context, care includes such acts as fireproofing, the installation of alarm systems, the avoidance of certain dangerous activities, and so on. In the context we are concerned with here, care would relate primarily to the characteristics of the assets acquired and the liabilities issued by a financial institution. The relation between the probability of loss and the amount of care is a fact of nature. But the relation between premium and care, or between indemnity and care, is a characteristic of the insurance policy. Taking care is costly to the consumer, in terms of current cash costs or foregone earnings.

Given the terms of the insurance policy, one naturally assumes that the consumer chooses the amount of insurance and the amount of care that maximize the expected value of a utility function. I have already stipulated that the consumer is supposed to be risk-averse (the utility function exhibits diminishing marginal utility of wealth), because otherwise there is no point in insurance. The insurance company or central bank, on the other hand, is quite naturally supposed to pool a lot of relatively small risks; it is therefore risk-neutral and is concerned only with the difference between its premium inflow and its average indemnity outflow. In designing an insurance policy, the insuror (in our case, the lender of last resort) must take account of the fact that consumers will react to the terms of the policy offered by choosing how much care to exercise, and choosing in their own best interest.

If it were not for moral hazard, the problem would be easy. Suppose the contingency in question were a pure act of nature, and care were entirely irrelevant. Then obviously the optimal insurance scheme is full coverage at an actuarially fair premium. With full indemnification in case of loss, everyone is completely relieved of uncertainty, and the law of large numbers guarantees that the insurance company breaks even. In practice, of course, there are administrative costs to be covered, but let us suppose them to be trivial.

The possibility of costly care and the consequent inducement of moral hazard make the problem more difficult. One can ask: What is the socially best insurance policy, taking account of the amount of risk that will actually be borne by the individual consumer and the amount of resources that will be used up in care, given that the insuror must break even (or meet some other specified budget constraint)? The precise answer depends on the precise formulation, but there are some general propositions that would seem to apply to a wide variety of circumstances.

First of all, let us suppose that the degree of care is unobservable by the insuror. That is to say, the lender of last resort cannot discover, ex ante or ex post, 'the quality of the assets acquired by insured banks and other institutions. Then neither the premium nor the indemnity can depend on the actions of the insured banks. Theory suggests, first of all, that some degree of insurance coverage is desirable, for standard risk-pooling reasons. The first little bit of insurance must gain more social utility by spreading risk than it loses by reducing the amount of care taken. But theory also suggests that insurance coverage should only be partial. A policyholder should be indemnified only for part of any loss suffered, so that some marginal incentive to take care remains. The optimal degree of coverage depends on the cost of care. If care is very expensive, then the policy should offer almost full coverage; the socially optimal amount of care will be small anyhow, and so the risk-sharing motive predominates. If the cost of care is very low, then once again the policy should offer almost full coverage; there will be few losses anyway. In between, partial coverage – coinsurance – is the rule.

An alternative form of coinsurance would be randomization. The contract could specify that a valid claim will be indemnified fully with probability q and partially (or not at all) with probability $1 - q$. Analogous schemes have appeared in the theory of optimal taxation. In principle, the introduction of another degree of freedom in the description of the insurance policy cannot be disadvantageous. But neither does randomization appear to be a practical possibility. Besides, because the object of insurance is the reduction of individual risk, the deliberate creation of additional risk in the insurance contract seems to be an unlikely form of coinsurance.

Now suppose that the insuror can observe the amount of care exercised by the insured. There are two cross-cutting distinctions to be made. The first is between ex ante observation, made at the time the policy is written, and ex post observation, made when a claim is filed. This distinction, which may be important in the ordinary insurance context, is almost empty in the application to financial institutions. Credit-worthiness standards can be stipulated ex ante, but the quality of loans actually made can be verified only ex post. Periodic bank examination is a compromise, though rather more like ex ante observation. The second distinction is between accurate observation and inaccurate observation. The usual theoretical assumption is that a standard of care is imposed in the insurance contract. In the case of ex post observation, the insuror studies each claim that is presented; indemnity is paid if and only if the standard of care has been met. If the observation is noisy, there is a risk that the insured will be judged falsely to have taken inadequate care and deprived unjustly of indemnity.

Suppose observation is accurate. The socially optimal degree of care depends on the cost and effectiveness of care and on the population's degree of risk aversion. Once the right degree of care has been calculated, the correct form of policy imposes that degree of care and then offers full coverage if the standard is met. Ex post observation is presumably cheaper and therefore appropriate. The rationale here is that accurate observation permits the optimal degree of care to be imposed. The danger of moral hazard is effectively eliminated, and risk aversion then calls for the complete elimination of uncertainty.

Even noisy observation is useful in the sense that it permits the design of a better insurance policy. There is some advantage to ex ante observation, because then the premium can be made to depend on the level of care. In the ordinary insurance context, a window-dressing problem may arise. Construction standards can be verified when a policy is issued and a premium agreed, but ongoing items of care (proper waste disposal, day-to-day safety precautions) can be allowed to lapse once the policy is in force. In the banking context, ex ante observation presumably means at least a continuing spot check on the credit-worthiness of accepted borrowers; I leave it to others to judge whether or not this degree of surveillance is reasonable and likely to be achieved.

When observation is imperfect, either in the nature of the case or because it is very costly, the best form of insurance policy is likely to call for partial coverage. Some incentive to take adequate care has to be provided for the insured, and this incentive is self-administered if the insured must share in any loss.

IV. Applicability to banking

How well does this insurance-inspired theory apply to the situation of the lender of last resort? Imperfectly, I think, but not trivially.

The important difference is in the source of the social value of insurance in the first place. In the context of accident insurance, for which the theory is designed, there need be no important externality. (I emphasize "need be" – Mrs. O'Leary's cow provides the counterexample.) Insurance is desirable because individuals are risk-averse, and everyone gains when risk is shared. There are some intrinsic difficulties with insurance markets, but, in general, one can imagine that the best policies will be generated by competitive insurance companies.

The lender of last resort is bound to be a public body, for several reasons. The most obvious one is scale; for credibility, the lender of last resort needs access to greater resources than any private lender can have. The more important reason is that the primary function of the lender of last resort is not to share default risks among private financial institutions. Banking is a business, not a religion; default risk belongs with stockholders just as fashion risk belongs with clothing manufacturers. The job of the lender of last resort is not to preserve individual banks from failure but to preserve the monetary-financial system from being forced into undesirable deflationary pressure by epidemic loss of confidence in its soundness.

The desirable degree of coverage is likely to be higher for that reason. To take an extreme case, if full or nearly full coverage were required to generate the necessary confidence, then presumably the lender of last resort would offer full indemnification and hope to combat the resulting deterioration of credit standards by other means. Bagehot's insistence that the Bank of England should lend freely but at a penalty rate fits in here. His explanation was that only "fundamentally sound" banks should be rescued, and a fundamentally sound bank would eventually be able to pay off, with interest. In our language, the fundamentally sound bank is one that has not allowed the availability of insurance to undermine its credit standards. Thus the penalty rate is a way of reducing moral hazard. It is a form of coinsurance

Unless there is strong evidence to the contrary, I think one should presume that complete coverage is not necessary for the safety of the monetary-financial system. The theoretical presumption in favor of partial coverage should certainly be the starting point for the design of a lender of last resort.

This impression (it hardly rises to the level of a conclusion) rests also on casual empiricism about the quality of observation. The theory suggests that if observation is cheap and accurate, standards of care should be imposed, and then full coverage offered. That suggestion would be strengthened by the public-good objective of safeguarding the financial system. I doubt that a central bank (or, a fortiori, an international agency) can judge accurately enough the quality of the credit issued by each insured bank. And even if it could, I doubt that it would, partly because of the tendency of regulatory bodies to be co-opted by the regulated via the "club" mechanism, and partly because there would arise issues of invasion of privacy and national pride.

I suggest that there should indeed be standards, but they will need to be reinforced be some degree of coinsurance. There is a tradeoff: The more stringent the standards, the nearer one can come to full insurance. In choosing a point on that tradeoff schedule, one should keep in mind that the object of the lender of last resort is stabilization of the monetary system, not the protection of bank managements from their own errors of judgment.

References

Bagehot, 1873 (reprinted 1962). *Lombard Street.* Homewood, Ill.: R. D. Irwin.
Friedman, M. 1960. *A Program for Monetary Stability.* New York: Fordham University Press.
Hicks, J. 1967. *Critical Essays in Monetary Theory.* Oxford: Clarendon Press.
Hirsch, 1977. "The Bagehot Problem." *Manchester School* 45:241–57.
Reisman, D. A. 1971. "Henry Thornton and Classical Monetary Economics." *Oxford Economic Papers* 23:70–89.
Shavell, S. 1979. "On Moral Hazard and Insurance." *Quarterly Journal of Economics* 93:541–62.
Thornton, H. 1802 (reprinted 1962). *An Enquiry into the Nature and Effects of the Paper Credit of Great Britain.* London: F. Cass.
Varvel, W. A. 1976. "FDIC Policy toward Bank Failures." *Federal Reserve Bank of Richmond Economic Review* September/October, pp. 3–12.
Zolotas, X. 1979. *The Dollar Crisis and Other Papers.* Bank of Greece Papers and Lectures No. 41. Athens: Bank of Greece.

Comment

JEAN-PIERRE LAFFARGUE

In the presence of moral hazard, no insurance may sometimes be socially better than 100%. However, as Solow noted, more imaginative second-best solutions may be found that give a fair compromise between some spreading out of risk and reasonable self-protection. Deductible or partial-coverage rates are examples of such devices. I do not agree with Solow that a random-coverage rate is not a practical possibility. To supply credit, French banks need central-bank money. The Banque de France supplies this to the money market at uncertain dates and in uncertain amounts. The aim of this policy is to make the cost of bank refinancing uncertain, in order to encourage banks to have a careful credit policy. Another example of the efficiency of a random policy is given by Matthews: The act of 1844 did not actually prevent the Bank of England from acting as a lender of last resort (LLR) but made its intervention uncertain enough to discourage speculation. A last example of the use of randomization as a policy is the ambiguity of the LRR to which McClam refers.

An efficient way of eliminating moral hazard is to ban insurance systems: A good device to decrease the number of fires is to ban fire insurance. Such a solution lacks a good deal of subtlety: First, it prevents any pooling of risk; second, it ignores the possibility that some moral hazard may be beneficial to an economy. People must not spend their whole time (as Solow points out) taking care that no burglar enters their home, and banks must not lend only to 100% safe firms. However, this view is close to the traditional one that financial crises must be left to run their course without any intervention of a LLR so as not to encourage banks and financial institutions (FI) to pursue too adventurous policies.

Now a difference with traditional insurance is that people who are to be protected are bank and FI customers, and those who are responsible for moral hazard are bank and FI owners and managers. The trick is to fully protect the first and to penalize the second when insurance systems have to intervene. Solow recalls Bagehot's idea that the LLR must lend at a penalty rate. Deposit-insurance systems and the LLR often accompany their action by restructuring measures and changes in management (which, of course, will limit the cost of their intervention).

Moral hazard can occur because a bank (FI) is more informed about itself than other banks (FI) and the LLR. But this lack of information is still more likely to hold for small deposit (bills, etc.) holders at the bank. Economic theory teaches that when buyers cannot discriminate between the various qualities of a commodity when they purchase it, the market for this commodity may collapse, or at least diminish.[1] Let us assume that deposit holders have a fair idea of the risk of holding bank deposits (bills, etc.) in general (based on the frequency of bankruptcies, newspaper articles, etc.) but that they are unable to compare the risks of holding deposits at various banks. Then, during a speculative mania, each bank (FI) may find that it is in its own interest progressively to increase the risk it assumes: The losses of its stockholders are limited to the value of their stocks, and if things turn out badly, most of the cost will be supported by deposit (bills, etc.) holders. Because of lack of information of these agents, the bank will not have to increase the return on its deposits, nor will it suffer a loss of deposits as a result of its own decisions. But if all banks adopt such a policy, the public will become aware that deposits are becoming more and more risky. This will induce a general increase in their yield (limited by banks' ability to pay for them) and a withdrawal of deposits from banks by agents who will try to shift these funds to other safe assets (gold, real estate, etc., and, of course, central-bank money). During this process the banking system will become less and less profitable and liquid, right to the occurrence of a financial crisis.

These considerations constitute one interpretation of Kindleberger's and Solow's idea that "a confidence-worthy . . . monetary-financial system is a public good" and that "as with any public good, the problem of the free rider intrudes." What devices does theory suggest to limit this process? One solution is that banks and FI create an association with standards of behavior imposed to its members (e.g., ratios, criteria for loans, etc.). These standards must be observable by experts of the association, and their maintenance must be able to reduce the risk of bankruptcy. They may be established by members of the association by the kind of process that has been developed for the revelation of preference for public commodities. If belonging to the association is not compulsory, the public may have difficulties in discriminating precisely between the risks of deposits at member and nonmember banks. The association might then collapse, or its standards could become insufficiently stringent for the same reasons that it was not in the interest of a bank to limit the risk assumed by its deposit holders when there was no such association. On the other hand, with an insurance scheme, compulsory adhesion and standards would limit moral hazard. When insurance is provided by a LLR, the latter must instruct and police the association and its members to limit the extent of moral hazard in the whole financial community (a good example is the French Commission de Contrôle des Banques).

The public-commodity feature of a confidence-worthy financial system is, of course, reinforced in the foregoing model, if we take into account the fact that evaluation of the risk of holding bank deposits (bills, etc.) is usually far from rational, but rather results from an unstable expectation-formation process. If one bank or a limited number of banks go bankrupt, deposit holders at other banks may overreact by shifting to exaggeratedly pessimistic expectations on the general risk of bank failures and may withdraw much of their deposits. It is on this basis that Solow develops the need for a LLR that prevents runs from cumulating and restores confidence. We can add that the LLR holds its power from the fact that it is the issuer of the only permanently safe asset: central-bank money. It is the legal tender that the public has to accept, and the LLR has no obligation to guarantee the convertibility of this money into any other asset.

Note

1   See, for example, Akerlof, G. A. 1970. "The Market for 'Lemons': Quality Uncertainty and the Market Mechanism." *Quarterly Journal of Economics* 84:488–500.

Comment

J. F. LEPETIT

According to Solow, "the function of the lender of last resort is to stop such a chain reaction in its earlier stages, before it has a chance to cumulate, by visibly providing ample credit to keep the weaker links from giving way. This protection need not extend to the weakest links."

I. The responsibility of central banks has increased with the development of the Euromarkets

As one responsible for foreign-exchange activities in a group whose bank, its branches, and subsidiaries deal with more than 1,500 banks situated in more than 40 countries, with a daily turnover somewhere around $2 billion, I need to believe, at least to sleep well at night, that in the event of big trouble the central banks will be prepared to rescue at least the sound links of the financial community under their responsibility.

As a matter of fact, it appears that banks are now borrowing from and lending to one another through domestic and Euromarkets more than they are dealing with customers; but when setting an interbank credit limit, it is very difficult to assess the value of a bank from the outside, and one has to rely partly on the belief that the central bank has been able to create an orderly national market.

Furthermore, the market deems it necessary for the central bank to intervene immediately, as soon as a bank in its market is losing its own credit.

This alleged responsibility of central banks results from three factors that have appeared during the last few decades, as discussed in the following sections.

II. Countries themselves are borrowers in the Euromarket

First, more and more countries are now depending on borrowing in Euromarkets in order to finance the deficits of their balance of payments.

It is generally considered that a bank failure in their domestic markets would affect the credit of the whole country if any loss was suffered by a foreign bank.

Germany or Switzerland could, to a certain extent, afford the bankruptcies of Herstatt or Sindona's Finabank (Geneva), but Italy was not strong enough and had to rescue the Italian banks of the Sindona group.

Contrariwise, the credit of a bank is closely linked to the credit of its own country: When banks in a country are facing liquidity problems because of the national political situation, one may expect that the central bank will make use of its reserves and credit to help everyone under its responsibility.

III. Herstatt lessons

Second, responsibility means regulation and controls, as we shall see later, but regulation and controls decrease private responsibility and increase public responsibility, especially when a bank in trouble has complied absolutely with its central bank's instructions.

The Herstatt bankruptcy convinced the German authorities that they must limit and control the foreign-exchange positions of German banks; I may be wrong, but I believe that we have seen, in that country, the last bank failure caused by foreign-exchange positions and involving foreign banking interests.

In the Herstatt affair, it seems that the German authority wanted to teach speculators, as well as banks dealing with speculators, a lesson. But the U.S. clearing system nearly collapsed with Herstatt on 26 June 1974; the CHIPS computer was switched off, and it was necessary for the clearing U.S. banks to barter checks during the whole night and afterward to use the impossible device of conditional payments.

To be sure, speculators and banks have been taught a lesson, but I feel sure that the monetary authorities of Germany have got the message as well.

Furthermore, national responsibility means that a nation on its way to socialism may choose to intervene directly in the banking sector by nationalizing the major banks' capital. This seems to be the case in more and more countries; it seems obvious that should a problem arise, the lender of last resort would have to come immediately to the rescue at the expense of the central bank or the nation's budget without involving other banks.

Hessische Landesbank Gironzentral lost something like 2 billion deutsche marks, but the loss had less effect than the 1.2 billion Herstatt bankruptcy, as everybody knew that the taxpayer of Hesse was richer than Mr. Yvan Herstatt.

IV. Euromarkets cannot afford the failure of a single large borrower

Last, but not least, it seems to me, in a world where banks and multinational companies may be bigger and more powerful than some cities or countries, that it is irrational to contemplate the possibility of the failure of such banks or multinational companies, as well as cities or countries, whatever the misconduct of such entities may be.

It may be dangerous for a large international bank to lend directly or indirectly to less developed countries more than its shareholders' total equity.

One could also argue against a recycling process that consists in borrowing money at short notice from an OPEC country to lend it for 12 years to underdeveloped countries.

Any failure in the credit chain would have tremendous repercussions. That is the way it is, however, and it makes me feel that every necessary step would be taken to prevent any bankruptcy that would affect the major banks of national or international markets.

For all these reasons, I go further than Solow in my appreciation of the need for a lender of last resort. I believe that our markets cannot afford to see a bankruptcy that would involve losses exceeding the overall profits of the first line of creditors.

Furthermore, I think that many situations would lead monetary authorities to intervene at the very source of the financial trouble in order to prevent bigger trouble somewhere else: They have rescued the City of New York in order to protect the credit of other U.S. cities. They coped with Franklin National Bank and the National Bank of San Diego problems to protect the U.S. banking system. England preserved the fringe banks to maintain the good name of the City of London. The authorities helped the iron and steel industry in France and Belgium to avoid a social crisis on top of bank failures, to say nothing of keeping the credit of these countries safe.

V. The consequences of the responsibility of central banks: regulations and controls are necessary

First of all, any responsibility of the monetary authorities involves regulation and controls in order to prevent any rescue action in the future and to punish the black sheep before rather than after the failure.

I don't believe, as Solow does, in the alternative of some sort of code of good behavior, the track of which leads to the insurance model; such a code implies that there is a majority of "sound" banks and a minority of "bad" ones and that God would save the good ones. But what the bank next door does is not always what is correct for my bank, even if it makes me feel safe to run in the middle of the herd; the flock of sheep might be led by the maddest one.

For example, before the Herstatt failure the majority of international banks underestimated the risks of foreign-exchange positions and transactions. More particularly, the majority thought that there were no delivery risks in spot transactions; just a few were caught, but all have learned.

Likewise, if Brazil, Mexico, or some Eastern countries went bankrupt, one may be sure that there would be a large majority of banks that would not be prepared or strong enough to face such a failure; but should such a thing happen, the U.S. Exim Bank, the French Coface, the German Hermes, and so on, would take the lead in the creditor's list.

Let us come back to regulation and controls. The subject is a very large one, but let me emphasize just two points. First of all, a central bank can regulate and control only its own market. Who can regulate the financial markets that have been created precisely to escape such regulations? Great progress has been made since Herstatt, when central banks unofficially accepted the responsibility for the misconduct of their national banks, but uncertainty remains about the risks involved in the foreign branches, subsidiaries, and consortium affiliates of these banks, especially those situated in beautiful and sunny islands. International banks know that central banks are doing a lot of homework on the regulations for consolidated balance sheets that will give them better results in the future than chasing the Loch Ness monster of global regulations for Euromarkets.

Lastly, everybody knows that it is always possible to get up regulations and controls on a national scale, but no one has yet found out how to enforce rules on a borrowing country, largely because nations are competing with each other more fiercely than are international banks.

VI. Banks are taking too much risk when lending in the international markets

My last comment will deal with the problem of moral hazard. Solow says that the existence of a credible commitment by the central bank to lend freely in time of trouble leads to the assumption of excessive risks by private banks.

I am afraid my own answer is that I agree. The truth of this remark is widely proved by the low margins taken by banks when they feel rightly or wrongly that there is a lender of last resort.

When lending money, a banker needs a threefold margin: one to cover his expenses, one to cover the commercial risk, the last to cover the liquidity risk, if any.

Now, when international banks are organizing balance-of-payments credits with margins around 0.5% or 0.625% one has to admit that these banks are just covering their expenses and must consider that it is not necessary to cover the liquidity risk and the commercial risk.

One must therefore assume that they feel that two lenders of last resort are ready for action, one for lending Eurodollars if the market become tight for them and a second one for lending to the country unable to pay back its debts or to reschedule them.

As a conclusion, I would like to tell you the opinion of my two previous bosses from different private banks about this problem of the lender of last resort.

The first one said: "I don't mind having to ask my central bank for money because of big trouble in the national or international markets. I just want to be the last of the private banks to need money."

Ten years later, the second said: "If I need money because of a crisis in the money markets, I will go straight to the central bank. I don't want to be the first private banker to knock at the door, but I don't mind being the second."

Both agreed on the need for a lender of last resort, the only difference being that the second banker was a little bit less proud than the first.

As a matter of fact, both might have been more anxious about their personal safety than the safety of their banks. If that were the case, it would prove that there is a human factor that limits the negative effect of the existence of a credible commitment of a lender of last resort.

11. Financial fragility and instability: monetary authorities as borrowers and lenders of last resort

WARREN D. McCLAM

The recent revival of interest in the history and theory of financial crises, and in their policy implications, has been a welcome development. Certainly, in the light of our experiences over the past 15 years, there have been reasons to suspect some systemic tendencies toward growing financial instability. Internationally we have witnessed the breakdown of the Bretton-Woods system, the generalized move to floating exchange rates, two major oil-price shocks, and, against this background, a serious intensification of world inflation and persistence of large external current-account imbalances. For many observers the sense of unease resulting from these developments has been intensified by concerns about the elasticity, and possible instability, of national and international monetary mechanisms: in particular, about the rapid growth of the Eurocurrency markets, the huge increase in international liquidity, and the continuing widespread buildup of individual countries' foreign indebtedness.

Much of the academic debate on financial crises has revolved around the theories of Minsky (1972, 1978), who has written extensively on this subject over many years. In addition, one has seen a resurgence of interest in the domestic and international causes of the Great Depression, as evidenced in the writings of Kindleberger (1973), Temin (1976), and Mishkin (1976). Recently, Kindleberger (1978), in his new book *Manias, Panics and Crashes*, has applied the Minsky model over a wide sweep of history and in the broad context of international as well as national developments. According to Kindleberger, the heart of his book is that "a synthesis of Keynesianism and monetarism, such as the Hansen-Hicks IS-LM curves that bring together the saving-investment (IS) and liquidity-money (LM) relationships, remains incomplete, even when it brings in production and prices ..., if it leaves out the instability of expectations, speculation and credit .... The omissions under particular circumstances may be so critical as to make both Keynesianism and monetarism misleading" (p. 23). In view

256

of this possibility and of the symptoms of financial strain evidenced in recent years, Allan Sproul's words on the dust jacket of Kindleberger's book seem particularly apt: "It would be an act of folly to disregard the possibility of a financial crisis, and a failure of prudence not to give thought to possible means of preventing it."

For Kindleberger, the essence of the problem lies in the inherent instability of the economy as reflected in its tendency toward recurrent boom–bust episodes. He is not concerned with the periodicity of cycles or crises but rather with the "speculative manias leading to crisis and collapse" (1978:14). In this respect, Minsky's version of the financial-instability hypothesis appears to be more general. It postulates the possibility that sectoral financial distortions may cumulate over long periods of times, within or across conventional business cycles, thus gradually rendering the financial system increasingly fragile and vulnerable to some external shock, large or small. Considerable emphasis is put on the endogeneity of elements contributing to fragility, and hence, as Kindleberger also stressed, on expectations, speculation, and credit. Although Minsky recognizes that his model is modified by the existence of large government, neither of these authors gives much credence to the view that structural and institutional changes affecting corporations, trade unions, and financial institutions have in any fundamental way altered the economy's inherent tendencies toward financial instability. The animal spirits remain.

In terms of policy prescription, both Minsky and Kindleberger stress the importance of a lender of last resort. They consider the monetarist attitude toward crisis situations, which would be to emphasize the maintenance of monetary growth, and presumably also the Keynesian view, which would rely largely on increased public-sector deficits, to be insufficient. After a speculative boom it may be impossible to prevent a collapse without providing liberal availability of lender-of-last-resort facilities in terms of both discounting and open-market operations. And in the international sphere, according to Kindleberger, the difficulties are even more pronounced, because it is not obvious whether or not there is, in fact, a lender of last resort and under what conditions, and on what scale, assistance would be made available.

The financial-instability hypothesis appears to represent a significant challenge to conventional modes of economic thought. Modern monetarism is based on the assumption of an inherently stable private sector and sees instability as deriving primarily from the failure of monetary authorities, whether from shortcomings of will or operational techniques, to exercise firm control over the supply of money. The Keynesian framework, though seemingly better suited for sectoral disequilibrium analysis in a long-term setting, has in practice typically been concerned with short-term equilibrium analysis stressing the stabilizing potential of demand management, in particular fiscal policy. As time has gone on, the limitations of these approaches have become increasingly obvious. National authorities have found themselves confronted more and more with financial problems of an essentially structural or institutional nature – problems the understanding of which would seem to require a new analytical approach in a long-term disequilibrium framework.

Broadly speaking, this chapter has a threefold purpose. First, it seeks to shed some light on the question of long-term financial trends, using evidence based on U.S. experience, on international trends in company profitability, and on cumulative external indebtedness positions of individual countries. Second, it discusses the question of the stability characteristics of the international monetary system in the face of severe deflation and possible crisis. Third, it examines the changing historical role of the lender of last resort, arguing that this role appears today to be different in a number of fundamental respects from its original classical conception.

I. U.S. historical experience: some stability comparisons

In essence, the Minsky/Kindleberger views concerning financial instability appear to postulate a process closely akin to the classical monetary theory of the business cycle. In this process, changes in expectations play a major role. Given some initial impetus, or "displacement," an upswing, either cyclical or secular, may lead gradually to a strengthening of confidence, culminating in excessive optimism and "euphoria," which then lead inexorably to a reversal and possible crisis. The demand for credit and the elasticity of credit supplies play major roles in this process. In the following paragraphs, based on U.S. experience, a simple test is suggested that seems to cast some doubt on the modern-day relevance of the classical model.

Let us first look at some broad statistical measures that are at least symptomatic of the degree of financial stability in an ex post sense. In the top panel of Figure 11.1 are plotted the annual percentage variations in gross national product and the income velocity of money (GNP/M_2) over the period 1917–78. It can readily be seen that the variabilities of both the gross national product and the income velocity of money were very great over practically the whole of the interwar period and, for that matter, during the period 1940–53 covering World War II, its aftermath, and the Korean War. Since that time, however, income velocity and the growth of nominal gross national product have settled down to a much narrower range of variation, although, of course, not without a strong underlying trend toward faster inflation.

In the second and third panels of Figure 11.1 a comparison is made

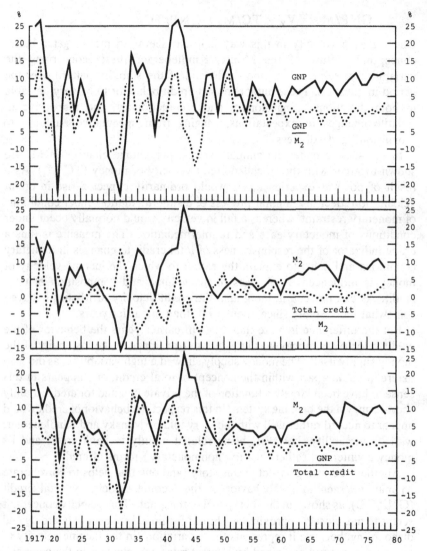

Figure 11.1. United States changes in money supply and velocity, 1917–78.

between the variability of the money supply (M_2) and two "elements" of the income velocity of money. For convenience, these two elements may be called the credit velocity of money (TC/M_2) and the income velocity of total credit (GNP/TC),[1] related to each other as follows:

$$GNP/M_2 = V_Y = TC/M_2 \cdot GNP/TC$$

Decomposing velocity in this way helps, it seems to me, to get a better conceptual picture of the Minsky/Kindleberger thesis concerning the variability of expectations and credit and of the stability pattern over the period in question. These authors depict credit behavior to be very unstable in both directions, expansionary and contractionary, and responsive to volatile changes in expectations, ranging from speculative euphoria to "revulsion" and "distress."

In the second panel the annual average percentage changes in M_2 are shown together with the so-called credit velocity of money (TC/M_2). As a result of postwar experience, we would ordinarily expect a rise in credit velocity to reflect the familiar process of disintermediation under conditions of monetary restraint, whereas a fall in velocity would normally occur under conditions of monetary ease and re-intermediation. The measure is thus a crude indicator of the responsiveness of total credit to changes in monetary conditions and helps to explain the extent to which the income velocity of money is influenced by changes in the volume and composition of total credit. As can be seen in the graph, the credit velocity of M_2 has behaved somewhat more stably since about 1950 than in earlier years.

But the difference is more than that. In earlier years the behavior of the credit velocity on money was largely a mirror image of the instability of the money supply itself. The money supply showed a high variability, as did also its credit counterpart within the concept of total credit, and appears in this sense to have been largely a function of the private demand for credit, mainly short-term, via the banking system. In this respect the behavior of credit would appear to accord rather well with the story told by Minsky and Kindleberger, with its variability, however, being related mainly to bank credit and its money counterpart rather than to "nonmonetary" forms of credit.

Another interesting aspect of this story (and one that helps to corroborate it) may be seen in the behavior of the income velocity of total credit (GNP/TC), as shown in the third panel of the graph. This velocity concept, it seems to me, closely approximates the old-fashioned concept of hoarding and dishoarding, because it represents those variations in the income velocity of money that are not explained by interest rates and changes in the composition of credit flows. As such, therefore, it is likely to reflect changes in confidence, euphoria and the like – indeed, expectations generally. For this reason it is striking to see that its variations from 1920 to 1941 are closely and positively related to variations in the rate of growth of money itself. This suggests that variations in the stock of money were being determined, via the credit-demand link, by the same confidence factors that influenced the hoarding demand for money.

This analysis, as far as the interwar period is concerned, accords very closely with Hicks's brief account (1976:5) of the classical cycle as depicted by Thornton, by J. S. Mill, and later, as the monetary theory of the cycle, by Hawtrey:

> The boom starts by businessmen becoming more "optimistic" and as a consequence of their optimism keeping less money idle. So the velocity of circulation rises and prices rise. The rise in prices engenders expectations of further rises; this further increases "optimism" and further increases the velocity of circulation. But the businessmen do not have the money to do all they want to do; so they borrow from the banks, who share their optimism, and are therefore very ready to give them the credit which they require. Thus there is an increase in bank credit, which we would nowadays reckon to be an increase in the supply of money.
>
> At last the point comes (so the story goes) when the banks (and perhaps some other businesses also) feel themselves to be overexpanded; credit is restricted and there is a crisis. Credit is shaken, confidence is shaken.

In terms of confidence, changes in the supply of money were seen to depend mainly on changes in the demand for credit, with the demand for credit responding to the same alternating waves of optimism and pessimism that motivate changes in velocity.

Thus, in the United States, over the years 1917–41, changes in the income velocity of total credit and in the money stock (M_2), though highly variable, showed a quite significant positive relationship. As far as variability is concerned, the standard deviation of changes in M_2 was 8.26%, and that of changes in the income velocity of total credit was 9.81%. A simple regression of the first variable on the second yields an $\bar{R}^2$ of 0.55 (D.W. = 1.61) for this 25-year period. I would conclude that, in line with the classical theory, the variations in the money stock over these years were largely demand-determined, that is, they were influenced by the same confidence considerations that motivated changes in hoarding and dishoarding.

In the postwar period, however, this statistical picture has changed completely. Over the years 1952–78 the standard deviation of changes in the money stock and the income velocity of total credit dropped off sharply to 2.92% and 1.37%, respectively. The same regression as for the earlier period gives an $\bar{R}^2$ of practically zero. Thus the income velocity of total credit and also the growth of M_2 show a far more stable behavior, and the money stock appears, to me at least, to have followed a path more determined by supply. Or, to put it another way, fiscal/monetary policy has been in a better position to accommodate the demand for money associated with high average levels of employment. In order to shed more light on these developments, it would perhaps be useful to look more closely at the historical behavior of total debt, and its components, in relation to income.

II. Debt burdens and the borrower of last resort

In the past, a principal element contributing to financial instability was the phenomenon of "debt deflation," as vividly described by Irving Fisher in the context of the Great Depression. In the interwar period and earlier, when prices and output generally fluctuated together, declining incomes meant a rise in the real burden of fixed-interest debt, which turned into a cumulative process as efforts were made, unsuccessfully, to reduce the burden of outstanding debt. The subsequent appearance of a large "borrower of last resort," particularly during World War II and after, transformed this situation. What I mean by this term is simply that central government recognizes the need for built-in fiscal stabilizers and accepts passively an increase in the budget deficit when an economic decline sets in, and vice versa. The role of discretionary fiscal policy is quite a different matter, and fine tuning in this sense has, in the opinion of many observers, contributed to destabilizing modern economies in the inflationary direction. To illustrate the changing trend in debt relationships, we may again turn to the historical experience of the United States.

In Figure 11.2 the second panel shows the relationship between total credit (or debt) and gross national product over the years 1929–78. In this panel the 1941–78 relationship is extrapolated backward over the period 1929–40, and in the first panel the same extrapolation is carried back over the period 1916–29. It can be seen that the actual relationship over the years 1941–78 was very close to the one for 1916–29, though with a much smaller variance.

It is clear, on the other hand, that the 1930s were years of highly abnormal debt behavior. In my opinion, one key to an understanding of the Great Depression is the fact that the sharp absolute declines in money incomes from late 1929 onward were associated either with a decline in the money stock through debt repayment or (and this was equally important) with a concomitant increase in the real burden of outstanding debt. Efforts to escape this situation through further liquidation or building up real cash balances simply tended to worsen it. The real money supply rose, it is true, but this was more a reflection of behavior than of policy. And, in any case, account would have to be taken of the fact that the business sector was, as is typically the case, a net borrower. What made matters worse was that the consumer sector had borrowed heavily in the 1920s, both for housing and for equity purchases, so that households contributed to the general liquidation and retrenchment.

The crucial question is this: Is it at all conceivable that when the burden of private debt relative to income was increasing as fast as or faster than nominal debt was being repaid, easier and cheaper money could have been expected to encourage borrowing and maintain money growth? In this

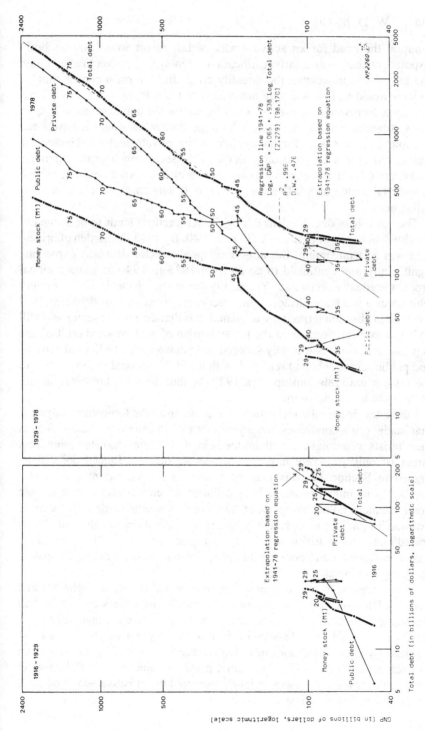

Figure 11.2. United States: money, debt, and gross national product, 1916–78.

263

situation the need for an active lender of last resort would not be hotly disputed, as there was clearly justification for monetary action to allay panic and help banks to weather the liquidity crisis. But the main contribution of Keynes would be lost if it were not recognized that there was a strong need also for a borrower of last resort. Only by having the public sector willing to run substantial deficits and undertake large borrowing would it have been possible to compensate for the decline in the private sector's demand for credit. In the Great Depression, with the public sector much smaller than it is today, there is serious question as to whether or not it would have been able to undertake such deficit financing quickly. In any case, there was not the willingness.

The key role of debt burdens during the contractions tends to be borne out also by debt behavior between 1933 and 1940. By 1933 the burden of private debt was at a maximum. But after 1931 public-sector debt was expanding significantly and continued to do so from 1933 to 1940 as gross national product gradually recovered. Yet during the whole of the 1933–40 period, which was a weak and disappointing recovery, private-sector debt remained flat even in absolute terms. One explanation is that the private sector was still trying to extricate itself from the heavy burden of debt imposed on it by the depression but was now finally succeeding in doing so. In 1940 total private- and public-sector debt had returned, with the gross national product itself, to the same overall relationship as in 1929. Within the total, however, public-sector debt had risen sharply.

I think the principal conclusion to be drawn from the foregoing analysis is that, under crisis conditions, money-supply growth cannot be maintained, as monetarists would have it, without the help of credit demand stemming from larger (if only passively larger) public-sector deficits. Indeed, as will be argued in Section IV, this may be true to a limited extent even under conditions of mild recession. In a deflationary environment, with private credit demand falling away, what the economy seems to demand is more "owned" liquidity via widening public-sector deficits rather than the "borrowed" liquidity available in a further cheapening of money. But, of course, easier monetary conditions could help, through wealth effects, to sustain spending and income.

In this argument, which is based on asymmetrical sectoral behavior and debt-burden effects, one of course runs head on into the view that deficit financing is ineffective because economic agents discount their future tax liabilities. I myself would not be inclined to attach great weight to this view, particularly under conditions in which the economy is sliding into recession or even depression. At the same time, it seems quite clear that changes in attitudes over the years have seriously impaired the effectiveness of activist, discretionary fiscal policies.

It appears, then, that U.S. financial stability, measured in terms of the variance of the money stock and velocity, was much greater in the years after the Korean War than before. What are the explanations for this? A principal reason, no doubt, has been the dramatic change since the 1930s in macroeconomic policy attitudes, both fiscal and monetary, and in the institutional environment, especially as far as banking legislation and deposit insurance are concerned. I would attach particular importance to what I have called the borrower of the last resort and would concur fully with Lawrence Klein (see Stein, 1976:51), who disagrees with the monetarist view "that induced (non-exogenous) actions of the treasury have no significant causal effects on real money income. [Rather] I believe that the built-in stabilizers are of enormous importance, quietly doing their work and keeping fluctuations within bounds." Hence, insofar as the monetarists are correct in saying that the private economy is stable, or responds in a stable way to policies consistently pursued, one reason may be that the automatic stabilizers have helped to make it so.

Have there also been changes on the supply side that might have contributed, at least on the down side, to greater economic stability? One factor is that wages and prices have gradually become less flexible downward, both because of the changed macroeconomic policy environment and because of the growing market strength of labor unions and business firms. This is reflected in the observed progressive worsening of the Phillips tradeoff between unemployment and inflation and, in recent years, in the "stability" implied in a situation of economic stagflation. In Figure 11.3 one can see that from 1890 up to the end of World War II, changes in real output and prices generally moved up and down together, whereas in the postwar period their rates of growth more often than not tended to move in opposite directions. At the same time, the problem of inflation seems to have become endemic. Although the point is not a new one, it seems that the more stable macroeconomic policy environment has, by affording a kind of employment and output guarantee, destabilized the system in the upward direction in terms of wages and prices. Insofar as this is true, it seems to me to imply a criticism much more of discretionary fine-tuning policies than of the automatic stabilization effects of the budget. It also implies, of course, the need for greater attention to be given to the long-run design features of fiscal policies, in terms of automatic stabilization parameters, the size of the public sector, and incentive effects at the micro level.

III. Budget deficits and money creation

Viewed in terms of money-stock behavior, the foregoing analysis comes into conflict with both monetarist views and the Minsky/Kindleberger instability

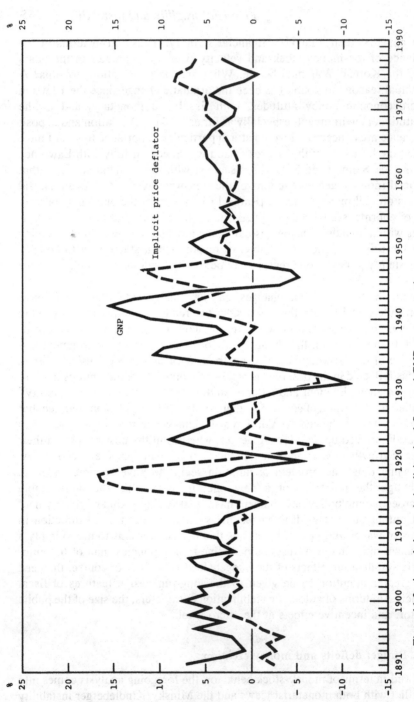

Figure 11.3. Annual changes in implicit price deflator and GNP at constant prices, 1918–78 (as percentages), centered three-month moving averages.

hypothesis. In contrast to monetarist views, I have argued that budget deficits may, in the event of a falling off in private credit demand, be a precondition for maintaining satisfactory money growth rates. Analogously, in contrast to the instability hypothesis, I have argued that borrower-of-last-resort functions, carried out via the mechanism of public-sector deficits, may be equally crucial if not more crucial for stabilization purposes than those of the lender of last resort, taking the latter to mean liberal policies with respect to discounting, open-market operations, and, internationally, the maintenance of open capital markets.

The validity of the analysis hinges partly on the question of the links between budget deficits and the money stock. Admittedly, this is still a much contested issue. Recently, for example, Buchanan and Wagner (1977) have forcefully argued that excessive U.S. money growth rates have been closely related to budget deficits, reflecting a political bias toward deficits of increasing size, financed by a compliant monetary authority. In a rejoinder, Barro (1978) formulated money growth equations purporting to show that the link perceived by Buchanan and Wagner did not appear in fact to have been operative.

My own approach views this question, admittedly in a rather simplistic way, from a somewhat different angle. It is fairly common practice, especially in countries other than the United States, to look at the money-creation process partly in terms of what is happening on the assets side of the banking system's consolidated balance sheet. Let us suppose, consistent with my argumentation, that public-sector deficits and their monetary financing had simply the function of "filling up holes" resulting from variations in the net demand for bank credit emanating from the private sector and from abroad. In such circumstances it seems immaterial that the decision about deficit financing is not independent of the decision to create money. Rather, the point is that the latter decision could not necessarily have been made operative without a prior decision to accept a deficit of a certain size. Thus the central bank's task of achieving a desired money growth rate may at times be feasible only if fiscal and monetary policy are operating together so as to compensate for cyclical reversals in private and foreign credit demand.

This point may be illustrated with the help of Figure 11.4, which shows 12-month rates of (broadly defined) monetary growth and the contemporaneous "contribution" to this growth of the expansion in bank credit to the private sector. In the United States and the United Kingdom, for example, private demand for bank credit dropped off sharply in late 1974 and 1975, but the money growth was, after an interval, stabilized at around 10%, reflecting inter alia the increased monetary financing of a growing public-sector deficit.[2] On a lesser scale, the same development occurred in other countries,

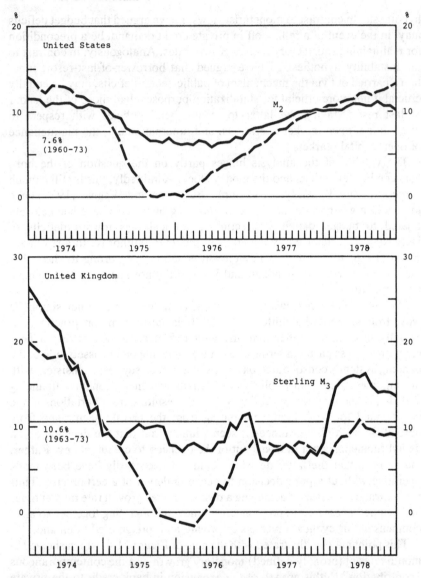

Figure 11.4. Changes in bank credit to the private sector: contribution to changes in the money stock. Solid line indicates money stock (M_2 or M_3): changes over 12 months (inset line represents average annual growth rate over period indicated). Dash line indicates credit to private sector: "contribution" to money-stock changes (change in private credit as a percentage of money stock 12 months earlier).

such as Germany, France, and Japan. In Italy, which has experienced a rapidly swelling public sector, a high rate of monetary expansion has reflected a growth trend toward greater public-sector recourse to bank credit and a concurrent decline in borrowing by the private sector.

Of course, there is often only a loose link between current budget deficits and changes in the banking system's claims against the public sector. This latter variable reflects both the financing of the budget deficit and the portfolio shifts induced by public-debt management. Figure 11.5 and Table 11.1 give the results of a simple regression of banking-sector claims on the public sector against budget deficits for six major countries over the period 1960–77. The $\bar{R}^2$ results show the relationship to be closest for Germany and Italy (the latter with a strong trend element), but fairly high also for the United States and Japan. That the coefficient should be very low for the United Kingdom is not surprising, given the relatively large volume of government debt outstanding and the volatility of funding operations.

Because these data provide no indication of overall changes in the money stock, additional information is shown in the two memorandum columns. Over the period 1960–77 the contribution of changes in claims on the public sector, on average, was highest in Italy and lowest in Canada and the United States. However, considerable care must be taken when interpreting these figures, because the coverage of the banking system and the nature of the financial markets differ considerably from country to country.

For a further piece of evidence, it is useful to look back again to Figure 11.2. As can be seen, the growth path of M_1 in the United States since 1929 has moved very closely in line with that of public-sector debt. There is no necessary reason why that should have been the case, because only a moderate proportion of total public-sector debt represented Federal Reserve acquisitions to expand the monetary base. Nor is such a close relationship evident in other countries. The most plausible explanation, perhaps, is that deficit financing during periods of economic slack, more often than not through sales of short-term Treasury paper, has been followed with a lag by a further monetization of public debt as private credit demand has recovered. It is under these conditions that money growth would appear to have been a clear decision of monetary policy. Whereas this sequence seems to support the Barro thesis more than the Buchanan/Wagner thesis, it would not appear to contradict my main point, namely, that a large infusion of monetary borrowing by the public sector may be indispensable for stabilization purposes during a period of sharply declining private credit demand. The size of the infusion, of course, is the crucial question, because the monetization of deficits in recession runs the risk of storing up trouble for the future.

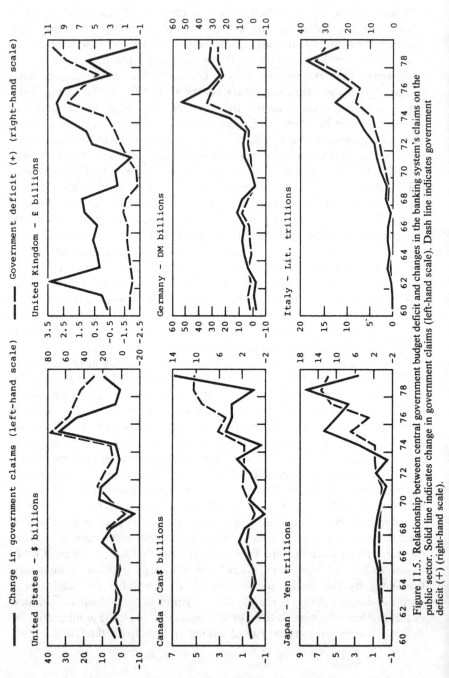

Figure 11.5. Relationship between central government budget deficit and changes in the banking system's claims on the public sector. Solid line indicates change in government claims (left-hand scale). Dash line indicates government deficit (+) (right-hand scale).

270

Table 11.1. *Relationship between government deficits (GD) and changes in the banking system's net public-sector claims, 1960–79*

Country	Equation	$\bar{R}^2$	D.W.	Normalized standard error	Average annual growth rates, compounded	
					(1) Money and quasi money	(2) Contribution to (1) of changes in claims on public sector
United States	0.44 + 0.31 GD (4.62)	0.518	1.63	1.002	8.56	2.35
Japan	0.36 + 0.45 GD (5.70)	0.624	1.91	0.923	16.69	7.84
Germany	0.65 + 1.27 GD (14.71)	0.919	1.16	0.351	11.94	6.47
United Kingdom	0.40 + 0.05 GD (0.51)	−0.041	1.36	2.930	9.96	3.88
Canada	−0.05 + 0.32 GD (3.68)	0.398	2.29	1.633	12.89	4.24
Italy	0.69 + 0.53 GD (14.44)	0.916	0.72	0.334	16.96	11.98

Source: Based on data from the International Monetary Fund: *International Financial Statistics.*

IV. Budgetary responses to incipient crisis: the 1970s

Does the safety net afforded by the borrower of last resort also extend to the international economy? What one may expect, I would suggest, has already been amply demonstrated by the experience of 1974–5 in the wake of the oil crisis. By postwar standards, the United States and many other countries had by 1973 developed considerable financial fragility, and the shock of higher oil prices, and the policy reactions to them, quickly plunged the industrial world into its sharpest recession since the 1930s. But, despite distress in many sectors, including financial ones and local government, the various economies stopped well short of the abyss.

The private-sector reactions were severe almost everywhere. Savings ratios increased sharply, investment fell off, and restructuring of balance sheets became the order of the day. What saved the situation, internationally as well as nationally, was that the governments of oil-consuming countries understood, and readily accepted, the need for unusually large shifts toward public-sector deficits. Private-sector credit demand was dropping sharply and had to be compensated in some degree by the intervention of a borrower of last resort.

As a matter of international policy coordination, OECD member countries concluded among themselves that the oil deficits had largely to be accepted and, by appropriate measures to sustain domestic demand, apportioned on an equitable basis among the countries concerned. In the event, countries reacted quite differently, with some, such as Sweden, Canada, Denmark, Norway, The Netherlands, and later the United States, being relatively expansionary, whereas Japan, Switzerland, Italy, and (after 1976) the United Kindgom were quite restrictive. Germany, France, and Belgium were more toward the middle of the spectrum. The differences in behavior were reflected largely in differences in the relative pressure of domestic demand, but the role of fiscal policy, at least in the ex post sense, is shown in Table 11.2. A new oil-price shock in 1979, when an incipient recovery was under way, may have helped to perpetuate high budget deficits.

Viewed in terms of last-resort functions, governmental responses on the fiscal front largely obviated the need for central-bank lending on an unusual basis. The exceptions are well known: Penn Central, Franklin National, the U.K. secondary banking crisis, etc. At the same time, as far as distressed industry is concerned, it should not be overlooked that in a number of countries a very impressive amount of support was given (and is still being given) via the national budgets. Government aid to industry of a last-resort nature has taken the form of loans, subsidies, grants, and even public-sector takeovers on a scale not seen since the 1930s. The industries receiving such help have been diverse, but they include shipbuilding, steel, textiles, and the

Table 11.2. *General government net lending, 1966–80[a]*

Country	Annual averages, in percentages of GNP					
	1966–9	1970–3	1974–7	1978	1979	1980[b]
United States	—	−0.1	−0.4	−0.0	0.6	−1.1
Japan	−2.8	−2.0	−2.5	−5.5	−5.2	−4.5
Germany	−0.3	0.2	−3.3	−2.7	−3.0	−3.3
France	—	0.2	−0.7	−1.8	−0.8	−0.7
United Kingdom	−0.6	−0.4	−4.3	−4.3	−3.3	−3.2
Italy	−3.0	−3.9	−9.2	−9.7	−9.4	−8.3
Canada	1.0	0.5	−1.2	−3.1	−1.7	−0.9
Belgium	−1.5	−2.2	−5.5	−6.0	−7.2	−8.2
Netherlands	−0.9	−0.1	−1.7	−2.1	−4.3	−4.1
Sweden[c]	4.0	4.6	2.9	−0.1	−3.6	−3.6
Denmark	1.3	3.7	0.4	−0.5	−1.4	−3.2
Norway	3.4	4.5	3.3	0.2	−0.8	4.3

[a]General government includes central and local governments plus social security funds. Nationalized industries and other public enterprises are excluded. Net lending is the difference between the sector's saving and its own investment. A minus sign signifies a financial deficit.
[b]Forecasts.
[c]Includes national pension fund.

chemicals sectors. Among the countries where such aid has been important are Italy, France, Belgium, The Netherlands, Spain, Sweden, and the United Kingdom. Although national authorities are loath to divulge the scale of such assistance, it figures in the size of the public-sector deficits shown in the table. In some cases the distressed industries are part of the nationalized sector; indeed, this has often been the route by which certain industries have become nationalized. In some instances, too, banks had to reschedule loans to domestic firms, even unwillingly, to provide additional credits and take over share participations.

As I see it, the oil crisis, preceded by a trend toward greater financial fragility and followed by deep recession on an international scale, provided most of the ingredients of a major crisis. However, actual developments, disruptive though they were, were quantitatively and qualitatively very different from those of the 1930s. Governments, acting on a national level as both borrowers and lenders of last resort, massively cushioned the shocks emanating from abroad and from the domestic private sectors. It is worth noting that crisis conditions of international dimensions did appear in certain industrial sectors such as shipbuilding, steel, and textiles. But it was generally at the national level rather than the international level that individual governments intervened with assistance of the kinds already mentioned.[3] The problems involved were not merely cyclical but implied as well a need to adjust to a changing international pattern of output and trade. Hence, the conflict between perceived financial needs and international adjustment considerations posed a difficult dilemma for governments as lenders of last resort.

V. The domestic economy: long-term financial trends

Despite the foregoing analysis, it is still pertinent to ask whether or not one can, in fact, detect long-term financial trends that render an economy increasingly fragile and vulnerable to a sharp reversal. The further question whether or not such trends are endogenous, though intellectually interesting, is not crucial from a policy standpoint. They may equally well be explainable partly as a consequence of major exogenous disturbances such as war, oil shocks, world recession, and the like. What seems more relevant is that policymakers should seek to make themselves aware of such long-term movements and act in a timely fashion to take remedial measures. In the sections that follow, two examples are given of what appear to be long-term domestic financial trends with implications for economic stability and growth. One of these is based on U.S. experience and the other on international comparisons of selected major countries.

The relationship of private debt and public debt. In the case of the United States, some broad evidence pointing to the existence of long-term financial trends has already been presented in Figure 11.2. There it has been shown that, except for the abnormal period of the 1930s, total net debt has been very closely related to the gross national product. Within this stable total, however, public debt and private debt have moved over long periods along quite divergent paths. If, as I have earlier assumed, private economic agents perceive public debt as a net addition to their financial wealth, the ratio of private debt to public debt may be taken as one rough measure of financial fragility. Even if we drop this assumption, however, the measure can still be taken as a rough indicator of illiquidity and risk that is itself highly significant in terms of the fragility thesis.

In Figure 11.6 the movements of the ratio of private debt to public debt, together with those in short- and long-term private-sector debts, are shown over the period 1919–78. This ratio rose sharply from 3.2 in 1919 to 5.3 in 1929, fell steeply to reach a low of 0.6 in 1945, and then rose fairly steadily, though with greater irregularity since the late 1960s, to stand at 3.5 in 1978. Even after a rise of more than 30 years, therefore, the ratio was still much below that of 1929 – a reflection partly of the relatively small size of the public sector in the 1920s.

The long-term financial cycle as measured by the private/public debt ratio

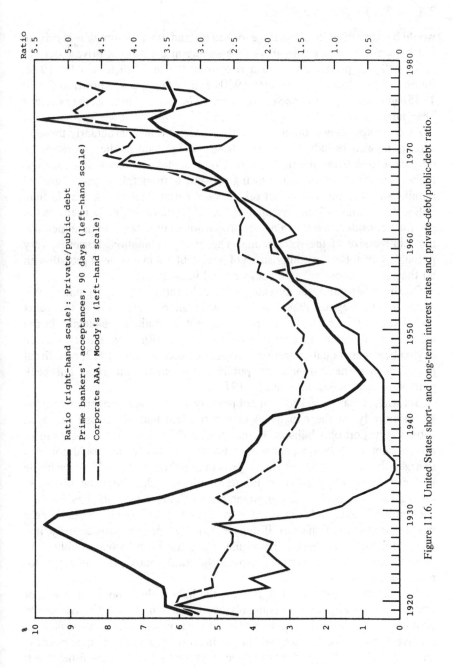

Figure 11.6. United States short- and long-term interest rates and private-debt/public-debt ratio.

Ratio

Ratio (right-hand scale): Private/public debt

Prime bankers' acceptances, 90 days (left-hand scale)

Corporate AAA, Moody's (left-hand scale)

would be somewhat different if we looked instead at a measure of real private indebtedness. For example, if we look simply at the ratio of private debt to gross national product, we see a rise from 1.2 in 1919 to 2.4 by 1932, followed by a decline in the later 1930s and during the war down to 0.7 in 1945, and then a gradual rise up to 1.5 by 1974. Since that time, the ratio has been fairly stable.

As the graph shows, the movements of interest rates, particularly those at short term, were broadly in line with those in the private/public debt ratio, the only exception being the mid-1920s. However, this exception is enough to make one very cautious in drawing too much from this broad historical parallelism. The mere fact that private debt entails higher risk premia than public debt seems of little explanatory value. Of more weight, perhaps, is the portfolio consideration that a higher proportion of private debt might increase the relative size of the risk premia. The main explanation, however, very probably lies not in the composition of total debt but in its rate of growth with all that that implies for price behavior and interest rates.

On the other hand, the private/public debt ratio may have great significance for the fragility thesis, as seen by its sharp increase over the years 1919–29. These years saw a steady, and not so gradual, weakening in the asset/liability pattern of private-sector finances, with economic expansion having been dependent entirely on private borrowing. After 1929, with fiscal policy at best neutral and the public sector small, the ratio fell back precipitously by 1933 to about its 1919 level.

But why, it may be asked, is it not possible to envisage an economy that is based entirely on the expansion of private debt and yet is one in which satisfactory portfolio balance is maintained over time? Does the ratio of private debt to public debt show anything at all? Clearly one would not wish to argue that some optimum rate of growth of public debt would be desirable in the interest of portfolio equilibrium. But, to judge from the historical record, there are periods during which private demand falls off considerably, even precipitately, and it is at these times that an expansion of public debt may be needed to fill the gap. If this mechanism functions satisfactorily, it is consistent with a gradual, fairly regular trend rise in the private/public debt ratio, though one that might approach the total debt/GNP line asymptotically as time goes on.

An interesting feature of the graph is the light it sheds on the question of financial "crowding out." Presumably one indication of crowding out would be a decline in the private/public debt ratio (inversely, a rise in public debt relative to private) coincident with a rise in interest rates. At no time over the entire period 1919–78 did that happen. It can be argued, on the other hand, that fiscal policy had not functioned so as to make sufficient room for private debt expansion during the upswing. Otherwise, the variability of interest rates in the upward direction would have been much smaller, particularly in recent years.

As a measure of financial fragility, the private/public debt ratio is at best a first approximation, and one must look further, as Minsky does, for evidence of financial distortion in individual economic sectors. Internationally, the company sector has in recent years commanded most attention in this respect.

Company-sector finances: international comparisons. In recent years the state of company-sector finances has become a principal source of concern in many countries. The main reason for this is the change in the trend of nonresidential investment that became increasingly evident in the course of the 1970s. One important factor was the oil shock of 1973–4 and disturbances in the international commodity markets, which, together with the move to floating exchange rates, may have substantially increased the risks attaching to long-term investment decisions. However, the alteration of the investment trend came in some countries in the late 1960s or early 1970s. Other factors, therefore, may have been the widespread acceleration of inflation during the 1960s, with emphasis on the cost side. Inflationary aspirations and expectations had already begun to contribute to a deterioration in the investment climate.

It is a fairly well established fact that company investment is closely dependent on the volume of retained earnings that companies are able to generate. In Table 11.3, retained earnings are not shown as such, but figures are given for five major countries on estimates of long-term trends in net profit shares and net profit rates, which may be viewed as an even broader measure of investment incentives. As the table shows, there appears to have been a marked downward trend in profits in all these countries, whether measured in terms of profit shares or profit rates. The only exception is the relatively small downward movement in the profit share of U.S. companies, whose higher rate of decline in profit rates might partly reflect the sharp drop in productivity gains evidenced over much of the last decade.

To a large extent, the declines in profit shares and rates must reflect the continuing upward pressures on costs in a world in which companies have not been able, readily, to pass on costs in higher prices. In this respect the environment had become one in which national authorities were continually seeking to moderate aggregate demand in order to hold down inflation. In a cyclical sense this development contributed to an inverse relationship between price inflation and output growth, and in a secular sense it contributed to the phenomenon of stagflation.

More particularly, as the table shows, the dropping off of the rate of growth in the period 1973–9 compared with 1960–73 appears to have been closely

Table 11.3. *Profitability, real investment, and real growth*

Countries	Net profit shares (%)[a]			Net profit rates (%)[a]			Average annual real private nonresidential fixed investment (%)		Rate of change in real gross national product (%)	
	1960	1978	Trend[b]	1960	1978	Trend[b]	1960–73	1973–9	1960–73	1973–9
United States	25.4	22.5	−0.16	34.1[c]	21.3[c]	−0.71[c]	5.4	2.1	4.1	2.5
Japan	39.3	25.6	−0.76	21.7[d]	11.1[d]	−0.60[d]	14.0	2.2	10.2	4.1
Germany	34.5	22.0	−0.73	28.2[c]	13.5[c]	−0.85[c]	4.6	2.7	4.5	2.4
United Kingdom	25.7	16.3	−0.52	14.1	5.4	−0.48	4.3	1.6	3.2	0.8
Italy	36.0	23.2	−0.75	21.5	12.6	−0.50	4.9	−1.6	5.1	2.8

[a]Based on Hill, T. P., *Profits and Rates of Return*, OECD. Profits are measured net of stock appreciation and capital consumption. These net profits are related to total net factor income arising in the industrial sector to give the net profit share, and to the net capital stock measured at current replacement cost to give the net profit rate. The figures are presented as trends rather than actual values.

[b]Average change per year, 1960 to 1978, in percentage points.

[c]Manufacturing.

[d]Gross profit rates.

associated with a broadly similar pattern of declines in the rate of non-residential investment. This bodes ill, of course, for the size of the capital stock and the rate of productivity growth. More than that, however, productivity was adversely affected in an immediate sense, merely because of the pronounced falling off of demand in the investment-goods sector, as a matter both of final demand and of the high productivity of that sector.

A number of other symptoms of fragility in the company sector can be observed. In the United States, for example, the ratio of internal funds to gross investment in 1979 was 0.71, against 0.99 in the years 1963–4, and would have been significantly lower still if the profits of oil companies were left out of account. In addition, short-term debt as a ratio of long-term debt has been on a rising trend, as has total debt to equity, whereas liquid assets as a ratio of short-term debt have been declining. A similar picture is seen in the case of the United Kingdom, where, leaving North Sea oil out of the picture, the profitability of British industry over wide areas is low or even negative. A similar concern about profits has been evident in a large number of European countries, including Italy, France, Belgium, The Netherlands, and Sweden. The case of Germany is interesting in that companies appear to pursue quite conservative balance-sheet practices. Thus the trend of internal funds to gross investment has been on a moderate uptrend over the past two decades, rising from somewhat over 0.70 in the early 1960s to nearly 0.90 in the late 1970s. The debt/equity ratio has risen substantially, as in most other countries, but the ratios of liquid assets to short-term debt and short-term debt to total debt have shown considerable improvement as a trend.

Although this section has focused on the company sector, other domestic sectors would also merit attention. The household sector, though asset-predominant in terms of financial balance sheets, is far from immune to financial fragility. This was seen in the late 1920s in the context of financing real estate and securities speculation. When asset values began to plummet, individuals were left stranded with heavy burdens of fixed debt. Strains of the same virus have been evident in the United States over the years 1977–9. Consumer debt relative to disposable income rose to an all-time high, and real estate hedging or speculation was widespread.

In the financial sector, the most exposed group in the event of incipient crisis has typically been the commercial banks. In the deep recession of 1974–5, it will be recalled how U.S. banks incurred heavy losses in their loans to REITs and were faced with rescheduling of loans to such borrowers as the City of New York, shipping companies, etc. In more recent years the main pressure appears to have fallen more on the savings banks. The heavy predominance in their portfolios of long-term, relatively low yielding fixed-interest claims, combined with the sharp rise in market interest rates and increased competition from new money-market instruments, brought them to a state of severe distress. Dangers of financial disintermediation exist also for other financial institutions, such as insurance companies, which are subject to withdrawals from the liability side without necessarily having sufficient liquidity on the asset side.

As far as the banking sector is concerned, the crucial question at the present time has more to do with their heavy commitment to international lending. The next section undertakes a brief survey of some of the issues in this area.

VI. Growth and stability of international financial markets

To most observers the international money and capital markets, and more particularly the Eurocurrency markets, have a strong Jekyll-and-Hyde tinge. On the one hand, they are recognized to facilitate trade and payments, channel compensatory capital movements, lower transactions costs, help recycle oil moneys, and foster portfolio diversification. On the other hand, they are said to add to the world money supply and hence world inflation, encourage speculation and exchange instability, lead to excessively easy credit availability and the postponement of adjustment, and, related to this, contribute to an overexposure to risks for banks lending internationally. Broadly speaking, however, the view that the markets are generally disruptive and potentially explosive seems exaggerated, though they may at times involve disturbances or inconveniences for individual countries.

By the end of 1979 the gross size of the market, based on statistics reported by banks in the Group of Ten countries, Switzerland, Austria, Denmark, and Ireland, as well as by the branches of U.S. banks in certain offshore countries, reached the neighborhood of $1,100 billion (American billion). The net size of the market, after adjusting for interbank lending within the reporting group, amounted to more than $665 billion. Considering that the market began to take hold only in the late 1950s, these aggregates are impressive, and, to some, disturbing.

There are grounds for caution, however, when one seeks to assess the meaning of Eurocurrency aggregates. One is that the procedure whereby interbank deposits are netted out is applied only with respect to the group of countries of the reporting banks. It is possible that interbank lending is also fairly significant between the reporting group and the rest of the world. Second, because changes in the Eurocurrency aggregates may, via outward and inward capital flows, already involve changes in national money supplies, they cannot be treated as an additional element in some concept of a world money supply. Third, depositing in and borrowing from the Eurocurrency market may to some extent be no more than a substitute for forward exchange transactions. To this extent the deposit claims involved cannot be considered as liquid funds. Finally, the funds held in the Eurocurrency market are generally fixed-time deposits and cannot as a rule be used to make current payments. Hence, they would normally be included only in the widest definitions of the money supply. As a fairly comprehensive matrix of international banking statistics, the data are helpful primarily to those interested in banking operations, market shares, and balance-of-payments flows. They are basically a measure of international banking activity, although some countries have also become interested in their possible relevance for the domestic monetary aggregates and domestic expenditure. To the banking community these statistics provide a ready and reasonably up-to-day picture of the changing sizes and patterns of markets against which individual banks can compare their own activities. In particular, because the data shed light on the broader puzzle of international indebtedness, banks can use the information to help assess their own risk exposure. Central banks and other supervisory authorities see similar advantages in the data for their own purposes.

From the general monetary point of view, however, estimates of gross size and net size of the market seem to be of limited significance, because they greatly exceed anything that could be realistically added, say, to some concept of the world money supply. With regard to the Eurocredit multiplier, there is considerable support for the view that the size estimates reflect little autonomous credit multiplication and, after making allowances for substitution effects, involve no grossly excessive lending on a global basis. Moreover, whereas available statistics show a considerable increase in liquidity via maturity transformation over recent years, this is probably a normal tendency as the market grows in absolute terms.

Misgivings about the Eurocurrency markets are likely to continue, however, until the factors underlying their growth are better understood. One pervasive factor, long recognized, is the existence of domestic monetary control biases, such as reserve requirements and interest-rate ceilings, that contribute to a shift, both cyclically and as a trend, to offshore lending and borrowing. Although official attitudes differ as to how countries as a group might deal with this problem (one proposal envisaged uniform global reserve requirements on Eurocurrency liabilities), they are alike in welcoming further unilateral efforts to reduce or eliminate the domestic biases, thus removing causes rather than treating symptoms.

A more interesting question, perhaps, has to do with the possible links between the financial side and the real side of the international economy. Among some analysts there is reluctance to view the growth of the Eurocurrency markets as being related in any close way to the growth of international trade and payments. Yet, over the past two decades, following the return to convertibility in western Europe, the volume of trade and payments has expanded by leaps and bounds. According to the IMF's *International Financial Statistics*, world imports increased from $120 billion in 1960 to nearly $1,550 billion in 1979, which puts their value at roughly 2.3 times the net size of the Eurocurrency market.

From the standpoint of financing needs, the external sector measured in gross terms (i.e., exports plus imports of goods and services) has everywhere grown substantially relative to the size of domestic production domestically consumed. What we may observe, therefore, may be a two-tier system of financial markets, domestic and international, with the international markets more oriented to "wholesale" business relating to trade and payments. The fact that financial transactions in the Eurocurrency markets can also conveniently be linked to currency hedging operations may provide an additional incentive. One might add that in current research efforts to augment money-demand functions by including certain Eurocurrency claims, it may be desirable also to adopt a new scale variable that would better measure transactions needs (e.g., gross national product plus imports of goods and services).

Another of the main reasons for the growth of Eurocurrency claims is that the reported data record capital movements of all kinds and hence partly reflect the size of world payments imbalances. Compare, for example, the change in the net size of the market with the gross current-account imbalances of the OECD countries, assuming the latter to reflect persisting one-way imbalances and also to act as a proxy for imbalances in non-OECD countries. The gross current-account imbalances of the OECD averaged $21 billion in the years 1970–3 and $63 billion in the years 1974–8, whereas the corresponding figures for the average net growth of the Euromarket were $29 and 67 billion, respectively.

But it is in this context, perhaps, that the financial-fragility hypothesis finds its international expression. If to a large extent the Eurocurrency statistics are simply registering streams of financing that are contributing to the buildup of vulnerable positions with respect to net international indebtedness, then the dangers may lie in the persistence of the large external imbalances themselves and in the ways in which these are financed. In the nature of things it is extremely difficult to know when a long-term financial trend will run up against the financial constraints imposed by the markets, but it is clear that the growth of international indebtedness has troubled the international financial world from the 1973–4 oil crisis onwards.

As far as the LDCs are concerned, developments up to now have been better than one might have expected. On the whole, individual countries have shown an aversion to running up a large volume of external indebtedness, and they have been able to maintain fairly satisfactory debt-service ratios. They have usually displayed a healthy willingness and capacity to adjust their domestic economies even at considerable cost in terms of output and employment. There has been no widespread evidence to suggest that the borrowing countries have used external credit in order to postpone adjustment unduly. Indeed, frequently the borrowing undertaken has been used mainly to bolster international currency reserves. And, from the creditor standpoint, it would appear that foreign lenders have to some extent covered themselves through interest-rate premia charged on loans to higher-risk countries and through spreading their country risks.

It is not the purpose of the present chapter to delve into questions of country-risk analysis. It is pertinent, however, to illustrate some of the trends in debt formation by broad geographic areas. For this purpose the most up-to-date sources are the international banking statistics published by the Bank for International Settlements, although by definition these statistics are limited to the external claims and liabilities of banks in the reporting countries. Table 11.4 shows the reporting banks' gross claims, together with claims net of deposit liabilities, in respect of four major geographic groupings, with a further breakdown of the non-OPEC LDCs into four additional groupings.

As the table shows, the reporting banks' net liabilities to OPEC increased from $37 billion at the end of 1975 to $82 billion by June 1980. Over the same period the banks' net claims on developed countries (outside the reporting area), eastern Europe, and the non-OPEC LDCs rose from $49 billion to $158 billion. Of the total claims against Latin America (i.e., $78 billion in June 1980), approximately two-thirds represented claims by U.S. banks and their offshore branches.

The broad picture is scarcely an auspicious one. Although in recent years export earnings have risen fairly well, often very well, the growing burden of indebtedness necessarily implies a greater vulnerability in the event of persisting high interest rates and a slackening of world markets. In recent years the most individual country difficulties have tended to be resolved through debt rescheduling or along traditional IMF lines. In the recent case of Turkey, however, a support package was viewed as necessary by governments acting as a group.

It can be argued, of course, that the figures in the table reflect nominal debt, the real burden of which is less after allowance for the effect of continuing world inflation on export earnings. This may well be true, but it is a ceteris paribus argument that is not altogether very reassuring. It assumes that a sufficient margin of export earnings over import requirements can be

Table 11.4. *Claims of the BIS reporting banks[a] with groups of countries outside the reporting area (amounts outstanding, in billions of U.S. dollars)*

	End 1975	End 1976	End 1977 I	End 1977 II	End 1978 I	End 1978 II[b]	End 1979	June 1980
Banks' gross claims on:								
Developed countries	40.8	54.5	70.2	55.5	64.5	63.9	72.4	79.6
Eastern Europe	21.6	28.8	32.9	38.3	47.6	47.5	55.9	57.6
OPEC[c]	14.3	24.1	35.4	39.1	57.2	56.4	64.1	63.2
Non-OPEC LDCs	63.0	80.9	92.0	98.7	122.5	120.8	157.1	172.2
Latin America[d]	43.5	57.4	63.8	65.9	80.8	79.9	103.5	114.0
Middle East	3.3	4.4	4.6	5.2	6.6	6.5	8.2	8.3
Other Asia	12.9	14.7	18.1	20.5	23.7	23.1	31.1	34.7
Other Africa	3.3	4.4	5.5	7.1	11.4	11.3	14.3	15.2
Total	139.7	188.3	230.5	231.6	291.8	288.6	349.5	372.6
Banks' net claims on:								
Developed countries	7.6	19.5	29.1	27.4	26.0	25.8	26.3	33.1
Eastern Europe	15.3	21.2	25.1	29.9	36.9	36.9	40.5	45.0
OPEC[c]	−37.2	−39.8	−41.9	−38.8	−26.7	−26.1	−56.2	−82.2
Non-OPEC LDCs	26.0	31.1	30.0	36.7	45.0	44.2	67.5	80.0
Latin America[d]	27.2	35.1	38.5	40.7	46.9	46.7	65.1	78.4
Middle East	− 2.7	− 2.9	− 5.4	− 4.8	− 7.2	− 7.3	− 7.7	− 9.8
Other Asia	2.3	− 0.2	− 1.9	0.4	1.3	0.9	5.1	6.7
Other Africa	− 0.8	− 0.9	− 1.2	0.4	4.0	3.9	5.0	4.7
Total	11.7	32.0	42.3	55.2	81.2	80.8	78.1	75.9

Note: The figures, which include domestic and foreign currency positions, are partly based on estimates.

[a]Up to December 1977 (I) the BIS reporting banks covered the Group of Ten countries including Switzerland, and certain offshore branches of U.S. banks. Since December 1977 (II) the figures include Austria, Denmark, and Ireland, which are no longer included under "Developed countries," as well as buyers' credits in domestic currency for banks in France and some domestic currency positions for banks in the United Kingdom not reported earlier.

[b]As from December 1978 (II) the figures for banks in the United States exclude all custody items except negotiable U.S. bank certicates of deposit held on behalf of nonresidents. Previously the only custody items excluded were nonresident holdings of Treasury bills and certicates.

[c]Including, in addition, Bahrain, Brunei, Oman, Trinidad, and Tobago.

[d]Including those Caribbean countries not considered to be offshore banking centers.

Source: BIS quarterly press releases on international banking developments.

generated from the investment financed by such borrowings. Depending on the circumstances, which may change, the assumption may or may not prove a valid one.

VII. The role of central banks as lenders of last resort

If we may speak of a "classical" view of the lender of last resort, it would be the view that evolved from the principles enunciated by Walter Bagehot (1924) in the late nineteenth century. According to this view, the central bank should stand ready in the event of a generalized liquidity crisis to "lend without stint," though at a penalty rate of interest. The purpose of such lending should be to meet the exceptional liquidity needs of the system so as to avert a major contraction of credit. It was not intended to rescue individual institutions from solvency difficulties arising from their own past management practices. Another element is that the reduction of risks implied by a lender of last resort should be no more than partial. Otherwise there would be an untoward degree of "moral hazard," an excessive degree of "insurance," which could undermine the lending standards of financial institutions (Solow, 1982). Hence there would need to be a certain ambiguity, uncertainty, and randomness about the conditions and terms under which such a facility might become activated. Finally, the lender of last resort was normally thought of as being the central bank.

How well does this view reflect the present state of affairs? Let us start with the international sphere, where the existence and role of an international lender of last resort has historically been less well defined.

We may first recall that on 10 September 1974, in the wake of the Herstatt revelations, the central banks of the Group of Ten countries and Switzerland felt it appropriate to issue a statement to reassure the markets. As far as the lender-of-last-resort function was concerned, it read simply: "They recognised that it would not be practical to lay down in advance detailed rules and procedures for the provision of temporary liquidity. But they were satisfied that means are available for that purpose and will be used if and when necessary."[4] On a general level, this is about all that central banks as a group have been willing to say on the subject. The wording of the statement is consistent with the traditional view that assistance should be extended only in the event of general liquidity difficulties, not to help individual financial institutions afflicted by solvency problems.

In the years following, however, a great deal was accomplished at the practical level of supervision and safeguards. What has been done, and is being done, has best been summarized by the governor of the Bank of England, Gordon Richardson:

My colleagues in Basle and I have long established the principle of parental responsibility; that is, that parents should have ultimate responsibility for subsidiaries, and that central banks should be responsible for supervising the lending activities of banks of their own nationality, wherever the lending is conducted. We are currently developing ways in which this principle can be extended, for the purposes of prudential supervision, by means of consolidated accounts for each bank on a worldwide basis. We are also discussing in Basle ways in which maturity transformation statistics, such as we have for a number of years collected and published in London, can be developed for other countries.[5]

Work along these lines is being carried forward by the Cooke (formerly Blunden) committee, the basic assumption being that transparent international markets are healthier markets. In addition, the BIS issues periodic press releases on international banking statistics, including country positions and maturity transformation data. Another development, an outcome of an earlier initiative by Arthur Burns, has been the publication of the BIS brochure collating available sources of information on international lending.[6]

The concept of parental responsibility, although up to now limited to supervisory functions, implies that there is as a rule no single international lender of last resort for the international banking community but rather many national ones, with shared responsibilities. It is based on the assumption, or rather the fact, that the international economy is simply an extension of national economies. Broadly speaking, the parent institution is viewed as responsible for the solvency of a fully owned subsidiary abroad, whereas the host country is responsible for liquidity provisions, at least as far as operations in the host country's currency are concerned. There are still some ragged edges of responsibility, such as that for partially owned subsidiaries abroad, but the general principle seems to be well established.

The other interesting development is the central banks' shift in favor of prudential supervision of individual bank balance sheets on a consolidated worldwide basis. Only a few countries such as the United States, Canada, and the United Kingdom, The Netherlands, and, more recently, Switzerland already do this, and in others new legislation might be necessary. Germany, for example, has no legal supervisory powers over its banks subsidiaries, Luxembourg being the main center, but relevant information is now being supplied on a voluntary basis. As a group, the central banks meeting regularly in Basle have now endorsed the idea of pushing ahead of this front. This is understandable, because one of the most pervasive concerns about the Euromarkets has to do with the gradual structural shift of banking business, or at least its domicile, to less regulated markets. In terms of market incentives, the problem is not unlike the problem that was posed by nonmembership of banks in the Federal Reserve System.

Thus, through the concept of shared responsibilities, the functions of lender of last resort trace back ultimately to individual central banks. In turn, however, as indicated in earlier sections, it is useful to view the functions of lender of last resort at the national level as being shared in certain respects by different branches of government. It is appropriate, in other words, to think of the "insurance" model of last-resort lending as applying to the monetary authorities as a whole and not just the central bank. In the first place, during a downturn, the government, as a borrower of last resort in the saving/ investment sense, contributes in a timely, substantial way to liquidity creation via the automatic stabilizers. Second, in many countries the government itself has acted as lender of last resort to troubled industries. Third, when we consider the safety net of deposit insurance, which Milton Friedman thinks is enough in itself, how much of the classical function of lender of last resort is left for the central bank?

Some observers, not surprisingly, view the entire concept of a generalized liquidity crisis with suspicion. Rather, what they see, assuming prudential controls ensuring wide distributions of risk, is a more limited role for central banks. This would consist largely of supervisory control, dealing with isolated cases of bank failures at the micro level, applying penalty lending rates, and acting as a last-resort provider of foreign exchange. In the postwar world, up to now at least, this view seems consonant with actual developments.

Applying an "insurance" model to the lender-of-last-resort function, one is led in the present-day world to ask if there is not a danger of being overinsured by way of such facilities. After all, the main question today concerns financial instability in the inflationary rather than the deflationary direction. In many countries we have seen modern governments moving gradually from their role as borrowers of last resort to that of borrowers of "first resort," increasingly giving rise to concern about real and financial crowding out. And, against the background of a generally more stable fiscal/monetary framework, we have also seen an alteration in the economy's price/output responses to changes in demand. For these reasons, it seems to me that we are far from having found the right "insurance mix" for the economy as a whole.

In a world of chronic inflation the penalty-rate function of the central bank as lender of last resort can also be said to assume a different guise. Instead of being an exceptional matter reserved for crisis lending only, the penalty rate should be viewed as having immediate relevance for daily operations. In the States, prior to 6 October 1979, the month-to-month setting of the Federal Reserve funds rate effectively constituted the penalty rate, in the sense that at the existing rate the market's demand for funds would be fully met. Seen in that perspective, the October change in operational techniques from a money-market orientation to a bank-reserves orientation had major implications for the Federal Reserve System's role as a lender of last resort.

The implications will also be far-reaching in the international sphere. Although, as indicated earlier, there are many potential international lenders of last resort, it will be agreed that the United States, with its large and open financial markets, has a special leadership role. Under the new system of bank-reserves targeting, interest-rate adjustment will be more flexible and more in keeping with the need for domestic and international price stability. A similar development appears to have occurred in the United Kingdom, where exchange controls have been abolished and vigorous efforts are being made to control money growth, not least by high interest rates.

In the international sphere, it has been argued, the lender-of-last-resort function should in the first instance be viewed as a national function. This would be true of a liquidity and/or solvency crisis in international banking, in which case parent banks and indirectly individual central banks and governments might be called to the rescue. But, as stressed earlier, the response, if any, of the official lender of last resort might be limited and conditional.

In today's world of open economies and chronic inflation, a single-country financial crisis is likely to express itself not as a domestic liquidity crisis but rather as an external exchange crisis. In these circumstances the failure of the country to apply a central-bank penalty lending rate, or its broader policy equivalent, simply shifts the locus of the lender-of-last-resort function to the international community. Under floating exchange rates the crisis will be resolved partly by a depreciation in the value of foreign private and official holdings of the currency, particularly if it is widely held abroad. In addition, central banks, governments, and international institutions may be called on, or may act in their own interests, to support the currency by exchange-market intervention and stabilization loans. If when doing so, they undertake to impose an element of conditionality, they may be considered, in effect, to be substituting for the penalty-rate function that had been defaulted at the national level.

VIII. Concluding remarks

This chapter has argued that economic stability characteristics, both domestically and internationally, have been fundamentally altered by the historical emergence of government as a large borrower of last resort. Added to this, developments regarding government assistance to industry, special credit institutions, and deposit insurance, together with often accommodative monetary policies, have helped to destabilize economic activity in the inflationary direction. In conseqence, the classical role of the central bank as lender of last resort has shifted away from dealing with general liquidity crises to concern over micro problems of isolated bank failures and problems of prudential supervision and to acting as a provider of foreign exchange of last resort. Moreover, in the face of chronic inflation, central banks have come increasingly to view the penalty-rate function not so much as an exceptional crisis measure but rather more as one of current operational significance in seeking to avoid excessively accommodative monetary policies. Developments in both the United States and the United Kingdom seem to confirm this view.

In the international sphere, cooperative efforts among the central banks have laid considerable stress on the importance of adequate supervisory systems aiming at prudential control. One positive step in this direction has been the endorsement of consolidated balance sheet reporting for banks engaged in international banking activity. In addition, the concept of parental responsibility has been extended to cover not only a parent bank's offshore branches but also its foreign subsidiaries, and efforts have been made to clarify the respective responsibilities of the parent bank and host country in respect of liquidity and solvency considerations.

The question of the availability of lender-of-last-resort facilities for troubled countries is another matter. Up to now these situations have been dealt with on an individual basis by various familiar means, including debt reschedulings, intergovernmental credits, and stabilization programs along conventional IMF lines. In this respect the IMF is a key international lender of last resort, and the conditionality of its lending, which is apparently undergoing certain modifications, is not unlike that which would be applied by a central bank to institutions in domestic difficulties.

At the present time the international economy faces a protracted period of painful adjustment. In the industrial countries the monetary authorities are showing renewed determination to bring inflation under control, with the result that in two center countries (the United States and the United Kingdom) interest rates stand at unusually high levels. In most countries economic activity is slackening, or even falling, although in the United States there are signs of moderate recovery. However, with budget deficits already very large, governments are showing reluctance, as borrowers of last resort, to see them swell still more elsewhere. There is the prospect of a huge OPEC surplus for 1980 as a whole, though on optimistic assumptions it is expected to decline over the next two years. Even at best, however, the outlook is for a continuing growth in the debt burdens of various deficit countries, particularly the non-oil LDCs and the smaller OECD countries. The prospect of high borrowing costs for variable-interest, rollover, and new credits, combined with slackening export growth, is a discouraging one. Much will depend on the adjustment capacities of the deficit countries, which in the past have generally displayed considerable resilience and adaptability.

Notes

1 The term TC refers to total credit, and for this purpose I have taken the U.S. Department of Commerce series on net public and private debt.

2 In the case of the United States, the 1974–5 experience contrasts sharply with that of 1930–3, when over four years bank lending to the private sector dropped by nearly 45% and was accompanied by a decline in M_2 by over 30%. With reference to the 1974–5 recession, it is noteworthy that money growth accelerated markedly in 1976–7, demonstrating the dangers of excessive stimulus during a recession/recovery phase.

3 Internationally, the OECD has sought by means of its Positive Adjustment Programme to establish recognized guidelines aimed at avoiding unduly defensive national assistance measures that would tend to freeze existing industrial structures.

4 The governors also "discussed the working of the international banking system. They took stock of the existing mechanisms for supervision and regulation and noted recent improvements made in these fields in the number of major countries.

   "They agreed to intensify the exchange of information between central banks on the activities of banks operating in international markets and, where appropriate, to tighten further the regulations governing foreign exchange positions."

5 Speech given at the annual banquet of the Overseas Bankers' Club, 5 February 1979.

6 Bank for International Settlements, *Manual on Statistics Compiled by International Organisations on Countries' Indebtedness*. Basle, March 1979.

References

Bagehot, W. 1924. *Lombard Street*. London: Clowes.

Barro, R. J. 1978. "Comment from an Unreconstructed Ricardian." *Journal of Monetary Economics* 4:569–81.

Buchanan, J. M., and Wagner, R. E. 1977. *Democracy in Deficit. The Political Legacy of Lord Keynes*. New York: Academic Press.

Hicks, Sir J. 1976. "Real and Monetary Factors in Economic Fluctuations." In: *The "New Inflation" and Monetary Policy*, edited by M. Monti, pp. 3–24. London: Macmillan.

Kindleberger, C. P. 1973. *The World in Depression*. London: Allen Lane.

   1978. *Manias, Panics and Crises. A history of financial crises*. New York: Basic Books.

Minsky, H. P. 1972. "Financial Instability Revisited: The Economics of Disaster." In: *Reappraisal of the Federal Reserve Discount Mechanism, Vol. 3*. Washington, D.C.: Board of Governors of the Federal Reserve System.

   1978. *The Financial Instability Hypothesis: A Restatement*. London: Thames Polytechnic.

Mishkin, F. S. 1976. "The Household Balance-Sheet and the Great Depression." Report 7639, University of Chicago, Center for Mathematical Studies in Business and Economics.

Solow, R. M. 1982. "On the Lender of Last Resort." This volume.
Stein, J. L., editor. 1976. *Monetarism. Studies in Monetary Economics, Vol. 1.* Amsterdam: North Holland.
Temin, P. 1976. *Did Monetary Forces Cause the Great Depression?* New York: W. W. Norton.

Index